Student Success in College

Doing What Works!

Christine Harrington
New Jersey City University

Cengage

Australia • Brazil • Canada • Mexico • Singapore • United Kingdom • United States

Cengage

***Student Success in College: Doing What Works!*, Fourth Edition**

Christine Harrington

SVP, Higher Education Product Management: Erin Joyner

VP, Product Management, Learning Experiences: Thais Alencar

Product Director: Laura Ross

Product Manager: Colin Grover

Product Assistant: Celia Smithmier

Learning Designer: Hannah Ells

Content Manager: Grace Thomas

Digital Delivery Quality Partner: Justin Stross

Director, Product Marketing: Neena Bali

Product Marketing Manager: Danielle Klahr

IP Analyst: Ann Hoffman

Production Service: Lumina Datamatics Ltd.

Designer: Gaby Vinales

Cover Image Source:
658984513: Klaus Vedfelt/Getty Images
1047699430: golero/Getty Images
1171003830: Klaus Vedfelt/Getty Images
1249078123: ferrantraite/Getty Images

For product information and technology assistance, contact us at
**Cengage Customer & Sales Support, 1-800-354-9706
or support.cengage.com.**

For permission to use material from this text or product, submit all requests online at **www.copyright.com**.

Library of Congress Control Number: 2022901066

ISBN: 978-0-357-79287-2

Cengage
200 Pier 4 Boulevard
Boston, MA 02210
USA

Cengage is a leading provider of customized learning solutions with employees residing in nearly 40 different countries and sales in more than 125 countries around the world. Find your local representative at: **www.cengage.com.**

To learn more about Cengage platforms and services, register or access your online learning solution, or purchase materials for your course, visit **www.cengage.com.**

Notice to the Reader

Publisher does not warrant or guarantee any of the products described herein or perform any independent analysis in connection with any of the product information contained herein. Publisher does not assume, and expressly disclaims, any obligation to obtain and include information other than that provided to it by the manufacturer. The reader is expressly warned to consider and adopt all safety precautions that might be indicated by the activities described herein and to avoid all potential hazards. By following the instructions contained herein, the reader willingly assumes all risks in connection with such instructions. The publisher makes no representations or warranties of any kind, including but not limited to, the warranties of fitness for particular purpose or merchantability, nor are any such representations implied with respect to the material set forth herein, and the publisher takes no responsibility with respect to such material. The publisher shall not be liable for any special, consequential, or exemplary damages resulting, in whole or part, from the readers' use of, or reliance upon, this material.

Printed at CLDPC, USA, 04/22

Brief Contents

Contents

Part 2   Mapping Out a Path and Developing Career Skills 65

Part 3   Achieving Academic Success   129

Exploring the Research in Depth Appendix: Full-Length Research Articles

Success Strategies at a Glance

There's something magical about the number seven. It's not just lucky; it's a number that researchers have found to be most productive in terms of memory. This is why there are seven chapters in this text. Findings from a famous psychological study tell us that seven chunks of information are what work best naturally within our memory systems (Miller, 1956). We've put this research into practice, using it to shape the organization of the text.

There's a lot to learn and do in this course. This introductory section is designed to get you on your way. It provides an overall organizational structure to guide you at the start of the semester and will continue to be a great reference tool throughout the entire semester. Before you start reading the first chapter, take a few moments to get familiar with this text to see how it can be helpful to you. This brief, powerful preview activity will familiarize you with the key concepts you need to know as you begin your college journey. Here's a great way to become familiar with the key success strategies:

- Flip through the Success Strategies at a Glance pages that highlight research-supported success strategies for each chapter.
- Write down strategies that you are already using. Think about how these strategies will help you in college.
- Identify at least three strategies you would like to learn more about. Go to their corresponding chapter, find the section that describes the strategy, and learn about the strategy.
- Choose at least one strategy that you can start using and try it out!

7 Success Strategies at a Glance

Chapter 1 • Exploring Your Identity

1 **Explore what factors contribute to how you define your identity.**

Your identity is influenced by many factors. Your group memberships such as race, ethnicity, sexual orientation, and gender are often core elements of who you are. In addition, your rolesand responsibilities such as parent, child, significant other, student, and professional play an important role. Finally, your personal characteristics and interests also shape your identity.

2 **Reflect on how your multiple identities connect.**

You are complex and cannot be defined by one or two parts of who you are. Instead, you are defined by your multiple identities that intersect.

3 **Acknowledge privilege and oppression.**

Some groups with whom you identify may be privileged, which means unearned advantages are given based on these group memberships. Other groups, however, may be oppressed and instead face disadvantages associated with group membership.

4 **Reflect on how your personal, academic, and professional roles influence your identity.**

Your role within your family often significantly influencesyour identity. In addition, your role as a student and as a current or future professional can also impact how you define yourself.

5 **Determine what matters to you.**

Identifying and evaluating your values will help you make decisions that you will feel good about. Your values drive your actions.

6 **Discover opportunities to engage in activism.**

Activism involves acting on what you believe is important and often targets social or political change. There are many ways to engage in actions aligned to your beliefs such as participating in peaceful protests, writing about issues on social media, and engaging with legislators.

7 **Elevateyour aspirations.**

You do not have to be limited by what you currently believe is possible. Look for mentors who have excelled at high levels and challenge yourself to aspire higher.

7 Success Strategies at a Glance

Chapter 2 • Evaluating Information and Thinking Critically.

1 Improve your information literacy skills.

Being able to determine what information you need, how to find that information, and then evaluate information is an important skill in college and careers. In the academic world, information literacy skills will help you successfully complete assignments. In many careers, you will also need information to make good decisions and complete projects.

2 Explore multiple sources when gathering information.

Information is everywhere. Although most of us go to the Internet first when we are seeking information, it is important to also explore scholarly sources such as peer-reviewed journals for useful content. In addition, social media can be used to gather academic information.

3 Evaluate credibility of websites and other sources of information.

One of the biggest information literacy challenges is being able to determine whether the information you find or come across has value. You can use the CRAAP test, which was developed by librarians, to help you determine if the information is credible. This involves evaluating currency, relevance, authority, accuracy, and purpose.

4 Follow professionals and organizations on social media.

Ask your professors for suggestions on which professionals and organizations to follow on social media. Reading posts by experts and organizations can help you learn about the current issues in the field.

5 Get confident reading and using scholarly sources.

College-level work requires you to use high-level information sources. Professors want you to back up your opinion with data and research. Learn how to understand and apply information you find in peer-reviewed journals. With the help of your professor and the resources in this text, you will gain skills and confidence in this area.

6 Build your foundational knowledge.

Having a strong foundational knowledge base is important. As described in Bloom's taxonomy, remembering key information is a first and necessary step before being able to engage in high-level tasks. Learn research-based study strategies that will help you build foundational knowledge.

7 Learn how to be a critical thinker.

Your professors expect you to engage in complex cognitive tasks. Discover what actions you can take to think critically. Learn about the importance of developing a strong knowledge base, believing in yourself, and being motivated. Embrace the challenges you will encounter in college and use available support to help you succeed.

7 Success Strategies at a Glance

Chapter 3 • Setting Goals and Choosing a Career Path

1 Establish short- and long-term goals.

Students who set goals are more likely to succeed. Long-term goals are valuable because they help you focus on the big picture, emphasizing your values and priorities. Short-term goals pave the way for success because they make it easier for you to monitor your progress toward your long-term goals.

2 Use the ABCS approach to goal setting.

Aim high! Research shows that students who have challenging goals are more likely to succeed. Believe in yourself—if you believe you can successfully achieve your goal, you will be more likely to continue working toward your goal even if you experience setbacks. Care and commit—students who care about their goals and are committed to achieving them are more likely to have successful outcomes. Specify and self-reflect—having specific goals makes it easier to monitor your progress and the self-reflection process allows you to adjust as needed so that you stay on track toward your goals.

3 Recognize the importance of engaging in active career exploration.

Deciding on a career path can be a challenging task. Unfortunately, many students choose a path without first engaging in significant exploration activities. Exploring before deciding will help you make a better decision.

4 Explore career theories.

Understanding theories behind career decision making processes can help youengage in productive actions and make decisions related to your career.Be aware of how your beliefs, experiences, values, actions, and interests play a role in your career decisions.

5 Reach out for assistance with career decision-making as needed.

Advisors or career counselors are available to assist you with exploring career options. They can point you to information that can influence your decision about which career path to pursue. Seeking out guidance can be especially helpful if you are still exploring options, but it can also help you further explore your field of interest if you have selected a career pathway.

6 Engage in self-assessment activities to make better career decisions.

Reflecting on your values is an important first step in the career exploration process. Also considering your skills, interests, and personality style will help you make good career decisions.

7 Check out career websites and conduct informational interviews.

In addition to learning about yourself, learn about various careers. Informative websites, such as the Occupational Outlook Handbook, give you a good overview of many careers. Informational interviews allow you to get a more personal view of careers and can help you build your professional network.

7 Success Strategies at a Glance

Chapter 4 • Strengthening Networking and other Essential Skills

1 Expand and strengthen your network.

One of the most effective ways to discover career opportunities is through networking. Building your networking skills and developing your network early on in your college career is advantageous. Find a mentor and discover ways to build your network. Because relationships take work, spend time strengthening relationships with current members of your network too.

2 Create a professional online presence.

Employers look at social media sites, so be sure that your online presence is positive and professional in nature. Be careful about what you post online—it may have negative consequences later. Before you look for a new job, delete inappropriate photos or posts. Use social media to promote a professional image of yourself by sharing your accomplishments online.

3 Develop an elevator speech.

An elevator speech is a very brief story about you, your accomplishments, and aspirations. Writing an elevator speech requires you to engage in self-reflection. Having an elevator speech ready will help you make the most of opportunities that come your way.

4 Practice professionalism.

Professionalism involves being honest, responsible, and hardworking. Always put forth high levels of effort and be respectful of others. Employers desire employees who act professionally and ethically.

5 Use time management strategies that work.

Document the tasks you need to complete on a to-do list, prioritizing the most important tasks. Block out time on your calendar to engage in required tasks, working ahead of deadlines. Focus on only one task at a time to maximize productivity.

6 Gain cultural competence and strengthen your interpersonal skills.

College is a perfect opportunity to develop and further enhance cultural competence and other interpersonalskills. Engage with others who are different from you and spend time learning about various cultures. Learn communication and conflict management skills, increase your emotional intelligence, and develop strong teamwork skills.

7 Seek out opportunities to develop leadership skills.

Employers value those who exhibit leadership skills. You can develop these skills via class activities such as group projects and through outside of class activities. Join on- and off-campus organizations, observe leaders, and volunteer for leadership roles.

7 Success Strategies at a Glance

Chapter 5 • Building Academic Skills

1   **Use a note-taking method that works.**

Taking notes ensures you will have the information you need when it is time to study. Explore the various note-taking methods, such as the Cornell Method, concept maps, outlines, and matrixes. Choose a method that works for you during class and then be sure to use a method that focuses on organization of content such as the matrix or concept map after class. By using the organizing strategies within these methods, you will increase your understanding of the content.

2   **Actively read your textbook—try the 3R, SQ3R, and SOAR techniques.**

To make the most of your reading time, engage in the 3R (Read-Recite-Review) technique, the SQ3R (Survey-Question-Read-Recite-Review) technique, or SOAR (Select, Organize, Associate, Regulate) technique. These approaches focus on you being an active reader by using your own words to summarize what you have read and interacting with the text several times. Taking notes while reading further increases learning.

3   **Learn how memory works.**

Knowing how memory works can help you make the most out of your study time. The goal is getting the information you are learning into your long-term memory so that it is available when you need it. Elaboration or identifying examples is one strategy you can use to strengthen memories.

4   **Study a little every day.**

Research shows that you learn more when you study over time. If you study a little each day, the memories will stick, and you will not have to spend hours cramming for an exam.

5   **Use a multisensory approach.**

Everyone is a multisensory learner. You learn best when you use several senses to take in information. Visuals are particularly powerful, so pay attention to charts, graphs, and images.

6   **Test yourself regularly.**

Research has shown that recalling information helps us learn. Take advantage of practice tests in your texts or on the textbook publisher's website, or you can create your own. Practice tests allow you to learn from your mistakes while not negatively impacting your grade in the course.

7   **Teach to learn and participate in study groups.**

One of the most powerful ways to learn is to teach someone else. In a study group, you can teach your fellow study group members part of a chapter and then learn from others teaching you content from other sections of the chapter.

7 Success Strategies at a Glance

Chapter 6 • Demonstrating Knowledge and Skills

1 **Discover the benefits of engaging in academically honest actions.**
Academic integrity is important. Dishonest actions not only negatively impact the individual and result in lower levels of learning, but also foster a negative image of the college or university. This can result in lost opportunities for current and future students.

2 **Know when and how to cite sources.**
Always cite sources unless you are presenting your own original idea or common knowledge. Learning how to cite appropriately helps you avoid unintentional plagiarism. Get familiar with APA and MLA citation styles. There are online tools that can help you with citing sources.

3 **Plan, write, revise, and proofread.**
Before you write a paper, carefully review the assignment and plan by writing an outline. Begin with a clear, strong opening statement that communicates your topic. Address your key points, adding supporting details and examples as needed. Connect all concepts to one another. Summarize your key points at the end, bringing attention to what you want to emphasize. Revise your work after you have had a chance to take a break from it. Start the revision process by looking at the big picture and then focus on the details when proofreading.

4 **Engage your audience when presenting.**
The more prepared you are, the easier it is to engage your audience. Maintain eye contact and highlight important points by changing your voice pattern, sharing a related story, or repeating information. Adding brief, active learning opportunities, such as a written reflection or a Turn and Talk, can also increase audience engagement and learning.

5 **Create effective visual aids.**
According to research, images are better than words. Limit the use of words on your slides and draw attention to the most important points. Avoid adding extra information or using bells and whistles that may distract from your main points. Use simple, conversational language.

6 **Manage performance anxiety.**
Performance anxiety is common. The best way to reduce anxiety is to prepare and practice. Know that a moderate amount of anxiety will lead to the best outcome.

7 **Use test-taking techniques that work.**
Preparing well for an exam is the single best way to improve exam performance. However, there are also some strategies you can use when taking a test. When taking a multiple-choice test, predict the answer before reading the options, read all the options, and eliminate the incorrect responses. Skip difficult questions and change your answer if you have good reason for doing so. When taking an essay exam, address the question directly using a clear organizational structure.

7 Success Strategies at a Glance

Chapter 7 • Mapping Your Path to Success: Plans and Action Steps

1 **Meet with your advisor regularly.**

Students who meet with their advisor are more successful than students who do not. Take advantage of the advising services offered at your college. Your advisor can help you map out an academic and career plan and serve as a mentor throughout your college experience.

2 **Understand curriculum and graduation requirements.**

Knowing what courses and experiences are required of graduates will help you plan effectively. Understanding the structure of a degree will be helpful to you as you map out an academic plan, making it more likely that you will be able to complete graduation requirements on schedule.

3 **Embrace internship, study abroad, and service learning opportunities.**

Internships not only enhance your skills and experiences but also give you a great opportunity to network with professionals in the field. Students who study abroad are more likely to graduate on time and perform well academically. Service learning can help you develop knowledge and skills while you make societal contributions.

4 **Regularly engage in academic self-regulation.**

Academic self-regulation involves three main phases: setting a goal, using learning strategies to work toward the goal, and self-reflecting on whether you are making progress toward your goal. Successful students ask themselves, "How am I doing?" regularly.

5 **Discover what it means to be resilient and have grit.**

Resilience and grit are needed, especially when you encounter challenges, to achieve your goals. Resilience is the ability to bounce back after facing a stressful situation. Having grit means you are committed to a goal and will stick to it no matter what.

6 **Practice good stress management.**

Keeping stress at a moderate level is best. There are many effective ways to manage stress. Practice the basics—eating nutritiously, sleeping well, and exercising regularly. Avoid unhealthy options, such as drinking alcohol or using other substances. Instead, engage in effective strategies such as mindfulness, positive thinking, talking with your support team, and taking breaks from stressors.

7 **Stay motivated.**

Motivation will fluctuate; this is normal. There are many ways to get and stay motivated. Reward yourself for accomplishments, interpret events productively, ensure your basic needs are met, and lean on others in your support system.

Preface

What Makes Student Success in College: Doing What Works! Unique?

A Personalized, Academically Rigorous, Research-Based Approach

- Explore Identity: Research-Based Self-Assessments Embedded in Text
- Discover Research-Based Success Strategies
- Explore the Research in Summary: Research Findings at the Beginning of Each Chapter
- Learn How to Read and Use Peer-Reviewed Research
- Explore the Research in Depth: Original Research Studies in Appendix

Rawpixel.com/Shutterstock.com

A Guided Pathways Framework That Helps Students Choose a Career Pathway

- Set Effective Career and Academic Goals Using the ABCS Goal-Setting Framework
- Explore Careers and Engage in Career Decision Making
- Stay on Track and Be Successful

iStockPhoto/BrianAJackson

Just Seven Chapters Allows for Meaningful Exploration of Success Strategies

- In-Depth Coverage of Content
- No Need to Rush
- Flexibility to Incorporate Personally Relevant Content
- Increased Opportunity for Critical Thinking and Information Literacy

Ron Dale/Shutterstock.com

About The Author

Dr. Christine Harrington is a professor and co-coordinator of the Ed.D. in the Community College Leadership program at New Jersey City University. Prior to this, she served a two-year term as the executive director of the New Jersey Center for Student Success at the New Jersey Council of County Colleges, where she used a guided pathways framework to improve success outcomes and decrease equity gaps at all 19 community colleges in New Jersey.

Dr. Harrington spent most of her career at Middlesex College, over 16 years, where she served in the following roles: professor of psychology, student success course coordinator, director of the Center for the Enrichment of Learning and Teaching, counselor, and disability service provider. Dr. Harrington was the 2016 recipient of the Excellence in Teaching First-Year Seminars award that was presented at the Annual Conference on the First-Year Experience. She also teaches graduate courses on teaching and learning at Rutgers University. Dr. Harrington

Christine Harrington

frequently shares her expertise and passion about teaching, learning, and student success at national and local conferences as well as at colleges and universities across the United States. She has authored or co-authored several other books including:

- *Why first-year seminars matter: Helping students choose and stay on a path*, Rowman and Littlefield.
- *Keeping us engaged: Student perspectives (and research-based strategies) on what works and why*, Stylus.
- *Designing a motivational syllabus: Creating a learning path for student engagement*, Stylus.
- *Dynamic lecturing: Research-based strategies to enhance lecture effectiveness*, Stylus.
- *Ensuring learning: Supporting faculty to improve student success*, Rowman and Littlefield.
- *Engaging faculty in Guided Pathways: A practical resource for college leaders*, Rowman and Littlefield.

Introduction

Student Success in College: Doing What Works! is set apart by its personalized, yet academically rigorous, research-based approach, its guided pathways framework that supports students as they define their career pathway, and its meaningful exploration of success strategies in just seven chapters.

A Personalized, Academically Rigorous, Research-Based Approach

● Exploring Identity through Research-Based Self-Assessments

Chapter 1 helps students explore the complexities of who they are and what matters to them so that they can identify a career path that aligns with their values. Students will have the opportunity to take numerous self-assessments that were developed by researchers such as the Multigroup Ethnic Identity Measure, Race Salience Subscale, Student Identity Centrality Assessment, Values Assessment, List of Values Questionnaire, Career Aspirations Scale, and the Cultural Humility Instrument.

● Research-Based Strategies

Moving beyond advice, *Student Success in College: Doing What Works!* provides students with research-based strategies so that they can "Do What Works!" and successfully achieve their goals. There are over 450 references, most from original research studies. Over 200 are new to this edition.

● Exploring the Research in Summary

Every chapter begins with a summary of a research study on a related chapter topic. This research article serves as a visual reminder that the strategies shared are based on research. Research article summaries can also be a great way to engage students with the chapter content.

- **Learning How to Read and Use Peer-Reviewed Research**

  In Chapter 2, students will learn about peer-reviewed research, the different parts or elements of research studies, and how professionals read peer-reviewed research so that students feel confident in their ability to use and apply research.

- **Original Research Studies: Exploring the Research in Depth**

  In the appendix, students will find numerous original research studies. Prior to each study, students will be guided through a four-step process:

  1. Engaging via prediction
  2. Reading for key points
  3. Critically thinking about the research
  4. Building information literacy skills

A Guided Pathways Framework That Helps Students Choose a Career Pathway

- **Setting Effective Career and Academic Goals Using the ABCS Goal-Setting Framework**

  A research-based alternative to SMART goals, the ABCS approach to goal setting helps students set and monitor progress toward goals: Aim high. Believe in yourself. Care and commit. Specify and self-reflect.

- **Career Exploration and Decision Making**

  Student Success in College: Doing What Works! goes above and beyond traditional coverage of career, bringing theory and research related to the career exploration process into practice. For example, students learn how to: expand and strengthen their network, create a professional presence, craft an elevator speech and resume, and develop essential skills such as professionalism, time and project management, interpersonal and leadership skills. After being introduced to career theories that describe how career decisions are made, students can reflect on their values, abilities, personality, and interests and find and evaluate career information. Students also engage in networking right at the start of college.

- **Staying on Track**

  Recognizing that life can sometimes get us off track, *Student Success in College: Doing What Works!* focuses on how to reflect on progress and make changes needed to accomplish goals. Learning about how to be resilient and gritty by managing stress and staying motivated will assist students with staying on track and achieving their goals.

Just Seven Chapters Allows for Meaningful Exploration of Success Strategies

- **In-Depth Coverage of Content**

  Rather than bringing just surface-level coverage of every possible success topic, the seven-chapter approach in *Student Success in College: Doing What*

Works! allows instructors and students to deeply explore the most essential success strategies. After an introduction that focuses on the value of a college education, financing education, return on investment and financial actions, the following chapters provide in-depth guidance and support:

- Chapter 1: Exploring your identity: Intersectionality, values, activism, and aspirations
- Chapter 2: Evaluating information and thinking critically
- Chapter 3: Setting goals and choosing a career path
- Chapter 4: Strengthening networking and other essential skills
- Chapter 5: Building academic skills
- Chapter 6: Demonstrating knowledge and skills
- Chapter 7: Academic planning and staying on track

No Need to Rush

Finally—a College Success text that can be adapted easily to your academic calendar! Instead of rushing through a chapter or more each week during a 15- to 16-week term, instructors can spend up to two weeks on each chapter. In a seven- to eight-week term, instructors can still spend a full week on each chapter. Research shows that learning is more likely when we really engage with the content, which is achievable with the seven-chapter approach used in *Student Success in College: Doing What Works!*

Flexibility

Having only seven chapters allows time for instructors and students to introduce other topics, especially personally relevant and institution-specific content, that are deemed important without sacrificing learning of key success strategies.

Increased Opportunity for Critical Thinking and Information Literacy

There is more time to deeply explore the research on success strategies using the original studies provided at the end of the book or students can search the library databases for additional research on topics of interest.

What's New in the Fourth Edition?

- Organized into three parts making it more streamlined for faculty to choose sections that align with their course learning outcomes:
  - Knowing Yourself and Being a Critical Thinker
  - Mapping Out a Path and Developing Career Skills
  - Achieving Academic Success
- New chapter on identity
  - Intersectionality
  - Values, Activism, and Aspirations
- Assessments included in text to encourage student engagement in self-reflection activities
  - Multigroup Ethnic Identity Measure
  - Race Salience Subscale
  - Student Identity Centrality Assessment

- Values Assessment
- List of Values Questionnaire
- Career Aspirations Scale
- Cultural Humility Instrument
- Increased emphasis on diversity, equity, and inclusion
- Over 200 new references, most from empirical studies
- A new glossary of key terms at the end of the textbook

Side-by-Side Comparison of Third and Fourth Editions

3rd edition	4th edition
Introduction: Getting Started • College Expectations (not included) • Value of the First-Year Seminar (not included) • Success Strategies at a Glance (still in Introduction)	Introduction: Getting Started • Value of a College Education (from Chapter 1) • Financing Your Education, Return on Investment and Financial Actions (from Chapter 6)

Chapter 1: Discovering the Value of Education and Sharpening Key Thinking Skills
 • Value of a College Education (moved to Introduction)
 • Decision Making (not included)
 • Information Literacy (moved to Chapter 2)
 • Critical Thinking (moved to Chapter 2)
	Chapter 1: Exploring Your Identity (new chapter)
	 • Intersectionality
	   • Group Membership
	   • Roles and Relationships
	   • Personal Characteristics and Interests
	   • Reflecting on Identity
	 • Values, Activism, and Aspirations

Chapter 2: Setting Goals and Choosing a Career Path • Setting Goals (moved to Chapter 3) • Career Exploration and Decision Making (moved to Chapter 3)	Chapter 2: Evaluating Information and Thinking Critically (moved from Chapter 1) • Information Literacy (moved from Chapter 1) • Critical Thinking (moved from Chapter 1)
Chapter 3: Building Academic Skills (moved to Chapter 5) • How Memory Works (moved to Chapter 5 and renamed Memory Process) • Active Reading Strategies (moved to Chapter 5) • Note-taking (moved to Chapter 5) • Note-taking Tips (not included as separate section) • Studying Strategies (moved to Chapter 5)	Chapter 3: Setting Goals and Choosing a Career Path (moved from Chapter 2) • Setting Goals (moved from Chapter 2) • Career Exploration and Decision Making (moved from Chapter 2; previously called Choosing a Career Path)
Chapter 4: Strengthening Soft Skills (still Chapter 4 but renamed to Strengthening Networking and Other Essential Skills) • What are Soft Skills? (Infused into Introduction; not separate section) • Professionalism (still in Chapter 4) • Time and Project Management (still in Chapter 4) • Interpersonal Skills (still in Chapter 4) • Leadership (still in Chapter 4; shifted to subheading under Interpersonal Skills)	Chapter 4: Strengthening Networking and Other Essential Skills (same chapter location; added networking from Chapter 6) • Networking (moved from Chapter 6) • Essential Skills (still in chapter; previously named Soft Skills)

3rd edition	4th edition
Chapter 5: Demonstrating Knowledge and Skills (moved to Chapter 6)	**Chapter 5: Building Academic Skills** (moved from Chapter 3)
• Purpose of Academic Tasks (not included as separate section) • Academic Integrity (moved to Chapter 6) • Papers and Presentations (moved to Chapter 6 as subheadings under assignments and tests) • Test-taking Strategies (moved to Chapter 6 as subheadings under assignments and tests)	• Note-taking and Reading Skills (moved from Chapter 3) • Memory and Study Strategies (moved from Chapter 3 and memory and study strategies were combined)
Chapter 6: Mapping Your Plans to Success: Plans and Action Steps (moved to Chapter 7)	**Chapter 6: Demonstrating Knowledge and Skills** (moved from Chapter 5)
• Creating an Academic Plan (moved to Chapter 7) • Career Planning: Discovering the Power of Networking (moved to Chapter 4; renamed Networking) • Financial Planning (moved to Introduction and renamed Financial Actions)	• Academic Integrity (moved from Chapter 5) • Assignments and Tests (moved from Chapter 5 and re-organized)
Chapter 7: Staying on Track and Celebrating Success (still in Chapter 7)	**Chapter 7: Academic Planning and Staying on Track** (same chapter location)
• Reflecting on Progress (still in Chapter 7; subheading under Creating Academic Plans and Monitoring Progress) • Staying Motivated (still in Chapter 7; now a subheading under Being Resilient and Developing Grit) • Managing Stress (still in Chapter 7; now a subheading under Being Resilient and Developing Grit) • Being Resilient and Developing Grit (still in Chapter 7) • Celebrating Success (still in Chapter 7)	• Creating Academic Plans and Monitoring Progress (same chapter location) • Being Resilient and Developing Grit (same chapter location; re-organized)

Organization of the Text

Student Success in College: Doing What Works! is organized into three parts. In Part I, students are invited to explore their identity and gain a deeper level of self-understanding as a foundational step in their path to success. In Part II, students consider their career pathway and related major. Last, in Part III, students are presented with research-based success strategies to achieve personal, academic, and professional success.

- **Part I: Knowing Yourself and Being a Critical Thinker**
  - Learn about how your group memberships, roles and responsibilities, and unique personality traits and interests define your identity.
  - Determine your values and how you can be an activist.
  - Build information literacy skills by learning how to read and analyze peer-reviewed research articles and determine credible sources.
  - Build critical thinking skills to use in conversation, courses, and meetings.

- **Part II: Mapping Out a Path and Developing Career Skills**
  - Learn about ways to set goals and choose a path.
  - Create an academic and career plan and get on track to a successful future early.
  - Strengthen networking and other essential skills for academic, career, and personal success.

- **Part III: Achieving Academic Success**
  - Discover and practice key strategies that will be useful to get a degree, land a position aligned to your interests and values, and advance in your career.
  - Showcase knowledge and skills with high-quality presentations, papers, and assignments.
  - Be resilient and gritty by practicing effective stress management and strategies to stay motivated.
  - Use the end-of-chapter note-taking methods to focus on most important concepts and learn success strategies.
  - Test knowledge with Quick Quizzes as a powerful way to study and learn.

Ancillary Package

Embracing Technology

MindTap College Success for *Student Success in College: Doing What Works!* combines tools like a robust self-assessment, readings, flashcards, practice research opportunities, quizzes, and other digital activities designed intentionally to guide students through their course and transform them into master students. This MindTap follows a "Research It, Apply It" structure that guides students through chapter-aligned research exercises, followed by authentic application opportunities.

- The College Success Factors Index (CSFI) is a personal success indicator that helps students identify their strengths and areas for growth in 10 key factors identified by researchers to affect college success. The CSFI kicks off MindTap for Student Success in College: Doing What Works!
- "Research It" activities align with the research studies found in the Exploring the Research in Depth appendix in the book. Each "Research It" folder includes a warm-up polling question, research study, and journal entry.
- "Apply It" activities are designed to bridge the understanding of chapter concepts with their real-world applications in both college and career.

Cengage Infuse for College Success is the first-of-its-kind digital learning platform that leverages Learning Management Systems (LMS) functionality so that instructors can enjoy simple course set up and intuitive management tools. Offering just the right amount of auto graded content — like Concept Checks and Chapter Quizzes — you will be ready to go online at the drop of a hat.

For Instructors

Additional instructor resources for this product are available online. Instructor assets include an Instructor's Manual, Educator's Guide, PowerPoint slides, and a test bank powered by Cognero. In addition, sample syllabi and teaching demos conducted by the author are provided. Sign up or sign in at www.cengage.com to search for and access this product and its online resources.

Acknowledgments

I am beyond grateful to my family, colleagues, students, and my amazing team at Cengage. Writing this book would not be possible without the never-ending support and encouragement provided by my husband, Dan, and two sons, Ryan and David, my niece Ashley, and of course my parents.

I would also like to thank my many FYE colleagues across the nation for believing in me and this resource and for their willingness to share their ideas about how to improve the book. I am honored that so many colleges and universities across the nation have chosen this text to support the work they are doing with first-year students. My students have always been, and will continue to be, a source of inspiration. I am also thankful to the many reviewers whose feedback was incredibly valuable and helped strengthen this text, and to Chris Genthe for her excellent proofreading skills.

Tom Peterson

Part 1

Knowing Yourself and Being a Critical Thinker

Getting Started

> Commit to your education, because every time you stretch your mind, you boost your confidence and add power and credibility to your voice.
>
> —Michele Obama

1 What are the benefits of getting a college degree?

2 What options are there to pay for college?

3 What does return on investment mean?

4 How can my financial behaviors today impact my future?

5 How can I establish and maintain a good credit score?

Value of a College Education

Going to college is one of the best decisions you can make! The knowledge, skills, and confidence you gain not only will increase your career opportunities but will also be beneficial to you and others in many ways. Students often view college as a necessary step to enter a desired career, and this is certainly one benefit of education. Some careers do require a college degree; however, there are other definite benefits to a college education.

iStockPhoto

Some countries focus almost exclusively on getting students prepared for the working world by only requiring coursework that is directly connected to a student's selected major or career. This is not the case in the United States. The U.S. higher education system was built on the idea that education can prepare individuals to be productive, contributing members of society. It is believed that to accomplish this task, knowledge and skills beyond a specialty area—often called a major—are needed.

You will learn major- and career-specific content and skills as part of your degree program of study but courses in your selected major may only be approximately one third of the required coursework. In addition to taking major-specific courses, you will also need to take general education courses and electives. In these courses, you will be exposed to a variety of perspectives and opportunities that can help you develop essential information literacy, critical thinking, and interpersonal skills needed to excel in various careers and as a citizen. As a college graduate, you walk away with not only a deep knowledge of the discipline you chose to major in but also a broad range of essential skills that will serve you well personally and professionally.

Civic Engagement

Civic engagement refers to being involved in your community and taking actions that can have a positive impact on others. Skills such as critical thinking, problem solving, working collaboratively in diverse teams, and communication are useful in careers and facilitate civic engagement (Sukkon, 2016). These skills are heavily emphasized in college.

Vesperstock/Shutterstock.com

"It is the participation in higher education, the interactions with peers, teachers and diverse forms of knowledge that will enable people to live richer lives and contribute to greater social justice through work and other social activities" (McArther, 2011, p. 746).

Sanders (2012) noted "so much of what you do in college, such as doing research and taking general education classes, is designed to help you become a more intelligent, capable, understanding, aware, and competent person—regardless of your major" (p. 4).

Researchers have found that college graduates are more likely to participate in community service, give to charities, and vote, as compared to individuals who did not attend college (Chan, 2016; Ishitani, 2009). Baum et al. (2010) reported that 43% of adults with a bachelor's degree volunteered, compared to only 19% of adults with only a high school diploma.

Well-Being

Education is connected to emotional and physical well-being. For example, Yakovlev and Leguizamon (2012) found that individuals with more education were happier than individuals with less education. Baum et al. (2010) also found that college graduates were more likely to be satisfied with their job and to report a sense of accomplishment with their work. More education was also found to be associated with fewer depressive symptoms in a study conducted by Sironi (2012). See Figure I.1.

College graduates were less likely to have physical health problems later in life (Goesling, 2007; Zhang et al., 2011). This may be in part due to college graduates being less likely to engage in unhealthy behaviors, such as smoking, and more likely to engage in healthy behaviors, such as exercising regularly (Ma et al., 2019; Baum et al., 2010). Getting an education helps you make better choices that will help you stay healthy and increases the likelihood that you will have access to health insurance benefits. Ninety-two percent of individuals with a bachelor's degree reported having health insurance as compared to only 69% of individuals with a high school diploma reporting that they have health insurance (Washington Higher Education Board, 2012).

Family and Future Generations

Getting a degree can also benefit your current and future family members. Baum et al. (2012) found that college graduates were more likely to exhibit better parenting behaviors, such as reading to their children and taking their children to community events. Ma et al. (2019) also found that higher levels of education were connected to increased parental engagement. The education you receive will help you make better parenting choices in the future, and these choices will have a long-lasting impact on your children and even your grandchildren. Your family will therefore benefit from you getting a college education.

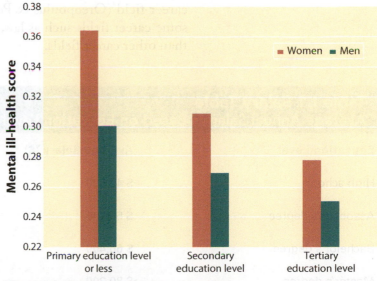

Figure I.1 Education and mental health.

Think Critically

1. What education and gender differences do you notice related to mental health?
2. What are some possible explanations for these education and gender differences?

iStockPhoto/Monkeybusinessimages

Finances

As you probably know, earning a degree will also increase your earning potential. See Table I.1 for a quick look at average salaries for full-time workers with varying levels of education (Ma et al., 2019). As you can see, earning a bachelor's degree increases the average salary by almost $24,500 per year. This means individuals with bachelor's degrees make approximately a million dollars more than their peers with only a high school education throughout the course of a lifetime. This turns into approximately 2 million more dollars in your lifetime if you get a doctoral degree.

Figure I.2 visually displays the positive financial consequences of higher education.

Although the cost of college has been increasing, research conducted by Abel and Deitz (2014) suggests that college is still a worthwhile investment. Over the past 40 years, the average wage has been consistently higher for those who earn a bachelor's degree. Likewise, individuals with an associate degree have been consistently earning higher salaries as compared to those with a high school diploma. Not surprisingly, there can be much variability in salary based on the career field (Oreopoulus & Petronijevic, 2013). Kim et al. (2015) found that some career fields such as law, business, and medical had much higher salaries than other career fields.

Table I.1 Salary Table
Average Annual Salaries Based on Education Level (Ma et al., 2019)

Education Level	Average Salary ($)
High school	$ 40,500
Associate's degree	$ 50,100
Bachelor's degree	$ 65,400
Master's degree	$ 80,200
Doctorate degree	$ 102,300

Think Critically

1. What is the key take-away from this graph on annual earnings by education?
2. Why do you believe the salaries vary so much by education?

Source: Adapted from: Ma, J., Pender, M., & Welch, M. (2019). Education pays: The benefits of education for the individual and society. College Board. https://research.collegeboard.org/pdf/education-pays-2019-full-report.pdf

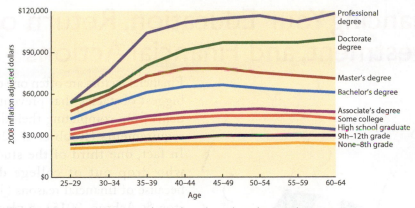

Figure I.2 Average annual earnings by education attainment.

College graduates are also less likely to be unemployed (Gillie & Isenhour, 2003; Ma et al., 2019) and are more likely to work for companies that provide higher-level benefit packages such as healthcare, paid vacation, and sick time. For example, in a study conducted by the Washington Higher Education Board (2012), 90% of individuals with a bachelor's degree indicated receiving paid vacation or sick leave as compared to only 75% of individuals who had a high school diploma or less.

Summary: Benefits of Higher Education

- Civic engagement
  - More likely to vote
  - More likely to volunteer and engage in community service
  - More likely to make charitable donations
- Overall well-being
  - Happier, less likely to become depressed
  - More likely to engage in healthy behaviors such as exercising
  - Less likely to have physical health problems and engage in unhealthy behaviors such as smoking
- Future generations
  - More likely to use effective parenting strategies, such as reading to children
- Career satisfaction
  - Increased satisfaction and sense of accomplishment
- Salary and benefits
  - Higher salaries
  - Less likely to be unemployed or need to rely on government support
  - More likely to have access to healthcare

Value of College Education Quick Quiz

1. How can you benefit from a college education?
2. How can your education benefit others?

Financing Your Education, Return on Investment, and Financial Actions

Mehaniq/Shutterstock.com

Financial factors are often one of the biggest obstacles that prevent students from completing their degree requirements (Robb et al., 2012). In fact, one third of the students who drop out of college do so because of financial reasons (Johnston & Ashton, 2015) so planning for financial success while in school is critical.

Understanding the long-term impact of financial choices you make while a college student is also important. Students who engage in good planning and decision making related to financial choices are more likely to succeed (Johnson & Ashton, 2015).

Financing Your Education

Many college students rely on student loans and need-based or merit-based scholarships or grants to pay for college. To be considered for all types of financial aid including loans, you will need to complete federal forms commonly referred to as the FAFSA (Free Application for Federal Student Aid).

Financial Aid Grants and Loans

The FAFSA paperwork needs to be completed every year and is used to determine your eligibility for federal aid,

iStockPhoto/Artisteer

including grants, work-study, and loans. Most traditional-aged students will need to provide financial documents and information from their parents or guardians. If you are a nontraditional-age student, you will likely be able use your own financial information to complete this form.

Many colleges offer students assistance with completing this paperwork. If you need assistance with this task, reach out to the financial aid office. After you complete this paperwork, you will be notified about whether you are eligible for grants or loans. Grants typically do not need to be paid back but loans do.

Most students rely on student loans to be able to attend college. The Institute

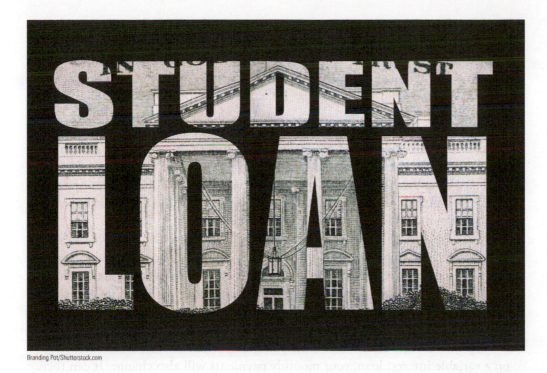

Branding Pot/Shutterstock.com

for College Access and Success (2013) reported, "Seven in 10 college seniors who graduated in 2012 had student loan debt, with an average of $29,400 for those with loans" (p. 1). While college is an exceptionally good investment in your financial future, having too much debt can be stressful and impact your ability to qualify for loans, such as mortgages, in the future. You will therefore want to minimize your debt to the extent that this is possible. Only borrow what you need.

There are two kinds of student loans: federal loans, which require you to fill out a FAFSA, and private loans. It is recommended that you apply for federal loans first and use private loans only after you have exhausted all other options because private loans often have higher interest rates and payments may be required immediately even though you are still a student. Typically, you have approximately six months after you graduate or stop attending college before you have to start paying back a federal student loan.

Before you take out a loan, it is important for you to understand how loans work and how they will impact you financially after graduation. Loans are composed of principal and interest. Principal is the amount you borrowed; interest is the additional amount you are paying to the lender as a service fee for lending you the money.

Loan repayment plans typically front-end the interest costs. In other words, when you start paying your loan back, most of your initial payments will be toward interest and not the principal of the loan. This means the overall amount that you owe does not decrease much in the earlier years of the loan.

According to Kantrowitz, a general guideline is that if your total student loan debt is less than your starting salary after graduation, you will likely be able to pay it off within 10 years (as cited in Ashford, 2014). The average student loan debt is approximately $30,000 (Bidwell, 2014).

According to a national survey, the average starting salary for college graduates in 2016 was projected to be just over $50,000 (Poppick, 2015). If your situation is similar, you will be able to repay your loans within the 10-year period with payments of approximately $300.00 per month. As the size of your loan grows, so do the monthly payment amounts. See Table I.2 for some examples of how long it can take to repay student loans.

Knowing the specific terms associated with your loan is important. **Subsidized loans** do not accrue interest while you are a student, meaning the amount you borrowed will be the same amount you owe at the time you have to start repaying the loan. **Unsubsidized loans** start to accrue interest from the moment you sign on the dotted line. In this case, by the time you finish school, your loan amount will be more than what you originally borrowed.

Loans can have either variable or fixed ratio interest rates. Variable rates tend to be attractive because they are often low at first, but as their name implies, the rate can go up or down at any time. Fixed ratios, on the other hand, are predictable because they are locked in, meaning your interest rate remains the same throughout the duration of the loan. Most federal student loans are fixed, while private loans are often variable.

The interest rate on the loan is incredibly important because when rates change on a variable interest loan, your monthly payments will also change. It can therefore be more challenging to budget as the loan payment amount will vary. It is strongly recommended that you meet with a professional in the financial aid office at your college so that your student loan questions can be answered, and you can understand the terms of your loan.

Borrow only what you need. You may qualify for a loan that will cover expenses beyond tuition costs. While having some extra cash can seem like a good idea at first, remember that you will be paying interest on this money. Whenever possible, consider paying for smaller expenses as you go along. This helps keep you from graduating with significant debt.

Scholarships   You may also be receiving merit-based scholarships. If so, congratulations! Merit-based scholarships are offered to students with exceptional academic performance. Some scholarships are one-time scholarships, meaning you receive the funding only once or toward one year of college. Other scholarships are renewable, sometimes providing you with funds for up to four years of college. Often, there are grade point average or other requirements that must be met to continue receiving the funding. If you are receiving a scholarship, investigate the terms of the scholarship.

Contact your financial aid office or visit websites such as Fastweb.com or Scholarships.com to learn about additional scholarship opportunities for which

Table I.2 Loan Repayment Table Examples of Student Loan Repayment Schedules and Costs			
Student Loan Amount	**Monthly Payment**	**Approximately, How Many Years to Pay it Off?**	**Approximately, What Will Be the Total Interest Paid?***
$ 30,000	$ 300.00	10	$ 6,500.00
$ 60,000	$ 600.00	10	$ 13,100.00
$ 100,000	$ 1,000.00	10	$ 21,800.00

*Based on a 4% interest rate

Fizkes/Shutterstock.com

you can apply. If you are planning to transfer to a different institution, be sure to contact its financial aid department to inquire about scholarship opportunities for transfer students. Many colleges and universities offer scholarships specifically for transfer students. Investing your time to explore possible scholarship opportunities might pay off!

Payment Plans Most colleges will also offer students the option to pay their tuition bill in monthly or quarterly payments instead of as a one-lump sum. Although it is not common for colleges to charge significant fees for this option, it is a good idea to find out how a payment plan option works at your college or

iStockPhoto/Milindri

university. This option is appealing to students who are working and plan to use their income from work to make the tuition payments.

Return on Investment

While college can be expensive, analysts have shown that education has a high return on investment (Carnevale et al. 2020). **Return on investment** refers to the financial benefits associated with investing your money in something such as education or the stock market. In other words, when someone is asking about return on investment, they are basically asking the question, "Is this a worthwhile investment that will lead to financial gain?" According to Abel and Deitz (2014), the return on investment for a college degree is much higher (14%–15% over the past 10 years for a bachelor's degree) than other financial investments such as stocks that typically have a return rate of approximately 7% or bonds that have a typical return of 3%. In other words, education is one of the best financial investments one can make.

Although getting a degree does significantly increase your earning potential (Julian & Kominski, 2011), the total cost of an education is an important consideration. Abel and Deitz (2014) discussed two types of costs associated with getting an education: direct costs and opportunity costs. **Direct costs** are any costs associated with obtaining the degree. Tuition, fees, and books are examples of direct costs. **Opportunity costs**, on the other hand, refer to what is lost because of attending college. The best example of an opportunity cost is the wage that you would have earned if you were working instead of attending college. Going to school part-time can often have a higher opportunity cost than attending full-time. This is because part-time students spend more years in college and although part-time students earn some income while in college, the pregraduation salaries are typically significantly lower than the postgraduation salaries. Graduating within four years can decrease both direct and opportunity costs.

Return on investment can vary by institution and by career field. According to a 2019 report, community colleges, not surprisingly, had the highest return on investment (Carnevale et al., 2020). You can visit websites such as payscale.com to better understand the return on investment at different schools and for different majors. Ash (2014) outlines the following steps to calculate the return on investment for college:

- Determine the net price for the college you are or will be attending. The net price is the total cost of tuition, books, fees, and room and board minus any grants or scholarships you receive.
- Determine the approximate debt you will have upon graduation. In other words, how much will you have to borrow by the time you graduate?
- Find out how long it will take you to earn the degree. Unfortunately, many students do not graduate in four years, the typical expected length of time for full-time students. In fact, only approximately 59% of undergraduates earn a bachelor's degree within six years (as cited in Ash, 2014). Attending college as a full-time student is advisable, if possible, because attending part-time means you will be in college for a longer period of time.
- Investigate your earning potential upon graduation. There are many websites that can help you identify starting and average salaries for various majors or careers.
- Identify missed opportunities for income. For example, if you are attending school full-time, you will be missing out on a full-time income.

Considering all these factors will help you determine if the investment is worth it. As mentioned previously, earning a college degree has a high return on investment; however, it is best if you can earn a degree without having significant debt after graduation. Evaluate the pros and cons of attending various colleges and universities.

Many of you may be attending a community college, which is a terrific way to get a quality education without accumulating as much debt. The average tuition and fees for community college are less than half of the tuition and fees at the public, four-year colleges. Specifically, in 2020–2021, the average annual community college tuition and fees were $3,770, while the average annual tuition and fees at the four-year public colleges were $10,560 (AACC, 2021). You might be surprised to learn that "nearly half of all undergraduates attend community college" (AACC, 2021). If you are attending a four-year college or university, you may want to consider taking summer classes at your local community college. Check with your college on transfer policies before you register. Community colleges have high returns on their investment, and starting at a community college before transferring to a four-year school can also be a way to reduce debt (Ma et al., 2019).

Financial Actions

Developing and practicing good financial habits while you are in college can help minimize debt and reduce stress. Establishing and living by a budget, engaging in financial planning, and establishing good credit are all important.

Budgeting and Financial Planning Budgeting can help you make good financial choices. The budgeting process is simple. First, determine how much money you have coming in, then deduct required expenses. You can then decide what to do with any additional monies. Unfortunately, when we do this exercise, many of us discover that our expenses exceed our income. This often results in credit card use that leads to unwanted debt.

Finding ways to reduce your monthly expenses can have long-term positive consequences. Start by evaluating whether all your expenses are essential. For example, instead of paying a membership fee for an outside gym, consider using the on-campus fitness center. Small actions such as brewing your own coffee versus stopping at a local coffee shop before heading to class can add up and make a big impact on your budget.

You can also evaluate whether you need every service or subscription you currently have. When you review all of your services, you may discover that you are not using all of them often or that two services are similar, and you can opt to have just one. Sometimes you can negotiate a better price for services you subscribe to by

Prostock-studio/Shutterstock.com

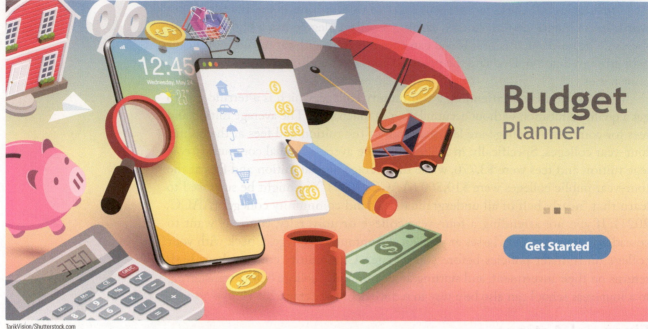

TarikVision/Shutterstock.com

contacting the providers. Instead of simply paying whatever monthly fee is being charged, periodically shop around and renegotiate pricing.

Take advantage of bundling discounts when available. Insurance companies will reward you for purchasing more than one type of insurance through their company, often giving discounts if you use their company for auto and home or rental insurance. Technology companies do this too—if you purchase Internet, phone, and television services through the same provider, you will likely benefit from a bundled rate. Contact providers and ask them for a better rate, or shop around and consider switching providers. Although these actions do require your time, you will likely financially benefit with reduced monthly expenses.

Even though we know that engaging in short- and long-term financial planning is beneficial, most do not focus enough time and energy on this important task. College students are particularly guilty of not engaging in financial planning, probably because many college students do not have much money to "plan" with! Yet, the financial choices you make today can have significant, long-lasting consequences.

As with all planning, it is best to start with the end in mind. What is your long-term financial goal? For most, it is financial security. This means you want to be able to afford to live the lifestyle you would like and not experience financial stress. As you know, education is the single most important action you can take to make this goal a reality.

After you have identified your financial goals, you need to determine what you need to do to accomplish these goals. This includes evaluating your current spending patterns and choices. It also involves saving for the future.

When making financial decisions, it is important to make logical choices that result in positive consequences. However, it is common to make emotionally based decisions. Mood plays a significant role in decision making, especially when making big purchase decisions (Gardner, 1985). As emotions go up, logic drops down. See Figure I.3. This is particularly problematic when you are making decisions

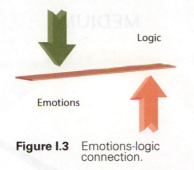

Figure I.3   Emotions-logic connection.

about expensive purchases such as a car, but it can also be a problem if you buy less expensive items frequently. When you are excited about a purchase, the logical part of your brain will not be as functional as it would be if your emotions were neutral. This results in what is often called impulse buying. Impulse buying often leads to debt and works against your long-term goals.

Wait before making a big purchase. With the passage of time, your emotions tend to become less intense, which allows you to make more logical decisions. This is why the car salesperson pressures you to make a decision now. The salesperson knows that you are more likely to sign the contract when your emotions are high, so they will push you to sign on the dotted line today. To increase your excitement, the salesperson will have you sit in a car that is your favorite color and tell you all about the bells and whistles. If you leave and your emotions decrease in intensity, your logic returns and you are more likely to make a financially wise decision.

Saving for big purchases such as cars, vacations, or homes and also saving for the future are advisable. Although it may often feel like it is impossible to save while in college, most can find a way to save something. This may mean not buying a cup of coffee every day or eliminating a technology service or two. You will be surprised and will likely feel proud when you see how much of a difference these small actions can make. Although it may be difficult to think about retirement now given your current financial obligations, saving just a small amount when you are young can turn into a significant amount when it is time for you to retire. Consult with a financial planner to help you develop a plan for saving for retirement.

Establishing Good Credit   Based on your financial behaviors, you will be assigned a credit score. A **credit score** communicates how well you are managing your finances. Lenders, such as banks, landlords, and credit card companies, use your credit score to determine eligibility for loans, interest rates, or even reward programs. It is therefore important to have a good credit score. Scores range from 350 to 850, and a score of 700 or higher is typically considered good while 800 or higher would be considered excellent. There are several agencies that conduct the credit evaluations to determine your score (FICO, 2011). These agencies determine your credit score based on several factors including:

- payment history (on-time vs. late payments), 35%
- amount owed (debt), 30%
- length of credit history (when first financial account was opened), 15%
- new credit (new accounts), 10%
- type of credit (variety in account types) 10%

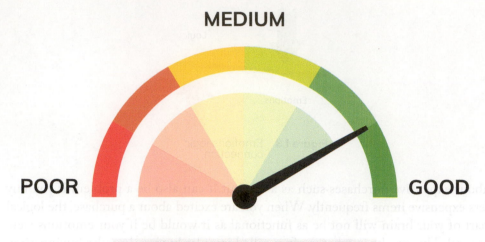

MEDIUM

POOR   **GOOD**

CREDIT SCORE

Kolonko/Shutterstock.com

The better your credit score, the more likely it is that you will be eligible for a loan or for a loan with the best interest rate. You are also more likely to get higher credit limits that will allow you to make big purchases, such as buying a car or home.

There are several ways to earn a good credit score:

- **Pay bills on time.** The most important way to build good credit is through on-time payments of bills. You can set up automatic payments from your checking account to be sure that you are not late or do not miss payments.
- **Get a credit card.** If you do not already have a credit card, you might want to consider getting one or two. Keep in mind that it is not a good idea to open too many credit card accounts, though.
- **Use your credit card wisely.** It is important to consider how much you owe on a credit card compared to your limit. The limit is the maximum amount you can charge. Maxing out your credit cards or charging close to the credit limit lowers your score. A good suggestion is to only charge up to 25% of your limit. If you have a $1,000 credit limit on a credit card, do not charge more than $250, and be sure to pay your bills on time (FICO, 2011).

Getting a credit card can be a wise financial decision if you are responsible. The Credit Card Act of 2009 made it more difficult for college students under 21 to get a credit card, though. To do so, you will either need someone to cosign for you or you will have to show proof that you can pay the credit card bill (Prater, 2010). Because you are only going to get one or two accounts, choose your credit card carefully. Thoroughly review the terms and conditions associated with the card. Several credit cards offer reward programs such as miles for flying or cash-back, but factors such as the interest rate and fee structures matter the most.

Remember, credit card companies are in the business of making money. They charge fees, such as annual fees, late fees, and interest on your purchases. They only require that you pay a minimum amount each month, and the interest charges quickly increase your debt. In fact, if you are only able to pay the minimum amount each month, it will take an awfully long time to pay off the entire balance and get out of debt. If you have a credit card balance of $1,000, make the minimum payment of $20 per month and have an annual interest rate of 18%, it will take you over seven years to pay it off and with interest, you would pay almost $1,800 to the credit card company. This is nearly double the original amount. Apps or online credit card calculators (www.creditcards.com/calculators/) are good resources if you want to see how long it will take to pay off a debt. See Table I.3 for an overview of the advantages and disadvantages of credit cards.

Financing Your Education, Return on Investment, and Financial Actions Quick Quiz

1. What options exist to pay for college?
2. What does return on investment mean? What is the return on investment for education and how does it compare to other investments?
3. What are some ways you may be able to reduce your monthly expenses?
4. What can you do to establish good credit?

Table I.3 Evaluating Credit Cards Table
Advantages and Disadvantages of Credit Cards

Pros	Cons
Builds credit if bills are paid on time, which will help later when making big purchases such as a mortgage for a home.	Interest adds up quickly.
Tracks spending habits easily.	If you don't pay off your balance each month, you will be paying more for the product because of interest.
You get the product now.	If you don't pay the balance on time, it negatively impacts your credit score.
Rewards may be associated with credit card use (e.g., cashback or airline miles).	Can easily create long-term debt if not paid off each month.

Chapter

1

Exploring Your Identity

We are more alike, my friends, than we are unalike.
— *Maya Angelou*

1. How do you determine and describe your identity?

2. In what ways do your group memberships define who you are?

3. What does intersectionality mean?

4. What roles and relationships influence your identity?

5. How do your interests and personal characteristics shape your identity?

6. What values are most important to you?

7. What is activism?

Exploring the Research in Summary

Research Study Citation:

Shell, M. D., Shears, D., & Millard, Z. (2020). Who am I? Identity development during the first year of college. *Psi Chi Journal of Psychological Research*, 25(2), 192–202. doi:10.24839/2325-7342. jn25.2.192

Introduction: The Research Question

What question did the research seek to answer?

1. How much change happens in terms of identity development during the first year of college?
2. Is identity development related to psychological well-being?

Method: The Study

Who participated in the study? What did the researchers ask the participants to do?

College students at a public university were invited to participate in the study. A total of 144 students completed surveys about their identity and well-being during their first year in college. Only 98 students completed the surveys in both the fall and spring semesters, so the results are based on their responses. Most students reported identifying as European Americans (91%). Ten percent identified as African American, 2% as Latinx, and 2% as American Indian or Native American.

Results: The Findings

Findings indicated there is much stability with identity exploration and commitment during the first year of college, meaning that students exploring their identity in the fall continued to explore in the spring and those who were committed to their identity in the fall remained committed in the spring. However, this did vary to some extent based on different aspects of identity.

Identity development was connected to overall psychological well-being. Global and friendship exploration were associated with lower levels of satisfaction with life. Romantic commitment was related to higher levels of life satisfaction.

Discussion and So-What Factor

How can YOU use this information as a student?

These findings show that identity development takes time and is not something that is achieved in one year of college. Identity achievement requires exploration followed by commitment. Seeking out opportunities for you to explore who you are can help you move toward identity achievement. Recognize that exploring can be associated with lower levels of life satisfaction and note that this is normal. Anxiety and stress are often higher when we explore and have not yet committed. Establishing a strong support system that includes friends and a significant other can be helpful and increase your satisfaction and life. Relationships are important source of support, but they take time to develop, especially when you have just entered a new environment such as college. Seek out opportunities to get to know others and build relationships.

Let us begin with an important yet complex question: Who are you? Taking time to explore who you are as you begin your college journey is a valuable activity. "Self-exploration is central to our growth as individuals, our relationships with others, and our ability to promote equity. Our various social identities—sex, race, ethnicity, sexual orientation, gender, age, socioeconomic class, religion, and ability, among others—are important aspects of our selves that shape our attitudes, behaviors, worldviews, and experiences" (Goodman, 2010, para. 1). In college, taking time to figure out who you are and who you want to be can help you make good academic, professional, and personal decisions.

In this chapter, you will learn about the importance of considering your multiple identities, a concept referred to as **intersectionality**. You will also explore groups in which you belong, relationships and social roles you have, and your personal characteristics. In addition, you will have the opportunity to consider your values, actions, and goals.

Intersectionality

Schwartz et al. (2010) emphasized the importance of exploring both your personal and cultural identity. According to Stirratt et al. (2007), there are three primary ways that we tend to describe our identity:

D.J Kirei/Shutterstock.com

1. Group membership
2. Relationships and social roles
3. Personal traits and characteristics

Intersectionality is a term that can help you see your many different identities and how these diverse aspects of your identity connect. The term intersectionality was first used in 1989 by Kimberlé Crenshaw, a scholar and activist, to bring attention to the experiences of Black females who belonged to two oppressed groups (Perlman, 2018).

Group Membership

Group membership is a key part of your identity. Race, ethnicity, sexual orientation, and gender are examples of group memberships that help you define who you are and are often core parts of your identity. Although these are terms that are used often, their definitions can vary. For our purposes, the following definitions will be used:

Melitas/Shutterstock.com

- **Race** is a **social construct** that refers to a group of people who have similar physical traits (American Psychological Association, 2019). The term social construct means that it is not biologically determined but rather determined by humans in society. Social constructs can have different meanings in different social contexts.

- **Ethnicity** refers to a shared ancestry, history, and culture (American Psychological Association, 2019).
- **Sexual orientation** refers to "a component of identity that includes a person's sexual and emotional attraction to another person and the behavior that may result from this attraction" (American Psychological Association, 2015, p. 22).
- **Gender** is defined as "the attitudes, feelings, and behaviors that a given culture associates with a person's biological sex" (American Psychological Association, 2015, p. 20).

It is important to recognize that the labels used do not fully capture who you are. Identities are complex, and your story will be best told when you acknowledge and appreciate your multiple identities. Chizhik and Chizhik (2005) cautioned that using simple definitions to describe identity can be problematic. They found that when you describe yourself in simple terms, you may also do the same for others. When this happens, you miss out on understanding all aspects of yourself and others.

It is important to understand how privilege and oppression can impact you and others.

- **Privilege** refers to advantages that are automatically given to you as a person because you are a member of a group. White individuals, males, individuals identifying as heterosexual, and as able-bodied individuals carry the most privilege.
- **Oppression,** on the other hand, refers to disadvantages associated with group membership. Examples of oppressed groups include BIPOC (Black, Indigenous, and People of Color), females, the LGBTQIA+ community, and individuals with disabilities.

One way you may characterize your identity is by how you are different from others. Stirratt et al. (2007) noted that you are likely to identify characteristics that make you unique when describing yourself. Individuals who are from privileged groups such as someone who is heterosexual may not immediately identify as such. However, individuals who identify as part of an oppressed group such as the LGBTQIA+ community are often more likely to indicate that sexual orientation is an important part of their identity. For those of you unfamiliar with the term LGBTQIA+, it is used to indicate someone who identifies as one or more of the following: lesbian, gay, bisexual, transgender, queer, intersex, asexual, and questioning. Another example relates to individuals with disabilities. For individuals who do not have a disability, being able-bodied may not be a term they would immediately use to

Shawn Goldberg/Shutterstock.com

define themselves. However, if someone has a disability, it is more likely that this part of their identify might be immediately identified as a core part of who they are.

The disadvantages and consequences associated with oppression are often felt very strongly and on a regular basis by members of oppressed groups. If, on the other hand, you are a member of a privileged group, the advantages given to you may not be noticed as easily. It is important to note that many from privileged groups work hard to achieve success. The difference, though, is that if two people work hard, one from a privileged group and another from an oppressed group, the positive outcome may be more likely for the person with privilege (T. Ayeni, personal communication, June 3, 2021).

Clifford (2020), who identifies as a White female, shared the following running metaphor to help students better understand privilege:

"As I started out, I felt like my feet were wings. I had gone for a longer-than-usual run a few days before and decided that must be the cause of my improvement. It's possible that I looked quite slow to anyone who saw me, but by my standards, I was zooming along. The Chariots of Fire theme song was going through my head. I felt like I reached the end of the first mile in no time. My hope had been to run the return route faster than the first mile, and I had no doubt in my mind I would be able to. But then I reached the end of the road and turned around. As I started my run back, I was gasping for breath and had to fight for each step. Remember, the road was pretty flat, so it's not that I was now going uphill. No, what I realized as I ran that first block in the return direction was that I was now running headfirst against the wind. I was aware of that wind every step I took and knew that I had to expend a lot of energy to simply move forward. It was very obvious to me that the wind was an obstacle to my running prowess. It took me a little while to realize, however, that the same wind that was now making it so difficult for me to run had a few minutes earlier been pushing me along on the first half of my run. What I thought was a major breakthrough in my development as a runner was really just nature giving me a push. While I was constantly aware of the wind on the second half of my run, I hadn't noticed it at all on the first half. Instead, in my mind my improved abilities were all because of me. I had thought I was becoming a damn good runner. As I was cooling down, I realized that this experience provides a metaphor for how privilege works in our society. Privilege is like the wind that was pushing me along. It surrounds us and gives some an added push—unearned benefits/advantages—that makes it easier to excel. The person running against the wind never forgets the wind is there. Similarly, many in our society can never forget that it is riddled with racism, sexism, class inequality, heterosexism, ableism, and religious intolerance. At the same time, others of us can go on blissfully unaware that the wind is at our backs. Our society is structured to keep that privilege invisible much of the time, and those with privilege often attribute their success to exactly the kinds of things I was thinking on the first half of my run: my success is because of my abilities, my hard work" (p. 75).

It is common for individuals to be part of both privileged and oppressed groups. Ayeni (2018) noted "an African American student at a predominantly White campus will have the experience of being part of a minority group. However, if that same African American student is a male majoring in one of the science, technology, engineering, and math (STEM) fields (a field in which women have traditionally been underrepresented), then, in the aspect of gender, he may also have experiences as part of a majority group" (para. 3).

In an interesting study by Chizhik and Chizhik (2005), they found that students who categorized themselves as non-White were more likely than White students to view themselves as having statuses associated with both privilege and oppression. The following are examples of student responses to a question about privilege and oppression that show the complexity of privilege and oppression.

"Both. I am oppressed because I grew up very poor, went to a school without any programs other than sports, and came from a one-parent home. I also grew up in an area that is mainly White or Hispanic, but I am both and never seemed to fit in. I am now a single mom, plus I am working my way through college. I am privileged because I had a family who valued education. My mother supplemented my education through PBS plus library materials. She has helped me whenever she could so that I could go to college and move from economic oppression to economic privilege" (Chizhik & Chizhik, 2005, p. 125).

"I must first say that both states of being are relative in my opinion. Nonetheless, I would consider myself to be both privileged and oppressed. I know that I am privileged because I have always had the "necessities" of life (i.e., a roof over my head, clothes on my back, food on my table, etc.) but beyond that, I have also had the opportunity to travel, pursue a postsecondary education, and the freedoms that accompany American citizenship. However, in the midst of the many positive aspects of my life is the negative and heavy weight of oppression. I say that I am oppressed because a major determining factor of my reality is the color of my skin. Another is my gender. And depending on what the latest societal norms are, those factors can, not will, limit my achievements. Now this is not to say that my capabilities do not play a role in shaping reality. I am just saying that they can be overshadowed by the factors mentioned above" (Chizhik & Chizhik, 2005, p. 125).

There are many differences among individuals within each socially constructed group. This is especially true when broader terms such as people of color are used but is also true with more specific labels such as Black or Latinx. Individuals identifying as Black or Latinx share some characteristics with others in their group but will also vary a lot on other characteristics. It is therefore important for you to consider not only what racial and ethnic groups you and others identify with but also in what way and to what extent. Categories are convenient ways to describe ourselves and others but cannot be relied on as they do not fully capture who you or others are.

There are, of course, many other kinds of group memberships that can also help define who you are. For example, your religious affiliation can be an important part of your identity. For some, this group membership is central to their identity. Individuals with disabilities may also define themselves in part by their disability or diagnosis. For example, it is common for individuals with a specific diagnosis to relate to others who have the same diagnosis, and this can be an important part of who they are. Team membership is another example. If you are an athlete or even a fan, being associated with a team can be another significant part of your identity.

Where you live also contributes to your identity. Your hometown or even the part of your hometown where you reside may play an important role in who you are. If you are residing on campus, your residence hall may also become a part of your identity. In a study by Garvey et al. (2020), student group membership in a residence hall positively impacted their sense of belonging.

Understanding yourself and others requires deep exploration and interaction. One way to get started is to complete self-assessment inventories. It is important that inventories you take have been studied by researchers to ensure they are effective tools. Roberts et al. (1999) developed a multigroup ethnic identity measure that has been published in a peer-reviewed journal and studied by researchers. See Table 1.1.

iStockPhoto/SDI Productions

Table 1.1
Multigroup Ethnic Identity Measure

These questions are about your ethnicity or your ethnic group and how you feel about it or react to it.

Please fill in: In terms of ethnic group, I consider myself to be _____

Use the numbers below to indicate how much you agree or disagree with each statement.

(4) Strongly agree; (3) Agree; (2) Disagree; (1) Strongly disagree

1. _____ I have spent time trying to find out more about my ethnic group, such as its history, traditions, and customs.
2. _____ I am active in organizations or social groups that include mostly members of my own ethnic group.
3. _____ I have a clear sense of my ethnic background and what it means for me.
4. _____ I think a lot about how my life will be affected by my ethnic group membership.
5. _____ I am happy that I am a member of the group I belong to.
6. _____ I have a strong sense of belonging to my own ethnic group.
7. _____ I understand pretty well what my ethnic group membership means to me.
8. _____ To learn more about my ethnic background, I have often talked to other people about my ethnic group.
9. _____ I have a lot of pride in my ethnic group and its accomplishments.
10. _____ I participate in cultural practices of my own group, such as special food, music, or customs.
11. _____ I feel a strong attachment towards my own ethnic group.
12. _____ I feel good about my cultural or ethnic background.

There are two subscales, and higher scores on each indicate stronger ethnic identity. The affirmation and belonging subscale refers to how strong your sense of group membership is, your pride associated with being a member, and your overall positive feelings related to your group. The exploration scale taps into how much time and effort you have spent getting to know more about the groups you relate to.

Affirmation/belonging scale: 3, 5, 6, 7, 9, 11, 12

Exploration scale: 1, 2, 3, 4, 8, 10

Source: Roberts, R. E., Phinney, J. S., Masse, L. C., Chen, Y. R., Roberts, C. R., & Romero, A. (1999). The structure of ethnic identity of young adolescents from diverse ethnocultural groups. *The Journal of Early Adolescence, 19*(3), 301–322. doi: 10.1177/0272431699019003001

In addition to determining how strongly you connect your ethnic identity, you can also consider how significant race is to your identity; Worrell et al. (2020) developed a five-question subscale on race salience. See the Race Salience Subscale in Table 1.2. **Race salience** refers to how prominent or important race is to you.

The better you know yourself, the better able you will be to make important decisions about your education and how you plan to use it. This includes reflecting on your group membership identities such as race and ethnicity. Researchers have found a connection between students who have a strong ethnic identity and several success factors such as the student's belief in their ability to be successful and their engagement in schoolwork (Kantamneni et al., 2018). This in-depth self-exploration process can therefore set the stage for your success. It will also help you appreciate the complex identities of others.

Group Memberships

- Race
- Ethnicity
- Sexual Orientation
- Gender
- Ability
- Religion
- Hometown or Residence Hall
- Sports Team

Roles and Relationships

Our social roles and relationships also factor into our identity, often in significant ways (Goodman, 2015). We all have numerous relationship roles. Here are a few examples of personal roles that may apply to you:

- Child
- Significant other

Table 1.2
Race Salience Subscale

Use a 7-point scale to indicate level of endorsement for each item with 7 being the highest level of endorsement.

1. _____ When I walk into a room, I always take note of the racial make-up of the people around me.

2. _____ When I read the newspaper or a magazine, I always look for articles and stories that deal with race and ethnic issues.

3. _____ When I have a chance to decorate a room, I tend to select pictures, posters, or works of art that express strong racial-cultural themes.

4. _____ When I vote in an election, the first thing I think about is the candidate's record on racial and cultural issues.

5. _____ During a typical week in my life, I think about racial and cultural issues many, many times.

Scoring: Higher scores indicate higher levels of race salience. Thus, the higher your score, the more important race is to you.

Source: Worrell, F. C., Mendoza-Denton, R., Vandiver, B. J., Phagen, P. E., & Cross, W. E. (2020). Incorporating a race salience subscale into the cross racial identity scale (CRIS). *Journal of Black Psychology, 46*(8), 638-658 (p. 645). doi: 10.1177/0095798420967598

- Parent
- Sibling
- Other family member
- Friend

Each one of these personal roles helps define who you are as a person. In some cases, this personal role may be one of the most central parts of your identity.

Your role as a student can be another critical part of your identity. Holmes et al. (2019) found that student identity has been associated with many positive outcomes such as

Kaspars Grinvalds/Shutterstock.com

- earning more credits,
- higher grades,
- increased confidence,
- improved sense of belonging, and
- overall well-being.

You can increase your sense of belonging and identity as a student by seeking out and connecting with others who are similar to you and hearing their stories of success. In an interesting study conducted by Williams et al. (2020), high school

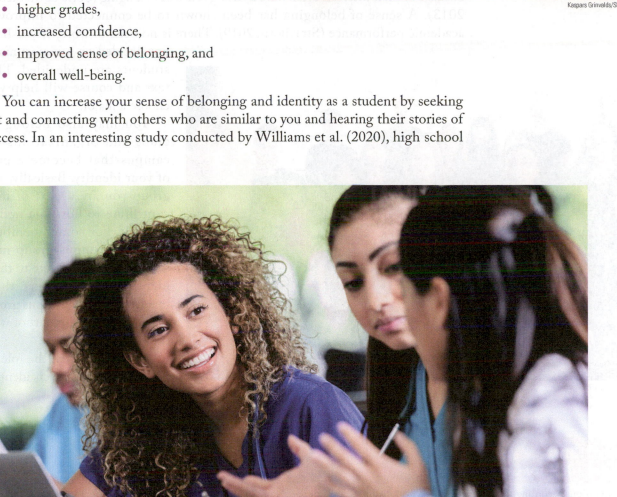

iStockPhoto/SDI Productions

students were assigned to one of two groups. In one group, students watched a video less than eight minutes in duration that featured students from minoritized and nonminoritized groups talking about how challenges decreased over time and then wrote a letter to a future student. In the other group, they watched a video on social media profiles. For students in the first video group where students shared their experiences, there were many positive outcomes including earning higher grades. It is important for you to know that you belong as a student at your institution even if you struggle at first; this is a common experience.

It can be helpful for you to understand how important your role as a student is to your overall identity. Student identity can be assessed with a three-item survey developed by Holmes et al. (2019). See Table 1.3.

As a student, you are a member of your college community as a whole and are also a member of more specific campus groups, too. For example, your academic major is part of your identity. Research shows that having an identity related to a discipline or major can contribute to student success. Students who choose a major because of their interests often have a strong sense of belonging (Soria & Stebleton, 2013). A sense of belonging has been shown to be connected to improved academic performance (Strayhorn, 2019). There is no need to worry if you have not decided on a major; many students are undecided. This text and course will help you choose a major.

You may also belong to clubs and organizations on campus that become a part of your identity. Basically, any group you are a part of may contribute to how you define yourself. For some, membership in a campus group may significantly contribute to their identity, but for others, their involvement in a campus group may not be a major part of who they are.

Even how much the role of being a student impacts identity

Monkey Business Images/Shutterstock.com

Table 1.3
Student Identity Centrality Assessment (Holmes et al., 2019)

Answer questions according to a 7-point scale, with 1 being strongly disagree and 7 being strongly agree.

1. _____ In general, being a student is an important part of my self-image.

2. _____ Being a student is an important refection of who I am.

3. _____ Being a student is unimportant to my sense of what kind of person I am.

Scoring: Reverse code 3 and then add scores. Higher scores indicate stronger sense of student identity.

Source: Holmes, J. M., Bowman, N. A., Murphy, M. C., & Carter, E. (2019). Envisioning college success: The role of student identity centrality. *Social Psychology of Education: An International Journal, 22*(5), 1015–1034.

can vary a lot from one person to the next. For those of you who are full-time students, this may be a primary part of your identity. For those of you who may be attending part-time and working full-time, being a student may be a less prominent part of your identity. Your student identity may be especially important if you are the first one in your family to attend college.

Professional roles also shape your identity. If you are employed, your identity probably also includes your role as an employee. As an employee, you have group membership related to your place of employment. Many of you will be more interested in having your future career as part of your identity. Being in a career field is usually a primary part of one's identity.

James Marcia, a renowned developmental psychologist, described different identity statuses, emphasizing that identity achievement requires both exploration and commitment (Karkouti, 2014). Culture plays an essential role in identity development (Karkouti, 2014). Exploring who you are and the possible options available is a critical part of making good career decisions. See Table 1.4 to see how these identity statuses can be applied to career decision making.

Personal Characteristic and Interests

In addition to group membership and social roles or relationships, your personal characteristics and interests also play an essential role in determining your identity. Personal characteristics describe your personality traits and attributes. There are many ways to describe personal characteristics. Some examples include:

- Adventurous
- Compassionate
- Courageous
- Creative
- Dependable
- Flexible
- Helpful
- Honest

Table 1.4 Marcia Identity Statuses
Marcia's Identity Statuses Applied to Career Decision-Making

Identity Status	Exploration	Commitment	Description
Identity moratorium	Yes	No	Actively exploring career options but has not yet decided; may be overwhelmed or anxious
Identity foreclosure	No	Yes	Career decision is made with little to no exploration; often decision is made based on parental influence or to avoid anxiety
Identity diffusion	No	No	Not yet invested in the career decision-making process
Identity achievement	Yes	Yes	Career path has been identified after careful exploration of many career options

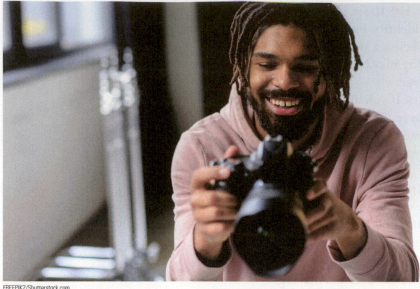

FREEPIK2/Shutterstock.com

- Loyal
- Responsible
- Patient
- Productive
- Social
- Trusting

Interests refer to activities that you enjoy doing. Sports, gaming, reading, traveling, fitness, gardening, cooking, drawing, and music are some examples. Interests usually guide what hobbies or activities you do. Interests also play a role in deciding on a major and career. Being in a career that aligns with your interests can increase the likelihood that you will enjoy working.

Some students have a good understanding of what they like to do and what characteristics best describe them, but for most students, college is a time to explore and develop interests. It is common for students to not yet fully know their interests and passions and be uncertain about what they want in the future. There is no need to worry if this is the case for you.

One effective way to better understand your interests, skills, and values is to engage in new activities every day. It is impossible to know if you like something if you have not experienced it before. Be open and try out new activities. College campuses have so many different types of opportunities for you to explore. Visit the website for your college and search for student organizations, activities, and events to see the vast array of options available.

After you engage in each activity, you can reflect by asking yourself the following questions:

1. What did you like about this activity?
2. What did you not like about this activity?
3. How did you feel when you engaged in this activity?
4. What about this activity made you curious?
5. How important was this activity to you? Why?
6. What did you do well when engaging in this activity?
7. What did you struggle with when engaging in this activity?
8. How interested are you in engaging in this activity again? Why?
9. What more do you want to know about this activity? Why?

The combination of your personal characteristics and interests helps differentiate you from others. Although you are similar in many ways to others, you also have characteristics that make you unique. It is the combination of your multiple identities that best describe your uniqueness.

Reflecting on Your Identity

Exploring and reflecting on your multiple identities is valuable. This deeper understanding of yourself can help you grow and develop. College is an excellent time to determine who you want to be now and in the future. Think about what aspects of your identity you want to strengthen and how you would like to incorporate new identities into your existing identity. For example, most college students want to develop or enhance their professional identity.

To help you explore and reflect on your identity, here are a few questions for you to consider:

Pathdoc/Shutterstock.com

1. How would you describe your identity? Be sure to include group membership, roles and relationships, and personal characteristics including interests.
2. What part(s) of your identity is/are most important to you? Why?
3. What part(s) of your identity is/are moderately important to you? Why?
4. What part(s) of your identity is/are not as important to you? Why?
5. What privileged groups do you belong to?
6. What oppressed groups do you belong to?
7. What part(s) of your identity do others notice the most?
8. What part(s) of your identity do you want to learn more about or develop?
9. What would you like to add to your identity?
10. What type of professional identity do you wish to develop?
11. In 5 or 10 years from now, how would you want to describe your identity?
12. What actions can you take toward this end?
13. What can you do to learn more about your identity?

In addition to helping you know yourself better, thinking about identity can also help you better understand others. When you have a deeper and more complex understanding of yourself, you will be more likely to acknowledge and appreciate that others also have multiple identities.

This recognition and appreciation of the complexity of others will increase your ability to be empathic and understanding. Increased empathy and understanding can translate into improved abilities for collaboration and teamwork, which are essential skills in college, careers, and in our personal life.

Researchers have demonstrated that having a balance between concern for self and others typically leads to the best outcomes. For example, Wayment et al. (2015) found that this balance is associated with improved coping and overall well-being. This self-other balance is desired by employers too.

Intersectionality Quick Quiz

1. What factors contribute to how you define your identity?
2. What is intersectionality?

Values, Activism, and Aspirations

Gustavo Frazao/Shutterstock.com

Values are an especially important part of your identity. **Values** refer to what you believe is important. In other words, what do you care about? What matters the most to you? Values motivate you to act and are used to evaluate yourself and others (Schwartz & Ciecicuh, 2021).

Values often stem from your family, community, and culture. Some cultures value individualism where independence and autonomy are encouraged, whereas other cultures value collectivism, where group needs are more important than individual ones (Triandis & Gelfand, 2012). These cultural values are often incorporated into your personal values.

Your family also plays an important role in shaping your values. For example, if education is highly valued in your family, enrolling in college was likely something you have always planned to do and you probably did not spend much time, if any at all, deciding on whether to attend college. Instead, you perhaps spent your energy deciding which college to attend. Another family value relates to caretaking. Living with family and taking care of other family members is a strong value in some families. If this value is important to you, you may be staying home and attending a community or other local college or may be at a college offering fully online degrees.

It is not surprising that the people you spend the most time with really shape your values. Although parents can play an important role in helping you decide on your values, other family members can also play a role. This was demonstrated in a study by Lee et al. (2016) where they investigated the value of work ethic in African American families. This study showed a connection between the work ethic of parents, siblings, and adolescents, finding that older siblings and fathers played an especially important role in developing the value of work ethic.

Schwartz (2012) identified 10 basic values (see Table 1.5). Researchers have been studying these values across cultures and found that Schwartz's framework is useful

Table 1.5
Basic Values (adapted from Schwartz, 2012)

Value	Description
Tradition	Commitment to customs in your religion, culture, or family
Conformity	Engagement in behaviors that are socially acceptable and unlikely to upset others
Security	Stability and safety in relationships and experiences
Power	Prestige and control
Achievement	Successful experiences
Hedonism	Pleasure and fun
Stimulation	Excitement, challenge, and new experiences
Self-direction	Independence and autonomy
Universalism	Enhancing nature and experiences of others
Benevolence	Helping and caring for others close to you

Table 1.6
Values Assessment (Dobewall and Rudnev, 2014)

The following questions should be answered using a 9-point scale with 1 being opposed to my values and 9 being of supreme importance.

1. _____ It is important to this person to think of new ideas and be creative, to do things one's own way.
2. _____ Adventure and taking risks are important to this person, to have an exciting life.
3. _____ It is important to this person to have a good time, to spoil oneself.
4. _____ Being very successful is very important to this person, to have people recognize one's achievements.
5. _____ It is important to this person to be rich, to have a lot of money and expensive things.
6. _____ Living in secure surroundings is important to this person, to avoid anything that might be dangerous.
7. _____ It is important to this person to always behave properly, to avoid doing anything people would say is wrong.
8. _____ Tradition is important to this person, to follow the customs handed down by one's religion or family.
9. _____ It is important to this person to help the people nearby, to care for their well-being.
10. _____ Looking after the environment is important to this person, to care for nature.

Scoring: Higher scores indicate higher values. List your values from most important to least important based on your score. Consider how these values can impact your actions and what experiences you can seek out that align with the values that matter the most to you.

Alignment to type of value is as follows: Q1- self-direction, Q2- stimulation, Q3- hedonism, Q4- achievement, Q5- power, Q6- security, Q7- conformity, Q8- tradition, Q9- benevolence, Q10- universalism.

Source: Dobewell, H., & Rudnev, M. (2014). Common and unique features of Schwartz's and Inglehart's value theories at the country and individual levels. *Cross-Cultural Research*, 48(1), 45-77. doi: 10.1177/1069397113493584

for many different populations (Dobewall & Rudnev, 2014). As you can probably imagine, there are numerous assessments you can take to explore your values.

McCarty and Shrum (2000) found that the best way to engage in assessments is to first identify the value that matters most and least and then rate the values. Dobewall and Rudnev (2014) developed a brief assessment to measure the values described by Schwartz (2012). See Table 1.6. Before you begin taking this assessment, use McCarty and Schrum's (2000) suggestion and decide which value matters the most to you and which value matters the least, and then rate each value.

Another useful self-assessment tool is the List of Values questionnaire, which was developed by Kahle (1988) and has been studied by researchers. See Table 1.7.

Table 1.7
List of Values Questionnaire (Kahle, 1988)

The following is a list of things that some people look for or want out of life. Please study the list carefully and then rate each thing on how important it is in your daily life, where 1 = not at all important and 9 = extremely important.

1. _____ Sense of belonging
2. _____ Excitement
3. _____ Warm relationships with others
4. _____ Self-fulfillment
5. _____ Being well-respected
6. _____ Fun and enjoyment of life
7. _____ Security
8. _____ Self-respect
9. _____ A sense of accomplishment

Higher scores indicate that the value is important to you. Consider which values matter the most to you and how you can seek out experiences and possibly a career that aligns with your most-important values.

Source: Kahle, L. R. (1988). Using the List of Values (LOV) to understand consumers. *Journal of Services Marketing*, 2(4), 49-56.

College is an opportunity for self-reflecting on personal values. Knowing what truly matters to you will help you make decisions that you will feel good about. Your personal values will be especially critical when you decide on a major and a career. Aligning your personal values with the values of the profession you choose is important and will likely contribute to higher levels of satisfaction. For example, if helping others is of high value to you, you may choose a major and career such as education, healthcare, or another service-oriented career.

Your personal values also matter when you look for employment. Organizations have values, too, and working for an organization with similar values will increase the likelihood that you are happily employed. For example, if the company where you work does not engage in environment-friendly actions and this conflicts with your value system, you may become unsatisfied at work. If, on the other hand, you are working for a company that emphasizes work–life balance and this is important to you, you will likely enjoy working there.

As you reflect on how important each of these values are to you, consider what values are not captured on these assessments too. No one tool is completely comprehensive. Thinking about all that matters to you can help you make good personal, academic, and career decisions.

Activism is a term that refers to acting on your values in ways that result in political or social change. For example, activism related to social justice and equity involves being a champion, advocate, and change agent for reducing the injustices faced by many underrepresented groups. Another example could be environmental activists who support green efforts. Activism can be an important part of your personal and professional identity.

Activism can come in many different forms. Some activists might engage in peaceful protests, while others might write or comment on social media posts to increase awareness of issues and encourage others to act. Other examples include writing to legislators or making statements on hearings for policies or regulations. Activism can also happen informally when individuals talk with family, friends, or co-workers, sharing knowledge and encouraging related actions. Students have a long history of being activists and have used numerous platforms, including social media in recent years, to voice concerns and push for change (Jason, 2018).

Activism begins with knowledge and passion. In college, there are many ways that you will expand your knowledge and find ways to act on what you care about. In an interesting study by Goldman et al. (2015), they found that students who were in majors that involved environmental concerns were more likely than students who were in majors where environmental topics were not addressed to engage in actions that address these concerns.

Find ways to learn more about what matters to you and then discover ways to be an activist in these

LouiesWorld1/Shutterstock.com

iStockPhoto

areas. In addition to using classes to increase your knowledge, you can also pursue outside of class opportunities on and off-campus. Organizations on campus may have already established programs that you can participate in. For example, Greek and other campus organizations typically center their philanthropy efforts on their core values. If you do not find an organization on campus that is doing the activist work you are interested in doing, most colleges and universities encourage students to start new clubs or organizations. You may also want to join efforts happening off-campus. There are many community-based organizations engaged in various forms of activism. Jason (2018) noted that using allies and partners can increase the likelihood of results.

Ways to Engage in Activism

- Peaceful protests
- Write blogs or other posts on social media
- Comment on social media posts
- Write to legislators
- Attend and speak at legislative hearings
- Explore on and off-campus opportunities to engage in activities aligned with your values

Your values not only impact your actions today but also play a significant role in your aspirations. Aspirations refer to who you hope to be or what you hope to accomplish. Your aspirations probably motivated you to attend college. For example, you may be attending college to learn the skills and earn the credentials related to your career aspirations. For some, attending and graduating from college is a way to improve socio-economic status or to pave the way for future generations. If you are the first in your family to go to college, your motivation may come from showing others in your family that education is possible.

Fit Ztudio/Shutterstock.com

When you think about who you hope to be and what you want to accomplish, look beyond your now and into the future. It is common to focus on your current network to see what your family members, friends, and community members have achieved and use this information to determine your aspirations. However, for many students, your now network may only provide you with limited examples of what is possible. For example, if most of your family and friends work in the same field or for the same employer, you may not see other options. Although this may be a good career choice, the best decisions are made when you explore and evaluate multiple options.

You can think beyond your now by seeking out conversations about possibilities with others. The more you talk with others, the more options you begin to see.

The over or under representation of your group membership in professions can impact your decisions. Researchers have found that role models, or others who you see in various careers, guide career choices (Quimby & DeSantis, 2006). In a study on science majors, Byars-Winston and Rogers (2019) noted the importance of giving Black college students the opportunity to watch and learn from Black mentors because this can help students feel like they are "science insiders versus science outsiders" (p. 40).

In addition to role models in our personal networks, you are also exposed to role models through television and social media. In a study conducted by Walters and Kremser (2016), they found that the career aspirations of first- and second-year students are more influenced by television and the media as compared to third- and fourth-year students. Seeing others who look like you in the field can make a difference.

There is no need to be limited by what is most visible. If you discover that there are few individuals from your race or gender currently in a career, search for

iStockPhoto/SDI Productions

role models or mentors who may help and support you as you challenge existing stereotypes. College is an excellent place to find a mentor. In fact, researchers have found that professors play an important role in career aspirations for third- and fourth-year students (Walters & Kremser, 2016). Professors are not the only resource.

Working professionals, especially alumni, are often willing to connect with students and support you with developing and reaching your goals. There is no need to be limited by what you currently see; stretch yourself and consider options you may have never thought about before. Your aspirations and related actions can have a long-lasting positive impact on you, your family, members of the groups in which you are a part of, and on future generations.

Aspirations go beyond what career path you choose and include whether you would like to move into a leadership position within your chosen field. It is not surprising that if individuals in the groups you identify with often have leadership positions, you may be more likely to aspire to higher levels within a career. Unfortunately, gender and racial gaps continue to exist in terms of salary and leadership positions. Yavorsky et al. (2019) found that education is connected to high income, but that men benefit more than women. Gaining knowledge and skills and challenging yourself to aspire to higher levels can position you well for success, even when there are obstacles to overcome. Take a few minutes now to complete the Career Aspirations Scale (see Table 1.8)

Table 1.8
Career Aspirations Scale

In the space next to the statements below, choose a number from "0" (not at all true of me) to "4" (very true of me). If the statement does not apply, enter "0." Please be completely honest. Your answers will be useful only if they accurately describe you.

0 = Not at all true of me
1 = Slightly true of me
2 = Moderately true of me
3 = Quite a bit true of me
4 = Very true of me

1. _____ I hope to become a leader in my career field.
2. _____ I do not plan to devote energy to getting promoted to a leadership position in the organization or business in which I am working.
3. _____ I want to be among the very best in my field.
4. _____ Becoming a leader in my job is not at all important to me.
5. _____ When I am established in my career, I would like to manage other employees.
6. _____ I plan to reach the highest level of education in my field.
7. _____ I want to have responsibility for the future direction of my organization or business.
8. _____ I want my work to have a lasting impact on my field.
9. _____ I aspire to have my contributions at work recognized by my employer.
10. _____ I will pursue additional training in my occupational area of interest.
11. _____ I will always be knowledgeable about recent advances in my field.
12. _____ Attaining leadership status in my career is not that important to me.
13. _____ Being outstanding at what I do at work is very important to me.
14. _____ I know I will work to remain current regarding knowledge in my field.
15. _____ I hope to move up to a leadership position in my organization or business.
16. _____ I will attend conferences annually to advance my knowledge.
17. _____ I know that I will be recognized for my accomplishments in my field.
18. _____ Even if not required, I would take continuing education courses to become more knowledgeable.
19. _____ I would pursue an advanced education program to gain specialized knowledge in my field.
20. _____ Achieving in my career is not at all important to me.
21. _____ I plan to obtain many promotions in my organization or business.
22. _____ Being one of the best in my field is not important to me.
23. _____ Every year, I will prioritize involvement in continuing education to advance my career.
24. _____ I plan to rise to the top leadership position of my organization or business.

(continued)

Scoring Instructions:

Reverse score items 2, 4, 12, 20, 22, so the responses are changed in the following way: 0=4, 1=3, 2=2, 3=1, 4=0. Place the new scores in the spaces below that correspond with the item. Place all remaining scores in the spaces with their corresponding item number below. Sum responses to each item for each scale. Higher scores indicate higher aspirations in each domain (achievement, leadership, education). Reflect on which area is most important to you and why. Determine if you might want to aspire higher in any of these areas.

The following are the numbers corresponding to each scale. The reverse scored items have an asterisk.

Achievement Aspiration items: 3, 8, 9, 13, 17, 20*, 21, 22*

Leadership Aspiration items: 1, 2*, 4*, 5, 7, 12*, 15, 24

Educational Aspiration items: 6, 10, 11, 14, 16, 18, 19, 23

FACTOR 1: LEADERSHIP ASPIRATIONS		FACTOR 2: ACHIEVEMENT ASPIRATIONS		FACTOR 3: EDUCATIONAL ASPIRATIONS	
1	_____	3	_____	6	_____
2*	_____	8	_____	10	_____
4*	_____	9	_____	11	_____
5	_____	13	_____	14	_____
7	_____	17	_____	16	_____
12*	_____	20*	_____	18	_____
15	_____	21	_____	19	_____
24	_____	22*	_____	23	_____
SUM	_____	SUM	_____	SUM	_____

Source: Gregor, M. A., & O'Brien, K. M. (provisional acceptance). Promoting career aspirations among young women: Improving instrumentation. The Journal of Career Assessment.

You are likely starting out on your college journey, so it may be difficult or perhaps overwhelming to think about your aspirations. If you are like many other college students, you may be struggling to decide on a major and may not know what career path you want to pursue. If this sounds like you, you are not alone; this is common. Learning about yourself and how to discover your aspirations is an important part of your journey. The better you know yourself, the easier the decision-making processes will be, but those decisions and that process take time.

Remember, aspirations are more than career choices. Think about what you want in the future personally as well as professionally. Considering who you want to be in 5, 10, or 20 years from now can help you determine what actions you can take today, tomorrow, and the next day to help you get to where you want to be. Engaging in this self-exploration process can also help you answer this question: What mark on the world can you make to make the world a better place?

Values, Activism, and Aspirations Quick Quiz

1. What does it mean to be an activist?
2. What influences our aspirations?

Chapter Summary: Note-Taking Model

Let's summarize what you have learned in this chapter. The Cornell model is used for this chapter. Remember, it is not expected that your notes will look like this right after class or reading. It takes time to organize your notes and repackage them. It is time well spent, though, because you learn the content better as you organize it, and you have a fabulous foundation from which to study for your exams! There are several ways to use this section:

- **Preview:** Read the model before reading the chapter to familiarize yourself with the content.
- **Compare:** Compare the notes you took on the chapter to the model provided.
- **Study:** The model along with your notes and other course materials are great resources for studying.

Cornell Method Model

How do we determine our identity?	Our identity is based on: • Group membership (race, ethnicity, sexual orientation, gender, religion, ability) • Some groups have privilege or advantages given because of group membership; some groups are oppressed and have disadvantages because of group membership • Relationships (parent, sibling, child, significant other) and social roles (student, career) • Personal traits and characteristics (interests and personality)
What is intersectionality?	How our many different identities connect and define us
How do we develop values and why do they matter?	Our families and culture play important roles in determining what we believe is important. Our values guide our actions and will factor into decisions such as which career we pursue.
What is activism?	Activism refers to standing up for what you believe in and taking action. This could involve engaging in a peaceful protest or writing or talking about what you are passionate about to increase awareness and to make a difference.
What influences our aspirations?	We are most influenced by others who are similar to us and those in our personal networks. We can expand our network and look beyond what is most commonly seen to see what can be possible.

SUMMARY: Exploring your identity is important. Your identity is usually based on your group memberships, your roles and responsibilities, and your personality and interests. Intersectionality refers to understanding the complexity of your identity. Your identity will be based on membership in several different groups, which may be privileged or oppressed. Taking time to determine your values is critical and can guide your actions and aspirations.

Chapter

2

Evaluating Information and Thinking Critically

> The value of a college education is not the learning of many facts but the training of the mind to think.
>
> —*Albert Einstein*

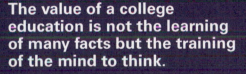

iStock/photo/Wavebreakmedia

1. Why are information literacy skills important?

2. Where can you find credible information?

3. What strategies will assist you in evaluating information?

4. How can you use social media for academic purposes?

5. What is a peer-reviewed journal? Why will learning about this scholarly source be helpful to you?

6. What is Bloom's taxonomy and how does it relate to critical thinking?

7. How can you become a critical thinker?

Exploring the Research in Summary

Research Study Citation

Head, A. J. (2012). Learning curve: How college graduates solve information problems once they join the workplace. *Project Information Literacy Research Report* (ERIC Document Reproduction Service No. ED536470).

Introduction: The Research Question

What question did the researcher seek to answer?

Information literacy refers to the ability to find, evaluate, and use information. Recognizing the important role of information literacy skills in the workplace, Head (2012) investigated the following questions:

1. What do employers expect from college graduates in terms of information literacy skills?

2. What challenges, if any, do recent graduates face in terms of information literacy skills in the workplace?

Method: The Study

Who participated in the study? What did the researchers ask the participants to do?

The researcher conducted interviews and focus groups with employers and recent college graduates. A total of 23 employer interviews were conducted. It is important to note that employers were from several different states and a variety of different career fields. Thirty-three recent graduates from four different public and private colleges and universities in the United States participated in one of five focus groups. During the interviews and focus groups, employers and students answered a series of questions related to information literacy. Specifically, the research investigated information problem-solving skills, which refers to an individual's ability to find and use information to address real-world issues or problems.

Results: The Findings

What were the answers to the research questions?

Employers rated the "ability to obtain and process information" (Head, 2012, p. 9) as being an essential skill, noting that their employees need to be able to search online, go beyond information found via Google, and use databases and data files. Some of the other important skills desired by employers included ability to work in a team, demonstrate excellent communication and decision-making skills, and be able to prioritize and plan work. Employers noted that these skills are related to information problem-solving and that students need to be patient as this process takes time. Almost all the recent graduates indicated that finding, evaluating, and using information were required skill sets in their job. Some of the challenges identified by recent graduates were the quick turnaround time needed, the lack of direction or structure with the task, and the social nature of the process, which referred to the need to talk with others to find necessary information. Recent graduates noted that their college experiences helped them become effective at critically evaluating information. Thus, graduates reported having a good foundation, but several indicated that further training, especially opportunities to practice finding information without much structure, would have helped them be better prepared for the working world.

Discussion and So-What Factor

How can YOU use this information as a student?

This research provides evidence that information literacy is an essential skill that is developed in college; however, a gap between the skills of recent graduates and the needs of employers exists. In other words, although graduates come to employers with some information literacy skills, additional skills are needed. To help bridge this gap, professors can engage students in information problem-solving tasks that are more complex and less defined. Students can also approach information literacy tasks from a broader perspective, thinking about how to access and evaluate information from a variety of sources, including other credible people. Students can also seek out opportunities such as being a leader of a club or organization where they will be able to practice information literacy skills. Finally, when students begin a new position as a recent college graduate, having a mentor can be quite helpful. Bouncing ideas around with another person who has strong information literacy skills can be helpful.

Information Literacy

We live in a world full of information. Learning how to navigate the endless amount of information available to find and use information for a task at hand is an important skill. Identifying, finding, and evaluating relevant and meaningful information will result in you making better academic and personal decisions.

According to the Association of College and Research Libraries (2016), "**Information literacy** is the set of integrated abilities encompassing the reflective discovery of information, the understanding of how information is produced and valued, and the use of information in creating new knowledge and participating ethically in communities of learning" (p. 12). Simply put, learning to sift through information and then find and evaluate information that will assist you with a task is important in all facets of your life.

Rawpixel.com/Shutterstock.com

According to the Association of College and Research (2016) framework, there are six essential components to information literacy. See Table 2.1. It is important to note that the components outlined are not sequential. In other words, you do not need to consider each one in order, but rather together they will assist you in developing information literacy skills.

Table 2.1 Information Literacy
Six Components of Information Literacy

Components of Information Literacy	Questions to Ask	Academic Example: Research Paper on Active Learning Teaching Strategies	Personal Example: Buying a Car
Authority is constructed and contextual *Authority typically relates to whether the person is recognized as an expert in the field.*	**Who might be an expert or credible source for this purpose? Why?**	• Educators' or teaching supervisors' personal experiences • Researchers with graduate degrees in field of education research studies • Authors of books on teaching strategies	• Independent researchers • Car salesperson • Owners of different car models • Online reviews
Information creation as a process *Experts look not only at the product that was created but also how this product was developed.*	**What was the purpose of this information product and how did this influence its creation?**	• Who funded the research? Was it an independent source or was it funded by a business with an interest in selling a product? • What benefit, if any, would the author of the information receive based on the findings?	• Car salesman will likely present only positive information • Difficult to know if an online reviewer has an agenda or has been compensated in some way
Information has value *Information products have been created by an author. It is essential that we give proper credit to the author for their work.*	**Who deserves credit for the information? What is intellectual property?**	• Cite sources to give credit to author, researcher, or educator (important to also cite personal communications)	• Independent researcher • Online reviewers
Research as inquiry *Information allows us to explore answers to questions.*	**What questions can shape research and discovery? What conclusions can be drawn from research?**	• Do active learning and teaching strategies lead to increased learning? What other benefits might there be? • Need to evaluate the nature of the study to see the validity and generalizability of the information (i.e., studies with larger number of participants may have stronger and more meaningful results)	• Which car has the features I need? • What is the cost difference between different options? • Need to exercise caution when interpreting anonymous reviews or information provided by someone who has a vested interest in which car you choose
Scholarship as conversation *By exploring all of the research on a topic, we can understand information within a context. In other words, we can evaluate how new information fits into what is already known.*	**What are the various perspectives? What best represents the current knowledge or thinking in this area?**	• What do supporters of active learning say? What do nonsupporters say? What evidence do they present? • What finding seems to be consistent across studies?	• What are the pros and cons of different models? • Is there consistency between what reviewers say and what the salesperson says?

Components of Information Literacy	Questions to Ask	Academic Example: Research Paper on Active Learning Teaching Strategies	Personal Example: Buying a Car
Searching as strategic exploration *It is important to determine what information is most relevant to the task at hand. Searching for information requires the use of strategies that are based on the reason for needing the information.*	**What information would be most useful to the task at hand? What search strategies will work best?**	• What research exists on this topic? What search terms might work best? How can I best narrow the results to find useful data? • What experiences have educators had with active learning strategies? What questions should I ask educators to get meaningful information?	• How can I find out the total cost including maintenance and gas? • What search terms can I use to find websites with the information I need?

Think Critically

1. In what ways have you engaged in these information literacy actions before?

2. How can you use this approach with upcoming tasks or decisions?

Being able to find and evaluate information will help you make personal decisions such as what major and career to choose, where to live, what car to drive, and which doctor to see. We seek out information from a variety of sources. According to survey results, 81% of individuals report they rely on their own search for information, 43% on family and friends, and 31% on experts before making big decisions (Turner & Rainie, 2020). In a study on how adults access health information, Yamashita et al. (2020) found that adults relied most on health professionals and the Internet, but also gathered information from other sources such as family and friends, books, and television.

Information literacy skills will also help you tackle academic tasks in college. Samson (2010) pointed out that academic assignments such as research projects help you develop and enhance your information literacy skills. A research project requires you to determine what information is needed, locate and evaluate information, and then synthesize and organize the information into a meaningful product. In addition to learning the content related to the research paper or presentation, you also benefit from information literacy skill development.

You will also need information literacy skills in your career. In a survey of college graduates, 78% indicated that learning how to find relevant information was an important work-related skill that was learned in college, and approximately 90% indicated that information literacy skills were being used at least monthly in their current job (Travis, 2011). As you can imagine, employers value employees who can skillfully engage with and use information. According to Bruce (1999), there are seven key facets of information literacy that relate to the world of work:

1. Using information technology to learn and communicate with others

2. Being able to identify appropriate sources of information

3. Engaging in problem-solving to sort through information

4. Organizing and bringing meaning to information

5. Developing expertise in an area of interest
6. Adopting new perspectives or novel approaches or ideas
7. Using information to benefit others

Although you sometimes intentionally look for information, it is also important to recognize that you are exposed to information every day that you did not seek out. Kohnen and Saul (2018) differentiated between intentional and incidental information. When you take action to learn something new such as when you search the Internet, this refers to **intentional information seeking**. You are intentionally looking to learn. **Incidental information**, however, refers to information that you encounter when not actively looking for it. You are bombarded with information on a daily basis. This information can come from many sources, but you are likely to encounter this type of information regularly via social media and the Internet. Head et al. (2018) noted that

> "For many college students in America today, the news is an overwhelming hodgepodge of headlines, posts, alerts, tweets, visuals, and conversations that stream at them throughout the day. While some stories come from news sites students choose to follow, other content arrives uninvited, tracking the digital footprints that many searchers inevitably leave behind" (p. 1).

Targeted advertisements based on your browsing history is one example of information that you encounter regularly. Another example is when you must watch an advertisement before you can watch a video online. A study conducted by Liu (2020) showed that people come across a lot more information in a passive way today, such as when you are browsing the Internet, than they did 20 years ago. It is therefore important to use your information literacy skills constantly so that you can determine what content is credible and of value to you.

Type of Information

- Intentional information is the information you actively seek out.
- Incidental information is information that you encounter such as advertisements.

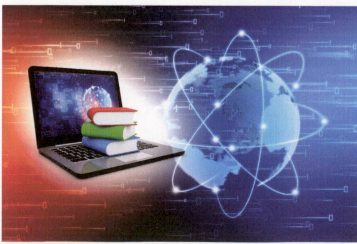

Sources of Information

There are many different sources of information. Most of us rely heavily on the Internet and social media. However, academic sources such as peer-reviewed journal articles and books are especially important sources of information in college.

Websites The Internet is one of the most widely used sources of information (Turner & Rainie, 2020). Not surprisingly, Google is often the first place most go to find information (Salisbury & Karasmanis, 2011). Internet searches can provide you with new information, increase your understanding, and help you compare and contrast information (Liu, 2020). Websites can help you gain a basic understanding of topics before investigating the topic more in-depth (Kim et al., 2014).

There are many highly credible websites that contain valuable information. Professional organizations often post research and reports for the public. For example, organizations such as the American Psychological Association share research findings and reports on mental health topics and WebMD provides valuable information on numerous health conditions for the public.

Social Media Social media is another one of the most frequently used sources of information. According to Head et al. (2018), 89% of students reported getting their news from social media, which was the second highest source of information. Peers were the most cited source for information, but much of the information communicated between peers stemmed from social media.

Although social media is primarily used for personal reasons, it can also be used for academic and professional purposes. An excellent way to learn more about a career field, for example, is to identify professionals and organizations in your field of interest and follow them on various social media platforms. You can consult with your faculty for suggestions on who to follow. Believing in the value of public scholarship, which means making research and related information easily accessible to the public, many professionals and organizations post links to research and reports that can be helpful sources of information. Many of these links can be found in blogs or news reports.

You can also request to join social media groups focused on issues or topics of interest to you. For example, most career fields will have social media groups and they often encourage students to join. Participating in social media groups is helpful for both information and networking purposes. Social media platforms that target professionals such as LinkedIn can be especially helpful if you want to gather information that can be beneficial to you in college and in your career. Checking these sites regularly is an excellent way to become knowledgeable about current issues in the field.

iStockPhoto/bigtunaonline

McCorkle and Alexander (2019) suggested that students use social media to create a digital personal learning network, which refers to a group of individuals who share information and collaborate to increase their understanding of concepts they wish to learn. They identified numerous benefits of this approach. "It can help students by providing content in their chosen career field to

(a) build why-to and how-to knowledge and learning,

(b) stay current and up to-date with news, trends, and career-specific practice,

(c) connect and learn from career-relevant influencers and thought leaders,

(d) maintain timely, focused, and relevant content for curation and social sharing,

(e) use social sharing to establish authority on a particular subject for strengthening a personal brand identity,

(f) stimulate and support creative thinking for creating original thought and content (such as blogging), and, most importantly,

(g) provide confirmation of a chosen career focus to potential employers" (McCorkle & Alexander, 2019, p. 110).

Students found the experience of creating a digital personal learning network to be valuable. Building expertise and skills were two of the main benefits they indicated (McCorkle & Alexander, 2019). In a review of over 100 research studies, Malik et al. (2019) also found that using social media for academic purposes had many benefits such as improved confidence, higher levels of engagement and sense of belonging, and better grades.

Peer-Reviewed Journal Articles One of the most scholarly sources is the **peer-reviewed journal article**, which can be defined as a theoretical or research-written work that has been deemed worthy of publication by experts in the field. These articles are published in journals that are monitored by professionals in that area of study. Most articles are based on original research. As a college student, you have access to this high-quality source of information through the library.

Information from original research studies can be quite helpful in academic and professional work. Professors prefer and expect students to use scholarly sources, such as peer-reviewed journal articles when conducting research (Valentine, 2001).

These high-level sources will also be of value to you in your career. On a survey conducted by Travis (2011), almost half of the graduates indicated that empirical research was needed in their career. Over 70% of alumni responding to another survey indicated that research skills were of value in their career, noting that undergraduate research experiences helped them build confidence, learn to work independently, and improved their ability for written and verbal communication (Mathew et al., 2019).

iStockPhoto

Unfortunately, only 14% of students surveyed indicated that they use the library database to find scholarly journal articles (Salisbury & Karasmanis, 2011). Part of the problem may be that students do not feel confident using the library databases and reading journal articles. Almost half of the college students in a research study conducted by Burton and Chadwick (2000) indicated that they did not receive training on how to use the library databases, and many students (45.2%) said they did not know the elements of a peer-reviewed article that qualified it for publication (Salisbury & Karasmanis, 2011).

The good news is that when students receive information literacy instruction during their first year, they do utilize a variety of sources beyond Google, including peer-reviewed research articles (Samson, 2010). As with most skills, learning is enhanced when you are challenged and supported. Research shows that information literacy skills significantly improve when students are given challenging, meaningful research assignments that require high levels of critical thinking and information literacy (Hayes-Bohanan & Spievak, 2008). As you would expect, student confidence with using information literacy skills develops over time. This was illustrated in a study where students reported higher levels of confidence in upper- versus lower-level courses (Henderson et al., 2011).

Students are often most successful with these high-level academic tasks when there is also a high level of support. Not surprisingly, Schroeter and Higgins (2015) found that students who were provided with guided instruction on information literacy skill development were more confident with their ability to determine what information is needed, find that information, and use the information in a meaningful way. In addition to being more confident, students who received guided instruction also demonstrated higher skill level in tasks requiring information literacy.

To fully appreciate the value of peer-reviewed research, it is important to look at the process an author must undertake to get a work published. See Figure 2.1. It starts with the author submitting the work to the editor of a journal. If the article is considered appropriate for that journal, the work is then anonymously distributed to several professional experts in that field. These professionals are called reviewers. The reviewers then provide feedback and a recommendation about whether the article should be published. Typically, the reviewers recommend numerous revisions before the work is published, and many times works are not accepted for publication. In fact, some journals have rejection rates as high as 90% (American Psychological Association, 2008). This means that 90% of the articles submitted are denied, and only 10% are published. The reviewers carefully attend to the research to be sure it is of high caliber, in keeping with the professional standards of the field, and that it adds a significant contribution to the current literature in that area. In a nutshell, an author must go through a rigorous peer-review process before the work ever makes it to print.

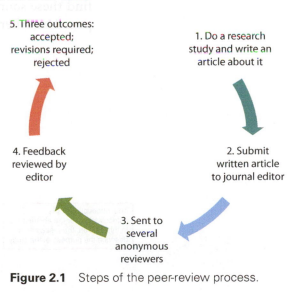

Figure 2.1   Steps of the peer-review process.

Think Critically

1. Why is it important for reviewers to be anonymous?

2. What is the value of this peer-review process?

Why is this important for you to know? Basically, it means that someone else has already evaluated this work. You can be confident that this is a reliable, credible source. However, no research is perfect, and you should still do your own analysis and critical thinking about the information presented.

Research articles can be broken down into parts. Each research article has the following elements: abstract, introduction, method (subjects and procedure), results, and discussion.

Abstract Abstract is another word for summary. It can be found at the beginning of the article and is sometimes in italics. In the abstract, the author briefly describes the nature of the study and the key findings. Because the abstract contains the purpose and main findings, reading this paragraph several times will help you understand the rest of the article. You can also return to the abstract whenever you find that you are struggling to understand the study as the abstract provides a basic overview of the reason for and results of the study.

Introduction **Introduction** is the first official section after the abstract. See Figure 2.2. Sometimes it is labeled "Introduction," but it most cases, the text simply begins without a heading. In the introduction, the author sets the stage for why this research was conducted, discusses why the topic is important, and describes research that has already been done in that area. You will notice that the author cites the sources within the body of the text according to APA (American Psychological Association) or MLA (Modern Language Association) style. The source citations clearly indicate where the information came from so that the reader could go directly to that source if a deeper understanding of the topic is desired (Raimes & Jersky, 2011). If you find these source citations distracting you as you read, block them out using a pencil or other method. Just be sure that you will be able to read them later if

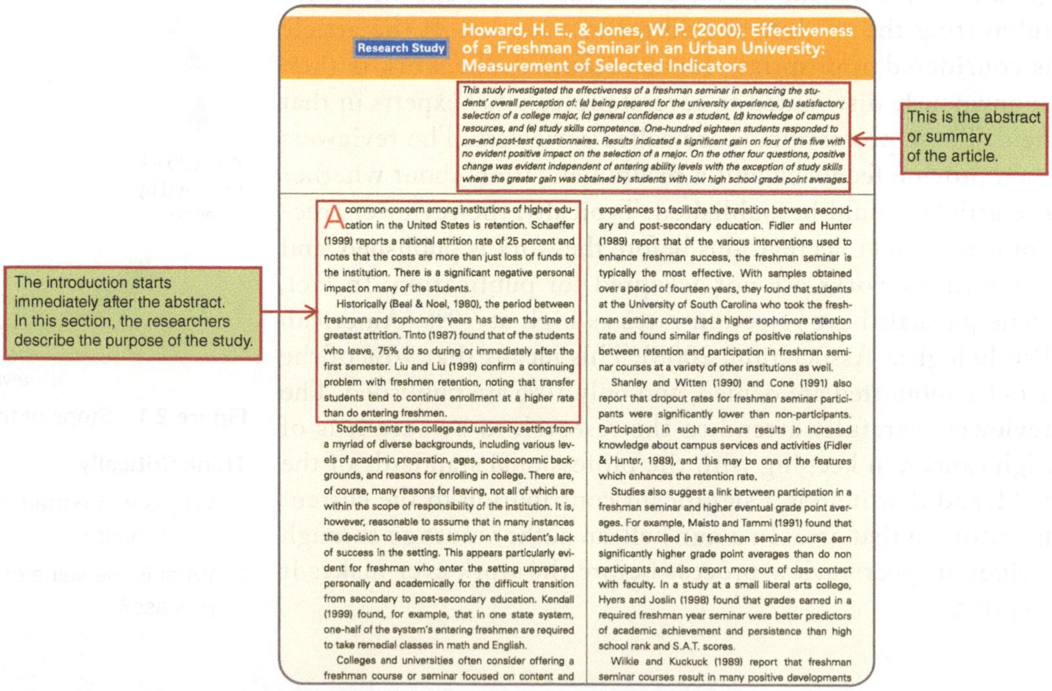

Research Study

Howard, H. E., & Jones, W. P. (2000). Effectiveness of a Freshman Seminar in an Urban University: Measurement of Selected Indicators

This study investigated the effectiveness of a freshman seminar in enhancing the students' overall perception of: (a) being prepared for the university experience, (b) satisfactory selection of a college major, (c) general confidence as a student, (d) knowledge of campus resources, and (e) study skills competence. One-hundred eighteen students responded to pre-and post-test questionnaires. Results indicated a significant gain on four of the five with no evident positive impact on the selection of a major. On the other four questions, positive change was evident independent of entering ability levels with the exception of study skills where the greater gain was obtained by students with low high school grade point averages.

A common concern among institutions of higher education in the United States is retention. Schaeffer (1999) reports a national attrition rate of 25 percent and notes that the costs are more than just loss of funds to the institution. There is a significant negative personal impact on many of the students.

Historically (Beal & Noel, 1980), the period between freshman and sophomore years has been the time of greatest attrition. Tinto (1987) found that of the students who leave, 75% do so during or immediately after the first semester. Liu and Liu (1999) confirm a continuing problem with freshmen retention, noting that transfer students tend to continue enrollment at a higher rate than do entering freshmen.

Students enter the college and university setting from a myriad of diverse backgrounds, including various levels of academic preparation, ages, socioeconomic backgrounds, and reasons for enrolling in college. There are, of course, many reasons for leaving, not all of which are within the scope of responsibility of the institution. It is, however, reasonable to assume that in many instances the decision to leave rests simply on the student's lack of success in the setting. This appears particularly evident for freshman who enter the setting unprepared personally and academically for the difficult transition from secondary to post-secondary education. Kendall (1999) found, for example, that in one state system, one-half of the system's entering freshmen are required to take remedial classes in math and English.

Colleges and universities often consider offering a freshman course or seminar focused on content and experiences to facilitate the transition between secondary and post-secondary education. Fidler and Hunter (1989) report that of the various interventions used to enhance freshman success, the freshman seminar is typically the most effective. With samples obtained over a period of fourteen years, they found that students at the University of South Carolina who took the freshman seminar course had a higher sophomore retention rate and found similar findings of positive relationships between retention and participation in freshman seminar courses at a variety of other institutions as well.

Shanley and Witten (1990) and Cone (1991) also report that dropout rates for freshman seminar participants were significantly lower than non-participants. Participation in such seminars results in increased knowledge about campus services and activities (Fidler & Hunter, 1989), and this may be one of the features which enhances the retention rate.

Studies also suggest a link between participation in a freshman seminar and higher eventual grade point averages. For example, Maisto and Tammi (1991) found that students enrolled in a freshman seminar course earn significantly higher grade point averages than do non participants and also report more out of class contact with faculty. In a study at a small liberal arts college, Hyers and Joslin (1998) found that grades earned in a required freshman year seminar were better predictors of academic achievement and persistence than high school rank and S.A.T. scores.

Wilkie and Kuckuck (1989) report that freshman seminar courses result in many positive developments

Figure 2.2 Abstract and introduction sections of a research article.

necessary. As you become more comfortable reading journal articles, you will naturally skip or jump over the citations as you read.

The author then talks about how this study adds to what is already known about the topic. The research question or hypothesis, which refers to an educated guess about the relationship between the variables, is also identified. This is the purpose of the study. Keep this purpose front and center in your mind as you read the rest of the article. Think of yourself as the detective seeking an answer to the research questions just posed. This helps you stay focused on the key point and not get distracted by the other content.

Method The next section is called **method**, which generally has two subheadings: subjects or participants and procedure. See Figure 2.3. In the subject or participants section, the author describes the people who participated in the research study. One reason why it is important for the author to do this is because it helps the reader understand how easily the results will generalize or apply to other populations. For example, if you are a college student and read an article that found pure memorization was the most effective study strategy, you might want to focus your energy on memorization. However, what if you discovered that the subjects in this study were second graders? Would you still want to use this information as a college student? Similarly, if the research study only used male students, would you be as interested in the results if you did not identify as a male? The size of the sample, defined as how many subjects were in the study, is also important. If only five people participated, would you feel as confident with the findings as compared to a study that had 500 participants?

The procedure section outlines exactly how the study was conducted. It should provide you with enough detail that if you wanted to do the same study, you would be able to do so. This is where the author tells you about the variables, which are defined as concepts or factors of interest, that are being investigated. The author also tells you when and how these variables were measured. In many cases, a questionnaire, assessment inventory, or test was likely given to measure the variables. This information allows a reader to critically evaluate the meaningfulness of the results. For example, you may be more interested in a research study

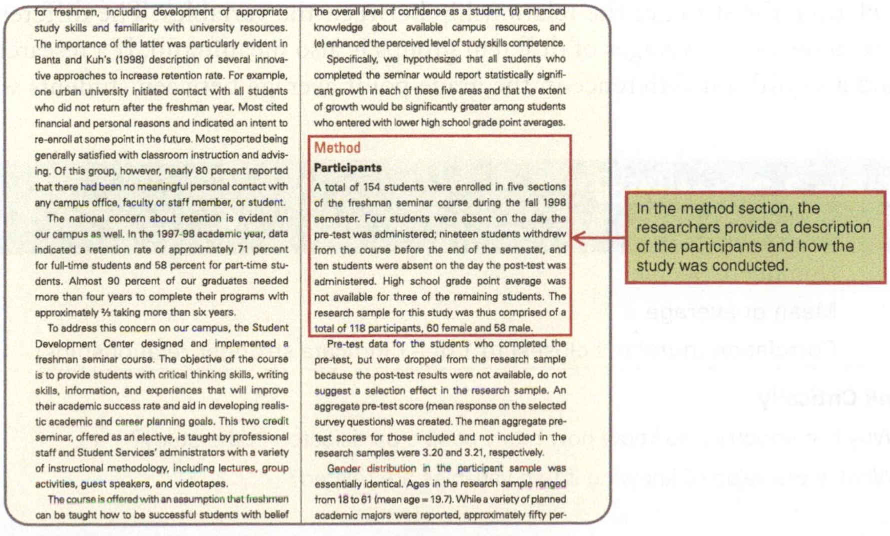

for freshmen, including development of appropriate study skills and familiarity with university resources. The importance of the latter was particularly evident in Banta and Kuh's (1998) description of several innovative approaches to increase retention rate. For example, one urban university initiated contact with all students who did not return after the freshman year. Most cited financial and personal reasons and indicated an intent to re-enroll at some point in the future. Most reported being generally satisfied with classroom instruction and advising. Of this group, however, nearly 80 percent reported that there had been no meaningful personal contact with any campus office, faculty or staff member, or student.

The national concern about retention is evident on our campus as well. In the 1997-98 academic year, data indicated a retention rate of approximately 71 percent for full-time students and 58 percent for part-time students. Almost 90 percent of our graduates needed more than four years to complete their programs with approximately ⅔ taking more than six years.

To address this concern on our campus, the Student Development Center designed and implemented a freshman seminar course. The objective of the course is to provide students with critical thinking skills, writing skills, information, and experiences that will improve their academic success rate and aid in developing realistic academic and career planning goals. This two credit seminar, offered as an elective, is taught by professional staff and Student Services' administrators with a variety of instructional methodology, including lectures, group activities, guest speakers, and videotapes.

The course is offered with an assumption that freshmen can be taught how to be successful students with belief the overall level of confidence as a student, (d) enhanced knowledge about available campus resources, and (e) enhanced the perceived level of study skills competence.

Specifically, we hypothesized that all students who completed the seminar would report statistically significant growth in each of these five areas and that the extent of growth would be significantly greater among students who entered with lower high school grade point averages.

Method

Participants

A total of 154 students were enrolled in five sections of the freshman seminar course during the fall 1998 semester. Four students were absent on the day the pre-test was administered; nineteen students withdrew from the course before the end of the semester, and ten students were absent on the day the post-test was administered. High school grade point average was not available for three of the remaining students. The research sample for this study was thus comprised of a total of 118 participants, 60 female and 58 male.

Pre-test data for the students who completed the pre-test, but were dropped from the research sample because the post-test results were not available, do not suggest a selection effect in the research sample. An aggregate pre-test score (mean response on the selected survey questions) was created. The mean aggregate pre-test scores for those included and not included in the research samples were 3.20 and 3.21, respectively.

Gender distribution in the participant sample was essentially identical. Ages in the research sample ranged from 18 to 61 (mean age = 19.7). While a variety of planned academic majors were reported, approximately fifty per-

Figure 2.3 Method section of a research article.

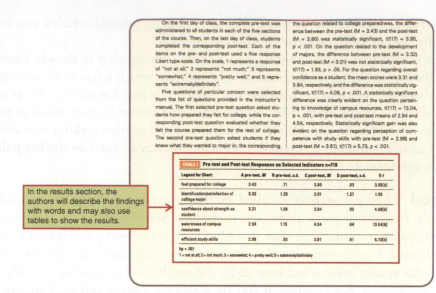

On the first day of class, the complete pre-test was administered to all students in each of the five sections of the course. Then, on the last day of class, students completed the corresponding post-test. Each of the items on the pre- and post-test used a five response Likert type scale. On the scale, 1 represents a response of "not at all;" 2 represents "not much;" 3 represents "somewhat;" 4 represents "pretty well;" and 5 represents "extremely/definitely".

Five questions of particular concern were selected from the list of questions provided in the instructor's manual. The first selected pre-test question asked students how prepared they felt for college, while the corresponding post-test question evaluated whether they felt the course prepared them for the rest of college. The second pre-test question asked students if they knew what they wanted to major in; the corresponding

the question related to college preparedness, the difference between the pre-test (M = 3.43) and the post-test (M = 3.80) was statistically significant, t(117) = 3.95, p < .001. On the question related to the development of majors, the difference between pre-test (M = 3.32) and post-test (M = 3.01) was not statistically significant, t(117) = 1.93, p > .05. For the question regarding overall confidence as a student, the mean scores were 3.31 and 3.84, respectively, and the difference was statistically significant, t(117) = 4.06, p < .001. A statistically significant difference was clearly evident on the question pertaining to knowledge of campus resources, t(117) = 13.04, p < .001, with pre-test and post-test means of 2.94 and 4.54, respectively. Statistically significant gain was also evident on the question regarding perception of competence with study skills with pre-test (M = 2.98) and post-test (M = 3.61), t(117) = 5.73, p < .001.

TABLE 1   Pre-test and Post-test Responses on Selected Indicators n=118

Legend for Chart:	A pre-test, M	B pre-test, s.d.	C post-test, M	D post-test, s.d.	E r
feel prepared for college	3.43	.71	3.80	.83	3.95[b]
identification/satisfaction of college major	3.32	1.20	3.01	1.27	1.93
confidence about strength as student	3.31	1.06	3.84	.92	4.06[b]
awareness of campus resources	2.94	1.15	4.54	.64	13.04[b]
efficient study skills	2.98	.93	3.61	.91	5.73[b]

bp < .001
1 = not at all; 2 = not much; 3 = somewhat; 4 = pretty well; 5 = extremely/definitely

In the results section, the authors will describe the findings with words and may also use tables to show the results.

Figure 2.4   Results section of a research article.

that used official grades as compared to one where they simply asked students to provide their grade because students may not provide information accurately.

Results   The **results** section tells you about the findings of the research study. See Figure 2.4. This section is often filled with statistics and numbers; however, you do not need to understand all the statistical information to walk away with the key findings. Your mathematical skills will increase as you take more courses, so this section will become easier to understand with time. The good news is that the authors also must use words to describe the results.

A very basic overview of statistical language can be helpful to you if you have not taken many math courses recently. See Table 2.2. When you see n, it typically refers to the number of people in the sample. When you see X, it stands for **mean**, which is another word for average. When you see r, it is telling you about a **correlation** or relationship between variables. Note that a relationship does not mean one variable caused the other. The numbers do however tell you about the size or strength of the finding, which is important. The larger the correlation, the stronger the relationship between the variables. The difference between means or averages of different groups is also meaningful. If a researcher found a significant difference in the grade point average between students who

Table 2.2 Statistics
Very Basic Statistics

n	Number of people
X	Mean or average
r	Correlation (numbers closest to 1 or –1 indicate stronger relationships)

Think Critically

1. Why is it important to know how many people participated in the study?

2. What is the value of knowing if two variables are related?

used electronic textbooks and students who used traditional textbooks and the average GPAs were 3.1 and 3.2 for the two groups, you may not care as much as you would if the GPAs for the groups were 2.5 and 3.0. The larger difference would be of more interest and have more value.

Discussion The last section is called the **discussion**. See Figure 2.5. In this section, the researcher puts the key findings into more everyday language, making it easier for everyone to understand. First, the researcher goes back to their original research question or hypothesis that was discussed in the introduction and then answers the question or tells the reader whether the hypothesis was supported. The researcher goes beyond just reporting the findings and also explains the findings. The findings are usually explained in the context of what is already known so you will likely see the researcher reference other similar studies and their findings. Then, there is a discussion of the study limitations, cautioning the reader to interpret the results carefully. Finally, in this section, the value of these findings are highlighted. When reading this section, think about how you can use the results and apply them to your life as a college student.

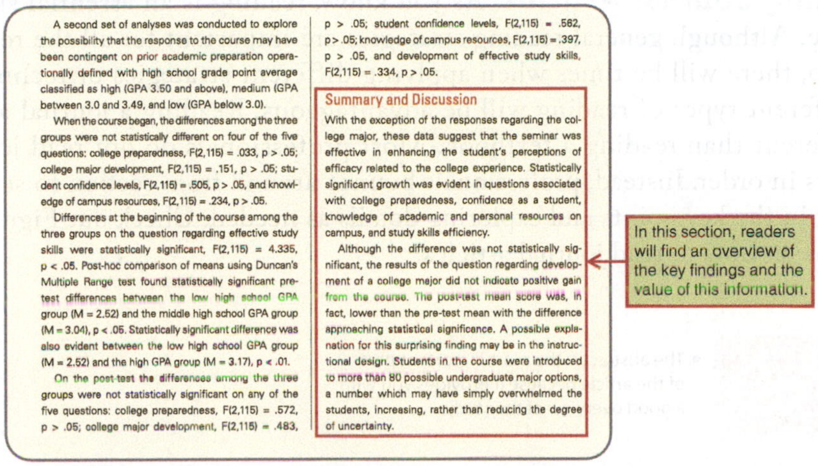

A second set of analyses was conducted to explore the possibility that the response to the course may have been contingent on prior academic preparation operationally defined with high school grade point average classified as high (GPA 3.50 and above), medium (GPA between 3.0 and 3.49, and low (GPA below 3.0).

When the course began, the differences among the three groups were not statistically different on four of the five questions: college preparedness, $F_{(2,115)} = .033$, $p > .05$; college major development, $F_{(2,115)} = .151$, $p > .05$; student confidence levels, $F_{(2,115)} = .505$, $p > .05$, and knowledge of campus resources, $F_{(2,115)} = .234$, $p > .05$.

Differences at the beginning of the course among the three groups on the question regarding effective study skills were statistically significant, $F_{(2,115)} = 4.335$, $p < .05$. Post-hoc comparison of means using Duncan's Multiple Range test found statistically significant pretest differences between the low high school GPA group ($M = 2.52$) and the middle high school GPA group ($M = 3.04$), $p < .05$. Statistically significant difference was also evident between the low high school GPA group ($M = 2.52$) and the high GPA group ($M = 3.17$), $p < .01$.

On the post-test the differences among the three groups were not statistically significant on any of the five questions: college preparedness, $F_{(2,115)} = .572$, $p > .05$; college major development, $F_{(2,115)} = .483$, $p > .05$; student confidence levels, $F_{(2,115)} = .562$, $p > .05$; knowledge of campus resources, $F_{(2,115)} = .397$, $p > .05$, and development of effective study skills, $F_{(2,115)} = .334$, $p > .05$.

Summary and Discussion

With the exception of the responses regarding the college major, these data suggest that the seminar was effective in enhancing the student's perceptions of efficacy related to the college experience. Statistically significant growth was evident in questions associated with college preparedness, confidence as a student, knowledge of academic and personal resources on campus, and study skills efficiency.

Although the difference was not statistically significant, the results of the question regarding development of a college major did not indicate positive gain from the course. The post-test mean score was, in fact, lower than the pre-test mean with the difference approaching statistical significance. A possible explanation for this surprising finding may be in the instructional design. Students in the course were introduced to more than 80 possible undergraduate major options, a number which may have simply overwhelmed the students, increasing, rather than reducing the degree of uncertainty.

> In this section, readers will find an overview of the key findings and the value of this information.

Figure 2.5 Discussion section of a research article.

Parts of a Peer-Reviewed Research Article

- Abstract—Summary of the study
- Introduction—Review of past research and current research question, which explains why the current study is being conducted
- Method—How the study is conducted, the number of participants, and what they were asked to do
- Results—Answers the research question, the findings, and detailed statistics are shared
- Discussion—Summary of key findings, cautions about interpreting results accurately, and the value of the research findings

Tatiana Frank/Shutterstock.com

Reading Journal Articles As you know, reading is an essential skill in college. Although general reading strategies are important for all the reading you do, there will be times when applying different strategies or techniques to different types of reading will be advantageous. Reading a journal article is different than reading a textbook. Most professionals do not read journal articles in order. Instead, professionals bounce around from section to section, taking in the key points and exploring details as needed. Check out Figure 2.6 for tips on how to read journal articles.

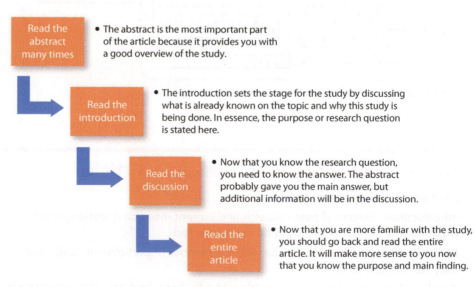

Read the abstract many times	• The abstract is the most important part of the article because it provides you with a good overview of the study.
Read the introduction	• The introduction sets the stage for the study by discussing what is already known on the topic and why this study is being done. In essence, the purpose or research question is stated here.
Read the discussion	• Now that you know the research question, you need to know the answer. The abstract probably gave you the main answer, but additional information will be in the discussion.
Read the entire article	• Now that you are more familiar with the study, you should go back and read the entire article. It will make more sense to you now that you know the purpose and main finding.

Figure 2.6   Tips on reading a journal article.

Think Critically

1. Why do experts read a journal article in this order?

2. How is reading a journal article different from reading a textbook?

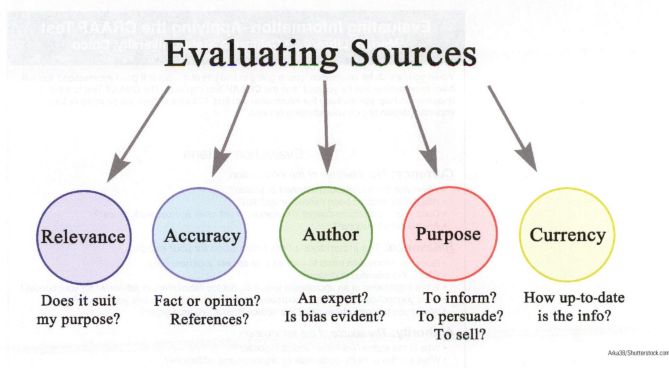

Evaluating Sources

Relevance — Does it suit my purpose?

Accuracy — Fact or opinion? References?

Author — An expert? Is bias evident?

Purpose — To inform? To persuade? To sell?

Currency — How up-to-date is the info?

Evaluating Sources

Determining whether a source is credible is challenging. Sources of information can be biased or even false. As you know, anyone can post information on the Internet, so although finding the information may not take very long, evaluating it can be a time-consuming task. One student in a study by Head et al. (2018) noted that it takes longer to find an unbiased source than it does to read it.

When you are looking for high-quality information online, it can be helpful to ask professionals in the field what resources they use. For example, your professors can point you to credible professional organization websites where you can find information you are seeking. Experts in a field can evaluate information related to their field more easily than others (Willingham, 2020).

One primary consideration when evaluating sources will be whether the person or organization that provided the information is qualified to do so. For example, if you found information on a psychological disorder, you would expect that the person who provided the information has an advanced degree in psychology. Another important consideration is whether the information you found seems to be consistent with other information. In other words, are many different sources coming up with the same conclusions? Kim et al. (2014) found that users often look for consistency not just across different sites but also with reviews or comments on the site being viewed. These are only a few of the questions you will need to ask.

To assist students with evaluating sources, Meriam Library at California State University (2010) developed the CRAAP test (Currency, Relevance, Authority, Accuracy, Purpose). This test provides you with a comprehensive list of questions to ask yourself when trying to decide whether a source is credible. See CRAAP test figure (Figure 2.7).

Evaluating Information—Applying the CRAAP Test
Meriam Library 📖 California State University, Chico

When you search for information, you're going to find lots of it…but is it good information? You will have to determine that for yourself, and the **CRAAP** Test can help. The **CRAAP** Test is a list of questions to help you evaluate the information you find. Different criteria will be more or less important depending on your situation or need.

Evaluation Criteria

Currency: *The timelines of the information.*
- When was the information published or posted?
- Has the information been revised or updated?
- Does your topic require current information, or will older sources work as well?
- Are the links functional?

Relevance: *The importance of the information for your needs.*
- Does the information relate to your topic or answer your question?
- Who is the intended audience?
- Is the information at an appropriate level (i.e., not too elementary or advanced for your needs)?
- Have you looked at a variety of sources before determining this is one you will use?
- Would you be comfortable citing this source in your research paper?

Authority: *The source of the information.*
- Who is the author/publisher/source/sponsor?
- What are the author's credentials or organizational affiliations?
- Is the author qualified to write on the topic?
- Is there contact information, such as a publisher or email address?
- Does the URL reveal anything about the author or source?
   examples: .com .edu .gov .org .net

Accuracy: *The reliability, truthfulness and correctness of the content.*
- Where does the information come from?
- Is the information supported by evidence?
- Has the information been reviewed or refereed?
- Can you verify any of the information in another source or from personal knowledge?
- Does the language or tone seem unbiased and free of emotion?
- Are there spelling, grammar, or typographical errors?

Purpose: *The reason the information exists.*
- What is the purpose of the information? Is it to inform, teach, sell, entertain, or persuade?
- Do the authors / sponsors make their intentions or purpose clear?
- Is the information fact, opinion, or propaganda?
- Does the point of view appear objective and impartial?
- Are there political, ideological, cultural, religious, institutional, or personal biases?

Figure 2.7   CRAAP Test evaluation criteria.
Source: Meriam Library-California State University. https://library.csuchico.edu/help/source-or-information-good

Information Literacy Quick Quiz

1. Why is information literacy important?
2. What is the difference between intentional and incidental information?
3. How can you use social media for academic purposes?
4. What is a peer-reviewed research article?
5. What criteria should you use to determine if a website is a credible source?

Critical Thinking

Critical thinking is one of the most important skills needed in life. For example, critical thinking is a skill that is highly valued by employers. Not surprisingly, researchers have found that critical thinking skills increase in college (Roohr et al., 2019). Throughout your college experience, you will have many opportunities to build critical thinking skills.

Critical thinking has been defined as the ability "to think in a sophisticated manner—to ask questions, define terms, examine evidence, analyze assumptions, avoid emotional reasoning, resist oversimplification, consider alternative interpretations, and tolerate uncertainty" (Wade, 2008, p. 11).

Ehrman Photographic/Shutterstock.com

According to Willingham (2020), "You are thinking critically if (1) your thinking is novel—that is, you aren't simply drawing a conclusion from a memory of a previous situation; (2) your thinking is self-directed—that is, you are not merely executing instructions given by someone else; and (3) your thinking is effective—that is, you respect certain conventions that make thinking more likely to yield useful conclusions" (p. 41).

While there are numerous definitions of critical thinking, Dunn et al. (2008) noted that most definitions have the following themes:

- Exploring and considering multiple perspectives and interpretations
- Examining and evaluating evidence
- Engaging in self-reflection
- Drawing conclusions

Critical thinking is a skill that is learned. Over time, with carefully crafted learning tasks, you will develop and strengthen this skill. According to constructivism, a learning theory, students cannot learn by simply memorizing facts. Instead, students must actively construct or create knowledge, making connections between new information and what has been previously learned (Dennick, 2012). "In other words, students arrive with pre-existing 'constructs,' and in order to learn, must modify these existing structures by removing, replacing, adding, or shifting information in them" (Hartle et al., 2012, p. 31).

Researchers have examined how students change their thinking during the college years. Perry (1970), for instance, studied intellectual development in college and discovered that students at the beginning of their college careers were more likely to think of information as being right or wrong, while students near graduation were more likely to recognize the complexity of information and the importance of considering many factors when evaluating the accuracy of information. In other words, college students move from simplistic to complex thinking.

Based on the work of Perry and several others, West (2004) identified the following four stages of intellectual development:

- Stage 1 (Absolute): Believes that there is a right and wrong answer. Also believes that professors or other authority figures know the correct answer.
- Stage 2 (Personal): After discovering there is not always a correct answer, believes that opinions are what really matter. Knowing is therefore based on personal experiences.
- Stage 3 (Rules-based): Values rules to compare and judge opinions or claims but will resort back to opinions when rules do not apply.
- Stage 4 (Evaluative): Uses more formal strategies to evaluate opinions and evidence. Can explain the process behind the evaluation, defending conclusions drawn.

The college experience fosters these high-level thinking skills and moves students toward the evaluative stage. The more open you are to looking at information from multiple perspectives, the more likely it is that you will develop these high-level cognitive skills. Challenge yourself to go beyond your opinion and to carefully examine the evidence.

Bloom's Taxonomy

One of the most well-known figures in the world of education and critical thinking is Benjamin Bloom (Anderson & Kratwohl, 2001). Bloom identified the various levels of knowing. He encouraged educators to think about what they really wanted students to be able to do with the information being learned. Did they want their students to simply memorize or remember the information, or did they want them to engage in a higher-level task where they had to apply the information to a new situation or make a judgment based on what was learned?

Being able to remember information is the first step. To engage in more complex cognitive tasks, you need to know the subject matter. Willingham (2020) noted that even experts may not be able to think critically about subjects outside of their area of expertise. The other levels are understanding, applying, analyzing, evaluating, and creating. Each level of knowing builds on prior skills and is more challenging in nature.

The concepts in the upper levels of the pyramid, analyzing, evaluating, and creating, are often thought of as critical thinking skills. One of the best ways to develop critical thinking skills is through questioning. See Table 2.3 for some examples of questions you can ask yourself to help you think more critically.

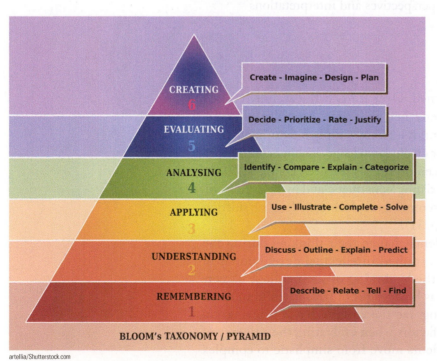

artellia/Shutterstock.com

Table 2.3 Critical Thinking Questions
Questions Aligned to Bloom's Taxonomy That Promote Critical Thinking Skills

Bloom's Taxonomy Levels	Questions to Promote Critical Thinking
Remembering	• What basic knowledge do I need to know?
Understanding	• How does this information relate (compare/contrast) to other information I already know? • How could I explain these concepts?
Applying	• How could this information be applied in different situations? • What are the potential positive and negative consequences of this information? • How useful is this information?
Analyzing	• What evidence or proof exists for or against the idea or finding? • What potential biases exist? • What distinguishes this finding from other findings?
Evaluating	• Why might this be true? • What other explanations might there be? • What would someone who disagrees with the finding say? • How consistent is this finding? • How does this finding or idea add value to the current knowledge base in the field? • Based on this knowledge, what recommendations would you make?
Creating	• How would this information guide your actions? • How might you modify or adapt products based on this information? • How can you take this information and create an original product? • How can this information be used to benefit others?

Creating is the goal. Your professors are going to want you to create academic products such as papers and presentations. As a professional, your employer will also likely want you to create products such as an advertising campaign, a lesson, a budget, or a written report. Thus, you need to be able to remember, understand, apply, analyze, and evaluate information to be successful at creating academic and professional work. It takes time and effort to get to the top of the pyramid. As you engage in cognitive tasks requiring critical thinking, you will discover that your thinking patterns will shift from simplistic to sophisticated.

The Process of Becoming a Critical Thinker

So how do you develop critical thinking skills? For starters, you need to focus on three foundational conditions. You need to know related content (knowledge base), believe in your ability to engage in critical thinking (self-efficacy), and be motivated to learn (desire/drive). The following two learning conditions are then needed: challenging learning tasks and support. See Figure 2.8.

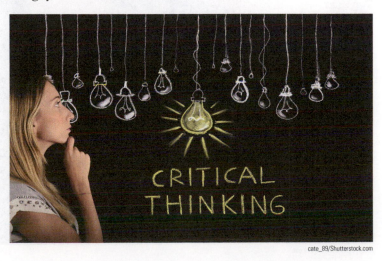

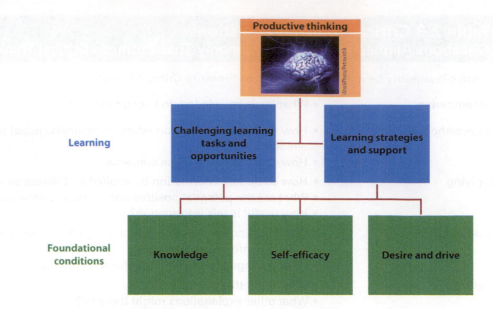

Figure 2.8 The process of becoming a critical thinker.

Think Critically

1. Why are knowledge, self-efficacy, desire, and drive essential foundational conditions for critical thinking?

2. What role do the learning conditions play in developing critical thinking skills?

Foundational Condition 1: Knowledge As indicated in Bloom's taxonomy (Anderson & Kratwohl, 2001), the first step is to remember the course content you are learning. Neuroscience research has demonstrated that it is easier to learn new information when you connect it to something you already know (Goswami, 2008). Thus, the more you know, the easier it is to learn. It is impossible to become a critical thinker without knowing information (Willingham, 2020). In

college, you will be constantly building this knowledge base because there is so much new information to learn—definitions, theories, concepts, and other important information in each field you are studying.

You are obviously entering college with knowledge. While you are in college, you add to or modify your current knowledge base. In some courses, you will be exposed to content that you have not yet encountered. In other courses, you may discover new information about a familiar concept or may even be challenged to think about whether the information you walked in with is accurate. Questioning the accuracy and

Table 2.4 Socratic Questions
Developing Critical Thinking Skills (based on the work of Paul, 1990, and Strang, 2011)

Purpose	Socratic Questions
Clarifying explanations	What do you mean by . . .? How does this compare and/or contrast to . . .? What are the potential advantages and disadvantages of . . .?
Questioning assumptions	What other explanations might exist? What are the assumptions behind this statement or finding?
Exploring additional evidence	How can I find out more about this topic? What additional evidence might support or refute this idea?
Multiple perspectives	What would someone who disagrees say? What are the cultural implications?
Real-world implications	What are the potential consequences or implications of this? What is a real-world example of this?
Self-reflective processes	Why does this matter? What is the importance of this information? What are the unanswered questions?

usefulness of information is an essential part of being a critical thinker. Critical thinkers do not take information at face value, but instead challenge, question, and seek out additional information before determining whether the information presented is accurate and has value. See Table 2.4 for examples of questions you can ask to develop your critical thinking skills.

Foundational Condition 2: Self-Efficacy Becoming a critical thinker involves more than just cognitively processing information. Our beliefs about ourselves also matter. The second foundational condition is self-efficacy. **Self-efficacy** refers to your belief about whether you can successfully complete a task such as critical thinking (Bandura, 1963). If you think you will be able to do a task successfully, you will be much more likely to put in the effort needed and will also be more likely to keep trying even if you experience some difficulties along the way. The way in which you think about yourself and your abilities drives your actions.

Foundational Condition 3: Desire and Drive The third foundational element is your desire and drive—otherwise known as motivation. You may know a lot about a topic and think you can do a critical thinking task successfully but not be interested in doing so. The truth is that critical thinking takes work. Why would you want to do the task if you do not think it is important or worthy? When you perceive the task as valuable and meaningful, you are more likely to have the desire and drive to work toward the upper levels of Bloom's taxonomy.

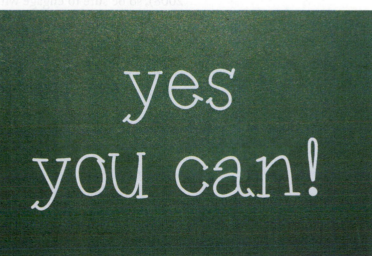

Eskemar/Shutterstock.com

Insta photos/Shutterstock.com

Learning Condition 1: Challenging Learning Tasks and Opportunities

One of the two learning conditions needed for the development of critical thinking skills is a challenging learning task. Fortunately, challenging learning tasks will be a natural part of your college experience. For example, your professors will require you to engage in discussions and debates, write research papers, and give presentations.

You will also find challenging learning opportunities outside of the classroom. For instance, you can seek out opportunities to work with faculty on research or other projects, become a leader of a club or organization, participate in campus-wide events, or get involved in community service projects. Many of these activities strongly encourage you to view the world from multiple perspectives. Research has shown that these out-of-class experiences can often play a more important role in developing critical thinking skills than traditional in-class learning experiences do (Loes et al., 2012).

Learning Condition 2: Learning Strategies and Support

It is important that you are supported as you strive to achieve success with the challenging tasks just discussed. Learning is a social activity, and you learn best when others assist you with tools and general support.

Professors, for example, can support you in many important ways, such as providing you with a good foundation of information, supplying guidelines about assignments such as grading rubrics or models, and being available during office hours, which are hours that faculty specifically block out to meet with and support students, or by e-mail. Professors can also pose challenging questions that require you to think about the issues from different perspectives and dive more deeply into research and theory. There are many other campus supports such as librarians and tutors available as well. Your classmates may also become a part of your support team. You learn best when you interact with others (Goswami, 2008), so be sure to engage with professionals and classmates frequently.

Once the foundational and learning conditions have been met, critical thinking will happen naturally. Your background and experiences will constantly play a role in your thinking. As your critical thinking skills develop, you will find yourself automatically analyzing and evaluating information to create amazing presentations, papers, and other work.

Critical Thinking Quick Quiz

1. What does it mean to be a critical thinker?
2. According to Bloom, what are the different levels of knowing?
3. What are the three foundational conditions needed to become a critical thinker?
4. What are the two learning conditions needed to become a critical thinker?

Chapter Summary: Note-Taking Model

Let's summarize what you have learned in this chapter. The Cornell model is used for this chapter. Remember, it is not expected that your notes will look like this right after class or reading. It takes time to organize your notes and repackage them. It is time well spent, though, because you learn the content better as you organize it, and you have a fabulous foundation from which to study for your exams! There are several ways to use this section:

- **Preview:** Read the model before reading the chapter to familiarize yourself with the content.

- **Compare:** Compare the notes you took on the chapter to the model provided.

- **Study:** The model along with your notes and other course materials are great resources for studying.

Cornell Method Model

Information Literacy: What is it?	Information literacy refers to your ability to determine what information is needed, find that information, and then evaluate the value and relevance of that information. Information literacy is a skill needed in careers.
What are good sources of information?	Websites—the Internet has a vast array of information; ask faculty for guidance on which websites are credible sources of information Social media—follow experts and organizations to learn about current issues Peer-reviewed research—scholarly, theoretical, or research work that has been deemed worthy of publication by professionals in the field • Parts of a research article: abstract (summary), introduction (purpose and research question), method (how study was conducted), results (answer to research question), and discussion (importance of key findings) • Reading journal articles: Read abstract several times, then introduction and discussion, and finally the entire article
How do you evaluate sources?	Good questions to ask are as follows: • Who might be an expert or credible source for this information? Why? • What was the purpose of this information and did the purpose influence its creation? • Who deserves credit for the information? • What conclusions can be made based on this information? • What are various perspectives on this topic? What information would be most useful? How can I find this information? The CRAAP test • Currency • Relevance • Authority • Accuracy • Purpose

Critical Thinking: What is it?	• Critical thinking is high-level thinking, which involves considering many perspectives, evaluating evidence, monitoring and reflecting, and making judgments or conclusions. • Constructivism theory focuses on how one creates knowledge by connecting new information to what's already known—active learning is a must! • Four stages of intellectual development: absolute right or wrong; personal opinions matter most; rules; formal evaluative strategies • Bloom's taxonomy—different levels of knowing (remembering, understanding, applying, analyzing, evaluating, creating)
How do you become a critical thinker?	Process to become a critical thinker: • Knowledge—need to know about a subject in order to think critically about it; add to or modify current knowledge • Self-efficacy—belief about whether one can successfully complete a task; high self-efficacy increases effort and achievement • Desire and drive—motivation is higher when tasks are perceived to be valuable and meaningful; need to care about the task and commit to it • Challenging tasks—assignments, class activities, out-of-class activities (work with faculty on research, leader of club, community service project) • Support—strategies to help learn and complete academic tasks; reach out for help

SUMMARY: Learning how to find and evaluate information is an important skill. There are many different sources of information such as websites, social media, and peer-reviewed journals. Evaluate the value and credibility of information using tools such as the CRAAP test. The process of becoming a critical thinker begins with knowledge, believing in oneself, and caring about the task, and then requires challenging tasks and support. College promotes the development of these high-level skills by providing challenging learning opportunities and high levels of support.

Chinnapong/Shutterstock.com

Part 2

Mapping Out a Path and Developing Career Skills

Chapter

3

Setting Goals and Choosing a Career Path

Shoot for the moon. Even if you miss, you'll land among the stars.

—*Les Brown*

iStockPhoto/Rawpixel

1 What are the benefits of setting short- and long-term goals?

2 What are the characteristics of effective goals?

3 How are career decisions made?

4 How can career theories help you understand the career decision-making process?

5 What contributes to career indecision and what can you do to move toward a decision?

6 What should you know about yourself before making career decisions?

7 How can you learn about various careers?

Exploring the Research in Summary

Research Study Citation:

Morisano, D., Hirsh, J. B., Peterson, J. B., Pihl, R. O., & Shore, B. M. (2010). Setting, elaborating, and reflecting on personal goals improves academic performance. *Journal of Applied Psychology, 95*(2), 255–264. doi:10.1037/a0018478

Introduction: The Research Question

What question did the researcher seek to answer?

Colleges are interested in developing interventions that will help students complete college successfully. Having effective goals is one area that has been associated with student success. In this study, Morisano et al. (2010) investigated the effectiveness of a goal intervention on academic success. The research question was: Does participating in a goal-setting intervention lead to positive academic outcomes such as improved GPA?

Method: The Study

Who participated in the study? What did the researchers ask the participants to do?

College students who were struggling academically were asked to participate in the research study. A total of 85 full-time students participated. Official grades were collected before the intervention and then one year later. Students were randomly assigned to the goal-setting intervention or another general intervention that did not address goals. The intervention was done online and lasted about two and a half hours. Students were then asked to complete a questionnaire 16 weeks later.

Results: The Findings

What was the answer to the research question?

There were three main findings. First, students in the goal group had higher GPAs after the intervention. Specifically, the average GPA for the goal group was 2.91, while the average GPA for the non-goal group was 2.25. See Figure 3.1. Second, students in the goal group were less likely to drop classes than students in the non-goal group. Finally, the goal group were less likely to experience negative emotions at the end of the study.

Figure 3.1   Goal intervention GPA: average GPA.

participated achieved their educational goal while 43% fell short of their goal. Only 8% of participants exceeded their goal. This is an important finding: it is not typical for individuals to achieve beyond the goal they set. Another reason to aim high from the start!

In addition to finding out information about their education level, Reynolds and Baird (2011) also assessed depressive symptoms to determine if there was an emotional cost associated with not achieving goals. They did not find any evidence of an emotional cost associated with not achieving goals. In other words, the participants who did not achieve their educational goal did not have more symptoms of depression than participants who did achieve their educational goal. Interestingly, they found that participants who had higher expectations at the start had lower levels of depression, even if they did not reach their goal.

iStockPhoto/martin-dm

Aiming high or creating challenging goals leads to the best outcomes. Given the limited research and mixed findings on the topic of realistic or unrealistic goals, it may not be worth your time to worry about whether it is realistic. Instead, focus on challenging yourself.

Believe in Yourself: Self-Efficacy Is Key! Self-efficacy is your belief in your ability to successfully complete a task (Bandura, 1997). According to researchers, self-efficacy plays an important role in goal setting (Zimmerman, 2002). In other words, your beliefs about yourself shape the goals you set.

Research has found that students who believe in themselves and exhibit high levels of self-efficacy set more challenging goals (Cheng & Cheou, 2010). Students who have low self-efficacy unfortunately set less challenging goals and, as you know, this can result in lower levels of achievement. Conkel-Ziebell et al. (2019) highlighted the role race can play in self-efficacy and goals. They found that students of color who expect to experience racism often have lower self-efficacy, which can in turn negatively impact their goals.

Successful experiences are one of the best ways to increase your self-efficacy. Researchers have found that individuals with a history of success will be more likely to challenge themselves with higher goals in the future (Spieker & Hinsz, 2004). One way for you to keep focused on your successful experiences is to keep track of your accomplishments. For example, if you have performed well on a paper or project, earned Dean's List status, or received an award, document these success stories, and refer back to them often. Keeping your successful experiences front and center can help you build your self-efficacy.

In addition to playing a role in goal development, self-efficacy also impacts goal accomplishment. If you believe that you can achieve your goal, you are much more likely to succeed. Travis et al. (2020) found that academic self-efficacy or one's belief that they could perform well academically was related to grade point averages. Why? You are more likely to work at something when you believe you can successfully complete the task. If you have low self-efficacy, you may avoid the task or not invest as much effort into it. This connection between self-efficacy and achievement was demonstrated in a research study conducted by Komarraju and Nadler (2013) in which they discussed how high self-efficacy enables students to continue to work and persist despite difficulties or failures.

iStockPhoto/Paul Bradbury

Care and Commit: Motivation Matters! Caring or being motivated to achieve the goal along with a strong commitment to do what it takes to succeed at the goal are important parts of the goal-setting and implementation process. Not surprisingly, students who are more motivated to achieve a goal are more likely to do so. Research conducted by Goodman et al. (2011) found that intrinsic motivation is the best predictor of academic success. Intrinsic motivation refers to factors within a person such as curiosity, interest, enjoyment, and excitement that encourage the person to start or continue doing a task (Deci & Ryan, 1985). Choose goals you care about, and you will be more likely to achieve them.

You must also be committed to achieving the goal. Being committed means you will do what it takes to achieve the goal. Angela Duckworth (2016), a renowned psychologist, has conducted several studies that show caring and commitment are related to successful outcomes. She refers to these qualities as grit or the passion and perseverance to complete tasks (Duckworth, 2016). In other words, commitment means you will put in the effort needed to successfully reach your goal.

Evidence for the importance of commitment comes from research conducted by Seijts and Latham (2011). In their study, participants had to indicate their commitment level to successfully complete a business simulation exercise. Participants with higher levels of commitment performed much better than participants who were not as committed to the goal. Turner and Husman (2008) found commitment to be particularly important when students experienced setbacks or failures. Your commitment is often higher when you also identify action steps related to your goal (Seo et al., 2018).

When you set a goal, researchers have found that it can help to share this with someone who is of a higher status such as a supervisor or mentor. In a series of research studies, Klein et al., (2020) found that commitment to the goal was higher when it was shared with others who were perceived to be of higher status.

Specify and Self-Reflect: Monitoring Your Progress Is Important!

Specific, measurable goals are connected to successful outcomes (Roney & Connor, 2008). Locke and Latham (2006) reported that over 1,000 studies found specific (and high-level) goals lead to the best performance. Specific goals are stated in measurable terms, defining the standard that will be used to judge whether the goal was accomplished. In other words, it will be easy for you or someone else to know if you have achieved your goal if it is specific.

iStockPhoto/Vladimir Vladimirov

Many students often say that they will "do their best" as an academic goal, but unfortunately, this type of goal is not effective. "Do your best" goals do not work because there is no specific target identified. This results in less effort being exerted and lower performance. Locke and Latham (2002) found that "when people are asked to do their best, they do not do so" (p. 706).

Students with specific academic goals such as "I will earn a 4.0 GPA this semester" will exert more effort than students with an "I will do my best" goal. Specificity leads to higher levels of achievement.

Specific goals allow for easier monitoring of progress. Self-reflection on your progress is an important part of goal setting and achievement. To determine whether you are on track with an "I will earn a 4.0 GPA this semester" goal, you can look at your grades thus far. Are your current grades consistent with your desired grade? Grade calculation apps or websites can help you understand your current grade and what grades are needed on future assignments and exams for you to reach your goal.

iStockPhoto/Rawpixel

If, on the other hand, your goal was to "do well" or "do your best," how would you be able to assess this progress? While no one could argue with the spirit of this goal, it is next to impossible to know whether you have achieved it. Do you need to get all As on your assignments to achieve the goal or do you simply need to earn passing grades on assignments and tests? Are Ds evidence of support for this goal? Hopefully, you are discovering the importance of being specific and how this makes it much easier for you to see if you are on track to accomplishing your goal.

As you evaluate your progress, you may need to make modifications or adjustments. For instance, if you were aiming for an A in your biology class and you currently have a B average, you will probably want to increase your studying time and perhaps even add new learning strategies into your daily routines so that you can achieve your goal. Students who actively monitor their progress and adjust as necessary are more successful than those who do not engage in self-reflection (Schloemer & Brenan, 2006; Zimmerman, 2002).

Setting Goals Quick Quiz

1. What are examples of short- and long-term goals?
2. What are action-based goals?
3. What are the ABCS of setting and implementing effective goals?
4. Do "do your best" goals work? Why or why not?

Career Exploration and Decision Making

According to a survey conducted by the Bureau of Labor Statistics (2019), the average person will have 12 jobs throughout their life. Given the likelihood that you will be in many different positions throughout your career, it is important for you to think broadly about what you are passionate about and how this may translate into success in a variety of positions. Many career opportunities you will

ESB Professional/Shutterstock.com

encounter in the future may not even exist today, so identifying a specific career goal is probably not as important as identifying a career pathway. A career pathway is a broader vision of what career field or type of profession you would like to pursue.

Career pathways often align with academic majors. A good first step, therefore, is to decide on a major. As you know, you have many options when it comes to choosing a major. Most colleges and universities have organized major options into broader categories such as business, arts, or health care. Within each major, there will be many more specific tracks. For example, business majors might include accounting, finance, marketing, management, or even more specific options such as supply chain management. Think first about which broad major category fits best for you and then explore the more specific options in that category.

Fortunately, there are many supports that can help students navigate the numerous options available. Reardon et al. (2021) reviewed over 200 studies that took place over a 45-year period and found that courses that focus on career exploration are very useful to students. Specifically, they found that students taking these courses had improved career decision-making skills, had better grades, were more likely to stay in college, and had higher levels of job satisfaction. This text is also a support to help you with this decision-making process.

How Do We Make Career Decisions?

According to the classic work of Parsons (1909), the three key steps involved in career decision making are the following:

1. Knowing about yourself
2. Knowing career information and opportunities
3. Using information about yourself and world of work to decide on a career path

While this classic framework is still used as a general guideline to help students or others make career decisions, career decision making is not this simple. It is a much more complicated process. Self-awareness and career information are still critical parts of the process, but other factors such as social networks also influence career choices.

Greenbank (2011) found that students tend to rely on intuition and readily available information from friends and family rather than actively engaging in a thorough process of exploring available career information. Not surprisingly, family and friends play a significant role in our decision making, with parents often playing the most significant role (Chinyamurindi et al., 2021; Workman, 2015). Significant others, other relatives, and teachers also impact our career decisions. See Figure 3.3 for a visual presentation of who influences our career decisions.

Oymak (2018) found that students from higher socio-economic backgrounds were more influenced by family members as compared to students from lower socio-economic backgrounds. However, teachers, and to some extent counselors, had a greater influence on career decisions for students from lower socio-economic backgrounds. College provides an opportunity to expand your network and explore career options that you may not have previously considered.

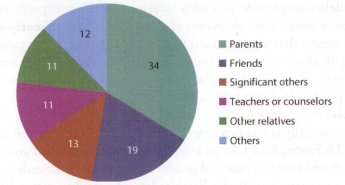

- ■ Parents
- ■ Friends
- ■ Significant others
- ■ Teachers or counselors
- ■ Other relatives
- ■ Others

Figure 3.3 Personal network career influence: who influences career decisions?

Think Critically

1. Why do you think so few students rely on professionals such as counselors to guide their career decisions?

2. How might the results be different if this study was conducted again today?

There are numerous career theories that help us better understand how we make career decisions. In this chapter the following four theories will be explored: social-cognitive theory, values-based theory, happenstance learning theory, and person-environment fit.

Social Cognitive Theory
Lent et al. (1994) proposed a **social cognitive theory of career** that can help you better understand how career interests develop, how career decisions are made, and what contributes to persistence and high-level performance. One of the basic premises behind this theory is that situational factors can play a major role in our decision making. Situational factors can include the people with whom you interact and the experiences you have.

Not surprisingly, you are more likely to consider careers that you know about or are visible to you. Your career decisions can be impacted both by role models with whom you have personal connections and those whom you see but do not know personally (Strasser-Burke & Symond, 2020). In other words, you can be influenced not only by your friends, families, and community members, but also by who you see portrayed in the media.

When you see others, especially those who look like you, working in various fields, it is easier for you to imagine yourself in those careers. For instance, interacting with teachers, doctors, or business professionals could result in you becoming interested in these fields. The visibility of these careers puts them on your radar for consideration.

There are many other career paths that may not be as visible, but that you may learn about because of a role model. For instance, having a neighbor who is a fragrance chemist, someone who studies odor molecules to develop perfumes, or a member of your church who is a voiceover artist, someone who is the voice for a cartoon character, a documentary or radio show might lead you to explore these options.

Role models also provide you with vicarious learning experiences that can directly impact your career decisions (Lent et al., 1994). **Vicarious learning experiences** means that you can learn from watching others. For example, if you hear others talk about how much they enjoy their career, or if you see them getting recognition or an award for their work, this might inspire you to consider options you previously did not think about.

You are also more likely to pursue a career path if you have seen others achieve and do well, especially if you perceive the role models to be like you in some way (Quimby & DeSantis, 2006). In an interesting study by Kofoed and McGovney (2019), they found that the race and gender of the mentor for cadets was related to their career requests. Specifically, Black cadets who worked with a Black mentor were 6% more likely to choose the same branch of their mentor than if their mentor was White. Similarly, female cadets were almost 5% more likely to choose the branch of their female mentor. Because you are most influenced by others who are like you, it can be important to actively seek out role models and mentors who identify with the same gender and race that you do.

Experiences also matter when it comes to the career decision-making process. Academic experiences and self-efficacy have been cited by students as playing an important role in career decisions (Chinyamurindi et al., 2021). When you take on tasks, you quickly discover what you enjoy and what you do not enjoy. Similarly, you find out your strengths. You are more likely to pursue careers if you have had successful experiences related to that path. For example, if you did well in science courses, you may pursue a health career.

In addition to social factors, Lent et al. (1994) emphasized that cognitive factors also play a central role in career decision making. Specifically, they noted that goal setting, expectations, and self-efficacy really matter when it comes to career decision making. You are most likely to pursue careers that you believe you will be successful in. This relates to the "B" in the ABCS of goal-setting framework. See Table 3.2 for a summary of factors that influence self-efficacy.

According to this social-cognitive framework, your career interests are shaped by your beliefs and social experiences. It is more likely for you to be interested in a task if you think you will succeed at it and believe that by doing so, positive things will happen. You are also more likely to believe this if you have experienced success previously or you have seen others experience success.

Table 3.2 Self-Efficacy
Factors That Influence Self-Efficacy

Factors	Description
Personal accomplishments	Experiencing success will increase self-efficacy while failure experiences will likely decrease self-efficacy.
Vicarious experiences	When you observe other people who are similar to you achieve success, your self-efficacy increases.
Social persuasion	You can be influenced by others encouraging and believing in you.
Physiological reactions	Your physical reaction when participating or completing a task also influences your self-efficacy. When you experience excitement or exhilaration, you will likely elevate your self-efficacy while, on the other hand, if you are exhausted or drained after completing a task, your self-efficacy can drop.

Rawpixel.com/Shutterstock.com

Values-Based Theory Brown's **value-based theory for career choice and satisfaction** (2002) emphasized that "cultural and work values are the primary variables that influence the occupational choice-making process, the occupation chosen, and the resulting satisfaction with and success in the occupation chosen" (p. 49). According to this theory, work values played an essential role in career decision making for individuals who identified with cultures that value individualism. Individualism refers to placing value and importance on the individual versus society. Brown (2002) noted that women, people of color, people from lower socio-economic backgrounds, and people with disabilities who identified with cultures where individualism was valued, often made career choices based on a more restricted list of options due to the realities of discrimination.

Work values are less important for individuals who identify with cultures that emphasize collectivism because they will be more likely to place the needs of the family or group first when making decisions (Brown, 2002). Brown (2002) believed that work satisfaction for individuals from cultures where collectivism is highly valued would be most influenced by whether there was a match between the cultural and work values of the employee, supervisor, and co-workers and if significant others approved of their work.

Not surprisingly, researchers have demonstrated that gender and race impact career values and choices. For example, in a study with over 30,000 college students, Duffy and Sedlacek (2008) found that men valued making money more than women and that women valued the opportunity to work with others and contribute to society in a positive way more than men. White students were more likely to value independence, and African American and Asian students were more likely to value salary and perceived availability of jobs. These differing value systems can lead to different career choices.

Antonio Guillem/Shutterstock.com

Happenstance Learning Theory Krumboltz (2009), a social learning psychologist, believes most career decisions are the result of **happenstance**. According to happenstance learning theory, career journeys do not necessarily follow a predicted path but rather happen as a result of planned and unplanned events.

Krumboltz and Levin (2004) discovered that many people are employed in careers that they did not plan to enter. In fact, they found that very few people followed a planned, predictable path and that many individuals were employed in areas that were not directly connected to their college major. Rather, individuals often choose careers based on experiences, networking, and being open to new opportunities. Because of this, Krumboltz (2009) is less interested in students deciding on a specific career and is more interested in whether they "engage in an active lifestyle to generate unexpected events, to remain alert to new opportunities, and to capitalize on the opportunities they find" (p. 152).

Krumboltz and Levin (2004) noted that people who engaged in action steps discover many excellent career opportunities. Here are some examples of action steps you can take:

- Talk to others (professors, friends, family, and coworkers) about career options.
- Take a variety of courses in college and talk with professors and classmates about your career aspirations.
- Participate in clubs and organizations and talk with the club advisors and members about your career goals.
- Seek out work experiences in a variety of settings and talk to coworkers about career issues.
- Participate in an internship program to gain experience in a work environment in your field of interest.
- Engage in a service-learning project.
- Conduct informational interviews with individuals from different careers.
- Ask others you meet at social events, conferences, and club meetings about their career journey.

Person-Environment Fit One of the most well-known career theorists is Holland (1997). His theory focuses on a **person-environment model**. According to this theory, interests, personality types, and work environments can be characterized according to six basic themes (see Figure 3.4):

- Realistic
- Investigative
- Artistic
- Social
- Enterprising
- Conventional

The basic premise of the person-environment theory is that if you can identify a work environment or career that matches well with your personality and interests, then you will be satisfied with your career choice (Smart et al.,

ASTA Concept/Shutterstock.com

2006). Holland refers to this as **congruence**. The better the match between your personality and interests, and the work environment and tasks, the higher the level of congruence (Leung, 2008). Higher levels of congruence have been connected to higher levels of satisfaction. Research studies have shown that there is indeed a connection between interest, job task, and satisfaction (Jagger et al., 1992; Nauta, 2010).

Figure 3.4 Holland's hexagon on person-environment fit.

Think Critically

1. What are some examples of careers that would be associated with each of the six components of Holland's theory?

2. How do the six components relate to each other?

Career Decision-Making Theories

- Social Cognitive Theory: Your beliefs and social experiences influence your choices.
- Values Based Theory: The driving force behind career decisions is your cultural and work values.
- Happenstance Theory: Career choices are a result of planned and unplanned events.
- Person-Environment Fit: A desire to work in an environment that matches your personality and interests influences your choices.

Career Indecision

It is not uncommon for students to enter college unsure of what major or career to choose. Some researchers have found that up to 70% of traditional-aged students, defined as high school student or recent graduate, and 65% of older students are undecided about their career choice (Albion & Fogarty, 2002). If this is the case for you, you are certainly not alone. Some career theorists have argued that deciding on a specific career may not be necessary, but rather determining what actions will lead to a satisfying career and personal life matters most (Krumboltz, 2009).

Edmondson (2016) stated that students should major in happiness, meaning that students should choose a major that matches their interests and values instead of trying to chase the latest employment trend

Alberto Andrei Rosu/Shutterstock.com

or identify a major that is associated with a high salary. He noted that when students choose a major that they are passionate about, success will follow. Discovering what matters to you and what will bring meaning to your life and the life of others will help you identify a major and actions you can take to have a successful career.

Making effective career decisions requires exploration. Engaging in actions such as reflecting on your values, interests, and skills, learning about career options, and talking with others about possible paths will help you make a career decision. With all the academic tasks on your plate, it is easy to put off the work associated with career exploration. However, there is no doubt that you will make a better decision if you make career exploration a priority and engage in actions that will help you determine a career pathway.

While it is important for you to explore before committing to a career path or major, choosing a major aligned to your career goals sooner versus later can help you stay on track with your graduation timetable. Waiting too long before choosing a major may have negative consequences in terms of time and money. It may take longer for you to earn a certificate or a degree. Taking longer to graduate also means you will be paying more tuition and perhaps more room and board, which can add to your student loan debt.

It is worth noting that choosing a major is not the same as choosing a career. In some cases, such as nursing, you will need to choose a major that is directly aligned with your career goal. However, in many cases, you can enter your career path through a variety of majors. For example, if you want to become a police officer, the major that would likely come to mind is criminal justice and this is, of course, a great option, but other majors such as psychology, sociology, communications, or a foreign language could also set you up for success in this field. It is therefore more important to identify a career path and then determine which major can best help you reach this goal.

As you are discovering, career decision making is complex. Gati et al. (1996), for instance, identified three primary types of career decision-making difficulties:

1. Lack of readiness. Some individuals may not be motivated to engage in the career exploration process and decide. Others may have a difficult time making decisions in general.

2. Lack of information. Individuals may lack information about themselves such as their interests and values, career information, or how to find information that will be helpful in this process.

3. Inconsistent information. Individuals may struggle to decide because the information they have is not consistent. For example, maybe you are excited about the job tasks and salary when reading about it online, but when you talk to professionals in the field, their description of the tasks and salary is not as positive. In addition, career options could cause internal or external conflict. An example of internal conflict could be if a career option matches many of your important values but conflicts with one value that is very important to you. An external conflict, on the other hand, could occur when your career choice does not match what your family or significant other had in mind for you.

Seeking professional guidance from career counselors who are experts at helping you with this process is recommended, especially if you are uncertain about your career goals (Greenbank, 2010). Unfortunately, only 8% of the students in a study conducted by Vertsberger and Gati (2015) reported meeting with career advisors even though this service was available free of charge. Students instead tend to get most of their career information from friends and family (Greenbank & Hepworth, 2008). While using your network is certainly important, seeking guidance from career specialists can also be quite helpful, especially if you are struggling with the career decision-making process. A career specialist can help increase your motivation to engage in the career exploration process, help you find additional information, or help you navigate and interpret inconsistent information.

Another benefit of reaching out for help is that you will be less likely to change your major if you work with a career expert (Vertsberger & Gati, 2015). As you can imagine, changing your major can sometimes increase the amount of time and money needed to graduate with a degree. Thus, investing your time and effort in this process now so that you make a choice after exploring options will help you save time and perhaps money in the future. You will also be more likely to choose a career path that will make you happy.

Self-Assessment

Self-assessment is an important part of the career decision-making process. Personality, values, interests, and abilities all play a role in career decisions. Even if you have a clear career goal and have declared an academic major, engaging in self-assessment can be a worthwhile activity. As a result of this process, you may feel more confident with your chosen career path, be clearer about which specialty area within a chosen field best fits for you, or you might question your initial goal and be interested in exploring different options.

Exploring Your Values Exploring your values is a great place to begin the career exploration process. Values are a driving force in your decisions (Balsamo et al., 2013; Sargent & Domberger, 2007). Values refer to what matters to you or what is high on your priority list of importance. Examples of career values include the following:

- Being able to help others or make a difference in society
- Functioning independently
- Room for creativity
- Working alone
- Working with others
- Salary
- Prestige
- Job security
- Engaging in a variety of tasks
- Having consistent, predictable job tasks
- Working in a competitive, fast-paced work environment
- Working in a calm work environment
- Flexible hours
- Consistent schedule, such as 9–5 workday
- Having reliable and likeable coworkers

Ehab Edward/Shutterstock.com

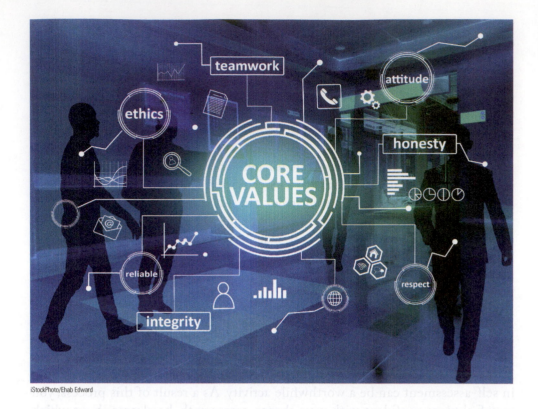

iStockPhoto/Ehab Edward

- Having fair and responsive supervisors
- Opportunity for advancement
- Recognition for achievements
- Opportunity to use strengths or talents
- Supportive work environment—easy to access help when needed
- Travel opportunities
- Leadership opportunities—managing or supervising others

Your values may change over time. For example, you might value the opportunity to travel now, but if you have a family in the future, you might then place a higher value on family time, and traveling may no longer appeal to you because it might mean you will miss out on important family events. Although it is difficult to predict what will matter to you in the future, spend some time thinking about what might be important to you in 5, 10, or even 20 years from now.

Unless you are in an extremely difficult situation, you will likely not take a job or enter a career that conflicts with your value system. For example, a person who is totally against smoking probably would not take an otherwise ideal position at a tobacco company. If a position clashes with your values, this will likely be a deal breaker.

Exploring Your Abilities Your skills and abilities are also important considerations as you engage in career decision making. Research has shown that ability is linked to career success (Judge et al., 2009). You are more likely to choose a career that builds on your strengths instead of highlighting your weaker areas.

Gardner's (1983) theory of **multiple intelligence** is a great way to start thinking about your abilities and strengths. He identified several different types of intelligence:

1. **Linguistic**—ability to use language
2. **Logical-Mathematical**—ability to use logic and solve mathematical problems
3. **Spatial**—ability to perceive spatial relationships
4. **Bodily Kinesthetic**—ability to use your body to perform tasks
5. **Musical**—ability to comprehend and create music
6. **Intrapersonal**—ability to engage in self-reflection
7. **Interpersonal**—ability to engage in social behavior
8. **Naturalistic**—ability to identify patterns in nature
9. **Existential/Philosophical**—ability to think deeply about philosophical questions such as the meaning of life

It is important to note that Gardner (1983) did not place a higher value on one type of intelligence as compared to another. Rather, he believed all types of intelligence are valuable and worthwhile. Gardner (1983) viewed these types of intelligences as being on a continuum, with everyone having some level of intelligence in each area but being stronger in some areas than others. This theory provides you with a great way to focus on where your strengths lie. Thinking about your strengths can help you choose a career that builds on these strengths, maximizing career success.

Employers are looking for both technical skills related to the career field and other essential skills that are important in most, if not all, careers. **Technical skills** vary from career to career. For example, teachers need to be able to write lesson plans while pharmacists need to know how medications may interact with one another. Essential skills can be used across all careers and include being able to communicate and work well with others. In a study conducted by Robles (2012), employers indicated that soft skills are very important. Specifically, employers were asked to rate 10 soft skills. As you can see in Figure 3.5, all the

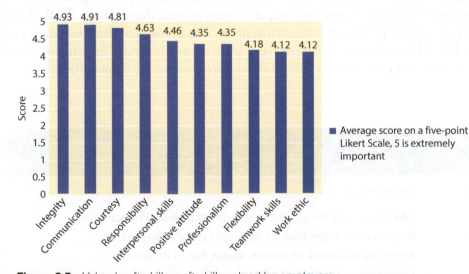

Figure 3.5 Valued soft skills: soft skills valued by employers

Think Critically

1. How might these findings differ across different careers?
2. What surprised you about these findings?

skills were highly valued by employers, with integrity and communication skills being the most important. You can increase your ability in these areas by seeking out assistance and relevant opportunities. For instance, if you want to increase your verbal or communication skills, take additional courses in this field, work with your professor or a tutor, or participate in activities where you can develop and use these skills.

iStockPhoto/SIphotography

Exploring Your Personality and Interests

Another important part of the process is to explore your personality traits and how these traits may play a role in your career decision making. Personality factors have been connected to career choice (Warr & Pearce, 2004) as well as career success (Rode et al., 2008). Although there are several personality theories, McCrae and Costa's (1990) Big Five Personality Factor trait theory is one of the most well-known and researched theories.

According to this theory, there are five distinct personality factors or characteristics: openness, conscientiousness, extraversion, agreeableness, and neuroticism. The mnemonic OCEAN can help you remember them. See Table 3.3 for an overview of the Big Five Personality Factors. The factors are on a continuum, meaning you will be low, moderate, or high on each dimension.

Holland's person-environment theory, which we have previously discussed, emphasized personality and interests and the importance of matching one's personality and interests to job tasks and work environment. See Table 3.4 for a description of each of the six themes and a few career choices linked to each one.

Your top three personality types or interest areas are often referred to as your Holland code. For example, SEC would be the code if your highest interest areas were the social, enterprising, and conventional dimensions. To find out your code, you can take an interest inventory. The Strong Interest Inventory and the Self-Directed Search are two very well-known interest inventories based on Holland's (1997) theory. Stop by the career center at your college and see

Table 3.3 Mccrae and Costa Personality
Big Five Personality Factors

Mnemonic	Personality Factor	Description
O	**O**penness	Like to try new things and enjoy doing a variety of activities
C	**C**onscientiousness	Responsible, organized, careful, and self-disciplined
E	**E**xtraversion	Enjoy the company of others, social, fun to be around
A	**A**greeableness	Cooperative, trusting of others
N	**N**euroticism	Worry a lot, anxious, high strung

Table 3.4 Holland's Theory
Holland's Theory and Related Careers

Theme	Description	Careers
Realistic	Athletic, prefers working with things and outdoors	Automotive technician, pilot, civil engineer
Investigative	Scientific thinker, prefers working with ideas	Chemist, Research Analyst, Industrial organizational psychologist
Artistic	Creative, prefers unstructured situations and working independently	Illustrator, Interior Designer, Journalist
Social	Helper, prefers working with others	Rehabilitation specialist, teacher, substance abuse counselor
Enterprising	Leader, prefers to influence and persuade others	Sales manager, buyer, politician
Conventional	Detail-oriented, prefers clerical and structured tasks	Administrative assistant, editorial assistant, tax preparer

Source: Adapted from: https://www.onetonline.org/

if there are career interest inventory resources available to you. There are also many resources available that describe careers using Holland's coding system. For example, O*NET OnLine (https://www.onetonline.org/) lists Holland's code for various occupations.

To understand your personality more fully, you may want to consider taking more comprehensive personality assessments. You can contact your Career Services department to explore your assessment options and to discuss the career decision-making process. The Myers Briggs Personality Assessment is one of the most widely used personality assessments and it is often recommended by career counselors (Kennedy & Kennedy, 2004). It summarizes your psychological preferences for interacting with the world. Knowing your preferences can aid you in the career decision-making process. For example, if you are extroverted, getting your energy from others, it will be important that you choose a career where you will have the opportunity to be around others. See Table 3.5 for an overview of the personality factors associated with this assessment tool.

Table 3.5 Myers Briggs
Myers Briggs Personality Factors

Extroversion: Gets energy from the external world (others, activities)	**Introversion:** Gets energy from one's internal world (thoughts, ideas, emotions)
Sensing: Prefers paying attention to what can be seen or sensed (what is real)	**Intuition:** Prefers to consider what might be rather than what currently exists
Thinking: Prefers to take in and organize information logically	**Feeling:** Prefers to take in and organize information based on personal values and emotions
Judgment: Prefers a life that is planned and well-organized	**Perceiving:** Prefers a life characterized by spontaneity and flexibility

Source: Adapted from: Hirsh and Kummerow (1992) as cited in Kennedy and Kennedy (2004).

Career and Your Self-Assessment

- Values—What is important to you? What will be important to you in the future?
- Abilities—What are your overall strengths? What are your soft or transferable skills? What technical skills do you have for various career choices?
- Personality—How would you describe your personality? What careers might fit best with your personality?
- Interests—What do you like to do? What is your Holland code? What types of careers might match your interests?

iStockPhoto/SDI Productions

Learning about Careers

Now that you have considered your values, abilities, personalities, and interests, it is time to explore career information. Knowing the education or training requirements, job tasks, salary information, and other important information about various careers will help you with the career decision-making process. It is difficult to know if a career is a good match for you if you do not know much about the profession. Finding and evaluating career information is therefore important.

Some students have many interests and therefore want to explore numerous careers. It is easier to decide on a career when you focus on a manageable number of options (Gati & Tikotzki, 1989). If you have too many options that match your interests and values, spend some time and energy thinking about your values and what matters most to you. You can then use your core values as way to screen potential options, eliminating career options that do not match your most important values. Once you have a list that is manageable, then you can start exploring (Gati, 1986).

However, some of you may begin the process with a narrow list of values or interests, and this can result in too short of a list of career options to pursue. If your list is too small, you will likely miss out on exploring options that could potentially be good matches for you. Seeking out new opportunities and experiences, talking with others, and exploring online career information resources can help you identify additional potential options you might not have previously considered. You can meet with a career specialist to help you expand or narrow your list before you start to research career information.

There is a wealth of information on careers available. The challenge is determining what information you need and then sifting through the vast amount of information out there to find this essential information. One of the most widely used information-gathering strategies related to career exploration is reviewing career websites. Another excellent approach is to connect with professionals in the field. Informational interviews and social media can be used for this purpose.

Career Websites Career websites provide you with basic information about the educational and other requirements needed to enter a specific career, an overview of job tasks and responsibilities, salary, and job outlook. Job outlook refers to the number of job openings expected in the future. Here are just a few credible resources you may want to explore:

- Occupational Outlook Handbook (www.bls.gov/ooh; see Figure 3.6)
- Career One Stop (www.careerinfonet.org)
- O-NET (http://online.onetcenter.org)
- National Career Development Association (www.ncda.org)

Most of the data presented on career websites is based on national data, so it is important for you to know that some of the information may vary significantly across different geographic areas. After gathering general information from these national resources, be sure to also look for information specific to where you plan to work. Salaries and job opportunities, for instance, can vary quite a bit based on location. See Table 3.6 for an example. Use websites such as salary.com for more specific information related to your geographic location.

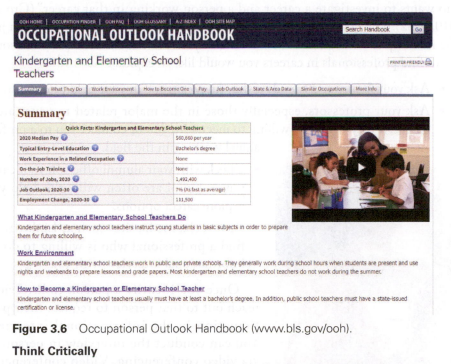

Figure 3.6 Occupational Outlook Handbook (www.bls.gov/ooh).

Think Critically

1. How could this information help you decide if this career is for you?
2. What additional information would you want to know about the career to help you decide on a career path?

Table 3.6 Teacher Salaries	
Example Job Summary on the Occupational Outlook Handbook Website	
Data Source	**Median Salary ($)**
National Average (*Occupational Outlook Handbook*)	$60,660
New York City, NY (Salary.com)	**72,086**
Rapid City, SD (Salary.com)	**52,006**

Source: U.S. Bureau of Labor Statistics. Retrieved July 17, 2021.

Although you probably do not yet have all the skills, knowledge, and credentials needed, job searching is a great way to find out valuable information about career fields. For example, you can explore what positions in your field of interest are available and the job requirements for these positions. Websites such as LinkedIn, indeed.com, or monster.com can work well for this purpose.

Looking at the necessary job requirements can help you determine what types of experiences you will want to seek out during college to build a strong resume. This increases the likelihood that you will be offered a position in the field of your choice in the future. You might even come across part-time opportunities that you are able to take advantage of now.

Informational Interviews Websites can provide you with a very clear overview of the career, but informational interviews can give you a more personal look at the career. "An **informational interview** is a brief meeting between a person who wants to investigate a career and a person working in that career" (Crosby, 2010, p. 22). The goal of the interview is to learn about the career, not land a job. The first step is to find someone working in your field of interest. Here are some tips to find professionals in careers you would like to explore:

- Ask your family and friends if they know anyone in your field of interest.
- Ask your professors, especially those in the major related to your career choice, if they would be willing to meet with you or connect you to a professional working in the field.
- Check with your alumni office on your campus—alumni are often willing to help you explore career options.
- Visit social media sites such as LinkedIn to find a professional who is willing to do an informational interview with you.

Once you identify a person to interview, reach out to that person to request their participation in the informational interview. You can conduct the interview in person or via video conferencing. Video conferencing may be more convenient and enables you to connect with professionals from across the world. However, attending an in-person

Vadym Pastukh/Shutterstock.com

informational interview provides you with the opportunity to also see the work environment.

Although most individuals are interested in helping college students with career decision making, professionals can be very busy. You may therefore want to have several individuals in mind to interview in case someone does not respond or is unable to do the interview due to their other responsibilities.

Conduct yourself professionally before, during, and after your informational interview. Prior to the interview, generate a list of questions you would like to ask. Keep the interview brief, approximately 15 to 30 minutes. Prioritize what questions you want to ask as you will likely only have time for a few questions. Here are some questions you might consider:

- How did you get started with this career?
- Describe a typical day in your position.
- What do you most enjoy about your career?
- What are the challenges associated with this career choice?
- What suggestions or advice do you have for someone who is interested in this field?

On the day of your interview, dress professionally, even if conducting the interview virtually. You want to make a good impression because this is also a networking opportunity. Arrive on time—or better yet a little early—and end the interview on schedule. In addition to thanking the person at the end of the interview, send a formal thank you e-mail or letter later that day.

These personal conversations can provide you with details about what it is like to work in that field. This is such valuable information, but you will not want to rely solely on this type of data because the experience of one person may not be representative of the experiences of others. As always, take in information from a variety of sources, and look for themes that emerge. This leads to a more comprehensive understanding of the career field.

Social Media Another great way to learn about careers is through social media platforms, especially those designed for professionals. Utz (2016) found that using social media, especially LinkedIn, increased knowledge of careers. You can look for and follow professionals in careers you are considering. By following professionals, you can often learn about their job duties as many professionals will post updates on their achievements. Social media posts can also provide you with some information about the personality and values of professionals in the field. In an interesting study by Rosen et al. (2018), they found that personality could be accurately predicted by reviewing Twitter feeds. In fact, many employers review social media to learn about job applicants.

In addition to following individuals, you can also follow organizations that relate to fields of

Vasin Lee/Shutterstock.com

interest. Organizations often post blogs, articles, conferences, reports, and other information that can help you learn about the field. You may discover some of these organizations when searching for career information, but it is also a good idea to ask professors or other professionals for suggestions of organizations to follow. Sampson et al. (2018) cautioned that just like all other sources of data, it is important to evaluate the information being reviewed. They noted that many only post positive aspects of their work, and the posts that you view may be unique and not representative of others in that career.

Career Exploration and Decision-Making Quick Quiz

1. According to social cognitive theory, what influences career decisions?
2. According to values-based theory, what influences career decisions?
3. According to happenstance learning theory, what influences career decisions?
4. According to person-environment fit theory, what leads to satisfaction in careers?
5. How can career specialists help with career decision making?
6. What are the Big Five personality factors, and how does personality influence career choice?
7. What is an informational interview and why is it valuable?

Chapter 3	Chapter Summary: Note-Taking Model

Let's summarize what you have learned in this chapter. The matrix model is used for this chapter. Remember, it is not expected that your notes will look like this right after class or reading. It takes time to organize your notes and repackage them. It is time well spent, though, because you learn the content better as you organize it, and you have a fabulous foundation from which to study for your exams! There are several ways to use this section:

- **Preview:** Read the model before reading the chapter to familiarize yourself with the content.
- **Compare:** Compare the notes you took on the chapter to the model provided.
- **Study:** The model along with your notes and other course materials are great resources for studying.

Matrix Notes Model

Use the ABCS of Setting and Implementing Goals to Achieve Success

Aim high	Goals should be challenging because the higher you aim, the higher you will achieve.
Believe in yourself	If you believe you can reach your goal, you will be more likely to succeed.
Care and commit	Being passionate about your goal and making a commitment to achieve increases success.
Specify and self-reflect	You will be more likely to achieve success if your goal is specific in nature. To help you achieve your goal, it is important to regularly monitor your progress and make changes as needed.

How Do We Make Career Decisions?

Social-cognitive theory	As a social being, important people in your life can influence career decisions by encouraging you or you can learn about options by watching others in various careers. Decisions are also based on our self-efficacy, which refers to whether you believe you can successfully achieve a task.
Values-based theory	Your cultural and work values strongly influence your career decisions.
Happenstance theory	Planned and unplanned events influence your career decisions. Being open to experiences and seeking out new opportunities is recommended.
Person-environment fit	Career decisions are based on your personality and interests.

Career Indecision

Reasons for indecision	Lack of readiness	Lack of information	Inconsistent information

What's Involved in Career Exploration?

Career Exploration Activities	Information Needed	Where to Access This Information
Self-assessment	<ul><li>Values</li><li>Abilities</li><li>Personality</li><li>Interest</li></ul>	<ul><li>Self-assessment surveys</li><li>Discussion with career specialist</li></ul>
Learning about careers	<ul><li>Basic information about careers (tasks, educational requirements, salary)</li><li>Personal experiences in the career</li></ul>	<ul><li>Websites such as *Occupational Outlook Handbook* (www.bls.gov/ooh)</li><li>Informational interviews</li></ul>

4

Strengthening Networking and Other Essential Skills

If your actions inspire others to dream more, learn more, do more and become more, you are a leader.

—*John Quincy Adams*

ASDF_MEDIA/Shutterstock.com

1 How can you expand your professional network?

2 How can you create a professional online presence?

3 What is an elevator speech and why is it important?

4 What behaviors demonstrate professionalism?

5 What effective time management skills can you use?

6 What skills are needed to effectively interact within a diverse community?

7 What do effective leaders do? How can you develop leadership skills?

Exploring the Research in Summary

Research Study Citation:

Clark, G., Marsden, R., Whyatt, J. D., Thompson, L., & Walker, M. (2015). 'It's everything else you do…': Alumni views on extracurricular activities and employability. *Active Learning in Higher Education*, 16(2), 133–147. doi: 10.1177/1469787415574050.

Introduction: The Research Question

What question did the researcher seek to answer?

Recognizing the need for students to develop essential soft skills desired by employers, Clark et al. (2015) were interested in the role that extracurricular activities play in the development of soft skills. Their research questions can be summarized as follows:

1. Are soft skills more likely to be learned through extracurricular activities or as part of degree requirements?

2. Are all extracurricular activities equal in terms of developing soft skills?

3. What role do extracurricular activities play in gaining employment?

Method: The Study

Who participated in the study? What did the researchers ask the participants to do?

A survey focused on extracurricular activities and the impact of these activities, if any, on employment was e-mailed to 14,538 alumni who graduated from Lancaster University between 1990 and 2010. The survey reached 14,215 alumni, was opened by 5,095, and a total of 620 alumni completed the survey. Those who responded to the survey were also invited to participate in an interview. A total of 320 agreed to be interviewed, and the researchers selected 25 from the list that represented diversity in terms of extracurricular activities, occupations, gender, and years since graduation. A total of 18 interviews were conducted.

Results: The Findings

What was the answer to the research question?

The first research question focused on where soft skills were learned, from extracurricular activities or as part of degree requirements. Results indicated that skills were learned from both extracurricular activities and course requirements, but alumni reported that communication skills, interpersonal skills, and self-confidence learned from extracurricular experiences were most critical to landing their first job. Interestingly, extracurricular and academic experiences led to different skill sets. For example, more alumni reported learning planning and analytical skills, time management, problem-solving, and creativity from their degree program. However, alumni reported that extracurricular activities led to increased skill development in almost all the other areas (communication skills, interpersonal skills, self-confidence, decision making, and leadership). Refer to Figure 4.1 for an overview of the findings.

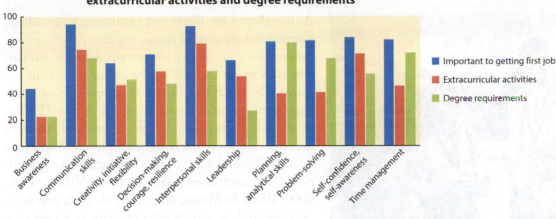

Percentage of alumni indicating development of skills through extracurricular activities and degree requirements

- Important to getting first job
- Extracurricular activities
- Degree requirements

Figure 4.1   Impact of extracurricular activities and degree requirements on soft skills development.

Think Critically

1. What type of class activities would help you develop these skills?
2. How do extracurricular activities provide you with opportunities to develop these skills?

The second research question focused on whether all types of extracurricular activities resulted in the same skill set. All types of extracurricular activities enhanced interpersonal skills, while most also improved self-confidence and leadership skills. However, alumni did report that certain activities facilitated the development of some skills more than others. For example, paid employment was the only activity they reported that developed business awareness. Confidence was reportedly most developed through sports, and interpersonal skills were most developed through social groups or organizations.

The last major research question focused on whether extracurricular activities played a role in employment. Survey and interview data indicated that participating in extracurricular activities did help graduates gain employment and perform well in the position. More specifically, 64% of the alumni indicated that the extracurricular activity helped them land their first job and 57% indicated that skills developed from participating in extracurricular activities helped them perform well on the job. Alumni consistently reported that participating in extracurricular activities helped them develop skills above and beyond those developed through the curriculum requirements.

Discussion and So-What Factor

How can YOU use this information as a student?

This research illustrates that the college experience involves much more than completing degree requirements. To learn and develop the soft skills that are desired by employers, participate in extracurricular activities. Because different types of activities can build different skills, consider participating in more than one type of activity. Participating in extracurricular activities such as sports, social clubs, arts- or music-related opportunities, volunteer work, or paid employment can enrich your college experience and help you build skills that will serve you well now and in the future.

Networking

Monkey Business Images/Shutterstock.com

Although you are likely just beginning your college journey and are several years away from starting your career, there are many important actions you can take now to set yourself up for career success in the future. Research has shown that networking has a long-term positive impact on career success (DeVos et al., 2009). Individuals with larger and stronger networks are more likely to be employed (Van Hoye et al., 2009) and have higher salaries, salary growth potential, and career satisfaction (Villar et al., 2000; Wolff & Moser, 2009). People with privilege, as compared to people who identify as a part of a marginalized group, are more likely to have these larger stronger networks (T. Ayeni, personal communication, July 22, 2021). According to Koss-Feder, approximately 70%–80% of jobs are found through networking rather than advertisements (as cited in de Janasz & Forret, 2008). There are many **"hidden" job opportunities**, jobs that are never advertised but are instead filled through connections (Violorio, 2011). Thus, one of the best career management strategies is to develop and use your network, and it may be especially important to do this if your current network is limited.

Networking involves establishing and maintaining personal and professional relationships with others. When most people think about networking, "who you know" comes to mind. Although who you know is critical, networking also involves who knows you and what you know. When you know someone in a career field, this person may be willing to make a connection for you. Sometimes opportunities present themselves in other ways. For example, if others notice your talents and contributions, they may seek you out to encourage you to apply for a position. What you know also matters because your knowledge and skills are needed in order to land the position and meet with success.

Networking

- Who you know—diversify and expand your network
- Who knows you—engage in behaviors that will get you noticed
- What you know—increase your knowledge and skills so you will be ready for success

Expanding and Strengthening Your Network

Networking is one of the primary ways to find employment and to advance up the career ladder. "Research has shown that the structure of social networks and the connections between key actors are just as important, if sometimes not even more important, as the knowledge and skills of the individual" (Özer & Perc, 2021, p. 46-47). Having a strong network has been associated with higher levels of employment, higher salaries, and increased career satisfaction (Van Hoye et al., 2009; Wolff & Moser, 2009). Unfortunately, many inequities exist with those from higher socio-economic backgrounds having stronger networks. People who identify as a part of marginalized groups may not know others with needed connections and may also not feel comfortable reaching out to individuals with privilege who can be of help to them. "For example, a woman in the STEM field who may have experienced perceived or real sexism from a male professor may be reluctant to visit his office hours, but a male in that same class may be more likely to get to know that professor and thus assimilate him into his professional network" (T. Ayeni, personal communication, July 22, 2021). Özer and Perc (2021) noted that education is an effective way to combat these inequities.

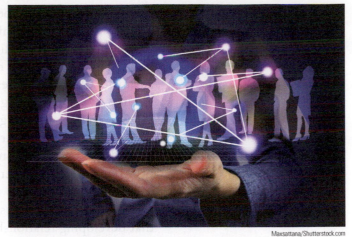

Maxsattana/Shutterstock.com

Students can start expanding and strengthening their networks as soon as they begin college. Stewart (2019) noted that students should use their identity as an asset when networking and should take advantage of networking opportunities offered by the college that have been designed with a diverse student population in mind. Consider what makes you unique and who might value your perspectives. You can explore the values of individuals and organizations by viewing their social media posts or websites. This can help you determine who you want to connect with, and the shared value you discover gives you a talking point to get a conversation started. Gaining confidence with developing and using social networks leads to increased success (Villa et al., 2000). The more you engage in networking behaviors, the more confident and skilled you will become.

Building Social Capital Networking is related to **social capital**, which "refers to the collective value of all social networks and the trust, reciprocity, information, and cooperation generated by those social networks" (Timberlake, 2005, p. 35). Another way to think about social capital is to focus on the structure and associated benefits of your relationships. Many opportunities will present themselves through your relationships, so it is important to establish professional connections with others.

Researchers have found that gender and race play a role in networks. For example, in a study conducted by Blommaert et al. (2020), it was found that women have less diverse networks, meaning many in their network hold similar types of positions. Having more diverse networks can provide increased access to varied occupations. Women were also found to have fewer higher status members such as managers in their network (Blommaert et al., 2020). This has also been found to be true for people of color (McGuire, 2000).

Trueffelpix/Shutterstock.com

Most of us prefer to be in situations where we are with others who are like us, because this is more comfortable (Greguletz et al., 2020). For example, research has found that women did not find it comfortable to attend networking events because there are often more males at these events, especially in positions of authority. Although researchers have found that connecting with others who are like you in terms of gender and race can provide you with valuable support (West, 2019), connecting with others who are different from you can help you expand and diversify your network.

College is a great time to develop and strengthen networks. One of the primary benefits of attending college lies with the networking opportunities with both higher-status members such as professors and with peers who will soon become high-status colleagues. Black and Latinx students have reported that developing relationships with their professors increased their social capital (Sandoval-Lucero et al., 2014). Research by McGuire (2000) found that although women and people of color initially had fewer high-status network members, once they were given "the opportunity to interact with high status employees, they were just as likely as White men to have high status network members" (p. 517). Take advantage of opportunities in college to connect with high-status professionals.

Social capital is not only influenced by the number of connections or relationships you have but the nature and strength of these relationships. Quality matters more than quantity when it comes to networks (PRNewsWire, 2013). It is therefore important to really get to know others and for others to really get to know you. If someone recommends you for a position, their reputation is at stake. The more they know and trust you, the more likely it is that they will be willing to take this risk and recommend you for a position when the time comes (Violorio, 2011).

You never know what experience or relationship might lead to a great opportunity. Sundheim (2011) argued that networking is also about who knows you and suggested that you engage in actions that help you stand out from a crowd. Always put your best foot forward, making positive first impressions. As you know, first impressions can be long-lasting (Clayson, 2013). As a college student, engage in actions that demonstrate your work ethic and values. You might be surprised at how much others will take note of your actions. Others will likely notice if you have a strong work ethic and are passionate about what you do. Similarly, Levin (2016) believed that the key element related to successful networking is your character and whether others like you. Most people are more likely to go above and beyond for others they like and admire and for those who seek to use their talents for the greater good rather than only being concerned with personal gain.

What you know also really matters, despite what the adage says. Higher grades have been linked to success at finding a job after graduation (Sulastri et al., 2015). When professionals in your network know about your skills and talents, they will be more likely to make you aware of opportunities related to your career interest and recommend you for a position. While a professional contact might be able to help you get an interview, you will need to have strong background knowledge and skills to be offered the position and to ultimately perform well. Gaining knowledge and skills will undoubtedly increase job opportunities and ultimate success in your desired career path.

Networking is a skill, and it takes time to develop it. Developing and enhancing your networking skills while in college is therefore critically important. Violorio (2011) suggested that networks be established long before it is time to engage in the job search process. As with all relationships, time is needed to develop trust and foster professional relationships, and as a college student, you have many opportunities to form new connections and strengthen existing relationships.

Most colleges and universities offer resources, such as a career center, that can assist you with developing this important networking skill set. McCorkle et al. (2003) suggested that students connect with the career centers at their college sooner versus later. This is because students who seek out assistance with networking skills benefit from doing so. According to results from the annual Gallup-Purdue University study of college graduates, graduates who visited a career center at their college at least once were more likely to be working full time. Specifically, 67% of college graduates who visited a career center were employed full time as compared to 59% of graduates who did not visit the career center (as cited in New, 2016).

Building Social Capital via Networking

- Develop relationships with professors and other professionals on campus.
- Connect with others who are similar and different from you.
- Connect with your peers who will be your future colleagues.
- Stand out from the crowd through your actions.
- Demonstrate good character; others will notice.
- Expand your knowledge and develop your skills.
- Work on developing your networking skills regularly; they take time to develop.
- Reach out to professionals on campus to help you develop these important skills.

Getting Involved Becoming an active participant or leader of a club, student organization, or sport is a great way to develop skills and make connections with others who share your interests. Not surprisingly, research has shown that students who are involved in extracurricular activities are more likely to find employment (Sulastri et al., 2015). This is likely due to both networking and skill development. Another great way to build your network is to take advantage of college- or community-sponsored events. For example, colleges will often host job fairs.

You may also want to consider joining professional organizations related to your career interests. If you need assistance with finding professional organizations linked to your goals, ask your advisor, a faculty member, or search the Internet. Many professional organizations have a student network within the larger structure and have several ways for you to learn about

iStockPhoto/SolStock

the profession. For instance, you might want to sign up for a newsletter or follow the organization on social media. If the organization sponsors a conference or meeting, consider attending. This is an excellent way to learn about careers and connect with professionals in the field. In fact, researchers have found that there is a connection between career success and attending conferences, business-related gatherings, and other in-person networking events (DeVry, 2015).

Stoatphoto/Shutterstock.com

Finding a Mentor One way to start networking is to seek out a faculty or professional mentor. If you have not already done so, investigate the areas of expertise for the faculty in your declared major. Determine which faculty member is engaged in work that matches your interests and values. For example, a faculty member might be looking for an assistant to help with a service project for a nonprofit organization or a research project on biofeedback.

If you are given the opportunity to work side by side with a faculty member, you will learn valuable skills while you also develop a professional relationship. You will tend to learn skills more quickly when supported by a mentor, especially when your mentor provides you with constructive feedback about your skills and performance (Ericsson et al., 2007). You never know what doors might open because of this relationship. For instance, you might be invited to co-present at a professional meeting or conference or be invited to coauthor a publication. Be open to experiences and opportunities that come your way.

Although professors make great mentors, you may also want to seek out a mentoring relationship with a professional who works full time in your field of interest. For example, if you are interested in becoming a lawyer, you may want to find a mentor who practices law in a specialty area that interests you. Reach out to the alumni office on your campus for assistance with identifying a potential mentor in your field of interest. Alumni are often interested in helping students from their alma mater.

Having more than one mentor can be helpful. Wild et al. (2017) noted that it is unlikely one individual will be able to meet all your needs and suggested having a mentoring network composed of several professionals and peers. Establishing a mentoring network means you can benefit from mentors who are both similar and different from you. Engaging with others who are similar can provide you with comfort and support (West, 2019). Researchers have found that students of color and women believed mentors were more helpful when they were from the same race or gender (Blake et al., 2011). Not surprisingly, you will likely be most influenced by others who look like you (Kofoed & McGovney, 2019).

However, it can sometimes be helpful to find mentors who are different than you. For example, if you are a female who is interested in a career that is currently composed of mostly males, having a mentor who understands the field may be more important than having a mentor from the same gender. Research has found that having a mentor who shares your values is more important than sharing demographic characteristics (Hernandez et al., 2017). Blake et al. (2011) did not find any differences in terms of academic outcomes associated with having a mentor of similar or different gender or race.

After you have identified a possible mentor, request a meeting to discuss their work and explore mentorship possibilities. Consider asking yourself the following questions before you request a meeting:

- What are your academic and career goals?
- What do you want to know about their work?
- How do their professional interests fit with your interests and goals?
- Why are you asking this person to be your mentor?

Strengthening Your Network

Relationships take work. Develop a plan to nurture your current network. For example, if you see a professional you already know at a meeting or event, reach out and have at least a brief conversation to find out how they are doing. Another simple but powerful strategy is to make a quick phone call or send a text or e-mail to see how they are doing.

The more frequently you interact with and support members of your network, the stronger the relationships will be. Small gestures such as sending a quick thank-you note when someone shared their wisdom or advice with you can go a long way.

Insta_photos/Shutterstock.com

Watch how professionals engage in networking and learn from their actions. You will discover that networking continues to be important throughout your career. Forret and Dougherty (2001), for example, found that survey respondents with an average of 15 years of work experience still engaged in many networking behaviors such as:

- Maintaining contacts (giving out business cards, sending thank-you notes)
- Volunteering for tasks that have high visibility (important committees or assignments)
- Participating in community events (events and projects)
- Engaging in professional activities (attending or speaking at conferences, writing articles or blogs)

A strong network can provide you with support and may be able to give you access to new career opportunities. Focus on the most important members of your network, and spend the time and energy needed to keep these relationships strong.

Creating a Professional Presence on Social Media

If you are like most students, social media is probably an important part of your life. College students spend a lot of time on various social media sites. Your social media actions can impact you both personally and professionally.

iStockPhoto/Stockcam

Although most students do not believe it is appropriate for employers to use social media in hiring decisions (Sánchez Abril et al., 2012), it is likely that a future employer will look at your online presence (Hartwell & Campion, 2020; Rosen et al., 2018). Employers have the right to access public information about a candidate and can choose not to hire someone with questionable character or moral values (Sánchez Abril et al., 2012). According to a recent survey, 93% of recruiters reviewed the social profile of a candidate before making a hiring decision, and 55% reported reconsidering a candidate after doing so (Jobvite, 2014). Facebook, Twitter, and LinkedIn are the most frequently checked social media sites (Mader, 2016).

Researchers have found that personality factors can be determined by reviewing social networking sites (Rosen et al., 2018). Reviews can lead to positive or negative impressions of you. Posts that illustrated volunteering and donating to charity, for example, were viewed positively by recruiters (Jobvite, 2014). Employers have noted several types of posts that have resulted in a negative impression. These included discriminatory comments, substance use, posts that depicted self-absorption and being opinionated, sexual content, profanity, and spelling and grammar mistakes (Hartwell & Campion, 2020; Jobvite, 2014; Tew et al., 2020).

Many employers have reported that they did not hire candidates due to content found on social media sites (Hartwell & Campion, 2020). In an experiment conducted by Bohnert and Ross (2010), it was found that individuals with a Facebook page that had an alcohol emphasis were less likely to be offered job interviews and were offered lower salaries than individuals with professional or family-oriented Facebook pages. Hartwell and Ross (2020) similarly found evidence that drug use negatively impacted hiring decisions. See Figure 4.2 for social media-related reasons for not being offered employment.

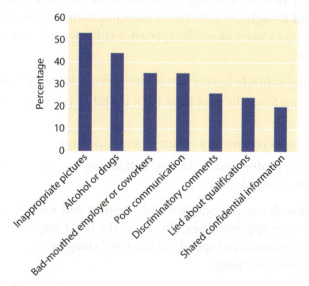

Figure 4.2   Social media reasons for not being offered employment.

Think Critically

1. How might the reasons for not hiring someone based on social media posts vary based on career field?

2. What additional reasons might there be for employers to not hire someone?

If you do not have a social media presence, employers may still make assumptions about you. In a study conducted with students who were asked to view social media as if they were employers, assumptions about no social media included believing the person was asocial or not skilled with technology (Melton et al., 2018).

Knowing your social media presence is important. Google yourself to determine what information about you is available on the Internet. Review your social media posts, especially those that are available to the public. Ask yourself the following questions:

- What messages do your photos and posts send about you?
- Who are your "friends" or "connections" and what do these relationships say about you?
- Based only on the information available via the Internet, how would someone describe you?
- If an employer were viewing this information, how might your social media presence influence whether they would hire you for a position?

If your social media presence is not communicating the professional message that you want future employers to see, take the following actions now to change and improve your social media image.

- Check your privacy settings and make decisions about what information you want public versus private. It is important to note, however, that your online friends or connections may share information you post or may even create their own posts about you. Thus, if there is something that you do not want public, it may be best to avoid putting this information on the Internet at all.
- Limit your online friend group to those whom you truly trust to help you convey a positive social media image. Talking with your friends about the importance of having a professional image can also help.
- Delete photos or comments that may not be viewed positively by an employer.
- Moving forward, only post content that you would be comfortable with a future employer or colleague reading or seeing. These actions can help you avoid a negative social media presence.

Social media can positively impact your career. Platforms such as LinkedIn were created to help you establish a professional online presence and make professional connections. Krings et al. (2021) found that both younger and older adults are using social media to promote themselves professionally.

If you do not already have a LinkedIn account, consider creating one. Use this account to share a professional photo, a profile summary, your accomplishments, and professional interests. Research has found that having a photo with facial prominence and a longer profile summary was connected to more job offers (Krings et al., 2021). Post updates to your account when you receive an award or honor, successfully complete a major project, learn a new skill that is relevant to your field of interest, or land a great internship or other work experience. By sharing your accomplishments, you are developing a professional presence on social media. Employers often look at your social media presence for evidence of professionalism and for additional details on your work experiences (Hartwell & Campion, 2020).

While it might be relatively easy for you to increase your network using technology, it is important to remember that quality really matters when it comes to networking. It is therefore not about making as many connections as possible, but rather developing meaningful relationships with others. Before sending or accepting requests to be connected, remember that you can be judged by the peers or colleagues with whom you choose to interact. Who you choose as your "friends" or "connections" says a lot about who you are as a person.

Social media can also impact you after being hired. Companies may monitor your social media presence, making sure that your actions are consistent with the company image. For example, some companies may prohibit you from making negative comments about the company. Although this is certainly a privacy issue, Sanchez Abril et al. (2012) reviewed legal cases and reported "it seems that U.S. employers may legally canvas social media sites for information on employees and candidates and act on the basis of the information found therein" (p. 95). Familiarize yourself with the social media policy at your place of employment to avoid engaging in actions that could jeopardize your employment.

Creating a Professional Social Media Presence

- Delete inappropriate posts.
- Check privacy settings and review what is public.
- Create a LinkedIn account.
- Use a professional photo and e-mail address.
- Write a profile summary that captures your achievements.
- Carefully choose your connections because your relationships, even online ones, can influence how others perceive you.
- Before posting, ask yourself if you would be comfortable with a future employer seeing the post.
- Share your accomplishments via social media.

Crafting an Elevator Speech and Resume

As you work toward creating a professional presence, it is important to think about what talents and skills you have to offer. You will want to communicate your strengths to others verbally and in writing.

One important way to share your talents verbally is through an elevator speech. An elevator speech is a very brief description of your skills and goals. **Elevator speeches** are often only about 30 seconds long (de Janasz & Forret, 2008), brief enough for you to share on a quick elevator ride.

Andrey_Popov/Shutterstock.com

An elevator speech can help you stand out from the crowd and develop connections (Petrone, 2018). Creating an elevator speech forces you to determine which strengths and values are most important to highlight. Students have reported that developing an elevator speech has helped them reflect on their strengths (Mou-Danha et al., 2019). Your elevator speech should clearly communicate key information about yourself in a way that sparks interest and questions. An elevator speech should also highlight what makes you unique (Petrone, 2018).

The elevator speech can be used as your introduction when you meet new people. You may want to develop different elevator speeches for different audiences because

Table 4.1 Elevator Speech
Tips on Creating Your Elevator Speech

1. Keep it simple and short.	Using simple language and avoiding complex jargon can make it easier for others to take in and understand your strengths, especially when pressed for time. Because we live in a world full of busy people, short messages are more likely to be heard.
2. Focus on one or two key accomplishments.	An elevator speech is not the time to share all of your accomplishments; your resume is the better place for a comprehensive list of your achievements. Instead, share one or two actions you took that resulted in successful outcomes.
3. Be creative and use your imagination.	Following public speaking guidelines, use a hook to grab the attention of others. Effective elevator speeches leave others wanting to hear more about you.
4. Know your audience.	Make connections between your strengths and what matters to the person with whom you are speaking. Because priorities and values will vary from person to person, you will want to create different versions of your elevator speech.

Source: Based on Howell's work (as cited in Hughes, 2010).

your purpose and closing ask may be different. If you are interacting with a potential colleague, you may be looking for a connection to a supervisor or manager. However, if you meet a supervisor or manager, you may want to find out when the next hiring event will be taking place or discover what types of experiences are highly valued by the company. See Table 4.1 for tips on creating your elevator speech. You can search online to find a variety of sample elevator speeches.

Documenting your strengths in writing is also important. Smith-Proulx (2018) noted that it is important to summarize strengths both on social media and in a resume. A **resume** is a snapshot of your professional skills and accomplishments and is used by hiring managers to decide if you should be interviewed for an open position. Having a strong online summary profile has been connected to positive outcomes (Krings et al., 2021). Some tips for writing your online summary include

- use first person,
- rely on short sentences, and
- emphasize key words related to your industry (Smith-Proulx, 2018).

Jacques (2017) recommended adding your personality to the summary profile as you describe who you are and what you want to do.

In addition to summarizing your strengths on social media, it is also important to be sure you have an up-to-date resume that captures your skills and experiences. Hiring managers or committees will likely be reviewing hundreds of applications for each job posting. It is therefore important that your resume is clear, easy to read, and succinctly highlights your most important work experiences or accomplishments.

Although the content and substance of your experiences matter most, organization and visual appeal are also important considerations. There are many resume templates available online that you can use to get started. You will find that most accomplishments or job experiences are presented in reverse chronological order, meaning your most recent experiences are at the top. This approach makes it easy for a hiring manager to see the timeline of your work experience to determine how long you were at different places of employment and whether you have taken on

Table 4.2 Resume Table
What to Include in a Resume

Contact information	Include name, phone number, and e-mail address (be sure you are using a professional e-mail). May also include a link to a personal Web page and LinkedIn.
Summary statement	Although this is not required, providing a brief one-paragraph summary of your key accomplishments and goals can help gain the attention of employers. Think of this as your written elevator speech.
Education	Indicate your college or university and date (or expected date) of graduation. If you graduated with honors, you can note this in this section.
Experience	This is often presented with most recent work experience first. You can include both paid and volunteer experience, which is also valuable. Provide place and dates of employment along with a brief description of what you accomplished in this position. Use action verbs and add outcome data that demonstrate your success where possible.
Extracurricular and community involvement	Share how you have been an engaged member of the community, noting leadership roles and key skills developed.
Awards and honors	If you have received any special honors or awards, include a section to highlight these accomplishments.

more challenging roles and responsibilities over time. However, some resumes are functional or skill-based versus chronological. A functional resume is organized by skill sets versus work experience. In this case, all positions related to certain skills would be clustered together. Meeting with a professional in Career Services for assistance with your resume is suggested. See Table 4.2 for a list of what is typically included in a resume.

Remember that employers will be looking not only at your academic qualifications but also at your work experiences and extracurricular activities (Cole et al., 2007). Thinking about what experiences you would like to showcase on your resume in the future can help you determine which opportunities to seek out as a college student.

When applying for a job, customizing your cover letter and resume will increase your chances of getting noticed and being offered an interview (Violorio, 2011). You will want to highlight different experiences and skills based on what the employer is looking for in a candidate. For example, if you are applying for a position that requires significant data analysis, you will want to emphasize jobs and other related experiences that involved working with data. In the cover letter, which accompanies your resume and is written to the hiring manager, you should directly address job requirements and duties outlined in the job posting and how your related experiences match these tasks and responsibilities. Your cover letter is another opportunity to emphasize why you are a great fit for the job.

Networking Quick Quiz

1. What is networking?
2. How can you expand your network?
3. What can you do to strengthen current relationships in your network?
4. How do employers use social media?
5. How can you develop a professional presence online?
6. What should be included in an elevator speech?

Essential Skills

A combination of career-specific skills, sometimes referred to as technical or hard skills, and other essential skills, sometimes referred to as soft or transferable skills, is needed. Career-specific skills are unique to the field. Examples of career specific or technical skills include using a special cooking technique if you are a chef, or using a special software editing tool if you are a video editor. Other essential skills needed across many fields include professionalism, work ethic, oral and written communication skills, interpersonal skills, time management, problem-solving, and leadership (Bowles et al., 2001; deCarvalho & Junior, 2015).

G-Stock Studio/Shutterstock.com

In a survey, 86% of mid-level to top-level executives agreed that these other essential or soft skills are very important to success in the world of work (Deepa & Seth, 2013). In fact, 77% of the human resource professionals who responded to a survey conducted by Career Builder indicated that soft skills were as important as technical skills and 16% indicated that soft skills were more important than technical skills (as cited in Russo, 2015). Fortunately, research has shown that teaching soft skills is effective. For example, Ritter et al. (2018) found that students and employers reported high levels of satisfaction with skill development when soft skills were integrated into the curriculum.

Which skills are most valued by employers? Based on an employer survey conducted by Barrington et al. (2006), the four most important skills needed by employees were:

- Professionalism and work ethic
- Oral and written communication
- Teamwork and collaboration
- Critical thinking and problem-solving

Other essential skills that have been identified as important by employers include integrity, confidence, planning and organizational skills, and decision-making skills (Archer & Davison, 2008; Robles, 2012).

College graduates have also reported that soft skills were important in landing their first job and with performing well in their career. Specifically, college graduates indicated that communication and interpersonal skills, along with self-awareness and confidence, were the most important skills when it came to getting their first job offer after graduation. They also noted that these skills helped them meet with success once hired. Interestingly, these graduates said that extracurricular activities really helped them develop these skills (Clark et al., 2015).

As you develop these essential skills, it is important to recognize the significant role of culture in skill development. Hora et al. (2018) noted "that human competencies are thoroughly situated in social and cultural dynamics, and that these dynamics can help or hinder students as they try to move into organizations and professions after graduation" (p. 36). They explained how different skills may be needed in different contexts and cultures. It is not enough to just have strong skills; you will also need to know when and how to use different skills depending on the situational and cultural factors.

Essential Skills

- Professionalism
- Time management
- Planning and organizational skills
- Work ethic
- Decision making
- Oral and written communication
- Teamwork and collaboration
- Leadership
- Critical thinking
- Problem-solving

Volha_R/Shutterstock.com

Professionalism

Employers expect their employees to act professionally. What does this mean? **Professionalism** refers to behaviors in the workplace that communicate you are:

- **Committed to achieving goals.** Cottringer (2015) noted that "a professional attitude involves a diligent, conscientious approach to doing what is necessary to help the organization demonstrate its values and accomplish its goals" (p. 26). Commitment to the mission of the organization happens naturally if the organizational mission aligns with your values. Therefore, it is important to learn about an organization before you accept a position. Choosing positions where you will be able to perform tasks that match your values makes it easier for you to engage in behaviors that demonstrate professionalism.

- **Responsible.** Being **responsible** means that your employer, professors, and colleagues can count on you. Responsible individuals show up on time, do what is needed to complete a task, and ultimately successfully complete those tasks. Responsible individuals are also responsive, answering e-mails and providing information requested in a timely fashion.

- **Hardworking.** Professionals will work hard and typically go above and beyond to achieve a successful outcome. Individuals with professionalism exhibit pride in their work and are willing to do what it takes to meet with success. This demonstrates a high level of work ethic. As a result, the final product is polished, professional, and on target.

- **Honest.** Employers want employees who will act ethically. **Ethics** refers to whether choices are morally right or wrong. Engaging in honest, ethical actions promotes a positive image of yourself and your organization. It will also make it more likely that others will trust you. For example, if you have access to company information, like a new product being developed, and your friend works for a competitor, it would be unethical to share what you know with them if this product has not been officially announced.

- **Respectful.** Individuals who exhibit professionalism are polite, respectful, and courteous of others. Being friendly is a simple yet powerful way to demonstrate professionalism. Demonstrating professionalism also involves doing your part to create an effective learning or working environment by minimizing distractions. For example, turning off electronic devices such as cell phones is a respectful action because the sounds of a cell phone can negatively impact the work of others such as coworkers or classmates (End et al., 2010).

- **Able to manage conflict.** When a conflict arises, disagreements are discussed calmly by listening to the viewpoints of others and using respectful language to communicate ideas and concerns. If the conflict escalates, professionals will seek the guidance and support of someone, such as a supervisor, who can assist with resolving the conflict.

- **Mindful of boundaries.** Professionals are mindful of boundaries and can determine which actions or behaviors are appropriate in which situations. For example, although you may become friends with coworkers, it is important that you keep your relationship professional while at work. This does not mean you have to completely refrain from discussing anything personal at work. An important part of getting to know your colleagues and establishing and maintaining good working relationships is sharing some personal information. For example, you may choose to share some general information about your family and significant other, your interests, hobbies, and activities you engage in. However, one of the most common unprofessional actions in the workplace is sharing too many details about your personal life, especially if you were involved in actions that would not be viewed positively by your colleagues or employer (Rawes, 2014). Professionals also recognize that there is a difference between professional and social communication. Although informal communication strategies such as emojis or abbreviations may be fine to use in social situations, these strategies are often not appropriate in professional and academic environments.

- **Able to learn from mistakes.** Everyone makes mistakes. Professionals handle their mistakes well. When mistakes happen, professionals acknowledge the mistake, take responsibility for their actions, and develop a plan to address the issue at hand. Most importantly, professionals learn from these experiences.

Time and Project Management

Effective time management, and relatedly project management, are essential skills that contribute to successful personal, academic, and professional outcomes. Ineffective time management is one of the most cited obstacles to student success. Numerous research studies have shown the relationship between time management and success, providing evidence that effective time management is related to higher levels of motivation and achievement (Demirdag, 2021; Orr et al., 2007).

Everyone is equal in terms of time, getting only 24 hours each day. However, some individuals are more productive than others when it comes to using their time. Some really struggle in this area. To make the most of your 24 hours per day, you can ask yourself the following questions:

- Am I using my time in a way that is consistent with my values and goals?

iStockPhoto/Brankospejs

- Do I have good work–school–life balance?
- Am I able to effectively plan and engage in actions so that I am successfully completing personal, academic, and professional tasks in a timely fashion?
- How might I improve my use of time?

Getting an accurate picture of how you currently spend your time can help you determine which activities in your life are taking up the most time, whether these activities are aligned to your goals, and where adjustments might be needed (Nonis et al., 2006). A powerful way to get a clear picture of how you currently use your time is to do what many call a time diary. Using a time diary involves documenting and categorizing how you spend your time over the course of a week. Determine how much time was spent studying, working, socializing, sleeping, and so forth in total for the week. Reflect on how you use your time and adjust as needed.

Time Traps When you evaluate your time, you may discover that you are engaging in many **time traps**, activities that take up a lot of your time and are often unproductive in nature. Some examples of time traps are using social media sites, surfing the Internet, watching television, and playing games. Not surprisingly, researchers have found that successful students spend less time on time traps, such as watching television and hanging out with friends (George et al., 2008). Although it is important to engage in social and relaxing activities, it is easy to lose track of how much time you spend on these activities. Often, it may be much more time than you originally planned on spending. Perhaps you have had the experience where you went to briefly check your social media apps only to discover that an hour passed by and you never returned to your studying. The following strategies can help you minimize time spent on these nonproductive time traps:

- **Raise your awareness of your time traps.** Complete the time diary and reflect on how you utilize time.
- **Ask others to assist you.** Tell others about your time traps and your goals. You can then ask your friends and family to remind you to get back on track if they see you distracted by a time trap.
- **Set self-imposed time limits for time traps.** Determine how long you would like to spend on the activity and then set a timer, or alarm on your cell phone, for that amount of time. This external reminder can help you stick to your plan and avoid letting the time traps take you on a detour from your goals. This strategy helps you take charge of your time.
- **Use fun activities as a reward for must-do activities.** For example, if you work on your presentation for an hour, reward yourself with one of your favorite time traps. Give yourself approximately 10 minutes for your reward, such as socializing time on a social media site, and then get back to your academic tasks.

Work–School–Life Balance In today's world, everyone is being pulled in many different directions. Family and friends want to spend time with you, professors want you to read and complete significant learning projects, and employers may want you to work more hours or complete tasks by a certain deadline. Making school a priority will increase the likelihood that you complete your degree in a timely fashion, but school may not always be your top priority if you have important family and work responsibilities that also demand your time.

Research shows that work–school–life balance is one of the biggest stressors facing students (El-Ghoroury et al., 2012). To achieve work–school–life balance, you do not have to necessarily choose between these different responsibilities. Rather, successful individuals have learned to effectively juggle their many different roles, finding balance among these competing needs and responsibilities. The key will be to keep your goals front and center.

Docstockmedia/Shutterstock.com

Time management can be especially challenging when different areas of your life demand increased attention at the same time. For example, if you work in retail, employers often need employees to put in more hours during the holiday season, which happens to be at the end of the fall term when academic pressures are highest. Remember, you and your employer do not necessarily share the same goal. Your employer will be looking out for the best interest of the company, but you must look out for your best interest and what will help you achieve your personal, academic, and career goals. Staying focused on what matters most to you can help you decide which tasks require more of your time and attention.

Working has been cited by student success professionals as one of the biggest obstacles to student success, and some research supports this claim. For example, Lammers et al. (2001) found that students who worked 23–60 hours per week studied less, had poorer concentration, slept less, and had increased absences in classes with optional attendance. Other researchers have also found that working negatively impacted academic success (Kulm & Cramer, 2006; Stinebrickner & Stinebrickner, 2004). However, not all research has found negative outcomes associated with working (Nonis & Hudson, 2006), and some research has even found that working can have positive outcomes. Dundes and Marx (2006), for example, found that students working 10–19 hours per week spent more time studying and performed better than students who did not work at all or worked 20 hours or more per week. In addition to the financial benefits, working can also help you build your skills, give you an opportunity to network with others, and create situations that demand you become good at time management (Larkin et al., 2007). Thus, according to this research, a balanced approach to work and school is best.

Some students do not have the luxury of attending school full time without the need to work. For many students, especially non-traditional aged students, work must be prioritized over school. This is especially the case for students who are supporting themselves and others. Academic success is still very possible for students who are unable to place school at the top of their priority list. The key is balancing to ensure that school does get some of your time and focus, and then making the most of that time. As you will discover in the next section, using time management strategies such as scheduling time for tasks and focusing on just one task at a time can help you meet with success.

Time Management Strategies There are many time management strategies that you can use to increase your productivity. The following time and project management tips have been offered by Shellenbarger (2009): make a to-do list of all tasks that need to be completed, develop a schedule to complete tasks, and stay focused on one task at a time to maximize the use of your time.

iStockPhoto/MichaelSvoboda

iStockPhoto/MokJinYoung

Make a prioritized to-do list Although simple in nature, creating a **to-do list** of tasks you must complete is a powerful planning and organizational strategy. To-do lists help you see the big picture of what you need to accomplish. Research has found that students who use a to-do list tool are more likely to complete tasks ahead of schedule (Cavanaugh et al., 2012). To-do lists can include personal, academic, and professional tasks. According to Shellenbarger (2009), your to-do list should include deadlines associated with the task and the level of importance of each task. There are many electronic tools available that allow you to easily organize your to-do list by deadlines or importance.

Break large assignments down into smaller tasks so that your to-do list is composed of manageable tasks. Breaking down larger tasks into smaller action steps will reduce the likelihood that you will procrastinate. You are more likely to avoid tasks that you perceive to be overwhelming but more likely to tackle tasks that can be done in a relatively short period of time.

After you have identified all the tasks you need to complete, focus on the importance of each task. This process is called prioritizing tasks and is an essential part of effective time management. Although there are many factors that will guide your decision making about which tasks deserve your attention first, your values and goals should be the driving focus here. Upcoming deadlines will also factor into this process of prioritizing tasks.

For academic tasks, the syllabus can be a great guide to help you start prioritizing. In the syllabus, you will find information about the nature of the assignments, their due dates, and how much the assignment counts toward your final grade. You can also request a meeting with your professor, advisor, or counselor to help you evaluate the tasks and decide on a time management plan.

To-Do List Tips

- Write down personal, academic, and professional tasks
- Assign level of importance to each task
- Indicate deadline for tasks
- Break larger tasks into smaller ones

iStockPhoto/Prostock-Studio

Develop a schedule Success does not happen by chance; success comes as a result of planning and hard work. Students who plan out their studying activities perform better academically (Krumrei-Mancuso et al., 2013). Professionals also rely heavily on their calendars to keep them on track.

There are a variety of planning tools available to assist you with scheduling. Many find apps or other online calendars work best for them, while others prefer good old-fashioned paper calendars. There are pros and cons associated with different planning tools, but the key is for you to choose a calendar tool that you will use regularly. It is a good idea to refer to your calendar at least once a day.

Start by getting class, work, and other already-scheduled meetings or appointments on your calendar. Scheduling time to study or work on assignments and tasks is also essential. We are more likely to do what is on our calendar or schedule. Rampton (2019) suggested that we calendar everything and put the most challenging tasks at the start of your day. Scheduling your time helps you stay on track toward your goals. Block out time on your calendar to complete all your assignments and learning tasks, including study time. Professionals often use this technique, scheduling working meetings or time to independently work on projects.

Sometimes unplanned events happen and impact our plans. For instance, you may get sick and be unable to complete academic tasks for other reasons. Working ahead of the due dates instead of waiting until the last minute will make it easier for you to adjust and still meet deadlines. A good practice is to pretend all assignments or projects are due several days or even a week earlier than indicated on your syllabus. Then, block out time on your calendar to complete your assignments according to this plan to ensure meeting official due dates.

Work on your most challenging tasks first (Rampton, 2019). Although students recognize the need to spend more time on tasks that they perceive to be difficult as compared to easy, they often spend their time on easy tasks (Son & Metcalfe, 2000). Diving into the most challenging tasks at the start of your day will ensure that these tasks get the time and effort needed for you to meet with success (Shellenbarger, 2009).

Scheduling Tips

- Choose a scheduling tool.
- Schedule in class, work, or other obligations.
- Block out time to work on assignments and complete other tasks, with challenging tasks scheduled in the morning.
- Plan to complete tasks ahead of deadlines.

Single-Task It! In today's world, the term *multitasking* is often heard. Appelbaum et al. (2008) distinguished between two types of multitasking: **task-switching** and **dual-tasking**. Task-switching refers to switching back and forth between two or more tasks. In other words, your attention shifts from one task to another. An example of task-switching would be reading and texting. Dual-tasking, on the other hand, refers to simultaneously working on two or more activities. An example of dual-tasking is having a conversation while cleaning your room.

Research shows us that tasks take more time, not less, when we multitask. May and Elder (2018) found that efficiency is reduced when we multitask even though students believed productivity was improved. In an experiment conducted by Bowman et al. (2010), it was found that students who engaged in another task while

Veronika M/Shutterstock.com

completing a reading task took much longer to read passages. This increase of time needed to complete the reading task did not include the time spent on the other task. In fact, students who engaged in multitasking while reading took 22%–59% longer to read, not including the time for the other task (Bowman et al., 2010). This is not an isolated finding. Other research has also found that individuals who multitask take much longer to complete tasks (Appelbaum et al., 2008; Fox et al., 2009).

In addition to increasing the amount of time it takes to complete tasks, there are other negative outcomes associated with multitasking. Researchers have found that academic performance was negatively impacted by multitasking in the classroom (Limniou, 2020; Demirbilek & Talan, 2018). Appelbaum et al. (2008) found that multitasking can also increase your stress and the likelihood of you making more errors, and it can decrease your ability to be creative and make good decisions. Individuals who multitask are also less likely to enjoy a task. In an interesting study conducted by Oviedo et al. (2015), it was found that individuals who used social media while watching television were less likely to enjoy the television experience as compared to individuals who only engaged in one task—television viewing.

Multitasking is not just detrimental for you; it also negatively impacts others. Researchers found that students sitting near a multitasker in class who was using a laptop for nonacademic reasons also suffered negative consequences (Sana et al., 2013).

Instead of multitasking, it is better to engage in **single-tasking**. Single-tasking requires you give your full attention and effort to one task at a time. When you are studying, keep focused on studying. When you are having fun, keep focused on having fun. When you are working, focus on doing the best job possible. This approach can save you time and increase your productivity. Practicing single-tasking will be beneficial to you personally and professionally.

Single Task-It Strategies

- Remove distractions—turn off notifications for e-mail, phone, or social media.
- Give your full attention to the current task.
- Write down other tasks you are thinking about so that you can relieve yourself of the pressure of remembering them.

Motortion Films/Shutterstock.com

Interpersonal Skills

Relationships are a key part of our lives. Being able to effectively communicate and collaborate with others, including those from different cultures, is a skill that is highly valued by employers. These relational skills will also help you with your personal relationships.

Diversity, Cultural Competence, and Cultural Humility Diversity refers to the differences among and between individuals. Although most people immediately think of race and ethnicity when they hear the word diversity, it is a much broader concept than that. For starters, we can talk about diversity in terms of culture, economic status, abilities, sexual orientation, gender, and age.

"**Cultural competence** is the ability to understand, communicate with and effectively interact with people across cultures" (T. Ayeni, personal communication, July 22, 2021). Burcham (2002) identified a total of six attributes of cultural competence that are identified in the literature most consistently. They included cultural awareness, cultural knowledge, cultural skill, cultural sensitivity, cultural interaction, and cultural understanding (as cited in Shen, 2015, p. 311).

Developing cultural competence often involves the following:

AJR_photo/Shutterstock.com

- Learning about various cultures and populations
- Becoming more aware of your own beliefs and attitudes and how these beliefs impact you and others
- Developing positive attitudes toward cultural differences
- Developing skills to effectively work with others who may be very different from you

Being culturally competent means you need to explore and address stereotypes and prejudices. **Stereotypes** are judgments you make about a person based on beliefs you have about a group. **Prejudice** refers to your feelings or attitudes about a group or members of a group. As you would expect, stereotypes and prejudice can negatively impact performance (Wolfe & Spencer, 1996).

It is also important to avoid **microaggressions** and know how to address them when they occur. Microaggressions are verbal or nonverbal insults related to a marginalized group status (Turaga, 2020). Microaggressions can be intentional but are often unintentional. On the surface, a microaggression might appear to be a compliment, but the underlying message is an insult. For example, saying "Wow, you are really smart, or wow, you can speak English well" implies that this is unexpected given their group membership. An example of a behavioral microaggression could be a male talking over a female coworker.

Microaggressions can lead to mental health challenges such as depression and anxiety and contribute to negative work environments (Turaga, 2020). It is therefore important to reduce microaggressions and intervene when they happen. When you notice a microaggression, Wood and Harris (2020) recommended the following actions:

1. Stop further harm by pausing the conversation and acknowledging that a microaggression just happened.

2. Ask questions to help the person making the statement understand the message behind the statement in hopes that the person will clarify what they meant and adjust what they said.

3. Focus on shared values of respect and the need for everyone to engage in comments and behaviors consistent with these values.

4. Share your thoughts and feelings related to what just transpired.

5. Determine what the individual who engaged in the microaggressive act can do to correct the situation and avoid this from happening in the future.

Discovering the cultural norms and customs associated with different cultural groups increases your diversity knowledge and prepares you to more effectively communicate and collaborate with others. According to Caligiuri and Tarique (2012), it is important to reduce ethnocentrism and be willing to approach tasks in new ways. Ethnocentrism refers to when individuals place a higher value on their own cultural perspective, viewing other perspectives and cultures as being inferior. You can be more productive when you value the perspectives of others, and you regularly engage with others from different cultures.

You can build your cultural competence by seeking out opportunities to interact and work collaboratively with others from diverse backgrounds and by taking courses focused on diversity. Seeking out experiential learning opportunities so that you can interact with others who are different from you will also increase your cultural competence.

Tervalon and Murray-Garcia noted that learning about and developing skills related to various cultures is a lifelong process and introduced the term **cultural humility** (as cited in Foronda et al., 2021). "Cultural humility is a process of being open, self-aware, egoless, and incorporating self-reflection when interacting with diverse individuals, groups, or communities" (Foronda et al., 2021, p. 399). You can take the Cultural Humility Assessment to better understand your skill development in this area. See Table 4.3.

The more you interact with others who are different from you, the less likely you will be to stereotype or pass judgments about a person based solely on group membership. Researchers have found that when you work in diverse groups on a task that requires cooperation, prejudice is reduced and you are more likely to view your peers positively (Walker & Crogran, 1998; Wolfe & Spencer, 1996). Likewise, others will be less likely to pass judgments about you. Interacting with others with different perspectives also exposes you to varied viewpoints that contribute to the development of more sophisticated thinking. As Schreiber and Valle (2013) noted, "collaboration with diverse others can be a vehicle for developing an appreciation of personal and cultural differences" (p. 396).

Communication and Conflict Management Communication is an extremely important skill and is the basic building block of relationships. Communication involves listening and clearly expressing your thoughts, ideas, or needs. Doyle (2016) nicely captured the key communication skills that will be helpful to you in the world of work. See Table 4.4 for a list and description of these essential communication skills. Practicing these skills will also help you communicate more effectively with your family, significant other, and friends.

Active listening requires that you give your full attention to the person. This means you eliminate barriers such as your phone, the computer, or other distractions. As you listen, you focus on the message that is being communicated. You also encourage the person to continue talking by sending nonverbal messages such as maintaining eye contact and nodding, which show you are listening. Asking relevant questions and paraphrasing, which basically means summarizing what you hear in your own words, are also powerful communication tools. When you paraphrase or summarize what was said, this gives the other person the opportunity to let you know if you accurately heard the message. If not, the person can clarify so that you can better understand.

Engaging in active listening communicates that the person you are listening to is important to you. Others will likely appreciate the time and energy you spent listening. When you listen and gain a good understanding of the person's ideas or

Table 4.3 Cultural Humility Instrument

Answer each question using the following scale: never/rarely (0), once in a while (1), sometimes (2), usually (3), and all the time (4).

Context for difference in perspective

1. _____ Do you consider diversity as a factor for difference in perspective?
2. _____ Do you consider the physical environment as a factor for difference in perspective?
3. _____ Do you consider the historical precedent as a factor for difference in perspective?
4. _____ Do you consider the political climate as a factor for difference in perspective?
5. _____ Do you consider the power imbalances as factors for difference in perspective?
6. _____ Do you consider situational context as a factor for the difference in perspective?
7. _____ Do you attempt to be open to considering the differing perspective?

Self-attributes

8. _____ Do you self-reflect and critique yourself afterward?
9. _____ Do you attempt to be flexible?
10. _____ Are you aware of your own biases?
11. _____ Do you attempt to shed your ego?

Outcomes of cultural humility

12. _____ Do you seek to establish respect?
13. _____ Do you seek to provide optimal care?
14. _____ Do you focus on the other person in addition to yourself?
15. _____ Do you seek to empower others?
16. _____ Do you work toward a mutual benefit?
17. _____ Do you seek to develop a partnership?
18. _____ Do you strive for a supportive interaction?
19. _____ Do you see yourself as a lifelong learner?

Scoring: Higher scores indicate higher levels of cultural humility in each area, meaning you will be better able to work with others who are different from you. The factor of context for difference in perspective may help bring awareness to the various contextual considerations that may influence a difference in perspective. The factor of self-attributes may guide individuals to reflect on what they can personally do to become more humble. The factor of outcomes of cultural humility may serve to demonstrate the benefits of cultural humility as well as what expected results will look like.

Source: Foronda, C., Porter, A., & Phitwong, A. (2021). Psychometric testing of an instrument to measure cultural humility. *Journal of Transcultural Nursing, 32*(4), 399–404. https://doi.org/10.1177/1043659620950420

concerns, you are then positioned well to engage in problem-solving if needed. In a research study by Coffelt and Smith (2020), they found that employers valued communication skills focused on relating to others and gaining an understanding the perspectives of others.

Being able to clearly articulate your ideas is also an important communication skill. What you say and how you say it can impact whether your message is heard and understood. Focusing on who you are speaking with will enable you to determine what is situationally and culturally appropriate (Hora et al., 2018).

As you would imagine, employers desire employees who are able to engage in effective conflict management. There are several steps involved in managing conflict effectively.

1. First, it is important to clearly define the problem or source of conflict. This typically involves all parties sharing their point of view and making a genuine effort to listen and understand the situation from the perspective of the other person or persons involved.

2. Next, possible solutions need to be discussed, with pros and cons being evaluated.

3. Then, a solution or decision will need to be made.

4. Finally, a timeline for assessing the effectiveness of this resolution needs to be established. By following up and evaluating whether the solution had the desired effect, it can make it less likely for future conflict in this area to develop.

Table 4.4 Communication Skills Table
10 Essential Communication Skills

Skill	Description
1. Listening	Active listening is when you are giving someone your undivided attention, really focusing on what they are communicating. As you actively listen, you can ask questions to clarify what is being said if you don't fully understand and periodically paraphrase what was said to be sure you are fully understanding.
2. Nonverbal communication	Most of what we communicate happens from how we communicate rather than what we communicate. Be mindful of your body language, facial expressions, and tone as you communicate with others.
3. Clarity and concision	Before communicating an important idea, plan what you want to say. This will make it more likely that you will be able to clearly communicate your ideas in a brief and concise manner. Brief, concise messages are more likely to be heard and understood.
4. Friendliness	Others will respond more positively when you communicate messages in a friendly, positive way. Simple actions such as a smile can enhance the communication process, making it more productive.
5. Confidence	It is more likely that others will respond positively to your ideas and messages if you communicate them with confidence. When you believe in your ideas, others will also be more likely to believe in your ideas.
6. Empathy	Empathy refers to being able to see the world from the perspective of another person. It does not mean you have to agree with the other person's perspective or point of view, but others will appreciate it if you can demonstrate that you understand how they see the issue.
7. Open-mindedness	Others will feel respected and valued when you demonstrate that you are open to different perspectives and ideas. This will also often result in more creative and positive outcomes.
8. Respect	Everyone wants to be treated with respect. There are a variety of ways you can send a message of respect including removing distractions, giving the other person your undivided attention, and thanking the person for sharing their thoughts and ideas.
9. Feedback	Being able to give and receive feedback is important. If you are in a position where you need to provide feedback to others, it is important to specifically share what the person is doing well and where and how improvements can be made. Feedback helps you grow and improve, so when you are given feedback, identify ways to take the feedback and put it into action.
10. Picking the right medium	In today's world, communication happens in so many ways: face-to-face conversation, online virtual meetings, e-mail, phone, text, and more. Determining the best mode for the communication is important. While technology tools such as e-mail can be very efficient, much can be lost because the nonverbal element of communication is missing. If a conversation is really important, it might be best to have the discussion face-to-face.

Emotional Intelligence Emotional intelligence can be defined as perceiving, understanding, and managing your own emotions as well as the emotions of others (Schutte & Loi, 2014). Individuals with high levels of emotional intelligence can skillfully interpret facial expressions and other nonverbal messages sent by others and are aware of the messages they are communicating to others.

Managing your emotions is a key component of emotional intelligence. To be emotionally intelligent means you are capably using stress management techniques so that negative emotions do not get in the way of you being productive.

Being emotionally intelligent also involves managing the emotions of others. This involves recognizing the feelings of others and determining how your behaviors can positively impact the situation. In some cases, this may mean giving a person some space and knowing that now may not be the right time to ask a question or make a request because the person is frustrated or angry. Recognizing when someone is in a good mood is also an important part of being emotionally intelligent. In these cases, the timing might be perfect to pitch a new idea.

Having high levels of emotional intelligence has been connected to positive academic and career outcomes. Sparkman et al. (2012) found that social responsibility, impulse control, and empathy were strong predictors of graduation. Empathy refers to the ability to identify and understand the feelings of another person. Impulse control refers to the ability to refrain from acting on feelings immediately and being able to manage one's emotions. Social responsibility refers to one's ability to work collaboratively with others to engage in meaningful and productive actions that benefit society.

Researchers have also found emotional intelligence impacts success in the workplace. Schutte and Loi (2014), for instance, found that employees with high levels of emotional intelligence were more likely to be engaged and satisfied. When employees have high levels of emotional intelligence, conflicts are more easily resolved and done so in more productive ways (Hopkins & Yonker, 2015). Emotional intelligence has been found to be particularly important in some positions. For example, Lopes (2016) found that the relationship between emotional intelligence and performance was strongest for managers, customer service positions, and healthcare providers. Being able to manage emotions in these positions is particularly important.

Research shows that emotional intelligence can be learned. Lopes (2016) conducted a thorough review of the studies on this topic and concluded that there is strong evidence that training related to emotional intelligence competencies works. Here are some strategies to improve your emotional intelligence:

- Increase the awareness of your emotional reactions and how you communicate when you are experiencing different emotions. Notice how others react to you when you are happy, sad, or angry.

- Practice good stress management daily, increasing the use of strategies when emotions are more intense.

- Notice the emotional reactions of others. How do your friends, family members, or coworkers act when they are happy, sad, or angry? Pay close attention to how your response or behaviors impact their emotions and behaviors.

Emotional
Intelligence

Chrupka/Shutterstock.com

- Engage in behaviors that have a positive impact on the mood or behaviors of others.
- Meet with a counselor or psychologist if you would like to better manage your own emotions and the emotions of others in your life.

Teamwork and Collaboration: The 5R Approach

Being able to effectively work with others is another important skill that will serve you well

iStockPhoto/Nensuria

personally and professionally. In college, you will likely work with your classmates on various types of projects. Research has shown that there are many benefits to group projects such as improved communication and interpersonal skills, increased knowledge and deeper thinking, and higher levels of motivation and achievement (Hansen, 2006). This is particularly true when students are taught about how to function effectively in groups before being required to do so, as evidenced by a research study conducted by Cranney et al. (2008). Thus, assignments that require you to work in groups are great experiences because they will give you opportunities to develop essential skills desired by employers.

To develop teamwork and collaboration skills, it is important that you approach group work productively. Unfortunately, students sometimes approach group work from a divide and conquer mindset, believing that each member of the group should be assigned a part of the project and should work independently on that part of the project to minimize the workload for all involved. This is not the best approach.

Group work is not designed to reduce your workload, but rather is a social learning opportunity where you can develop skills and support one another as you work toward a goal. Approaching group work from a collaborative framework is best. Collaboration, which means working together to achieve a desired outcome, is the key to effective group work. When using a collaborative approach, members will likely have different roles or may have more responsibility for certain parts of the project, but the work is still primarily done with others in the group. When you work collaboratively, you will typically produce a higher quality product.

Collaboration often takes place using virtual team spaces. Virtual platforms allow you to collaborate with other students or colleagues who do not live nearby or who have schedules that make meeting face to face challenging. In a study conducted by Deem et al. (2020), students and faculty identified several factors that contribute to the success of virtual teams. Factors included:

- having clear goals at the start,
- engaging in regular communication with others,
- being respectful of others, and
- having a balanced workload approach.

Although these factors were specifically identified for virtual teams, they would be relevant for in-person team meetings, too.

Groups do not always function well, and this can be quite frustrating to all members involved. One of the most frequently cited problems with group work is when not everyone does their fair share of the work. Sometimes there is a member or two who do not do any work or only a limited amount of work. This is referred

Table 4.5 5R Approach to Group Work
Strategies for Productive Groups

The 5R Approach to Group Work	Description
Establish **R**apport	Get to know group members.
Determine **R**ules	Agree upon ground rules for working in the group.
Determine R**o**les	Assign roles such as group leader, note taker, visual aid leader, finishing touch specialist, and rehearsal director.
Get **R**eady to work and support one another	Work individually on tasks before meetings. Come prepared and challenge one another with questions to more deeply explore content.
Remember to evaluate	Monitor progress and address conflict immediately.

to as social loafing (Hansen, 2006). Other problems cited by researchers are a lack of skills, lack of group leadership, conflicting schedules, time management difficulties, and behavioral or attitudinal problems (Deem et al., 2020; Hansen, 2006). When these problems exist, frustration levels can run high, relationships can become strained, and teamwork skills are not developed. Fortunately, there are effective strategies you can use in groups to help you have a productive, positive experience.

For groups to function effectively, there are several key strategies that need to be used. The 5R approach to group work describes these strategies. See Table 4.5. These skills are not only essential in college but also in the world of work. According to research by Klonek et al. (2021), you adapt and learn from engaging in group work. In their study, they found that group members were better at processes such as conflict management after regularly participating in virtual teams due to the COVID-19 pandemic.

Establish rapport Before you begin working on the task at hand, take some time to get to know your group members. When engaging in group work as a student, ask one another about career goals, interests, and work experiences. Knowing something about each member can help you understand their perspective better. Edmunds and Brown (2010) suggested that spending time on this activity promotes a positive social climate for the group. The amount of time you spend on this part of the process will vary depending on the nature and scope of your group work.

Develop group rules Establishing ground rules is "probably the most important, yet overlooked, action needed to create an effective group" (Armstrong, 2004, p. 34). Rules set clear expectations and provide members with a way to handle conflict that may arise. It is one of the best ways to prevent problems.

All group members should participate in the creation of the group rules. Rules may relate to communication and respect as well as to contributions and deadlines. It is particularly important to establish a timetable for completing the major tasks associated with the project. Some suggested group rules are:

- Attend all group meetings, or call or text if there is an emergency and you must miss a meeting.
- Come prepared to meetings, having read materials and produced what was expected according to an established timetable.
- Respond to e-mail, text, or other communication within 24 hours.
- Respect one another.

Assign group roles In addition to ground rules, establishing group roles for each member can help groups function productively. The nature of these roles will vary depending on the assignment. Group roles provide clarification of expectations for each member. Students report that having assigned roles within the group is valuable (Wise et al., 2012).

Assigning roles helps to ensure that all members contribute to the final project and that the work is evenly distributed. Here are some possible roles for a group that is working on a presentation:

- *Group leader*—Arranges meeting schedule, facilitates group meetings while allowing all members an opportunity to discuss their thoughts, and helps make sure there is an even distribution of work.
- *Note taker*—Takes meeting notes and shares the notes with everyone, clarifying tasks assigned to members.
- *Visual aid leader*—Takes work from group members and puts it together into one cohesive document or presentation.
- *Finishing touch specialist*—Reviews the document or presentation and any handouts for errors and makes sure the product matches the assignment expectations.
- *Questioner*—Asks group members questions about their contributions, often playing the role of devil's advocate to encourage all members to explore the content more deeply. This role is particularly important because it encourages critical thinking.
- *Rehearsal director/timer*—Organizes the rehearsals and the timing of the presentation, perhaps even recording it for review.

Get ready to work and support one another

After the rules and roles are established, it is time to start working on the project. One of the biggest challenges associated with group work is finding times when all members are available to meet. You may want to consider using technology tools for scheduling and communication purposes. You probably also have communication tools within your online course learning management system that you can use.

To make the most of your meeting time, assign tasks that need to be completed prior to the meeting. Researchers have found that doing work individually before gathering as a group improves functioning and increases productivity (Sarfo & Elen, 2011). For example, you may decide that members should read and summarize material before the meeting.

During the meeting, support one another by explaining concepts to one another and questioning. Teaching someone else content is one of the most effective ways to learn (Schwartz et al., 2011). Challenging one another with questions is also important because it fosters critical thinking skills for all members. Wise et al. (2012) found that having a questioner in the group enhanced the learning experience. Strang (2011) also found that students learned more when they asked each other challenging questions. Some examples of challenging questions are the following:

- What would be another example of this concept?
- Why do you think that is the case?
- How does this relate to...?

- What data support or contradict this idea?
- What are other possible explanations?

Remember to evaluate   Monitoring your progress is a must. As a group, refer to the timetable you established at the start of your project to determine if you are on track to achieve the goal by the deadline. If not, readjust the schedule by establishing new deadlines.

In addition to evaluating progress as it relates to the group, it can also be helpful to evaluate the progress and effectiveness of individual group members. Hughes et al. (2008) noted, "For students to develop skills in teamwork, team members must learn to give and receive feedback effectively" (p. 5). Thus, incorporating peer feedback about individual performance into the evaluation process can enhance skill development. Feedback that is specific and constructive, providing suggestions on how to improve, is most useful.

Leadership   Employers often indicate that leadership is a highly desired skill. Being a leader means you influence or persuade others to do the work needed to achieve a goal. McCallum and O'Connell (2008) noted that "**leadership** involves the ability to build and maintain relationships, cope with change, motivate and inspire others and deploy resources" (p. 152). Leaders also exhibit cultural humility, "being aware of the unique challenges and perspectives faced by the different types of people they are leading" (T. Ayeni, personal communication, July 22, 2021).

A **transformational leader** inspires others to engage in creative and collaborative problem-solving aimed at achieving a common goal that is highly valued by all members of the team. Arnold (2017) conducted an extensive review of the literature and found a positive relationship between transformational leadership and the psychological well-being of employees.

According to Bass, there are four primary characteristics associated with being a transformational leader. Transformational leaders are:

- **Charismatic.** Transformational leaders are role models whom others admire and want to follow. They clearly and passionately articulate a vision that immediately makes sense to others.
- **Inspiring and motivational.** Transformational leaders exude enthusiasm about their vision and get others excited about making this vision a reality.
- **Intellectually stimulating.** Transformational leaders not only share their ideas but also encourage others to consider creative ways to meet with success and actualize the shared vision.
- **Respectful of individual differences.** Transformational leaders care about the individuals with whom they work. They attend to the needs and ideas of all members of the group and create a supportive working environment where varying ideas and approaches are respected and appreciated (as cited by Stewart, 2006).

How do you develop leadership skills? Becoming a leader obviously requires much practice and time on task. Take advantage of opportunities you have in and outside of the classroom to work with a group of peers. For example, each student club or organization has several leadership positions you can explore. You can also look for leadership in your local community or even with a professional organization. You can start by being a member and observing what leaders do.

Then as you learn more about the organization, you can volunteer to take on a leadership role. When working on projects, practice articulating the goal, listening to others, identifying strengths of each member, planning tasks, and monitoring progress. As with all other skills, the more you practice, the better you will become at being a leader.

Strategies for Developing Leadership Skills

- Use classroom tasks such as group work as an opportunity to develop skills.
- Get involved in on- and off-campus organizations.
- Observe leaders in action.
- Volunteer to take the lead on tasks.

Essential Skills Quick Quiz

1. What essential skills do employers value most?
2. What are some behaviors that demonstrate professionalism?
3. What are some examples of effective time management strategies?
4. What does the research say about multitasking?
5. How can you develop cultural competence?
6. What is cultural humility?
7. What is emotional intelligence?
8. What is the 5R approach to group work?
9. What are the characteristics of a transformational leader?

| Chapter 4 | Chapter Summary: Note-Taking Model |

Let's summarize what you have learned in this chapter. The Cornell model is used for this chapter. Remember, it is not expected that your notes will look like this right after class or reading. It takes time to organize your notes and repackage them. It is time well spent, though, because you learn the content better as you organize it, and you will have a fabulous foundation from which to study for your exams! There are several ways to use this section:

- **Preview:** Read the model before reading the chapter to familiarize yourself with the content.
- **Compare:** Compare the notes you took on the chapter to the model provided.
- **Study:** The model along with your notes and other course materials are great resources for studying.

Cornell Method Model

How can you expand and strengthen your network?	Connect with professors and other professionals and your peers. Get involved in activities to meet others. Ask someone to be your mentor. Send thank-you notes and check-in regularly with those in your network.
What is important in terms of your professional presence on social media?	Use a professional image and informative profile summary. Share achievements. Choose connections wisely. Only post content that you would want an employer to see. Delete content that may be perceived by employers negatively.
What is an elevator speech?	A very brief story about you and your accomplishments and aspirations (approximately 30 seconds)
What are essential skills?	Skills that are important in many different careers and in life. Examples include: • Professionalism • Time management • Interpersonal skills • Leadership
What does professionalism mean?	Engaging in behaviors that communicate you care about achieving goals, are honest and responsible, hardworking, respectful, able to manage conflict, mindful of boundaries, and that you learn from mistakes
What time management strategies work best?	• Evaluate your time and determine if you are spending your time in a way that matches your goals. • Avoid time traps, activities that take up a lot of your time and do not help you achieve your goals. • Balance work, life, and school priorities. • Make a to-do list with specific tasks, prioritizing most important tasks. • Create a schedule. • Break large tasks into small ones to combat procrastination. • Single-task it, focusing on one task at a time.

What interpersonal skills are important to employers?	• Cultural competence: Ability to interact effectively with individuals and groups from other cultures; increase cultural competence by engaging in experiential learning opportunities to learn about different cultures, become more aware of your own beliefs and attitudes, and develop skills • Cultural humility: Being aware of culture, being open to different perspectives, and regularly reflecting on how culture influences our interactions with diverse individuals and communities • Communication and conflict management: Actively listen; Remove distractions and give your undivided attention to the task; Send clear messages; Address conflicts by hearing different perspectives and determining a solution • Emotional Intelligence: Being able to identify, understand, and manage your emotions and the emotions of others • Teamwork and collaboration: Use the 5R approach to group work—establish Rapport, develop group Rules, assign group Roles, get Ready to work and support one another, and Remember to evaluate • Transformational leadership: Leaders who are charismatic, inspiring, motivational, intellectually stimulating, and respectful of individual differences

SUMMARY: Networking is an essential skill that takes time to develop. You can expand and strengthen your network by connecting with professors, professionals, and peers and staying in touch with those in your network. Creating an online professional presence is recommended. Articulating your unique talents and strengths in writing and orally is important. Other essential skills, such as communication and teamwork, are skills that are needed across many different careers. Employers consistently indicate that they prefer candidates who possess strong soft skills. College is an opportunity to develop essential time management, communication, interpersonal, and leadership skills. Although you will develop some of these skills through coursework, it is a good idea to participate in extracurricular activities, as these skills are often best learned through out-of-class experiences.

Part 3

Achieving Academic Success

Chapter

5

Building Academic Skills

> All the so-called "secrets of success" will not work unless you do.
>
> — *Author Unknown*

1. What note-taking approach works best?

2. What reading methods work best?

3. How are memories formed?

4. What does the research say about cramming?

5. How can you use a multisensory approach to learning?

6. What is the testing effect? How can you use this approach to have long-lasting learning?

7. What are the advantages of establishing a study group?

James Woodson Getty Images

Exploring the Research in Summary

Research Study Citation:

McDaniel, M. A., Howard, D. C., and Einstein, G. O. (2009). The read-recite-review study strategy: Effective and portable. *Psychological Science, 20*(4), 516–522.

Introduction: The Research Question

What question did the researcher seek to answer?

Which reading strategy (re-reading, note-taking, or read-recite-review) works best?

Method: The Study

Who participated in the study? What did the researchers ask the participants to do?

The researchers conducted two experiments. In both experiments, 72 college students were assigned to one of the following three groups:

- Re-read (students read the passages twice)
- Note-taking (students took notes on the passages while reading but were not able to use notes at the time of testing)
- 3R: Read-recite-review (students read the passages once, then recited what they remembered, and finally read the passages again to review, determining if they accurately captured all the information)

All the students read several passages and then answered test questions about what they read immediately after the task and then again one week later. Some of the questions were fact-based and others required higher-level cognitive skills such as inference and problem-solving.

Results: The Findings

What was the answer to the research question?

Students who used the 3R method performed better on the fact-based recall questions as compared to the note-taking and re-reading groups (see Figure 5.1). This finding was true for the immediate test and the testing that occurred one week later. The students in the 3R method and note-taking strategy groups performed equally well on problem-solving tasks, both performed better than the re-reading group. However, the 3R method was less time-consuming (13.4 minutes in experiment 1 and 21.5 minutes in experiment 2) than the note-taking method (17.5 minutes in experiment 1 and 25.4 minutes in experiment 2). The re-reading group took an average of 9.2 minutes in the first experiment and 20.9 minutes in the second experiment (see Figure 5.2).

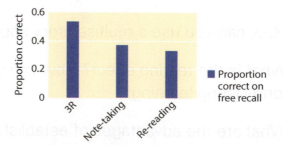

Figure 5.1   Reading strategy: proportion correct on free recall.

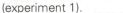

Figure 5.2   Reading strategy: time to complete task (experiment 1).

Discussion and So-What Factor

How can YOU use this information as a student?

These findings show that simply reading and re-reading your textbook will not lead to high performance on exams. The 3R method is the better option to maximize your success. The note-taking strategy is also very effective for more challenging test items. The act of recalling information, verbally or through writing, is what will really assist you with mastering the material. The 3R method does not take much longer than simply re-reading the chapter (less than a minute in the second experiment), and it leads to much better results. It therefore seems worthwhile to add in this additional step of reciting what you recall before you read the material again. In your classes, you will have to master much more information than what was asked of students in this study. Taking notes, while not looking at the book, may therefore be the best strategy to use so that you can refer to and use these notes when you are studying. If you are crunched for time, though, simply adding in a verbal recall activity can work!

Note-Taking and Reading Skills

Making the most of your in- and out-of-class learning experiences is important. As you know, actively participating in class and reading are two of the best ways to learn. During class, your professors will share their expertise and engage you in learning tasks. Outside of class, your professors will assign you readings from books, articles, and other sources. There are several strategies you can use to maximize your learning during lectures and other class activities as well as from reading tasks.

Note-Taking

You will likely forget most of what you learned in class unless you take good notes and actively use or re-package these notes after class (Murre & Dros, 2015). See Figure 5.3 for a visual image of how quickly you can forget information.

Research has shown that students who take good notes learn more, better understand the material, and ultimately perform better in their classes (Salame & Thompson, 2020). Taking notes in all learning environments,

Tom Peterson

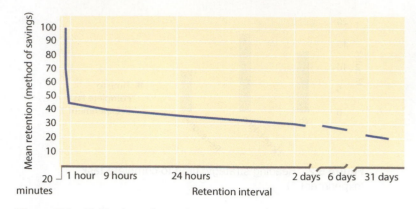

Figure 5.3   Ebbinghaus forgetting curve.

Think Critically

1. Why do you think you forget so much so quickly?

2. How can you use the information from this research to improve your memory and study approaches?

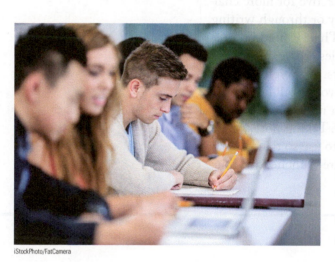

iStockPhoto/FatCamera

including online courses is important. Unfortunately, many students do not take notes in their online courses (Morehead et al., 2019). This is problematic because an organized set of notes serves as an excellent study tool.

Luo et al. (2018) found that different note-taking approaches can work well in different learning environments but that learning depends on whether notes are reviewed. This was illustrated in an interesting study by Knight and McKelvie (1986) where students were assigned to one of the following learning conditions:

- provided with lecturer notes,
- take your own notes, or
- do not take notes.

The results showed that studying from notes was connected to the highest performance, with those who studied from lecturer notes performing the best. This result highlights the importance of having good notes to study from when preparing for a test or exam. Interestingly, students who did not review their notes did not perform any better than students who did not take any notes at all. This finding emphasizes that the act of note-taking does not result in learning, but rather that learning happens when you use your notes as a study tool. One particularly effective after-class strategy is to combine your notes from the lecture and the readings. Organizing concepts from your notes enhances your learning.

The cognitive processes associated with note-taking and studying are what matter most. In a study conducted by Wong and Lim (2021), they found that students who took their own notes outperformed those who took photos of lecture slides or did not take notes. They indicated that students were often less engaged in the lecture and that their minds wandered more when using the photo approach as compared to taking their own notes.

There are several different note-taking methods. Salame and Thompson (2020) noted that the key is to use a strategic note-taking process that involves:

- actively listening during class,
- processing what is being learned, and
- documenting what is learned in writing.

Some students prefer to take notes in their notebook, while others like to use technology tools such as their laptop or tablet for note-taking. Both can be effective (Luo et al., 2019).

Note-taking should not be an in-class activity only. Taking notes on the reading prior to class is also important. Re-packaging your notes after class to combine your notes from the reading and from the lecture is also an excellent use of your time. Because this is a high-level cognitive task, this action can be considered a study technique. In fact, some of the most effective note-taking methods such as the matrix or concept map are best used after class when you have time to think deeply about the content. You may therefore use one note-taking method during class and then a different note-taking method after class. This approach is very effective.

Linear Notes   The **linear note-taking method** consists of phrases, sentences, or perhaps paragraphs. See Figure 5.4. In many cases, linear notes look like a long narrative. This method is not recommended because it is not very effective. Unfortunately, this method is frequently used by students because it is very easy to use this method during class. If this is the note-taking method that you have been using, try a different method and see if it helps you better achieve your goals. If you want to rely on this method during class, be sure to take your notes and re-package them into a more effective format after class.

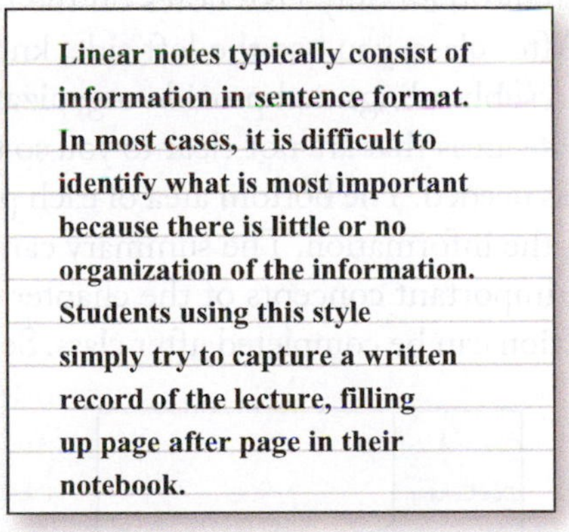

> Linear notes typically consist of information in sentence format. In most cases, it is difficult to identify what is most important because there is little or no organization of the information. Students using this style simply try to capture a written record of the lecture, filling up page after page in their notebook.

Figure 5.4   Linear note-taking method.

Think Critically

1. Why do students use the linear note-taking method?

2. Why is this note-taking strategy not as effective as most other strategies?

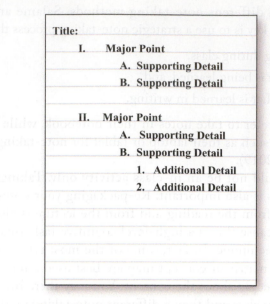

Figure 5.5   Traditional outline format.

Traditional Outline   With the **traditional outline format**, the main headings appear toward the top left of the page, and subheadings and information about the subheadings are indented and written below the main headings. This traditional outline method allows one to easily see the structure of the lesson. See Figure 5.5. It can sometimes be difficult to determine the main headings. If your professor shares PowerPoint slides ahead of time, this might help you identify the main points or ideas, making it easier for you to organize content during class. Research has shown that the outline method of note-taking approach leads to good recall of the information but is not as effective as the matrix approach (Kiewra et al., 1988).

Cornell Method   The **Cornell method** is another effective note-taking method (Pauk & Ross, 2008). In this method, you draw a vertical line about one third of the way across the paper and then only take notes on the right side. The left side remains blank at first. After class, you use the left side, known as the cue area, to identify the headings and subheadings and provide organizational structure to your notes. You can also indicate areas that are not clear to you so that you will remember to revisit these concepts as needed. The bottom area of each page is then used for the purpose of summarizing the information. The summary can simply be a paragraph or two, highlighting the important concepts of the chapter or lesson. Like the cue section, the summary section can be completed after class. See Figure 5.6.

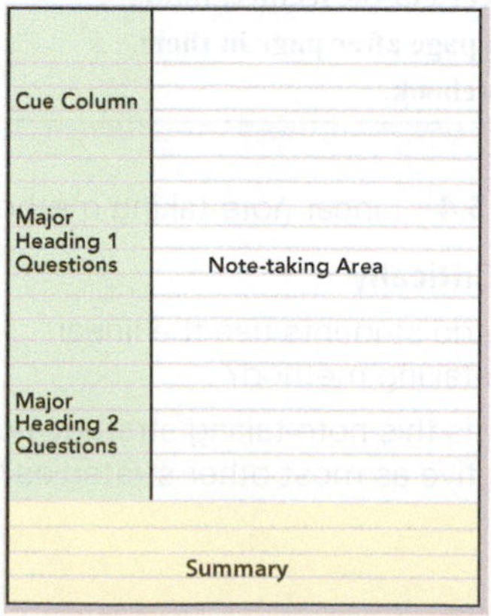

Figure 5.6   The Cornell method.

Figure 5.7 Concept mapping example

Concept Maps Another method is **concept mapping**. This method emphasizes visual connections between concepts. First, you indicate the main idea and put a bubble or box around it. Then, concepts that are connected to the main idea are put in different, often smaller boxes, with lines connecting the boxes that are related to one another. See Figure 5.7. Most students find it difficult to accomplish this type of note-taking during a lecture and instead use it after class as they reorganize their notes in a personally meaningful way. Research has found that students who create concept maps have higher levels of academic achievement as compared to those who do not use this approach (Chiou, 2008). There are several different computer programs and applications for mobile devices available that can help you create visually effective concept maps.

Matrix Notes According to research conducted by Kiewra et al. (1988), the matrix note-taking approach works the best. For the **matrix method,** you create a table where the main topics are on the top and subtopic headings are listed on the left. See Figure 5.8. For example, if you were going to use this note-taking approach to summarize the different note-taking methods, you could list the methods (i.e. outline, Cornell, concept map, and matrix) down the first column on the left and subtopics such as description, advantages, and disadvantages across the top. You then take pertinent notes in each box. Advantages of this approach include focusing on the connections between concepts and the easy-to-read visual format. It is particularly useful for comparing concepts or theories. It is often very difficult to use this approach during class because you may need more processing time to figure out the best organizational structure and to see how concepts are connected. However, re-packaging your notes after class in a table or matrix is a great idea. It gets you thinking more deeply about the concepts and provides you with a fabulous tool for studying.

Overall Topic	Main Topic I	Main Topic II	Main Topic III
Sub-Topic I			
Sub-Topic II			

Figure 5.8 Matrix note-taking approach.

iStockPhoto/Zephyr18

Active Reading

Class time is limited, and there are many important concepts and theories that you will need to learn. Professors will therefore expect you to also learn from the textbook or other sources. Reading and using your textbook as an information resource has been found to be positively connected to grades (Rawson et al., 2000).

You have probably discovered that college textbooks can sometimes be challenging to read. A research study conducted by Williamson (2008) found that even students who were reading very well as graduating high school seniors experienced a big drop when it came to comprehending a college-level textbook. This is because college textbooks contain complex content on material that is likely new to you. Fortunately, there are strategies you can use to help you learn from reading high-level texts.

Power of Prior Knowledge Researchers have found that one of the best predictors of how well you will be able to comprehend what you read is how much you know about the subject. This was illustrated in a classic study conducted by Recht and Leslie (1988). In their study, students were assessed in terms of their reading skills and their knowledge of baseball. Students were then asked to read a passage on baseball. After reading the passage, students answered questions related to the story and re-created the story nonverbally.

As you would imagine, the students who were good readers and who knew a lot about baseball performed the best. Similarly, the students who were poor readers and did not know much about baseball had the poorest performance on the tasks. But here is the fascinating finding: Students who were good readers but had low baseball knowledge performed almost as poorly as the poor readers with low baseball knowledge, and the poor readers with high baseball knowledge performed almost as well as the good readers with high baseball knowledge. The key finding of this study is that prior knowledge about baseball, not reading skill, was the best predictor of reading comprehension (Recht & Leslie, 1988).

As a college student, you will not have extensive prior knowledge related to all your courses. Although this will make it more challenging to comprehend the textbook content, there are several strategies you can use to help you get the most out of reading. Building at least an introductory knowledge base before you begin reading will serve you well.

1. Start by reviewing the table of contents, which provides you with an outline of the chapter content. This can provide a helpful organizational context for the information you will be reading and helps you see the relationships between concepts that will be discussed.

2. Next read the end of the chapter summary. The summaries can serve as previews for the chapter much like a movie preview. Familiarizing yourself with the key points from the summary will help you take in the more detailed information from the chapter.

iStockPhoto/Metamorworks

3. With textbook content that is particularly challenging, you can also search for a video on the topic before you read the chapter. You can also review websites such as Wikipedia to gain some basic background knowledge before you read the more detailed textbook. Students reported that Wikipedia provided easy to understand information (Blikstad-Balas, 2016).

Jacob Lund/Shutterstock.com

The 3R, SQ3R, and SOAR Reading Methods One simple yet effective reading strategy is the **3R method** (McDaniel et al., 2009). The 3R method involves the following three steps:

1. Read the material.

2. Recite the material—close the book and say what you remember (or better yet, write it down!).

3. Review or read the material again (add to your notes, filling in missing content and write key concepts in the text, a process called annotating).

Active readers use the 3R technique after reading small sections of a chapter. Research illustrates that being actively involved with information as you go along rather than waiting until the end of a chapter works best (Linderholm, 2002; Rawson et al., 2000). It is therefore a good idea to identify a short section of the chapter to read using this method rather than trying to use this technique with an entire chapter at once.

After reading the identified section, close your book before you begin the second step—recite. During the recite step of the process, you simply recall what you just read without looking at the text. It is important that your book is closed during the recite part of the process so that you are truly retrieving the information from your memory. Closing the book before you take notes forces you to put the information into your own words. When you summarize information in your own words, you learn more (Dickinson & O'Connell, 1990).

During the third R—review—go back and review how well you summarized the content. If you missed any content, this is the perfect opportunity to add to your notes, filling in any information gaps. Researchers have found that reading comprehension increases when students annotate (Azmuddin et al., 2020) so you may want to consider engaging in annotation during this step of the process. Annotating simply means you are summarizing key points. Writing in the margin of the text or using an electronic tool allows the summary to be visually connected to the text. Annotations typically include:

- a brief summary of the concept,
- a note on how this concept relates to something you already know, and
- your thoughts or reaction to the content.

Another well-known reading strategy is the **SQ3R method**. You will notice that there are two letters or steps added to the process. This technique involves the following five steps:

1. Survey

2. Question

3. Read

4. Recite

5. Review

For the first step, survey, preview the chapter. Survey means you scan the chapter as a whole and take in the big picture. Start by looking at the table of contents for the assigned chapter, headings, images throughout the chapter, and the chapter summary. Doing this provides you with an overview of the chapter content. These actions set the stage for success by helping you understand the organization of the information that will be presented in the chapter.

The second step in SQ3R involves creating questions about the content. You have probably already discovered that this textbook comes with chapter opener questions that appear on the first page of every chapter. If your other texts do not have this feature, create your own questions based on the survey you did of the chapter. What questions do you think will be addressed in the chapter? What are you curious about after scanning the chapter? Searching for answers to questions is an active reading strategy and will result in increased learning. The final three steps involve the same read, recite, review steps of the 3R method. Research has shown that the SQ3R method has been connected to increased reading comprehension (Artis, 2008) and improved exam performance (Carlston, 2011).

Another reading strategy that has been shown to be even more effective than SQ3R is the SOAR method (Jiaram et al., 2014). The SOAR method involves the following actions:

1. Select

2. Organize

3. Associate

4. Regulate

The first task is to select the key points or important information from the text. During the second step of the process, organize the content using a matrix or other graphic organizing tool. Associating, the third step, involves identifying how concepts relate to one another. Rather than trying to learn each concept independently, looking for connections or associations between concepts can help you learn the content. Connecting new content being learned to what you already know is also recommended. Regulate is the last step and refers to monitoring your learning progress. Assessing how much you have learned via a

practice test, for example, can help you determine if you need to spend more time and engage in different learning strategies to learn the content you just read. Results from a research study that compared the SOAR and SQ3R methods found that "The SOAR group learned about 14% more facts, 20% more relationships, and 13% more concepts than the SQ3R group" (Jairam et al., 2014, p. 416).

Highlighting   Most college students highlight their texts as they read. Researchers have found that students comprehend what they read at higher levels when important text is highlighted (So & Chan, 2009).

Unfortunately, most students are not engaging in effective highlighting practices. Because students are novice learners and do not know a lot about the textbook content, it is extremely difficult for them to differentiate the important from the less important and thus determine what to highlight. As a result, students either highlight too much or too little. This does not result in increased learning and has been found in some cases to even result in poorer performance (Dunlosky et al., 2013; Gier et al., 2009). Thus, ineffective highlighting is worse than not highlighting at all.

Some researchers have found that teaching students to highlight or underline main ideas works. For example, Hayati and Shariatifar (2009) found that students who participated in a one-hour training session on how to highlight effectively performed well on a reading comprehension test. Students were taught to read the passage first without highlighting and then to go back and underline the main ideas. As you can imagine, it would be next to impossible to truly figure out what is important on a first read of a passage or article.

If you want to highlight, wait to do so until the last R, reviewing, of the 3R or SQ3R methods. This way you will be deciding what is most important after you have already interacted with the text a couple of times. If you are still unsure about what is important, rely on other strategies instead and avoid highlighting.

Note-Taking and Reading Skills Quick Quiz

1. Which note-taking method works best?
2. What did Recht and Leslie (1988) discover about what most impacts reading comprehension?
3. What should you do during the second R in the 3R and SQ3R reading methods?
4. How can you use highlighting as an effective reading strategy?

Memory and Study Strategies

In college, you are exposed to extraordinary amounts of new information. Each course you take will be packed with new concepts and theories. As a college student, you are expected to engage in many sophisticated cognitive tasks, such as critically evaluating information and applying recently learned material to new and varied situations. Gaining content knowledge is a must. Learning how memory works and what study strategies are most effective will help you meet with success.

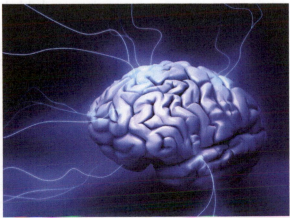
iStockPhoto/Petrovich9

The Memory Process

Remembering takes work. According to the classic informa-tion processing model (Atkinson & Shiffrin, 1968), there are three main processes within the memory system: encoding, storage, and retrieval. Research has shown that this process is multidirectional, meaning that all parts

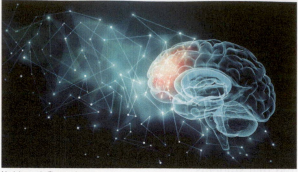

MattLphotography/Shutterstock.com

of the process can influence other parts (Willingham, 2009). Your prior memories, for example, play a role in how you encode and store new memories. The more you know about how these processes work, the more efficient you will be.

Encoding
Encoding refers to how you get memories into your memory system. To purposefully encode material, start by paying attention to it. You are constantly exposed to sensory information. For example, today in class your professor was probably talking to you about a topic (memory perhaps!), your classmates were taking notes, students were walking in the hallway or family members were moving about in your home if you were in a virtual classroom, and technology tools may have been making humming noises.

You must decide what information is worthy of your attention. Your past experiences can influence this process. If you have previously found information to be useful, then you will be more likely to attend to content that seems similar in nature. Your focus also guides this process. Actively attending to what your professor says during a lecture means it is much more likely for this content to get encoded and stored in your memory system.

Multisensory approaches to learning can assist you in encoding information more effectively (Myers, 2014). For instance, if you encode information using both visual and auditory inputs, you have increased the likelihood that the information will get into your memory system.

This **dual-encoding process** also makes it more likely that you will find the information in your memory system when you need it. You have probably had the experience where you could not remember something for an exam, but then suddenly, you were able to visualize where it was in your notebook. In this example, the visual encoding process helped you retrieve the information. Using more than one sense to input information into your memory system will improve your encoding and retrieval. Intentional interventions can improve memory. For instance, as you are learning a new concept, thinking of a related image can improve memory for that concept.

Storage
The second part of the memory process is **storage**, which refers to how you hold onto and save your memories. If you are like most others, you have probably had the terrible experience of typing a paper (the words got into the computer—they were encoded) and then turning the computer off without saving it. Saving information in your memory system is similar. Within your memory storage system, you have two main subsystems: working memory and long-term memory. Willingham (2009) nicely visualizes this process via a simple model shown in Figure 5.9.

The great news about long-term memory is that it seems to last forever, and you can store an endless amount of information (Villiness, 2020). Unlike your computer hard drive, which has limited capacity, your brain allows you to store more information than you will ever need during your lifetime. Long-term memory is clearly the goal when it comes to knowledge, but it takes effort for content to get there.

To get information into long-term memory, working memory is needed. Working memory refers to the workspace of your brain where new information is temporarily held. Psychologists used to think that memory was like a

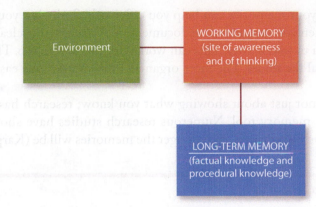

Figure 5.9   Simple memory model

one-way street. First, you encoded a new piece of information, and then you stored it temporarily until you housed it permanently in long-term memory. However, research has shown that your memory system is much more interactive in nature (Artuso & Palladino, 2019).

What you already know plays a big role in how you learn new information. You search your long-term memory for information that might help you encode or store the new information. For example, if you are trying to learn the names of your classmates, you will likely think about others you know with names or features similar to your classmates. This prior knowledge can help you bring the new knowledge into your memory system and keep it there.

Working memory is limited in terms of duration and capacity. In other words, you can only hold onto information for a short period of time, often only seconds, and can only hold onto a few chunks of information at a time. A famous psychologist, George Miller, demonstrated this limited capacity through a research experiment. He asked participants to remember a list of nonsense syllables (so the words could not be simply linked to other memories) and found that the average number of items participants could remember was 7 ± 2. In other words, you can only hold five to nine items in short-term memory at a time (Miller, 1956). This is not good news, since your professors will likely expect you to remember much more than that from each lecture.

Fortunately, you can expand your working memory capacity by **chunking** information. When you organize or chunk information, you can accommodate more than five to nine pieces of information at a time. An example would be a phone number. Typically, you remember area codes as one chunk rather than three independent numbers. Actively working with the new information and using memory strategies can help you hold on to important concepts you need to know (Hartshorne & Makovski, 2019).

Retrieval   **Retrieval** has traditionally been thought of as the last stage of the memory process. To show what you know, you need to retrieve or find the memories you have previously stored. You have probably had the experience when you knew you saved a document in your computer, but when you needed it later, you could not locate it. This is called retrieval failure, meaning you were not able to find what you needed when you needed it. This is obviously problematic when it happens during a test because it can negatively impact your grade.

Organizing your memories can help you efficiently find what you need when you need it. When you save an online document in a folder with a clear title, it will be easier for you to find it later. This can work with memories, too. Think of your brain as a mental file folder. The more organized the content, the easier it will be to retrieve.

Retrieval is not just about showing what you know; research has shown it is also a powerful memory tool. Numerous research studies have shown that the more you retrieve information, the stronger the memories will be (Karpicke, 2016).

Memory Process

- Encoding—Getting information into your memory system
- Storage—Saving information
- Retrieval—Finding stored information when you need it

Bo1982/Shutterstock.com

Study Strategies

Research has shown that the amount of time you study matters. When you spend more time learning, you will likely perform better (Cole & Butler, 2020). However, utilizing strategies that have been shown to be highly effective will help you make the most of the time you invest in studying. Some strategies work better than others.

Reviewing

Reviewing involves looking over your notes, text, and other resources. Reviewing is the most-used study technique by college students (Engin & Korucuk, 2020; Gurung, 2005), but it is not the most effective one. Reviewing your notes and other study materials can help you hold on to new content, but only for a short period of time (Karpicke & Roediger, 2006). Research has shown that student learning is not high when the reviewing technique is used by itself (Su et al., 2021).

Unfortunately, many students believe reviewing works well (Engin & Korucuk, 2020). Karpicke and Blunt (2011) found that students overestimated the effectiveness of the reviewing or restudying strategy. This is probably because as information is reviewed, it becomes more and more familiar. Familiarity can be misinterpreted as learning. This is problematic because it will likely lead you to stop studying too soon.

Reviewing can be effective when combined with other more powerful strategies such as elaboration and testing yourself. Students who learn about study strategies are more likely to use strategies that work well. Brown-Kramer (2021) found that students who read articles about effective strategies such as practice testing were more likely to use these strategies as compared to their peers who did not read these articles. Perhaps most importantly, they found that students who read about and used these effective strategies earned grades that were a full letter grade higher than their peers who did not learn about and use effective study strategies.

Elaboration

Elaboration happens when you attach meaning to new content being learned (Bartsch & Oberauer, 2021). To elaborate, find connections between information you know and new information you are learning. Learning is enhanced when new concepts are linked to previously learned content (Goswami, 2008). Seeing the relationships between new information and previously learned information enhances and strengthens learning.

TypoArt BS/Shutterstock.com

Researchers have found that by engaging in elaboration, long-term memory improves (Bartsch & Oberauer, 2021; Hall et al., 2004). Cole and Butler (2020) found that students who used elaborative study strategies where examples of concepts were emphasized had higher scores on a test as compared to students who were simply asked to memorize the information.

In an interesting study conducted by Dickinson and O'Connell (1990), they focused on mental processes whereby students:

- put information into their own words,
- created links between concepts via a hierarchical structure, and
- created examples to help the concepts come alive.

When comparing high- and low-performing students, Dickinson and O'Connell (1990) found that high-performing students spent approximately one hour or more per week studying. They also found that high-scoring students spent an average of 43.13 minutes using these mental processes compared to only 10.28 average minutes per week by the low-scoring group. Interestingly, high- and low-performing students spent similar amounts of time reading and reviewing. See Figure 5.10. Thus, the difference lies in total study time and the use of elaboration, which the researchers called organizing, as an important study strategy. Unfortunately, researchers have found that students are not frequently using these highly effective study strategies (Engin & Korucuk, 2020).

Testing Your Knowledge

One of the most effective ways to learn is by testing your knowledge (Einstein et al., 2012; Karpicke & Roediger, 2006). This is known as the **testing effect**. Rodriguez et al. (2021) found that self-testing was associated with higher academic performance as measured by final course grades.

Most individuals do not think of tests as learning opportunities but rather as the final step in learning—showing what you know. However, tests can be used for both purposes. You can demonstrate knowledge when taking a test, but you will also learn from testing your knowledge.

The testing effect was illustrated by a classic study conducted by Karpicke and Roediger (2006). In this study, students were randomly assigned to one of the following three groups:

- Study, Study, Study, Study
- Study, Study, Study, Test
- Study, Test, Test, Test

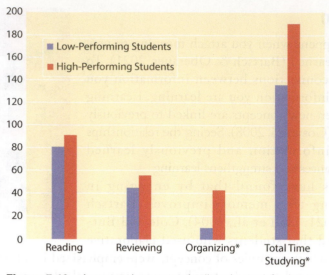

Figure 5.10 Average time on tasks (in minutes) for low- and high-performing students.

Think Critically

1. Why do you think low-performing and high-performing students differ on the use of the elaborating/organizing strategy?

2. How else might low-performing and high-performing students differ in terms of their study approaches?

*Statistically significant difference

ESB Professional/Shutterstock.com

In all groups, students were asked to learn content from a passage. The first group of students was given four study sessions of five minutes each to learn the content. Participants in the second group were given three five-minute study sessions and then were asked to write down what they could recall from the passage. Students in the last group were allowed to study the passage content for five minutes and then had three opportunities to write down what they recalled. On a delayed recall test, students in the Study, Test, Test, Test group performed the best, recalling 61% of the content. The Study, Study, Study, Test group remembered 56% of the content while the Study, Study, Study, Study group performed the worst, remembering only 40% of the passage content. See Figure 5.11.

You can test yourself by taking quizzes provided by textbook publishers, or you can create your own. Working with a classmate or study group to test one another is another great way to put the testing effect into practice. There are online platforms that allow you to share and co-create quizzes with your peers.

You can also use good old-fashioned flash cards. While some students like to use index cards for this purpose, there are also many apps or online tools that can also be used. The advantage of using an app is that it is accessible on your phone, so you can study anywhere, anytime.

Many students who use flash cards make use of their study time by putting aside the concepts they believe they know well so that they can focus their studying on the more difficult concepts. This sounds like a good strategy, but it may not lead to the best outcome. Kornell and Bjork (2008) conducted a series

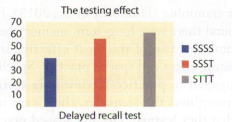

Figure 5.11 Results of the testing effect study.

Think Critically

1. Why do you think the students who were in the study, test, test, test group performed the best?

2. How can you apply these research findings to improve your studying practices?

of experiments on flash card use and found that dropping cards from the study pile was not beneficial. In fact, dropping cards resulted in poorer performance. Retrieving the material several times makes it more likely for the content to stay in your long-term memory. Although you may need more time on cards with content you do not yet know well, it is still important to quiz yourself on all the cards several times.

Another way that you can put the testing effect into practice is by engaging in a "Dusting off the Cobwebs" exercise. To engage in this exercise, recall everything you can remember from the prior class or reading for that week without looking at your notes, book, or other materials. Once you remember as much as you can, pull out your notes and other resources to fill in any gaps. This act of practicing retrieval strengthens the memory and makes it more likely that the concepts find a home in your long-term memory. Doing this exercise with a classmate enhances your learning even further because you can then discuss what you learned.

Testing Your Knowledge

- Pretend you have a test after every class.
- Frequently take practice tests.
- Use flash cards.
- Recall what you learned from class and reading assignments.

Spaced Practice

To maximize your learning, it is best to study a little each day. Studying in small chunks over time is referred to as **spaced practice**. Research shows that memories are more likely to stick when you study content numerous times versus studying in one longer session, which is often referred to as massed practice

iStockPhoto/Prostock-Studio

or cramming (Dunlosky et al., 2013). Hopkins et al. (2016) found there were long-term memory benefits when students combined two of the most effective study approaches: the testing effect and spaced practice. Specifically, when students engaged in practice retrieval via testing numerous times throughout the semester, they were more likely to retain what they learned. Despite spaced practice being one of the most powerful study strategies, many students do not report engaging in spaced practice (Gurung et al., 2020). Carving out even 15-30 minutes per day to review and re-package your notes and quiz yourself on what you have learned will help you achieve at high levels. Establishing daily habits that put evidence-based study strategies into practice will help you achieve your goals.

Multisensory Learning

Although you have probably heard of learning styles such as auditory, visual, and kinesthetic, there is not much research support for learning styles (Pashler et al.,

Magic pictures/Shutterstock.com

2008; Rohrer & Pashler, 2012). Rather, neuroscience research has shown that everyone is more similar than different in terms of how they learn best and that everyone typically learns best when they are using multiple senses (Goswami, 2008; Willingham, 2009). In other words, you remember more if you see, hear, and do something with the information. This is because you are engaging different neural pathways at the same time, which strengthens learning and memory.

Visual images appear to be particularly powerful in the learning process. Based on numerous experimental studies, Mayer (2009) found that adding an image to text resulted in significantly better memory for the concept. Other researchers have found that you are able to process pictures more quickly and efficiently than words (Seifert, 1997), and your memory for pictures is better than it is for words (Foos & Goolkasian, 2008). This phenomenon is referred to as the **picture superiority effect** and is connected to the encoding and retrieval processes (McBride & Dosher, 2002). Paying extra attention to the graphs, charts, and images that connect to the content you are learning about and studying is therefore a good approach. Your textbooks are filled with these powerful images, and you can also create visual matrixes, charts, or other images to maximize your learning. Fernandes et al. (2018) found that drawing simple figures related to content only took a few seconds and improved memory.

Study Groups

Another extremely powerful way to learn is to teach the content to someone else (Galbraith & Winterbottom, 2011; Srivastava et al., 2015). Research has shown that students who taught their peers indicated that this activity helped them learn and increased their confidence with the content (Johnson et al., 2015; Srivastava et al., 2015).

One effective way to use this study approach is to participate in a study group where different members take turns teaching content to one another. For example, you could each choose a section of a chapter to teach to the other study group members. This process would require you to prepare well so that you can clearly communicate your assigned part of the chapter to your peers. Being cognitively and socially engaged increases learning (Garrison et al., 2000; Prince, 2004).

According to research (Hendry et al., 2005; McCabe & Lummis, 2018), students have identified the following benefits of study groups:

Monkey Business Images/Shutterstock.com

- increased motivation,
- increased support, and
- the opportunity to clear up confusing concepts.

Despite their benefits, students often report that group work can be challenging. One of the biggest challenges associated with group work is finding time to meet. Research conducted by Roychowdhury et al. (2020) found that students have been able to use technology to address the challenge of complex schedules. Synchronous and asynchronous technology tools can be used to help students connect for studying purposes.

There are several strategies you can use to increase productivity and learning when using study groups.

1. **Group size.** Shimazoe and Alrich (2010) recommend a group size of three to four members. A small group size makes it more likely that your group will stay on task and be productive. Identify others who share your commitment to learning and success.

2. **Preparation.** Millis (2002) emphasized the importance of all group members being individually accountable for learning when engaged in group work. Everyone needs to contribute. Assigning a task to do prior to attending the study group session can increase accountability for all. For example, each member might need to come prepared to teach a section of the chapter. Doing independent work first helps everyone be ready to discuss topics more deeply, maximizing your study group time (Sarfo & Elen, 2011).

3. **Ground rules and roles.** Establishing ground rules and roles helps keep everyone focused on the task at hand. An example of a ground rule could be that the first 10 minutes are purely social and then you will start focusing on the topic of study. Another example could be that all members need to either come to the session prepared or post materials in an online space prior to the study session to stay in the group. You might also want to assign different roles. See Table 5.1 for some examples of group roles. Rotate roles so that different members have different responsibilities each time.

An effective study plan consists of the following five approaches:

1. **Use a multisensory approach to learning.** Using a multisensory approach will increase the likelihood that you effectively encode and retrieve information. Because memory for images is more powerful than it is for words, identifying and using relevant images will help you learn the content.

2. **Organize.** Use organizing techniques to create an effective study guide. Create written notes by putting key concepts into your own words, identifying examples, and finding connections between concepts you are learning.

Table 5.1 Study Group Table
Study Groups Roles

Role	Tasks
Agenda maker	Identifies the topics to be covered and what all members should do to prepare for the study session. The agenda should be distributed to group members approximately a week in advance. This might involve assigning each member a section of the chapter or content to teach others during the study group.
Facilitator	Starts the study session, makes sure everyone participates, and keeps the conversation moving along productively. The facilitator may begin with unclear concepts and then move into the other content areas identified on the agenda.
Time keeper	Ensures the study session time is maximized by following the schedule and keeping group members on track.
Quiz creator	Creates 5 to 10 quiz questions about the material. This gives members an opportunity to benefit from practice retrieval and also helps members of the study group assess how well they are learning the content.

Combine the notes you took during class and while reading the chapter into one comprehensive document that makes explicit connections between concepts being learned. Use an effective format such as the matrix table and concept map, or tools (bold, larger font) to bring attention to the most important points.

3. **Review.** Next, review your organized notes. For optimal performance on the exam, review your notes multiple times over the course of several different study sessions. Spaced practice, studying many times over a period of time, works best (Schwartz et al., 2011).

4. **Test.** Now, quiz yourself over and over again. Use publisher-provided assessments when available or create your own. Track your progress and modify your studying habits as needed.

5. **Teach.** Finally, teach the content you have learned to someone you know. Teaching is an extremely powerful way to learn!

Memory and Study Strategies Quick Quiz

1. How much information can you typically hold in working memory?
2. What is the testing effect?
3. What is the picture superiority effect?
4. Is it more productive to study alone or in a group? Why?
5. What strategies can make study groups function more effectively?

Chapter Summary: Note-Taking Model

Let's summarize what you have learned in this chapter. The concept map model is used for this chapter. Remember, it is not expected that your notes will look like this immediately after class or reading. It takes time to organize your notes and re-package them. It is time well spent, though, because you learn the content better as you organize it, and you will have a fabulous foundation from which to study for your exams! There are several ways to use this section:

- **Preview:** Read the model before reading the chapter to familiarize yourself with the content.
- **Compare:** Compare the notes you took on the chapter to the model provided.

- **Study:** Use the model along with your notes and other course materials as great resources for studying.

Concept Map Model

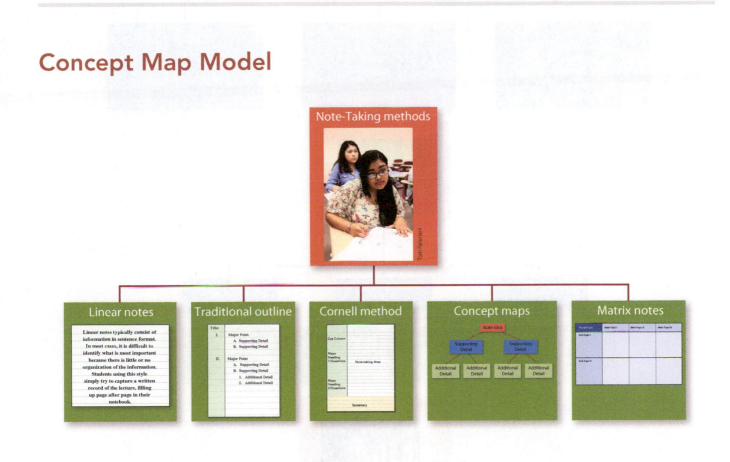

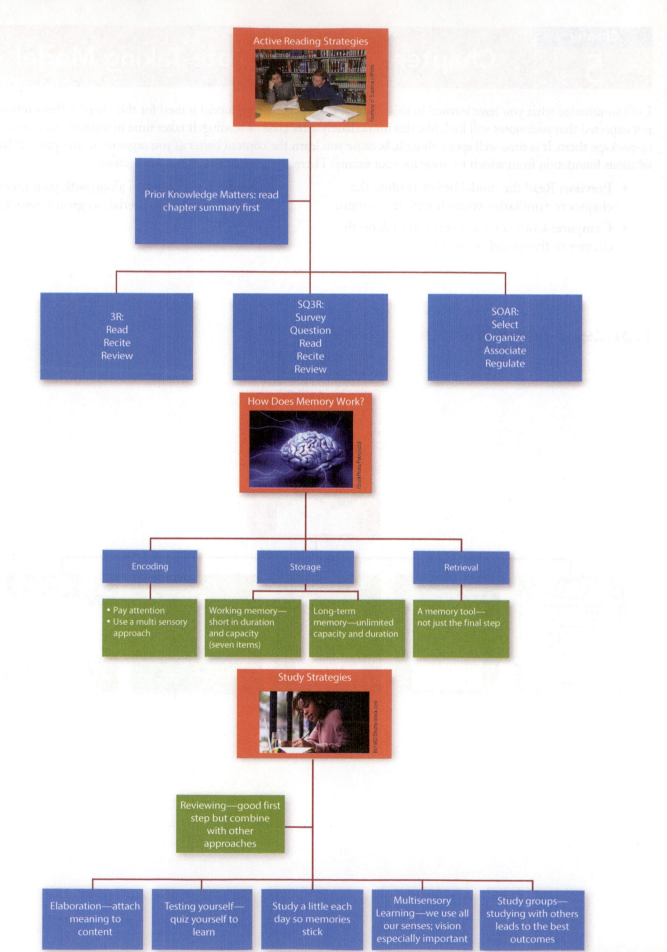

Active Reading Strategies

Courtesy of Susanna LeRoss

Prior Knowledge Matters: read chapter summary first

3R:
Read
Recite
Review

SQ3R:
Survey
Question
Read
Recite
Review

SOAR:
Select
Organize
Associate
Regulate

How Does Memory Work?

iStockPhoto/Petrovich9

Encoding

Storage

Retrieval

• Pay attention
• Use a multi sensory approach

Working memory—short in duration and capacity (seven items)

Long-term memory—unlimited capacity and duration

A memory tool—not just the final step

Study Strategies

B61962/Shutterstock.com

Reviewing—good first step but combine with other approaches

Elaboration—attach meaning to content

Testing yourself—quiz yourself to learn

Study a little each day so memories stick

Multisensory Learning—we use all our senses; vision especially important

Study groups—studying with others leads to the best outcomes

This is your moment to shine. Embrace it.

— *John Smith*

Tom Peterson, Middlesex County College

1 What is academic integrity? Why does it matter?

2 What can you do to avoid unintentional plagiarism?

3 What steps are involved in writing a paper?

4 How can you engage your audience when giving a presentation?

5 What makes a visual aid effective?

6 How can you manage performance anxiety?

7 What do the best students do when they take a test?

Exploring the Research in Summary

Research Study Citation:

Issa, N., Schuller, M., Santacaterina, S., Shapiro, M., Wang, E., Mayer, R., & DaRosa, D. (2011). Applying multimedia design principles enhances learning in medical education. *Medical Education, 45*(8), 818–826.

Introduction: The Research Question

What question did the researcher seek to answer?

Does learning increase when PowerPoint slides are based on multimedia learning principles?

Method: The Study

Who participated in the study? What did the researchers ask the participants to do?

Medical students (n = 130) participated in a lecture on shock as part of their curriculum. Ninety-one students participated in the revised PowerPoint condition, where the PowerPoint slides were developed based on multimedia research. A total of 39 students participated in the lecture where the original PowerPoint slides were used. The revised PowerPoint condition used the multimedia principle (use images rather than words), the signaling principle (draw attention to main points), and the coherence principle (only include essential content).

Pretests were given prior to the lecture so that groups could be compared on prior knowledge. One hour after the lecture, a posttest was administered to assess learning that took place during the 50-minute lecture.

Results: The Findings

What was the answer to the research question?

Both groups had similar levels of background knowledge, and both groups had experienced significant learning as a result of the lecture. However, the students in the revised PowerPoint condition outperformed the students in the original PowerPoint condition on a posttest measuring how well they remembered the lecture content. See Figure 6.1 illustrating test performance.

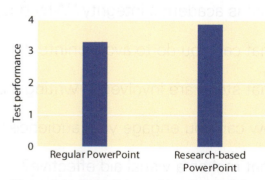

Figure 6.1 PowerPoint multimedia principle: test performance.

Discussion And So-What Factor

How can YOU use this information as a student?

These findings show that the multimedia principles identified by Mayer (2009) really do work in the classroom setting. When creating PowerPoint slides or using multimedia, it is important to only put the essential information on the slides and to use images rather than words whenever appropriate to do so. Eliminating distractions, such as animations, can also increase learning. This research reminds us of the importance of visual images and that PowerPoint slides are visual aids, not documents on slides.

Academic Integrity

Before you turn in any work for a course, it is important to understand academic integrity. You will want to become familiar with what it means to engage in academically honest work and the college policies related to academic integrity. Learning about academic integrity will make it less likely for you to unintentionally engage in dishonest actions.

What Is Academic Integrity?

Academic integrity refers to engaging in academically honest behaviors. It involves doing your work without using unapproved aids and creating your own academic product, such as a paper or presentation, while giving appropriate credit to those who shaped and influenced your work. Giving credit to these sources for their contributions is a must and involves using in-text citations and a Reference or Works Cited page. Academic

Rawpixel.com/Shutterstock.com

dishonesty can be intentional or unintentional, but either way it can have significant negative consequences. One of the best ways to avoid unintentional dishonest actions is to fully understand plagiarism and cheating. Chu et al. (2020) found that students often have misperceptions about academic integrity and dishonesty. See Table 6.1 for descriptions of terms associated with academic dishonesty.

Academic integrity benefits everyone at college. It is important for others in the community to have a positive image of your college or university so that the work you and others do there is valued. Negative mindsets about your institution or program that stem from dishonest actions can be detrimental to both current and future students. For example, negative views about your institution may result in fewer outside learning opportunities for students, such as yourself, or reduced employment options for graduates. Local businesses and other community services are less likely to partner with an institution with a questionable image.

Being honest matters not only in school but also in your personal and professional life. Guerrero-Dib et al. (2020) found that students who engaged in dishonest behaviors in school were more likely to engage in unethical actions in the work environment. Integrity is highly valued by employers.

Table 6.1 Academic Dishonesty Table
Types of Academic Dishonesty

Type of Academic Dishonesty	Definition	Examples
Plagiarism	Presenting someone else's work as your own	• Putting your name on a work (entire paper or small sections) that someone else created • Not using quotation marks when using another person's words • Using quotation marks when using another person's words but not citing the source • Only changing a few words in a sentence even if you cite the source • Paraphrasing the idea of another person and not citing the source • Submitting the same paper or work in two different classes without professor approval—this is referred to as self-plagiarism
Cheating	Engaging in any activity that gives you or another student an unfair advantage	• Using unapproved materials or resources when completing an assignment or exam • Working collaboratively when an assignment is supposed to be completed independently • Discussing exam content with another student who has not taken the exam yet

Everyone needs to do their part to encourage a culture of honest behaviors. McCabe et al. (2012) found that peers had a major influence on whether students cheated. Specifically, they found that students were less likely to cheat when they thought their peers were being honest and would not approve of cheating behavior. You can help promote a positive culture on your campus by caring about academic integrity and talking about the importance of it with your peers.

Your character and learning matters much more than the grades you earn (Sanders, 2012). The goal of assignments such as papers and presentations is for you to learn content and develop skills. When students are dishonest, they lose out on valuable learning that will help them perform well in their career. Although a degree may be the minimum requirement for a position, employers are much more interested in the learning that was connected to completing the degree.

There are several ways you can avoid engaging in dishonest academic actions. Perhaps most importantly focus on learning. Students who care about learning are more likely to engage in honest behaviors (Miller et al., 2011). Preparing well for tests and using good time management on assignments also makes it less likely that you will be tempted to be dishonest. Learning about academic integrity and how to effectively cite sources can help you avoid unintentional dishonesty (Belter & du Pré, 2009). Finally, do not forget to seek out help from others when needed. Sometimes students engage in dishonest actions when tasks are challenging. The better approach is to seek the help you need so that you can learn the knowledge and skills associated with the task while also being honest.

Strategies to Help You Be Academically Honest

- Know the definitions of plagiarism and cheating.
- Focus on learning as your goal.
- Prepare well for exams.
- Use effective time management strategies.
- Learn how to cite sources appropriately.
- Consult tutors, librarians, and professors as needed.

Citing Sources and Paraphrasing

Citing sources is important regardless of the product you are creating. Most students know that they need to document the source when writing a paper, but they may not realize that citations are also needed in all other academic products, too. Providing proper credit for images, videos, or other media tools is essential. If you do not cite the source, this is considered **plagiarism**; therefore, it is important that you learn when and how to cite sources appropriately.

To avoid plagiarism:

iStockPhoto/Oleksii Didok

- Cite all ideas unless they are purely your own or are considered common knowledge, which means that most people would know the information.

- If you are using someone else's exact words, use quotes, which clearly indicate that this is the direct work of someone else. Because your professor wants to hear your ideas, use quotes from others sparingly.

- Always cite the source whenever you are paraphrasing someone else's thoughts or ideas.

How you cite sources depends on the format and style your professor expects. Different disciplines use different styles. The Modern Language Association (MLA) and the American Psychological Association (APA) are two of the most common citation styles used in college settings. With both styles, it is essential that you reference citations in the body of the text and then provide complete citations on the Works Cited or References page. There are many Internet resources that can help you get your source information into the correct format. Check out Table 6.2 for an example of APA and MLA citations.

Keeping track of your sources helps you cite them appropriately. Whenever you take notes from a book, article, or website, write down the entire citation next to the content. In most library databases, you will see a citation tab where the citation appears in a variety of formats. You can then copy and paste the citation into your notes, making it easier for you to cite your sources when you are finalizing your paper or presentation. There are also citation management tools that may be helpful to you, especially if you are working on a paper or project with numerous citations. It is important to note, though, that these tools are not always completely accurate, so double check the formatting of citations you get from online tools.

Table 6.2 Citation Examples Table
Examples of Citations: APA and MLA

	APA	MLA
Paraphrase	College students will typically be expected to use either MLA or APA style in their papers (Harrington, 2023).	College students will typically be expected to use either MLA or APA style in their papers (Harrington 157).
Quote	"The Modern Language Association (MLA) and the American Psychological Association (APA) are two of the most common citation styles used in college settings" (Harrington, 2023, p. 157).	Harrington indicated that "the Modern Language Association (MLA) and the American Psychological Association (APA) are two of the most common citation styles used in college settings" (157).
Works Cited	Harrington, C. (2023). *Student success in college: Doing what works* (4th ed.).: Cengage Learning.	Harrington, Christine. *Student Success in College: Doing What Works.* 4th ed., Cengage Learning, 2023, p. 157.

When it comes to **paraphrasing** ideas from others, researchers have found that students are not always paraphrasing effectively. Howard et al. (2010) found that most students focused on sentences versus key points from the entire source. Paraphrasing is about summarizing ideas in your own words, so you should be paraphrasing ideas from an entire document, not just ideas from a sentence within the document. Students in this study conducted by Howard et al. (2010) relied on changing a few words and inserting synonyms, which is not enough. When students only change a few words, this may be due to students not fully reading or comprehending the source material.

Paraphrasing is a skill that gets better with practice. It is most difficult to paraphrase when you do not understand the content. In these instances, get help from a tutor, librarian, or professor. Accessing help not only helps you avoid plagiarism but also helps you learn the content!

Learning how to paraphrase well also reduces the likelihood that you will unintentionally plagiarize. One of the best ways to practice paraphrasing is to read an article, chapter, or report and then close the book or minimize the window on your computer while you write a summary of what you just read. If you use this strategy, you will not be tempted to copy words used in the original work or only change a couple of words. Research has found that when students summarize content without referring to the text, they are more likely to paraphrase better than if they refer to the text while writing (Kamimura, 2019).

Academic Integrity Quick Quiz

1. What is the definition of academic integrity?
2. Why is academic integrity important?
3. When do you need to cite sources?
4. What is the definition of paraphrasing?

Assignments and Tests

Assignments and tests are opportunities for you to demonstrate how much you have learned and what skills you have developed. In college, your professors will likely ask you to complete a variety of assignments and learning tasks. You will probably be asked to complete traditional assessments such as exams and papers, but your professors may also ask you to complete other types of assessments such as performances, multi-media projects, and reflection journals. Regardless the type of task, you want to show off all that you have learned and earn a grade that helps you achieve your goals.

Jacob Lund/Shutterstock.com

Papers

Being able to effectively communicate in writing is a skill that will serve you well personally and professionally. In fact, communication is one of the most desired skills by employers (Robles, 2012). Papers are great opportunities to build your information literacy, critical thinking, and writing skills (Albitz, 2007; Breivik, 2005).

Purpose Begin by focusing on your outcome or destination. Why did your professor assign this paper to you? What is the goal or purpose of the paper? Consider writing down the assignment in your own words to ensure you fully understand the task. Having a very clear understanding of the professor's expectations will assist you in knowing what you need to accomplish. If provided, carefully review rubrics, which are detailed explanations of how assignments will be graded, and ask your professor for clarification as needed. As you work on the project, it is a good idea to periodically review the assignment and its purpose.

Robert Plociennik/Shutterstock.com

Choosing a Topic If you have the freedom to choose the focus for the paper, the next step will be to select a topic. Students often underestimate what is involved in this process and the importance of choosing well. Identifying a topic that is too broad seems to be the most common student mistake (Head & Eisenberg, 2009). Suppose you choose stress management as a topic for a presentation. You may soon become lost in the vast amount of information available on stress management, and, as a result, your paper will be generic in nature and may not provide the level of depth and detail expected at the college level.

underverse/Shutterstock.com

One way to help you narrow your search is to focus on specific populations. For example, you could focus on stress management in children, college students, individuals about to have surgery, or individuals who recently became unemployed. In addition to narrowing your search by population, you could also zoom in on one aspect of the topic. Perhaps you want to learn about a particular stress management technique, such as progressive muscle relaxation, or you want to know more about the connection between stress and heart disease. You could even combine these approaches by looking at the connection between stress and heart disease in individuals who are unemployed. After you engage in this process, you will have a clear, concise topic that provides you with focus and direction, making it much easier to write a fabulous paper. Choosing a clearly defined topic helps set the stage for your success. See Table 6.3 for some ideas about how to choose a topic.

Gathering Information You will then need to use your information literacy skills to determine what type of information you will need to complete the assign-

Rawpixel.com/Shutterstock.com

ment, find the needed information, and evaluate the credibility of the information found. In most cases, you will find more information than you will need. As you know, there are a variety of sources for information including journals, books, newspapers, and the Internet. Where you look for the information will depend on the task at hand and whether your professor has any specific requirements about sources. Learning to navigate the massive amount of information available is a skill and you will get better at this skill with time and practice.

The best place to go for assistance with finding the information you need is the library. Visiting the library in person is ideal because you can easily ask the reference librarians for assistance as needed, but many college students rely on the online databases that can be accessed from anywhere there is an Internet connection. If you need help while working online, you will be happy to know that many college libraries offer telephone and Internet-based support. In fact, you may even have 24/7 online access via tools like chat available. Accessing help from the information experts will help you build important skills needed now and in your future career.

Table 6.3 Identifying a Topic Table
Strategies to Identify a Well-Defined Topic

Identifying a Well-Defined Topic	Strategies
To get started	• Look at the table of contents in related textbooks. • Review chapters that catch your interest, focusing on the subheading topics. • Google topics that capture your interest, looking for specific areas you could target. • Go to broad sources like encyclopedias, but do not stop there. • Conduct a literature search in the library databases.
To further define your topic	• Use search features that are built into database search engines. • Focus on specific populations or aspects of the topic. • Identify key words related to the topic. • Work with a librarian or your professor for additional tips.

As you find sources, it is helpful to do an **annotated bibliography** for each source. An annotated bibliography involves

- writing down the citation,
- summarizing the key take-aways or points, and
- thinking about how this source might be used in this paper.

Escorcia et al. (2017) found that taking notes before writing a paper was associated with better written products. Although annotated bibliographies do take time to complete, this approach saves you time in the long run. It can take a significant amount of time to read the original sources you plan to use in your paper. By writing down the summary immediately after reading it, you are processing the information more deeply and creating a much shorter synopsis that you can use when it is time to write your paper. Researchers have found that re-reading the source during the writing process is extremely time-consuming (Escorcia et al., 2017), so you avoid the need to do this when you complete annotated bibliographies. Students have reported that annotated bibliographies help with time management (Mostert & Townsend, 2018). See the following Annotated Bibliography.

After you have completed annotated bibliographies on the sources you plan to use, a synthesis matrix can help you organize your content (Clark & Buckley, 2017). Creating a synthesis matrix involves creating a table where the sources you found

Annotated Bibliography

Source:
Issa, N., Schuller, M., Santacaterina, S., Shapiro, M., Wang, E., Mayer, R., & DaRosa, D. (2011). Applying multimedia design principles enhances learning in medical education. *Medical Education*, *45*(8), 818–826.

Summary:

The researchers conducted an experiment to determine if PowerPoint slides developed based on research helped students learn the material better than traditional PowerPoint slides. The evidence-based PowerPoint slides had images instead of words, drew attention to main points, and only included essential content. Medical students completed a pretest and a posttest after the lecture. Results showed that students performed better on the posttest if they participated in a lecture that used the evidence-based PowerPoint slides, as compared to the traditional slides.

Reflection:

This research will help me make the case that the type of visual aid used matters. This research combined with the other studies I have found on the power of images in learning will show the reader the impact that presentation slides can have on learning. The study does, however, focus on medical students, and they did not provide demographic data so it is unclear whether these findings are relevant to the field of business which is my focus area.

go in the first column and then key themes are listed on the top of subsequent columns. This is a visual tool where you package all the content you have gathered from your sources. See Table 6.4.

Your professors will expect you to synthesize your content. This means you will need to share what you have learned from all the sources combined rather than reporting information from one source after another. The themes that emerge in the **synthesis matrix** can provide an organizational structure for your paper.

iStockPhoto/Tinpixels

Organizational Tools Good organization is an essential element of papers and presentations. Students often start writing without first mapping out the organizational structure of the paper. This is not advisable. Would you go on a trip to a place you have never visited without directions, a map, or GPS? Probably not! Knowing where you are headed and how you plan to get there is also important when writing papers. Researchers have found that the actions you take prior to writing can lead to better outcomes (Escorcia et al., 2017).

You can use a variety of organizational tools such as outlines or concept maps. Many students report not using an outline because of the time it takes to do so (Baker, 2019). This is unfortunate because outlining is a good investment of your time and will help you write a higher-quality paper. Researchers have found that using tools, such as graphic organizers, improve writing skills and decrease mental effort (deSmet et al., 2011; Brown, 2011).

List the main concepts you want to address in the paper as the major headings in an outline or as large circles in a concept map. Then, add subtopics and details. Think about how the topics are connected and which concepts are most important. Research has shown that outlines are most effective when students focus on both content and organization (Baker, 2019). When students learn how to effectively outline, they are more likely to do so (deSmet et al., 2011).

Table 6.4 Synthesis Matrix

Sources	Theme 1	Theme 2	Theme 3
Source 1			
Source 2			
Source 3			
Provide a brief summary of what the source contributes to the theme in each cell, if applicable. Not every cell will have content because not every source will connect to every theme.			

Think Critically

1. How might you use a synthesis matrix?

2. How can completing an annotated bibliography help you complete a synthesis matrix?

Drafts   After you have mapped out an organizational plan for your paper, it is time to start writing. Remember, this is just a first draft, so focus on getting your thoughts and ideas documented. Gezmiş (2020) noted that students will likely find this stage more challenging if they did not devote enough time to the prewriting tasks of reading and outlining. To get started, take the ideas you outlined and expand on them, describing concepts in more depth and providing more detailed explanations. There is plenty of time later to make modifications and edits.

Arcady/Shutterstock.com

Here are some suggestions for when you write your paper:

- **Begin with a strong opening.** Your opening should clearly address the purpose of the paper and your main idea. It should also gain the reader's attention and interest. After reading your first paragraph, your professor should have a clear understanding of the purpose and scope of the paper and should be excited to read it.

- **Keep your outline or concept map in front of you.** As you work, review it regularly. This can help ensure that you address all your key points. You may find that you need to modify your original plan as you start working and discover that there were additional points that you would like to include. Your paper will likely grow and develop as you continue to work on it. Revisit the actual assignment periodically to be sure that you have met all the expectations set forth by your instructor.

- **Begin each paragraph with a key sentence.** The key sentence, often referred to as a **topic sentence,** describes the focus for the paragraph. Sticking to one main idea per paragraph is advisable. Supporting details for each main idea are then provided in the body of the paragraph.

- **End with a strong conclusion that summarizes the key points.** The conclusion or summary is your opportunity to remind the reader of the main ideas presented in your paper. It refocuses the reader back to your most important points. This last part of the paper is often what is best remembered, so make the most of this section.

Revising Your Work   First drafts are not final products; they are just the beginning. After you have completed a draft, the critical process of revising begins. Culham (2018) noted, "No one writes their best, most coherent thoughts in a first draft—no one" (p. 96).

Revising a paper involves adding, deleting, and modifying the information in your first draft for the purpose of improvement. See Figure 6.2 for an overview of the writing process. Before reviewing and revising your work, it is often a good idea to give yourself a little space from the project. In other words, do not expect to plan, write, and review your assignment in one day. Instead, allow yourself time to reflect on what you have done before you begin revising it. You are often tired by the time you reach the end of the first draft. Take a day or so to rest and re-energize, and you will find that this results in being able to revise and proofread more effectively.

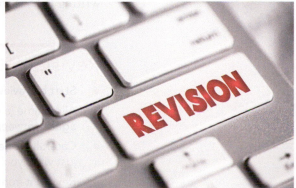

dizain/Shutterstock.com

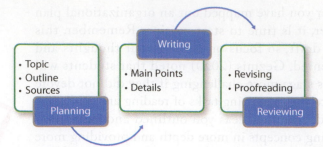

Figure 6.2   The flexible writing process.

When revising your work, first look at the big picture and then focus on the details. Wallace (1990) conducted an interesting research study where college students were asked to revise a written document. Half of the students were simply told to revise it, while the other half were first given an eight-minute lesson on how to effectively revise work. The lesson focused on the importance of:

- reading the entire written work before making any revisions;
- considering the document as a whole; and
- emphasizing global factors, such as the intended audience, purpose, and general organizational structure.

Students who participated in the brief revision training created documents that were judged to be of higher quality compared to the students who were simply told to revise the work (Wallace, 1990). Escorcia et al. (2017) also found that students who revised their work were more likely to create higher-level products.

As you review and revise, focus on whether your primary message was clearly communicated. The purpose of each section or paragraph should be easy to identify. Investigate whether your main ideas were supported by details and examples and backed up with citations. Did you provide the reader with enough information and examples to get your point across? It is also important to explore whether it will be easy for the reader to see the connections between topics you discussed. Adding transition statements such as "next" or "as a result" can assist the reader in seeing the connections and will make your paper flow well.

After you are finished, give yourself some more time and space and then revise it again. To produce high-quality work, you will want to write several drafts. By carefully engaging in this review process, you will enhance your work to create a polished product that reflects your knowledge and skills. Researchers have found that engaging in the revision process is connected to higher levels of confidence in writing (O'Sullivan Sachar, 2020).

Revision Tips and Strategies

- Start by reviewing the assignment expectations.
- Allow time (a day or so) to elapse before beginning the revision process, and again between drafts.
- Carefully review the document, focusing on what is actually in the paper and not just what you think you wrote down.
- Review it from a global perspective, focusing on whether you clearly addressed your key points in an organized fashion.

- Look for supporting details and examples.
- Determine whether you need to find additional information on the topic.
- Find your topic sentence for each paragraph.
- Explicitly make connections between concepts being discussed.
- Review the organization of the paper and make modifications as needed.
- Be sure you cite everything except your own ideas and general knowledge.

Proofreading The final step in the process of writing an academic paper is **proofreading.** When you proofread your work, you check for accuracy and the presence of grammatical or spelling errors. This is when you shift from the global focus to the more specific focus.

Take advantage of resources that can help with this step. Your computer, for instance, has many built-in tools that can help you with the proofreading process. The most obvious ones are the spelling and grammar checks that are often turned on automatically. Experiment with the other tools like Outline View in Word documents to check out your organizational structure. Use other resources

Lamai Prasitsuwan/Shutterstock.com

such as a text from your English class to help you with the proofreading process.

This is also a great time to go back over your written work and be sure that you have not unintentionally plagiarized. Ask yourself the following questions:

- Did I provide in-text citations according to MLA, APA, or other professor expectations?
- Did I always cite information that was not my own idea or general knowledge?
- Did I use quotes and citations when using the words of another?
- Did I include a Works Cited or Reference page with complete citation information using MLA or APA style?

Remember, you can also seek tutoring or writing support. Tutors do not typically proofread or edit your paper for you, but they will assist you with becoming good at these tasks yourself. Research has found that consulting with a tutor can contribute to improved performance on writing tasks (Dansereau et al., 2020; Oley, 1992).

Presentations

Effectively communicating information verbally is also important in college and careers. Professors and employers will ask you to present on a variety of topics. As you know, presentations can be in-person or be done virtually. Either way, there are several strategies that you can use to manage performance anxiety and deliver effective presentations.

iStockPhoto/SolStock

iStockPhoto/Fizkes

Managing Performance Anxiety When many students hear the word "presentation," they often start to feel anxious. **Performance anxiety** is normal. Some anxiety is desirable because it motivates us to perform our best. Majali (2020) found that high performing students had a moderate amount of anxiety. However, for some students, anxiety can spiral and become debilitating. When anxiety becomes debilitating, your performance is negatively impacted (Raffety et al., 1997).

The best way to manage performance anxiety is through preparation. It is easier to feel confident and less anxious when you know you have adequately prepared for the task ahead of you. For example, Menzel and Carrell (1994) found that the amount of time spent preparing for a speech was significantly linked to how well students performed on the presentation. Specifically, they found that all the following were positively connected to high-level performances:

- Total time preparing for the speech
- Total time spent practicing
- Amount of time spent on preparing the visual aid
- Total number of rehearsals
- Time rehearsing silently
- Time rehearsing out loud

You can use a variety of rehearsal methods when preparing. For instance, you can rehearse in front of a mirror, in front of family members or friends, or in front of anyone else who is willing to listen. Another effective strategy is to record yourself giving the presentation and then watch the recording. Technology tools make this easy to do. In a research study conducted by Tailab and Marsh (2020), students who video recorded themselves giving a practice speech were more confident and less nervous during the graded presentation.

If you present to others, ask for feedback from those who just watched the presentation. In addition to overall feedback, try asking content-based questions to see if the members of your audience understood the material you presented. This is a great way to assess your effectiveness. You can also encourage audience members to ask questions of you so that you can become comfortable responding to questions before the actual presentation.

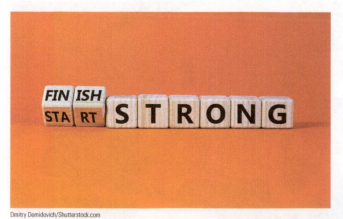

Dmitry Demidovich/Shutterstock.com

Beginning and Ending Strong There is a concept in the world of public speaking called the **Golden Rule** (Sellnow, 2005) that involves:

1. Telling the audience what you are going to say
2. Saying it, and then
3. Telling the audience what you just said

Using a strong opening and conclusion are very important. The opening sets the stage for the audience by preparing them for what is to come. **Priming** or talking about what is coming next gets the audience ready to take in or encode the information you will be presenting. Effective presentations begin with a strong opening that grabs the attention of your audience and draws them into your presentation. After just the first few minutes, your audience members should have a clear understanding of what you will be discussing, understand why you are discussing it, and be interested in hearing more. There are several opening strategies, also often referred to as hooks, that you can utilize. Here are some examples of hooks:

- Interesting statistics that speak to the importance of the topic
- Stories that help the audience connect to the material on an emotional level
- Audience involvement through questioning techniques or activities
- Humor (when used appropriately)

After you are finished presenting your content, go back and summarize the key points from your presentation. A strong conclusion is essential. Audience members can often get overwhelmed by the amount of information presented, especially when it is presented in a short period of time. By drawing their attention back to the main points, you increase the likelihood that they walk away with the most important content. Audience members are most likely to remember the first and last part of your presentation. This is referred to as the **primacy and recency effect** (Logan, 2021). Be sure to start and end strong!

Audience Engagement

Audience engagement refers to the involvement and attentiveness of your audience members. There are many strategies you can use to increase audience engagement. For example, maintaining good eye contact is a great way to stay connected to your audience (Tsang, 2020). Practice and preparation play a key role here because it is very difficult, if not impossible, to have good eye contact when you are not well prepared. The more comfortable you are with the material, the less likely you will feel a need to look at your notes or the PowerPoint slides when presenting.

Fizkes/Shutterstock.com

Speaking with enthusiasm and confidence can also engage your audience (Tsang, 2020). When your passion and excitement for the topic is evident, others are more likely to attend and may also get excited. On the other hand, it is very difficult for an audience to stay engaged if the presenter is speaking in a monotone voice or reading the presentation.

Using active learning strategies throughout your presentation will also help you keep the attention of your audience and make it more likely they will remember the concepts. As the presenter, you want to help your audience members focus on what is most important. When students are listening to numerous presentations in one class period, or professionals are listening to several presentation pitches in a row, they may have difficulty remembering key take-aways from each one. To combat this problem, try the following strategies to emphasize or highlight important concepts:

- Comment on the importance of the topic.
- Become more animated or change your voice pattern.

- Repeat the information.
- Use a dramatic pause.
- Connect concepts to a gesture or image.
- Spend a significant amount of time on the topic.
- Use several examples.
- Share stories related to the material.
- Use visual tools like charts or graphs.

Active learning techniques move the learner from a passive to an active role. Although student presentations are generally short in duration, you can still find quick ways to engage your audience. Many strategies may take only a minute or two but can significantly help your audience process and remember the information you are sharing with them. Here are some active learning strategies you can use:

- Give a brief one- or two-question quiz.
- Poll the audience, using a show of hands or a polling tool, about their opinion or experiences.
- Pause for questions or brief comments.
- Ask members to engage in an independent written self-reflection activity (i.e. What have you learned from the presentation so far? What questions do you have?). This is often called a one-minute paper.
- Encourage the audience to do a Turn and Talk, turning to a classmate and summarizing what they have learned from the presentation. Breakout rooms can be used for this purpose during virtual presentations.

Using Multimedia Effectively

Knowing how to best utilize multimedia can help you create high-quality presentations. Mayer (2009) has conducted numerous experimental studies investigating best practices in multimedia. See Table 6.5 for research-based strategies based on this work.

Creating a visual aid that consists primarily of an image can increase learning. In an interesting study conducted by Moen (2021), students in a class where only images were on slides outperformed students in a class where slides consisted of both images and text. Interestingly, students in this study thought they learned more when both pictures and text were used, but exam scores were higher when only pictures were used. Similar results were found by Smith-Peavler et al. (2019) where students also performed better with PowerPoint slides containing only images versus images and text.

Images can also enhance business presentations. Anic and Wallmeier (2020) found that adding a probability histogram, for instance, led others to find the products more attractive. Knowing the research and applying it to professional presentations will help you in your career.

Wachiwit/Shutterstock.com

Table 6.5 Multimedia Best Practices Table
Best Practices for Using Multimedia

Principle	Description
The Multimedia (or the Images Are Powerful) Principle  kurhan/Shutterstock.com	According to Mayer's (2009) research, adding an image significantly increased learning. According to this research, a fabulous slide could simply include a title and a relevant image.
The Coherence (or the Less Is More) Principle  Shutterstock.com	Students often add background music, sounds, or even videos, believing these make the presentation more effective. However, Mayer (2009) found that these additions can actually reduce learning because they sometimes distract and overload the brain. These tools may not help the learner differentiate between important and less important content. Instead, keep the slides focused on one or two main points.
The Signaling (or the Bring Attention to Main Points) Principle  iStockPhoto/ISerg	According to research conducted by Mayer (2009), highlighting or emphasizing main points through tools such as arrows or larger, bold font increased learning.
The Personalization (or the Conversational Language) Principle  Yummyphotos/Shutterstock.com	Mayer (2009) found that learning improved when simple conversational language was used instead of more formal language. Avoid complex terminology and use easy-to-understand explanations (this is why the principles have been renamed!).
The Modality (or the Be Quiet) Principle  WAYHOME studio/Shutterstock.com	Basically, Mayer (2009) found that when learners were presented with a lot of text and the presenter spoke about the topic, less learning took place. He attributed this to split attention. The learner is not sure whether they should listen or read—both are competing for the learner's attention. To increase learning, use only images or very few words with a narrated description. If there is a need to put a lot of words on the screen, then let the learner read the slide silently and "be quiet." After giving them ample time to take in the information, you can then discuss additional content on that topic.

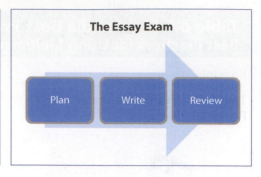

The Essay Exam

1. Planning is the first step of writing an effective essay response. It involves outlining or mapping out what you want to discuss.

2. Write your main ideas and support them with details.

3. Review your work by proofreading and making sure you fully addressed the question.

The Essay Exam

Plan → Write → Review

Figure 6.3 The power of SmartArt.

When it is difficult to find an image that conveys the main point or when some words are essential, you can consider using SmartArt. SmartArt is a tool that visually packages key words. See Figure 6.3 for an example. Another tool within PowerPoint that can help you create visually effective slides is the Design Ideas tool. This tool will show you several options for conveying the information effectively on your slide.

When slides have complex graphs or text, it can be helpful to engage in signaling, which means you are drawing the viewer's attention to the part of the slide that relates to the content being discussed. Arrows, inking, or highlighting are ways to use signaling. Based on a review of numerous studies, Alpizar et al. (2020) have found that signaling is connected to higher levels of learning.

Some presentation formats are more effective than others. The **Pecha Kucha method**, an alternative to a traditional PowerPoint presentation of text, bullet points, and images, requires students to conduct a fast-moving presentation with 20 slides consisting of only images. Each slide auto-advances after 20 seconds. Warmuth (2021) found many positive outcomes associated with the Pecha Kucha presentation style. Specifically, students in classes where this approach was used reported being more engaged, creative, and collaborative as compared to students in classes where traditional presentation formats were used.

Reflecting on Your Performance After you finish your presentation, reflect on your performance to maximize learning and enhance your skill development. Researchers found that students who watched and reflected on videos of their presentations produced higher-quality presentations as compared to students who did not watch and reflect on their initial performance (Sterling et al., 2016). This reflective practice also resulted in higher levels of confidence. Specifically, Sterling et al. (2016) found that students who engaged in these reflective practices felt more confident in their ability to prepare and conduct presentations as well as being more able to differentiate between effective and ineffective presentations.

fizkes/Shutterstock.com

Tips for Effective Presentation Delivery

- Practice! Practice! Practice!
- The Golden Rule: Tell your audience what you will say, say it, and then tell them what you said.
- Grab their attention with a good hook.
- Maintain eye contact with your audience.
- Integrate active learning techniques, such as brief quizzes, questions, or discussions.
- Create effective visual aids.
- End with a compelling conclusion.

Test-Taking Strategies

Tests are powerful learning tools. First, tests provide you with motivation to engage with and study the material after class. The studying actions you take will increase the likelihood that you will remember the content. Second, the act of retrieving the content helps strengthen memories (Karpicke & Roediger, 2006). Therefore, tests or exams are great learning opportunities. A test is also a way for you to demonstrate what you have learned. There are some test-taking techniques that can help you perform your best.

iStockPhoto/Ferrantraite

Stereotype Threat   Unfortunately, student performance on assessments such as tests is often undermined because of stereotype threat. **Stereotype threat** refers to when a member of a group performs lower because of their awareness of a stereotype. The pressure to not confirm a stereotype leads to anxiety that results in lower performance. For example, Steele (2011) shared research illustrating how White individuals performed more poorly on sports tasks, women performed more poorly on a math assessment, and Black students performed more poorly on a task believed to measure intellectual ability despite all these individuals having high ability in these areas. Fortunately, there is a significant body of research showing that the impact of stereotype threat can be reduced and even eliminated when individuals performing the task are explicitly told that gender or race do not impact the results of the assessment (Steele, 2011).

Learning about stereotype threat can help you recognize it when it happens and perform better on assessments (Johns et al., 2005). Research has shown that engaging in self-affirmations where you acknowledge your achievements and abilities can reduce the impact of stereotype threat (Jones, 2011). Nelson and Knight (2010) conducted an interesting study where they found that students who were instructed to think and write

M-SUR/Shutterstock.com

Table 6.6 Reducing Stereotype Threat Strategies to Minimize the Impact of Stereotype Threat on Performance Adapted from Casad and Bryant (2016)	
Environmental strategies	Surround yourself with positive images and examples of success of others who are similar to you. Using the gender stereotype of math as an example, have photos and success stories of women being successful on mathematical tasks and in careers that require high-level mathematical skills.
Role models and peer group	Find role models or mentors who are similar to you. When possible, attend events with others who are similar to you so that you are not the only one representing your group. Engage in group work that requires all members to work toward a common goal. Surround yourself with others who value you and provide you with feedback that is performance-based.
Attribution training	Meet with a counselor or psychologist or attend a workshop focused on attribution training. Attribution training targets our perception of what contributes to our success or failure and helps us focus on internal, changeable factors such as effort.

about a successful experience before taking a quiz had less anxiety and better performance when compared to students who were instructed to write about their morning. Recalling a successful experience before taking an exam can also help you perform well.

See Table 6.6 for research-based strategies identified by Casad and Bryant (2016) that can reduce stereotype threat and the negative consequences of it.

Multiple-Choice Tests According to research (LoSchiavo & Shatz, 2002; McClain, 1983), all the following multiple-choice test-taking strategies are connected to better exam performance:

iStockPhoto/PeopleImages

- **Anticipating answers.** Read the question and come up with an answer before looking at the possible choices. You will be less likely to fall victim to the distracter items when you use this strategy. Distracter items have been specifically designed to take you off track, but if you are clear on the question and have formulated your own answer, you will be more likely to answer correctly.

- **Reading all choices.** You have probably had an experience where you thought your answer was correct, but your professor indicated that another choice was the better option. If you do not read all the choices, you will not be able to consider all options and determine which is best.

- **Eliminating wrong answers.** Eliminating wrong choices helps to visually remove options you are no longer considering. This can save you time because you will not be tempted to reread and rethink answer options that you know are incorrect.

- **Skipping difficult questions.** If you spend too much time on a difficult question, you may not have enough time to answer questions that might be much easier for you. Before you move on, make your best guess based on the time and cognitive investment you have already made in case you do not have time to return to it later. Skipping difficult questions can also help reduce anxiety. Spending time on difficult questions brings attention to what you do not know, making you more anxious. Skip the difficult questions and find the ones you know to increase your confidence and decrease your anxiety. You may also come across questions later in the exam that trigger a memory, helping you correctly answer the original, difficult question.

- **Changing your answer if you have good reason.** You have probably heard the advice "Stick to your gut and go with your first answer." If you have heard this advice before, you may be surprised to find out that research suggests that changing your answers is often a good, not bad, idea. Students make more wrong to right switches than right to wrong switches when changing their answers (Di Milia, 2007). Shatz and Best (1987) also found that answer changing can have a more positive than negative impact on academic performance if there was a good reason for making the change. Individuals who changed their answer because they misread the question or because of a clue discovered later in the exam made a wrong to right change in 72% of the cases. Based on this research, change your answer whenever you have a good reason.

Multiple-Choice Exam Tips

- Prepare as if you were taking an essay exam.
- Carefully read questions while removing answers from view.
- Highlight key terms.
- Anticipate the answer before reviewing options.
- Read all answer options.
- Eliminate wrong responses.
- Skip difficult questions.
- Change your answer if you have a good reason for doing so but not if you are only guessing.

Short-Answer and Essay Exams Short-answer and essay exams give you the opportunity to articulate and apply your knowledge. You are generally not confined to focusing on one piece of information as you might be in a multiple-choice test question. Instead, you can use your overall knowledge about the topic to produce a good response. This is likely one of the reasons why students prefer short-answer exams over multiple-choice ones (Mingo et al., 2018). Use the following steps to write a good essay response:

iStockPhoto/Ferrantraite

- Planning
- Writing
- Proofreading

All good products start with a plan. Unfortunately, students often forget this important step when answering short-answer or essay questions and start to dive into their response without first thinking about how to best respond. The first step is to fully understand the question. Read the question carefully, underlining key words to keep focused on what the question is asking. For example, if it says compare and contrast, you need to discuss both similarities and differences between the concepts. Despite how thoroughly you discuss the similarities, if you forget to address the differences, it could result in losing half the points.

Spend approximately one fifth of the time you have for the question on this planning stage. Think about what you want to say and how you plan to organize your thoughts. Consider making a quick outline or concept map before you start writing. Start by jotting down the main points you would like to cover and then add details that support these points.

Most of your time will be spent on writing the response. Begin with a strong opening that directly relates to the question. This is often referred to as a topic sentence. This allows the reader to know where you stand with the issue or what you believe is most important.

Each subsequent paragraph should also have a clear opening sentence that tells the reader about the focus for that paragraph. Add more specific information about the topic through examples and supporting details. Writing an organized response is important.

Ending with a strong conclusion is an effective way to reiterate or emphasize your main point. Be sure you use this opportunity to leave the reader with a clear understanding of what you perceive to be most important. It is what the professor will remember most when grading your exam, so show what you know.

After you finish writing your response, there is one more very critical step you must do before you hand in your exam—proofreading your work. You should give yourself approximately one fifth of the time you have to complete the question for this important step.

Begin the proofreading process by rereading the question, carefully focusing on what is being asked. It is not uncommon for students to get off track when answering a question, writing about concepts that were not directly asked about in the question. Also, make sure that you have answered all the subparts of the question. Check off each sub-question as you review your response so that you are certain you gave a complete response. If you miss something, it could negatively impact your test score. Finally, check your organizational structure, spelling, and grammar.

Essay Writing Tips

- Read the question carefully.
- Plan effectively by jotting down main ideas and supporting details.
- Begin with a strong opening that sets the stage for your response.
- End with a solid conclusion that directs the reader back to your main point.
- Read the question again and check off the parts you answered.
- Proofread for spelling, grammar, and organization.

Take-Home and Online Exams   Take-home and online exams, although sometimes similar in format, can be a very different experience from in-class exams. Although many students often report less anxiety when taking tests outside of the classroom setting (Stowell & Bennett, 2010), it is important that you still prepare well. Take-home and online exams can be quite challenging in nature, and students often underestimate how much studying and preparation is needed. This can result in poor performance.

iStockPhoto/insta_photos

In addition to being challenging, take-home or online exams may also be more time-consuming than traditional tests. It is therefore essential that you carve out enough time to successfully prepare for and complete the exam. Look at your syllabus, or ask your professor for details about the testing process so that you can plan accordingly.

Knowing what to expect with these different test formats is important. Online testing can vary quite a bit from class to class. Know the technology requirements, and be sure you are using a computer and web browser that provides you with what is needed. You may also want to inquire about what you should do if you have a technology problem when completing the test.

Before an online test, ask how the test will be set up. Sometimes you may only be allowed one attempt at the test, but in other cases you may be allowed to take the quiz or test more than once. You may be able to go back and change your answers, but this may not always be the case. Some online quizzes or tests may be timed while others may be untimed. When tests are timed, a clock may be running on the computer screen or you may have to watch the time yourself.

Many online testing programs will immediately grade your test upon completion. Students really appreciate the immediate feedback associated with online tests (Nardi & Ranieri, 2019). Learning from your mistakes is a great way to increase your knowledge.

As with all testing, it is essential that you uphold the academic integrity of the course and engage in appropriate test-taking behaviors when completing take-home and online exams. Be sure you are clear about what materials, if any, you are permitted to use. To avoid the temptation to engage in academically dishonest behaviors, practice good studying skills and focus on the goal: learning. Strong preparation leads to successful outcomes—no matter what the test format!

Reflecting on Exam Performance After you get feedback on your test performance, it is a good idea to engage in reflection. Determine what you did well and where improvements are needed. This reflection will help you improve performance in the future. **Exam wrappers** are reflective assignments that students complete after an exam. In a study by Hodges et al. (2020), students answered the following questions:

iStockPhoto/Chainarong Prasertthai

1. Did you feel prepared for the exam?
2. What did you do to prepare for the exam (i.e. read before class, come to class, thinking, answering questions or doing practice problems)?
3. Did you use certain assignments or resources as learning tools or just get them done as fast as possible?
4. How many problems or questions did you complete before the exam?
5. Did you miss questions due to not reading carefully (or a subject-specific reason)?

6. What was the main reason for missing exam questions?

7. What type of question did you miss the most?

8. Did you know how to get help in the course?

9. Do you feel that you have made a good assessment of your learning habits and know how to adjust your approach? (p. 70-71).

Results showed that students in several different science courses had higher overall course grades when they completed exam wrappers. Edlund (2020) also found that exam wrappers led to improved course performance for students taking psychology courses. Thus, engaging in this reflective process after an exam will help you perform better on future learning tasks.

Assignments and Tests Quick Quiz

1. When revising your work, what should you focus on first?

2. What is the best way to combat performance anxiety?

3. What are some strategies you can use to engage the audience during a presentation?

4. What PowerPoint strategies did you learn from Mayer's (2009) multi-media research?

5. What strategies do high performing students use when taking a multiple-choice test?

6. What are the three steps associated with writing a good response to a short-answer or essay question?

7. How do take-home and online exams differ from traditional exams?

Chapter 6

Chapter Summary: Note-Taking Model

Let us summarize what you have learned in this chapter. The Cornell Map Notes model is used for this chapter. Remember, it is not expected that your notes will look like this right after class or reading. It takes time to organize your notes and re-package them. It is time well spent, though, because you learn the content better as you organize it, and you will have a fabulous foundation from which to study for your exams! There are several ways to use this section:

- **Preview:** Read the model before reading the chapter to familiarize yourself with the content.

- **Compare:** Compare the notes you took on the chapter to the model provided.

- **Study:** The model along with your notes and other course materials are great resources for studying.

Cornell Method Model

What is academic integrity?	Creating work products that are based on your ideas, citing sources that helped shape and guide your work.
How can I avoid unintentional plagiarism?	• Learn about academic integrity and dishonesty. • Learn how to cite sources using MLA or APA style. • Practice paraphrasing.
What strategies should I use to write a paper?	• Focus on the purpose of the paper first. • Choose a topic that is narrow versus broad. • Use information literacy skills to find and evaluate information. • Write annotated bibliographies. • Create a synthesis matrix. • Create on outline. • Write several drafts. • Focus on big picture first when revising and then proofread.
What is the best way to manage performance anxiety?	Prepare and practice.
What are tips to create an effective presentation?	• Start with an interesting hook. • Maintain eye contact and use active learning strategies such as the Turn and Talk. • Create PowerPoint slides that are based on multimedia principles (rely mostly on images, draw attention to most important part of the slide, only include essential content). • End with a clear summary.
What is stereotype threat?	If you are a member of a group and are aware of the stereotypes associated with that group, you will likely experience anxiety because you do not want to confirm the stereotype; as a result, you may perform more poorly.
What are some test-taking tips?	• For multiple-choice tests, predict the answer before reviewing the options, read all options, eliminate incorrect choices, and skip difficult questions. • For essay exams, first map out a plan, then write your response and review it. • For take home and online exams, find out what is expected and determine how much time you will need to prepare and take the exam. • Reflect on your performance after you receive your grade so you can increase learning and perform well in the future.

SUMMARY: Academic integrity is extremely important. Students who learn about how to engage in honest actions, and learn how to cite and paraphrase will be less likely to engage in unintentional dishonest behaviors. There are many different types of assignments. It is important to engage in preparation and planning before writing a paper. Preparation will also reduce performance anxiety for other assignments such as presentations and exams. When giving a presentation, use engagement strategies and develop slides with multimedia principles in mind. There are many different strategies for performing well on tests such as predicting an answer before reviewing the options and planning before writing an essay response.

Chapter 7

Academic Planning and Staying on Track

You're on the road to success when you realize that failure is only a detour.
— *Source Unknown*

iStockPhoto/FluxFactory

1 Why is it important to meet with your advisor and develop an academic plan?

2 What requirements do you need to fulfill to graduate?

3 What are experiential learning opportunities and what is their value?

4 What is academic self-regulation? What strategies can help you determine whether you are on track to achieve your goals?

5 What does it mean to be resilient and have grit?

6 What stress management techniques work?

7 How can you stay motivated?

Exploring the Research in Summary

Research Study Citation:

Iglesias, S. L., Azzara, S., Squillace, M., Jeifetz, M., Lores Arnais, M. R., Desimone, M. F., & Diaz, L. E. (2005). A study on the effectiveness of a stress management programme for college students. *Pharmacy Education, 5*(1), 27–31.

Introduction: The Research Question

What question did the researcher seek to answer?

Knowing that college students often experience stress, Iglesias et al. (2005) explored whether teaching students about how to manage stress reduced their stress levels. Specifically, the research question was: Does a stress management program for undergraduate students decrease stress levels?

Method: The Study

Who participated in the study? What did the researchers ask the participants to do?

A total of 136 second-year college students completed a questionnaire about a variety of psychological factors such as stress and anxiety. Eighty-nine of these students indicated they wanted to improve their stress management skills, and a group of 10 students was randomly selected to do so. The other students had an opportunity to participate after the study was over. The selected students participated in a stress management program that taught them about various coping skills such as deep breathing, relaxation, visual imagery, time management, and challenging thoughts. In addition to completing the questionnaire, these students also had their psychophysiological stress levels measured through saliva and a computer-based polygraph. Stress levels were assessed prior to and after the intervention.

Results: The Findings

What was the answer to the research question?

At the end of the stress management program, students had lower levels of stress and anxiety. This was evidenced by lower scores on anxiety inventories and lower levels of salivary cortisol. See Figure 7.1.

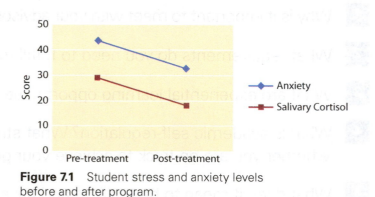

Figure 7.1   Student stress and anxiety levels before and after program.

Discussion and So-What Factor

How can YOU use this information as a student?

These results suggest that learning about stress management techniques does reduce stress levels in college students. College students can take advantage of stress management workshops or individual counseling to learn how to use techniques such as relaxation, deep breathing, visual imagery, time management, and shifting negative thoughts. Workshops on these topics may be offered through the counseling or student activities office. Learning these skills can improve your ability to manage stress and can also positively impact learning in general.

Creating Academic Plans and Monitoring Progress

Academic planning involves mapping out a plan for completing all the academic requirements needed for graduation. This includes identifying which electives to take and determining what additional learning opportunities such as co-curricular activities and study abroad you would like to take advantage of as a college student. Planning can also help you complete your degree in a timely fashion.

As you know, you will need to complete a variety of required courses to graduate and many of these courses are sequential in nature. This means that there will be some courses that need to be taken in a certain order. If you do not take some of the required courses in the beginning of the sequence early on in your college journey, you may have difficulty graduating on schedule. Mapping out an academic plan will help you see when courses need to be taken so that you can stay on track with your graduation timeline. In addition, there may be amazing opportunities such as internships and study abroad experiences that need to be planned well in advance.

GOAL ACHIEVED

0% [OOOOOOOOOOOOOOOOO] 100%

iStockPhoto/anyaberkut

Connecting with Your Advisor

Most colleges or universities will assign you an **advisor**. Colleges and universities use a variety of different job titles, such as advisor, counselor, student development specialist, mentor, and coach, to describe this position. We will use the term *advisor* in this section as it is still the most widely used title. Advisors serve as your academic and career mentor, helping you determine your academic and career goals and then assisting you with mapping out a plan to achieve these goals.

iStockPhoto/Drazen

Too often, students rely solely on information from their peers instead of getting information from campus experts such as advisors. Your advisor has professional and institutional expertise that your friends may not have. Students who use advising services, as compared to students who do not, have an increased knowledge of resources and academic requirements, higher grade point averages, are more likely to continue in college, have higher levels of self-efficacy, and are more likely to graduate (Alvarado & Olson, 2020; Kot, 2014).

Using their professional experiences and background, advisors provide you with a wide array of support and services. Advisors can engage you in self-assessment, help you identify your goals, help you develop strategies to monitor your progress and achievement, connect you to academic and career resources, encourage and support you, help you make networking connections, and assist you with mapping out an educational and career plan.

By meeting with your advisor, you will be better informed of opportunities aligned to your goals so that you can take full advantage of the offerings and experiences at your college. For example, advisors can share information about upcoming events related to various career fields or new internship opportunities. Attending career days and finding opportunities to learn skills and network will help you reach your goals.

In a study conducted by Christian and Sprinkle (2013), students noted that advisors also provided students with motivation. This can be particularly helpful and important if you are struggling with an academic task or are feeling overwhelmed. Your advisor can serve as a great source of support throughout your college journey and beyond.

How Advisors Can Help You

- Help you determine your interests, values, and abilities
- Assist with identifying possible career pathways
- Provide access to academic and career resources
- Inform you of academic and professional opportunities
- Provide encouragement and motivation, especially when challenges are encountered
- Expand your network
- Assist with course selection
- Serve as a member of your support system

Understanding Curriculum Requirements

Knowing the curriculum structure at your institution provides you with valuable information you can use to make good academic choices. Although curriculum structure will of course vary from institution to institution, there are some common elements that are generally true at most institutions. Most degree programs can be broken down into three main components: general education or core requirements that all students must take regardless of selected major, major courses in your area of interest, and electives (see Figure 7.2). Students who understand curriculum structure will be more likely to graduate on schedule because they will choose courses that fulfill these graduation requirements.

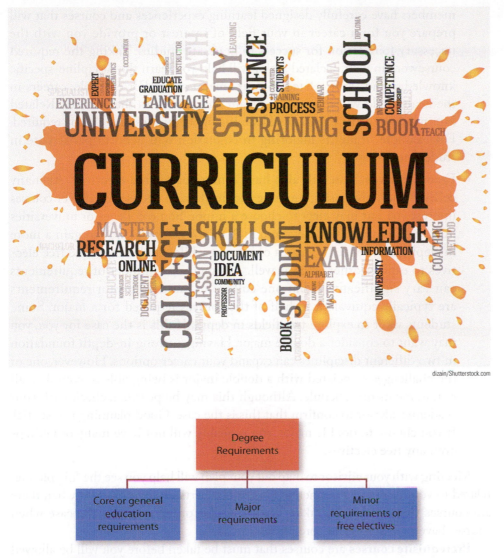

dizain/Shutterstock.com

Degree Requirements

Core or general education requirements

Major requirements

Minor requirements or free electives

Figure 7.2   Structure of degree requirements.

- **General education.** The **general education** coursework is designed to help you develop general knowledge and problem-solving skills that will help you be a productive citizen while also benefiting you in your desired career (Beckam, 2020). The general education or core requirement structure varies from college to college; however, most colleges and universities require standard categories such as communication, math, sciences, social sciences, and humanities. Some students struggle with understanding the value and purpose of general education or core courses that may not on the surface seem to be directly related to their major. However, research has found that general education courses are beneficial. Specifically, a liberal arts education has been found to positively connect to lifelong learning, intercultural effectiveness, the ability to be a leader, and overall well-being (Seifert et al., 2008). Understanding the value of general education course and major requirements can increase your motivation to succeed.

- **Major courses.** As you would expect, you will also need to complete a series of major-specific courses to graduate. Every discipline or field requires specific skills and background knowledge to be successful, and faculty members have carefully designed learning experiences and courses that will prepare you for a career in your field of interest or provide you with the necessary foundation for success in graduate studies. Taking the required coursework in your declared major will help you learn the discipline-specific knowledge and skills related to your area of study. For example, careers in the health field will require significant coursework in the sciences. Related internships or other experiential learning opportunities may also be required. For example, students majoring in education will need to participate in student teaching.

- **Free Electives.** You will also have a number of free electives. At many colleges and universities, you have the freedom to choose whichever courses interest you but may elect to choose a minor. Some colleges or universities may require you to choose a minor. A minor is a great way to gain a more in-depth knowledge in an area of interest while still having some free electives to explore other areas as well. Although the number of requirements can vary significantly from one college to another, minor requirements are typically equivalent to half of the courses required for a major. Some students want to explore two fields in depth. If this is the case for you, you may want to consider a double major. Having a strong in-depth foundation in two different disciplines can expand your career options. However, one of the challenges associated with a double major is being able to complete all requirements on schedule. Although this may be possible, check with your academic advisor to confirm that this is the case. Good planning is essential. If you choose to double major, you probably will not have many or perhaps even any free electives.

Meeting with your advisor to map out your plan will help you see the "big picture" related to your degree requirements. This can be particularly important when there are courses that need to be taken in a particular order, which is the case when courses have prerequisites or corequisites.

Prerequisite courses are courses that must be taken before you will be allowed to register for and take another course. For example, English I is typically a prerequisite for English II, and Introduction to Psychology is often a prerequisite for most other psychology courses. **Corequisites** are courses that you need to take at the same time, or before, as another desired course. For example, you may need to take a math course at the same time as, or before, a science course. This is because the content is related, or the skills will be needed for success in the current course.

In some instances, there could be a series of courses that need to be taken in a specific order. In these situations, if you do not start the first course in the sequence early enough, you may not be able to graduate when originally planned. Therefore, it is critical that you start meeting with your advisor during your first semester. Effective planning will help you meet your goals in a timely fashion.

You can find information about prerequisites, corequisites, and sequencing issues related to your curriculum on the college or university website. It is usually found in the college catalog section but may also be on the department's website. Ask your advisor or academic department for assistance if you have difficulty finding the degree requirements for your major or have questions about the required courses or experiences.

You can also explore the pros and cons associated with double majors and minors. The sooner you decide on whether you want to choose a minor or double major, the better. This will enable you to plan well and graduate on schedule.

Remember, you do not make it to the graduation ceremony based on how long you are a student or the number of credits you have earned. Instead, graduating is based on whether you have completed the required courses, so learning what is expected of you during your first semester is very helpful.

To complete a bachelor's degree in four years, you will need to take approximately 15 credits per semester or 30 credits per year. The exact number of courses can vary based on your institution and major-specific requirements. You can, of course, attend part-time but it will then take you much longer to meet the graduation requirements.

Ask your advisor to help you map a multi-year educational plan. Most colleges have mapping or planning tools built into their online registration system. Many systems allow you to try out "what-if" scenarios. For example, the online system may be able to map out how your plan would change if you decided to change your major, added a minor, opted not to take summer courses, or if you needed to go to school part time due to personal or family issues. Planning is critical so that you get the most out of your college experience and complete your degree requirements on schedule.

Exploring Experiential Learning Opportunities

Experiential learning typically refers to learning skills and knowledge beyond what the traditional classroom experience offers. Examples of experiential learning opportunities include internships, service learning, and studying abroad. Your college or university may require you to participate in one or more types of experiential learning to graduate. If you are not required, you will still want to explore these amazing opportunities and determine whether you would like to take advantage of these incredibly valuable experiences. Talk to your advisor about what options are available and build them into your educational plan.

According to a national survey, 52% of college students are participating in experiential learning experiences (Association of American Colleges & Universities, 2010). Many college graduates reported that their experiential learning experiences were the most valuable part of their college experience (Stone & Petrick, 2013). Researchers have found that students reported higher levels of connection to classmates and their instructor, increased motivation, and improved learning when they

engaged in experiential learning (Fedesco et al., 2020). Experiential learning may be especially helpful to students who identify with a marginalized group and feel disconnected to the campus community because through these experiences, they can make important connections and expand their network (T. Ayeni, personal communication, July 22, 2021).

Employers have indicated that they are more likely to hire college graduates with experiential learning experiences (Association of American Colleges & Universities, 2010). Employers especially value the problem-solving, project management, and communication skills that students learn during experiential

Undrey/Shutterstock.com

HowLettery/Shutterstock.com

learning opportunities such as internships (Galbraith & Mondal, 2020). They also value employees who exhibit timeliness, initiative, commitment to quality work, and who accept criticism, skills often developed via internships and related experiences (Gault et al., 2010). Consider adding experiential learning opportunities such as internships or study abroad to your educational plan.

Internships

Internships are opportunities for you to gain work experience in your field of study while also earning credit toward graduation. Internships enable you to apply what you have been learning in your coursework to a real work environment. Based on a review of 57 different studies, Velez and Giner (2015) found that internships benefit students, employers, and colleges and universities in many ways.

- **Student benefits.** Students benefit through increased employment opportunities, improvement of skills needed in their future career, and receiving guidance related to the career decision-making process. In a study conducted by Barnett (2012), students who took advantage of internship opportunities learned the importance of communication, autonomy, and teamwork, leaving their internship with more realistic expectations about what it takes to be successful in the workplace. Other researchers have found that students increased their skills and strengthened their commitment to and identity with their chosen field of study (Lucero et al., 2021). Internships can provide you with valuable work experience that can strengthen your résumé. Internships are also connected to an increased likelihood of being employed full time after graduation and earning higher salaries (Blair & Millea, 2004; Gault et al., 2010). In a study conducted by Callanan and Benzing (2004), it was found that 51% of seniors who did an internship had a job offer after graduation while only 13% of students who did not do an internship had secured a job. Weible (2009) also found that students who participated in internships received more job offers.

- **Employer benefits.** By hiring interns, employers benefit from their enthusiasm, creative ideas, and eagerness to learn new skills. It also costs less to hire an intern versus a professional staff person, so it is a financial savings to employers. Internships also provide companies with an opportunity to see if an individual is a good fit for a permanent position after their graduation. As you can imagine, many employers prefer to hire a current intern or former intern for a full-time position over an external candidate whom they have never met. In research reviewed by Galbraith and Mondal (2020), it was reported that 62% of interns were offered employment.

- **College or university benefits.** Colleges and universities benefit from internships because they are seen as essential marketing tools to attract students. Students are more likely to attend colleges and universities with strong internship programs. Thus, internships can enhance the college or university's reputation.

Most students participate in internships in their junior or senior years of college, but there may be opportunities to get involved with this type of experience even as a first-year or second-year student. Gaining internship or related work experience earlier versus later can help you determine if you are on the best career path. Working in your desired field is a great way to get a first-hand look at the working environment. This hands-on learning experience may validate your career choice, strengthening your desire to work in the field. Or you may discover that this career is not what you expected, and you may even decide to change your major or career goal. Either way, the experience is valuable.

Internships require time and therefore can be a challenge to many students who have limited time. Students working full-time, for example, may not have any additional hours to devote to an internship experience. Even for those working part-time, the internship schedule might conflict with current work, school, or family responsibilities. In these situations, creative solutions may be needed. For example, investigate virtual internship experiences, which significantly increased because of the COVID-19 pandemic, as these experiences would not require travel time and may offer flexible hours. Explore whether there is an internship or job shadowing, where you learn about a career by following someone in that career for a day or so, opportunity within your current organization. For example, if you are a marketing student working at a restaurant, ask your supervisor if you might be able to do a flexible internship with the marketing department for that restaurant chain (T. Ayeni, personal communication, July 22, 2021). For smaller companies without a marketing department, you can inquire about if they would be interested in you developing or enhancing their social media presence. You might be able to complete these tasks on your breaks or before or after your shift.

In addition to internships, another way to gain work experience in college is cooperative education programs, often referred to as co-ops. Co-ops are often full-time, paid practical working experiences, whereas internships are often part-time and may be paid or unpaid. Both internships and cooperative education programs can take place during a regular fall or spring semester or during a summer session. Consult with your advisor or the career services department to find out what types of internships and cooperative education programs are available at your college or university.

Study Abroad

Studying abroad involves going to another country to learn and continue your studies. When you study abroad, you are not only immersed in the culture and language of another country but will continue to make progress toward your degree requirements

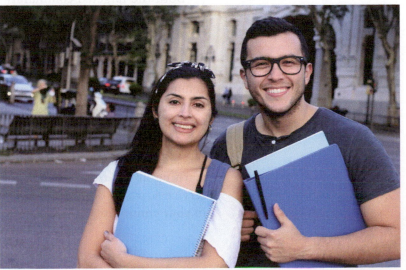

AJR_photo/Shutterstock.com

iStockPhoto/Izusek

because you will be taking college courses. Many colleges offer study abroad opportunities in a variety of formats such as full semester or year-long experiences, and briefer experiences in the summer, winter, or even during spring break.

Although some students may eagerly jump at study abroad opportunities, others may be more hesitant to do so. This new learning experience may be outside your comfort zone, but remember, you learn more when you engage in new experiences. When deciding if studying abroad is the right choice for you, consider the research. Researchers have found that students who engaged in study abroad were more likely to graduate on time and with a higher grade-point average than students who did not (Bell et al., 2021). According to this large-scale study, the benefit was greatest for students of color (Bell et al., 2021). Other researchers have found that the benefits of studying abroad included having a sense of increased independence, being more open-minded, and having increased cultural awareness and competency (Earnest et al., 2016; Hadis, 2005). The skills developed while studying abroad will serve you well in all aspects of your life.

Service Learning

Service learning is another way to learn beyond the classroom walls. "Service learning is a teaching and learning strategy that integrates meaningful community service with instruction and reflection to enrich the learning experience, teach civic responsibility, and strengthen communities" (National Service-Learning Clearinghouse, 2013). Learning skills and knowledge about the course content is a key component and the service is integrated into the course curriculum.

Both the targeted community and the student benefit from service learning (DeLaune et al., 2010). Students find service learning to be quite rewarding because they know that they are making a difference through their community service work. Researchers have found that benefits of participating in service learning included improved skills, confidence, motivation, and awareness of and commitment to social justice issues (Marco-Gardoqui et al., 2020).

The targeted agency or organization also benefits. For example, Trail-Ross (2012) required students in a gerontology course to facilitate programs in an Adult Day Program for the late adulthood population. This project benefited the individuals at the Adult Day Program while assisting the students with learning about this population and building communication skills. Explore service-learning opportunities at your college to learn while making a difference in your community.

who participated in a one-hour training on the importance of focusing on change-able, internal factors had course grades and overall grade point averages that were almost one letter grade higher than students who did not participate in this training. This is amazing—a one-hour training course and almost an entire letter grade higher! To take advantage of this research finding, simply invest a little of your time to focus on the importance of attributions.

Shifting to a Productive Attribution Style

Ask yourself: What factors within my control might have played a role in my success or failure?

For academic tasks, focus on:

- The amount of time you invested and your study schedule
- The strategies you used when reading, note-taking, and studying
- Whether or not you asked for help or support
- Overall effort

Creating Academic Plans and Monitoring Progress Quick Quiz

1. Why is it a good idea to meet with your advisor?
2. What are the typical requirements needed to earn a bachelor's degree?
3. Why are internships or co-ops valuable?
4. What are the steps involved in academic self-regulation?
5. What is attribution theory?
6. What is the most productive way to interpret mistakes?

Being Resilient and Developing Grit

Life can be challenging sometimes. However, these challenges do not have to stop you from meeting with success. In fact, many individuals can persevere despite being faced with numerous adverse or challenging situations. Resilience and grit are two important concepts that explain what contributes to successful outcomes even when you are faced with significant challenges.

Resilience is a person's ability to bounce back after experiencing diffi-cult, stressful, or even traumatic events.

iStockPhoto/Ridofranz

iStockPhoto/AntonioGuillem

Being resilient is connected to your overall well-being (Schuur et al., 2021). **Grit** is related to resilience because in part it is about your ability to be resilient when faced with adversity, but it requires more than resilience. Grit also involves being deeply committed to something and sticking with it on a long-term basis (Perkins-Gough, 2013). Duckworth et al. (2007) define grit as "perseverance and passion for long-term goals" (p. 1087), meaning individuals continue to work toward goals even when faced with failure or challenges along the way. Grit has been found to be associated with graduating on schedule (Goyer et al., 2021).

Effective stress management and high levels of motivation are needed to be resilient and gritty. Developing effective stress management strategies can help you reduce stress levels and cope with the stressors that you encounter so that you can continue to work toward and achieve your goals. Putting motivational theories into practice so that you can get and stay motivated will help you stick with your goals despite challenges you may face.

Managing Stress

Stress is a part of life. Everyone has experienced stress from positive events and situations such as starting a new job and negative events and situations such as a relationship ending. Change is stressful, so just starting a new journey, such as college, is reason enough to feel some level of stress. A research study conducted by Pierceall and Kiem (2007) found that most college students reported having a moderate amount of stress so if you are feeling stressed, know that you are not alone. Rix et al. (2021) found that stress levels often increase throughout the semester.

Keeping your stress at a moderate level will lead to your best performance (Rath, 2008). Some anxiety is good because it can serve as energy to help you perform well. Aydin (2017) found that stress was positive because students who were experiencing stress did better academically. Stress related to tasks that are connected to goals and perceived to be challenging but doable improves performance (Travis et al., 2020). This positive type of anxiety is referred to as **facilitative anxiety**. Researchers have found that when students view their anxiety as facilitative, this leads to improved academic performance (Strack & Esteves, 2015).

Too much anxiety, however, is not good and can hinder your performance (Raffety et al., 1997). This is referred to as **debilitating anxiety**. In a national survey conducted by the American College Health Association, college students identified "stress as the number one impediment to academic performance" (as cited in Ramler et al., 2016, p. 179). Often students from marginalized populations can experience higher levels of stress. Hernández & Villoda (2020) found that Latinx students, for example, experienced high levels of stress due to racial microaggressions, and this can be connected to increased mental health issues. Students who learn about how to effectively manage their stress report having fewer symptoms of anxiety and stress (Iglesias et al., 2005; Stallman et al., 2019).

To help you keep anxiety at a moderate and productive level, you can use a variety of stress management techniques that work.

Sleep, Nutrition, and Exercise

Sleeping well, eating healthily, and exercising are all essential stress management strategies. Practicing these basic stress management techniques can help you keep stress at a manageable level and cope effectively. Sleeping, eating, and exercising habits impact your academic success.

iStockPhoto/andresr

Studies show that poor sleep patterns are associated with lower academic performance (Trockel et al., 2000). In a study by Orzech et al., (2011), students reported that poor sleep affected the quality of their schoolwork. Specifically, poor sleep led to students dropping a course, earning a lower grade on an important assignment or the overall course, falling asleep in class and skipping class. They also found that students who did not report having an all-nighter, skipping sleep for an entire night, had higher grade point averages (3.26) than students who did report pulling all-nighters (3.05).

Unfortunately, most college students are not sleeping the optimal number of hours per night. Sleeping too much or too little has been linked to physical and mental health issues (Peltzer & Pengpid, 2016). Based on a survey with students from 26 countries, it was found that 39.2% of students reported getting less than six hours of sleep per night, 46.9% reported getting seven to eight hours per night and 13.9% got more than nine hours per night. Students also struggle with getting good quality sleep. In a study conducted by Abu et al. (2020), only 38.3% of participants in the study were good sleepers while 45.5% were poor sleepers, and 17.2% were very poor sleepers. Sleep is important, so take time to focus on how you can ensure you are getting the right amount of sleep and that it is of high quality.

To improve your sleep quality, try the following:

- Stick to a consistent sleep schedule, going to sleep and waking up at similar times each day
- Establish a sleeping environment that is free of distractions and is quiet and dark
- Avoid caffeine in the evening hours
- Engage in relaxing activities such as reading or listening to music prior to going to sleep
- Avoid use of technology prior to going to sleep
- Exercise regularly

Researchers have also found that eating healthy meals has been linked to increased school performance and higher self-esteem (Kristjánsson et al., 2010). Students often face challenges with healthy eating habits due to limited time. Latinx students in a study conducted by Rowland (2008), for example, reported that it was easier to choose unhealthy options because they were more easily accessible in vending machines or the cafeteria and they did not have time to prepare healthy meals.

To improve your eating habits, try the following:

- Pack a healthy snack or lunch so you are not tempted by unhealthy options from the vending machines.
- Choose healthy food options instead of sugary or salty snacks.
- Notice when you eat and why. Eat when you are hungry. We often eat for emotional reasons such as feeling stressed. When this happens, choose a stress management strategy that will help you manage your emotions.

Exercise can also help us prevent and combat stress. Schultchen et al. (2019), for example, found that exercise improved mood and affect. Physical activity has also been found to be connected to higher self-esteem and better academic performance (Kristjánsson et al., 2010). Unfortunately, many college students are not engaging in physical activities on a regular basis, but instead are spending significant amounts of time sitting. Lee and Kim (2019) found that sitting for long periods of time was connected to higher levels of stress, depression, and anxiety.

Exercising for just 30 minutes a day can significantly improve your mood and ability to cope (Hansen et al., 2001). Although any type of physical activity can be beneficial, Olafsdottir et al., (2020) found that walking in nature was an especially effective strategy. Walking in nature reduced stress and improved mood more than walking on a treadmill. Consult your doctor before you begin an exercise program to confirm that the program you select is a good one for you.

To increase your physical activity, try the following:

- Talk a longer route to walk to class
- Check out the fitness center on campus
- Establish a consistent schedule for exercising and stick with it
- Ask a friend to exercise with you

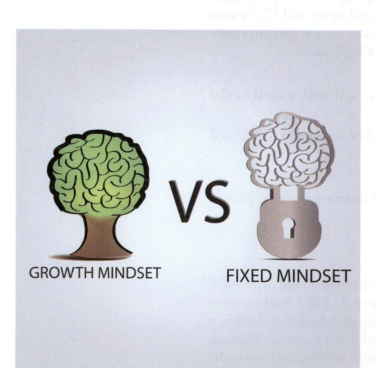

GROWTH MINDSET   VS   FIXED MINDSET

Teentoinks/Shutterstock.com

Mindset

Having a positive, productive mindset is one of the most powerful factors associated with being resilient. Individuals who are hopeful or optimistic about the future are more likely to persevere when faced with challenging situations.

Researchers have found that being optimistic is linked to improved academic performance (Seirup & Rose, 2011; Henry et al., 1993) and lower dropout rates among college students (Nes, 2009). Being optimistic and hopeful about the future can therefore help you meet with success in college. The good news is that the feelings of hope and optimism can be learned (Marsay, 2020; Forgeard & Seligman, 2012). Feldman and Dreher (2012), for instance, found that a 90-minute session on hope resulted in higher levels of hope and purpose.

There are several ways you can become more optimistic. Remember, it takes time and effort to change your thinking, but it can be done. Here are some strategies:

- Focus on the positive. For instance, keep a journal and write down three to five positive events from each day.
- Start each day with positive self-affirmations or thoughts such as, "I can and will accomplish my goals today."
- Talk about positive events with others. When you catch yourself talking about something negative, force yourself to think of a positive part of the situation, too.
- Surround yourself with optimistic people—happiness can be contagious!

Carol Dweck has conducted numerous, fascinating research studies on mindset about intelligence and how this plays a critical role in success. Dweck identified two different types of mindset:

- **A fixed mindset.** Individuals with a **fixed mindset** believe that intelligence is something they are born with and there is not much, if anything, that can be done to increase their intelligence. In essence, it is viewed as fixed or set in stone. If you experience failure and have a fixed mindset, it is likely that you will give up because you think you are not smart enough to successfully complete the task, so there is no point in even trying.
- **A growth mindset.** Individuals with a **growth mindset** view intelligence as something that is changeable or malleable, believing intelligence can be improved with practice, effort, and learning. If you have a growth mindset and experience failure, you will likely exert more effort or try different strategies, viewing the failure experience as a learning opportunity. Because you are engaging in productive thoughts and actions, you are more likely to experience success with a growth mindset (Dweck et al., 2014).

Research has found that students who learn about growth mindset are more successful. In a study by Broda et al. (2018), for example, they found that Latinx students who participated in a growth mindset intervention improved their academic performance, with grade point averages climbing by 0.4 in one semester. The intervention involved reading a short article on how intelligence is malleable, reflecting and writing about times they used a growth mindset, and sharing what they learned in a letter to another student. Thus, learning about how you can increase your intelligence can help you meet with success.

Challenging nonproductive thoughts is an important mindset stress management strategy. Much of our stress caused by our interpretations or perceptions of events rather than the events themselves. Not everyone experiences the same level of stress following the same event. Individuals who perceive situations as being more negative tend to experience higher levels of stress. Sometimes you can catastrophize an event, believing a situation is much worse than it truly is.

Shifting from negative interpretations to more realistic and productive ones can reduce your stress level and increase your motivation. Ask yourself questions to help keep situations in perspective and to focus on the positive. Here are a few questions you can ask yourself:

- What evidence is there that my thoughts are true?
- What would I tell a friend if they were experiencing the same thought?
- What would someone who views this situation positively say?
- How much will this matter in the future?

iStockPhoto/MangoStar_Studio

Support System

Regardless of what type of challenging or stressful situation you encounter, being connected to others is one of the best predictors of whether you will be resilient (Ungar, 2013). According to the American Psychological Association (2019), "emotional support is an important protective factor for dealing with life's difficulties" (para 2). Sharing your thoughts and concerns with someone you trust can significantly reduce your stress level. According to Duckworth (2016), every person she interviewed who was gritty "could point to someone in their life who, at the right time and in the right way, encouraged them to aim high and provided badly needed confidence and support" (p. 220).

Research has found that having a strong support system can help you stay in school and achieve academic success (Wilcox et al., 2005). It is also associated with better mental health. Hefner and Eisenberg (2009), for instance, found that students who had a low-quality support system, compared to students with a high-quality support system, were six times more likely to be depressed.

Quality matters more than quantity when it comes to support systems. Werner (1989) found that resilient individuals had at least one person in their lives who provided a high level of support. It is not how many people you have in your support system, but rather whether you are receiving the support you need. Some individuals may need only one or two important, supportive people in their lives. Others may need to expand beyond a few people and rely on a larger support network to meet their various needs. Researchers have shown that individuals with a high level of support were more likely to be resilient (Bonanno et al., 2007).

Although most students reported relying primarily on friends and family when they experience stress (Bledsoe et al., 2018), expanding your support system to include others who understand your situation can help. For example, a classmate may understand the challenges associated with school-related stress while a co-worker might better understand work-related stress (American Psychological Association, 2019). During college, it can therefore be helpful to expand your support team to include faculty, staff, and classmates who understand challenges related to being a college student.

There may be times when you need to talk with a professional about your personal stressors. If this is the case, you can seek out a psychologist or counselor at your college or university. Colleges often offer confidential counseling at no cost. Referrals to outside agencies or psychologists in private practice can also be shared with you. If you are struggling with significant issues, adding a mental health professional to your support network can be helpful. Researchers have found that students who have used counseling services improved their grades (Cholewa et al., 2015).

Relaxation and Mindfulness

Two excellent stress management strategies are muscle relaxation and mindfulness. Because we often have physical tension in our bodies when we experience stress, **muscle relaxation strategies** can also help reduce stress. To use this technique, concentrate on one muscle at a time, tensing and relaxing the muscle before moving on to the next muscle. The contrast between the tension and state of relaxation can be quite significant. Research has shown that learning progressive muscle relaxation techniques can help you better cope with the stressors in your life (Pluess, 2009).

iStockPhoto/francescoch

Mindfulness "is most commonly defined as the state of being attentive to and aware of what is taking place in the present" (Brown, 2003, p. 822). Mindfulness requires you to draw your attention to what is happening now and your reactions to what is happening. When practicing mindfulness, pay close attention to breathing sensations. Focusing on your breathing brings your attention to what is happening at this moment, which is the primary goal. Robin et al. (2013) suggested the following ways to be mindful:

- Direct all your attention to one task you are doing at that moment.
- Remove distractions such as your phone when eating or working.
- Practice taking deep breaths throughout the day.
- Pay attention to information coming in through your senses.
- Respond to your body, stretching and breathing when you experience tension.

Researchers have found that mindfulness is associated with positive academic outcomes such as improved grades (Tope-Banjoko et al., 2020). College students who practiced mindfulness were also more likely to make decisions that were aligned with their goals (Brown, 2003) and less likely to engage in negative coping strategies such as abusing alcohol (Bodenlos et al., 2013).

Researchers have found that first-year students benefit from engaging in mindfulness-based stress reduction training. Ramler et al. (2016), for example, found that participating in mindfulness training as part of a first-year seminar course resulted in better adjustment to college and reduced stress levels as compared to students who were taking courses that did not include mindfulness training.

Researchers have been investigating the neuroscientific evidence behind the practice of mindfulness. Tang et al. (2015) noted that "there is emerging evidence that mindfulness meditation might cause neuroplastic changes in the structure and function of brain regions involved in regulation of attention, emotion and self-awareness" (p. 222). As a result, individuals who practice mindfulness are less likely to experience high levels of stress and are more likely to experience improved well-being.

iStockPhoto/Juanmonino

Combatting Microaggressions and Racial Battle Fatigue

Microaggressions are subtle verbal or non-verbal negative messages based on one's marginalized group membership. The cumulative experiences of microaggressions over time can result in **racial battle fatigue**. According to Franklin et al. (2014), racial battle fatigue refers to "the psychological (e.g. frustration, anger, resentment), physiological (e.g. headaches, a pounding heart, high blood pressure), and behavioral (e.g. stereotype threat, impatience, poor school performance) responses from racism-related stressors that are often associated with being a person of color" (p. 306).

Research has found that students identifying with marginalized groups can combat stressors, especially those connected to racial microaggressions, by engaging in reflective coping strategies. "When students use reflective coping, they tend to approach problems by examining causal relationships, being systematic, planning, and engaging in behaviors for producing changes in the external situation, affective states, or cognitive processes" (Hernández & Villodas, 2020, p.407).

According to their research, students who used this problem-solving, reflective coping style, as compared to reactive or suppressive styles, tended to have higher levels of psychological health. A reactive style where individuals confront microaggressions can reduce microaggressions, but this often comes with a high emotional cost. The intense emotion experienced when using this reactive style can take a toll on individuals of color and negatively impact their ability to cope with future stressors. Individuals who use a suppressive coping styles avoid or ignore the problem (Hernández & Villodas, 2020). As a result, microaggressions will continue to occur and this can contribute to racial battle fatigue. Thus, the most productive coping strategy is to reflect on the situation and engage in problem-solving and activism to address microaggressions.

Holder et al. (2015) and Quaye et al. (2019) found that Black female professionals reported using the following strategies to cope with microaggressions:

- **Pride.** Being proud of their identity and culture and using internal markers to determine success helped these professionals cope with microaggressions.

- **Support network.** Having a support team comprised of individuals who were also Black female professionals and who understood microaggressions provided helpful guidance and support. For some, seeking counseling support was also beneficial.

- **Mentor.** A mentor helped participants focus on overall career goals and served as a partner in problem-solving when needed.

- **Prayer and meditation.** Faith and meditation empowered them to cope, forgive, and keep focused on what matters most.

- **Self-care.** Practicing overall good stress management techniques such as exercising, unplugging, or disconnecting from negative situations, and spending quality time with family provided needed breaks to re-energize.

Avoiding Unhealthy Behaviors

When you experience stress, especially high levels of stress, you may make unhealthy choices. Unfortunately, these unhealthy choices can sometimes have long-term negative consequences. Alcohol and other drugs, for example, might serve an immediate need of reducing stress but can take you off track from your bigger goal of academic success. This is particularly true for individuals who become addicted to a substance.

There is a stereotype that all college students consume alcohol on a regular basis. Although it is unfortunately true that alcohol consumption is higher during the college years than other developmental periods, you might be surprised to hear about how many college students do not drink alcohol at all or do so at minimal or moderate levels. According to a national survey, 53% of 18-22-year-old students reported drinking in the past month, which means that 47% reported *not* drinking in the past month (National Institute on Alcohol Abuse and Alcoholism, 2021).

The use of alcohol has also been connected to other risky behaviors, such as casual sex (Brown & Vanable, 2007) and an increase in unprotected sexual encounters (MacDonald et al., 2000). In fact, the use of alcohol was identified as one of the main factors by college students who looked back at their sexual experience with regret (Oswalt et al., 2005).

To recognize the signs that you or someone you care about needs help, go to online resources such as the National Council on Alcoholism and Drug Dependence (www.ncadd.org) or the National Institute on Alcohol Abuse and Alcoholism (www.collegedrinkingprevention.gov). You can also express your concerns to family and friends, reach out to a psychologist or counselor at your college or a mental health professional in your community, and attend a self-help or support group on your campus or in your community if you would like help with substance use or abuse.

Stress Management Strategies

- Choose healthy options rather than sugary or salty snacks.
- Bring healthy snacks to class to avoid the vending machines.
- Exercise daily for at least 30 minutes. Check out the fitness center at the college.
- Leave early for class and take the scenic route.
- Establish consistent sleep patterns by going to bed around the same time every night.
- Practice mindfulness and focus on what is happening in the moment.
- Regularly take deep breaths.
- Try progressive muscle relaxation.
- Think positively and challenge nonproductive thinking.
- Challenge negative thoughts with questions.
- Talk about stressors with family, friends, significant others, or professionals.
- Find a mentor.
- Be proud of who you are and your cultural groups.
- Take breaks from stressful situations to spend quality time with loved ones.

Staying Motivated

Motivation, the drive that gets us to begin and complete tasks, is an important part of being resilient and gritty. Not surprisingly, there is extensive research showing that motivated students perform better academically (Algharaibeh, 2020; Walker et al., 2006). This is in part because motivated students exert more effort on tasks (Goodman et al., 2011). Exerting high levels of effort, even when obstacles are encountered, can help you meet with success.

Dirima/Shutterstock.com

iQoncept/Shutterstock.com

Your motivation level will fluctuate—this is normal. Rix et al., (2021) found that motivation is high at the beginning of the semester but lower at the end of the semester. New beginnings offer an opportunity for a fresh start, and this can foster high levels of motivation. It is difficult, however, to maintain this high level of motivation throughout the entire semester. Using the following theory-based motivational strategies will help you get back on track when your motivation begins to drop and will assist you in developing grit.

Behavioral Theories

One of the most widely known and utilized motivational strategies is the reward. Rewards are at the heart of the behavioral approach to motivation. **Behaviorism** is the belief that consequences guide actions. More specifically, behaviorists believe that you will continue to engage in behaviors that have positive consequences or rewards, and you will stop doing behaviors that have negative consequences.

Research has demonstrated the value of rewards, especially in situations where interest in the task is low (Hidi, 2016). Students were more likely to complete tasks when incentivized with a reward such as bonus points and this resulted in improved final exam performance (Ingalls, 2018).

We are often motivated by a combination of intrinsic and extrinsic factors. **Intrinsic motivators** are internal rewards such as enjoying a task. **Extrinsic motivation** stems from external rewards such as receiving a good grade or a paycheck for doing the task. Research has shown that both intrinsic and extrinsic factors can impact performance, but intrinsic rewards tend to have more long-lasting effects (Irvine, 2018). To put this behavioral theory into action, focus on what you enjoy about the task and reward yourself when you complete tasks. Choose a reward that matters to you and one that matches the task.

Reward Strategies

- Celebrate the positive feeling of accomplishing a task.
- Reward yourself with a fun activity after working hard on a task.
- Share your accomplishments with friends and family so that they can celebrate with you.
- Be sure the reward is personally meaningful to you.
- Match the reward to the task—small rewards for small tasks and big rewards for big tasks.

Cognitive Theories

Cognitive theorists believe that thoughts impact mood and behaviors so they aim their interventions on the thinking process. According to this approach, it is your interpretation of the event, not necessarily the event itself, that will lead you to have different levels of motivation.

According to this cognitive perspective, you can increase motivation by looking at your thought patterns and reducing negative thoughts. Looking at the situation from a positive yet productive viewpoint can significantly increase motivation levels. Keeping the situation in

Anson0618/Shutterstock.com

perspective is an important part of the process. If you miss the mark on one assessment and fail a test or assignment, this is not the end of the world.

How you interpret your experiences impacts your emotions and actions. For example, because students who identify with marginalized populations often feel less connected to campus, they may interpret minor setbacks as evidence that they do not belong (T. Ayeni, personal communication, July 22, 2021). Fortunately, researchers have found that these beliefs can be shifted. Walter and Cohen (2011) and Williams et al. (2020) found that by helping students see that minor setbacks are a typical college student experience, their interpretation of setbacks shifted, and this resulted in positive outcomes. Hearing from others that they too experienced minor setbacks can be helpful to all students, but this has been found to be particularly helpful to students from marginalized populations (Williams et al., 2020). In their study, Black students who recognized that minor setbacks were common had higher graduation rates, increased levels of happiness, and improved health.

Another important cognitive concept that relates to motivation is self-efficacy. Most people are familiar with the term *self-esteem*, which refers to how you view or feel about yourself. You may be surprised to find out that research has not always found self-esteem to be predictive of academic performance (Stupnisky et al., 2007). Self-efficacy, on the other hand, has been found to be a very powerful predictor of academic success (Waseem & Asim, 2020). Self-efficacy is your beliefs about your ability to effectively perform a task. You can have different levels of self-efficacy for different tasks. For example, you might have high self-efficacy in math, but lower self-efficacy in writing.

According to cognitive psychologists, having a high self-efficacy is connected to higher levels of motivation. In fact, Lynch (2006) found that self-efficacy was the most powerful motivating factor in student success, for both first-year and upper-level students. It makes sense that you would be more interested in doing tasks that you believe you can do successfully.

Can you increase your confidence or self-efficacy levels? Yes, you can! Think about why you are confident in some areas of performance. Did someone believe in you? Positive messages from others are a good start on this road to higher self-efficacy. However, you have probably had experiences where someone said, "You can do it!" but you did not believe it. Messages from others are not always internalized or actualized, especially if you do not agree. Although positive messages from others can sometimes be useful, having successful experiences is the best way to build self-efficacy. To build confidence through successful experiences, start by doing the following:

- **Have the courage to take risks and try new tasks.** Whenever you attempt a new task, you do not know whether you will meet with success or failure. It therefore takes courage (sometimes lots of it!) to even try something new. The fear of failure can easily lead you to avoidance because if you do not try, you cannot fail. Courage is necessary for growth.
- **Identify action steps you can take now to move toward your goals.** Map out the steps you need to take to accomplish your goal, identifying actions you will need to take to meet this goal with success. Experiencing success along the way builds your self-efficacy and confidence.
- **Reflect on your academic experiences.** Consider keeping a journal to capture your progress on your academic journey. When you go back and review how much your writing and other skills have increased throughout the college years, you will be amazed.

Marko Aliaksandr/Shutterstock.com

• **Expect mistakes to happen from time to time.** No one is perfect. Using mistakes as learning opportunities can set you up for successful experiences in the future. In fact, we often learn a lot from mistakes. The uncomfortable feeling associated with making a mistake often goes away relatively quickly, but the learning that transpired because of the mistake is likely to be long-lasting.

• **Access help when needed.** In most cases, tasks do not need to be completed independently. Seeking help to achieve success can be an important part of this process. Research shows that accessing help is connected to improved performance (Algharaibeh, 2020). Because colleges and universities want their students to be successful, they offer a variety of support from professors, counselors, and tutors.

Humanistic Theories

Humanists believe in a concept called self-actualization, which basically refers to your desire and ability to achieve your potential. Humanistic psychologists believe that you will strive to achieve self-actualization as long as your needs are met (Winston, 2016). If your needs have been met, it is easier to be motivated. If, on the other hand, some of your basic needs are not met, it can be quite a challenge to motivate yourself to achieve at high levels.

Maslow, a humanistic theorist, created a pyramid to illustrate how needs impact our motivation. The most basic needs are at the bottom of the pyramid, and self-actualization is at the top. The needs he identified (starting with the most basic) are as follows: physiological, safety, love and belonging, esteem, and **self-actualization**. According to Maslow (1987), everyone strives to reach their potential if their basic needs are met.

From this perspective, to increase motivation you must attend to each level of need, seeking assistance when appropriate, to get and stay motivated.

• **Self-actualization:** Addressing all your lower-level needs and staying motivated leads you to reach your potential and achieve your goals.

• **Esteem:** Students who feel good about themselves and their accomplishments are more likely to stay motivated and move toward self-actualization. If you are struggling in this area, tutors and counselors may be able to help.

• **Belonging:** The need for belonging is strong and can be met through a variety of ways, such as a sense of community in the classroom or being a part of a sports team, club, fraternity, sorority, or other campus organization. Living in a residence hall is another great way to facilitate a sense of belonging.

• **Safety:** College campuses emphasize safety, but individuals may have safety concerns that need to be addressed. If this is the case for you, seek support from campus security, police, or the counseling department.

• **Physiological needs:** Be sure to eat a good breakfast and sleep well to strive toward self-actualization.

Self-actualization
desire to become the most that one can be

Esteem
respect, self-esteem, status, recognition, strength, freedom

Love and belonging
friendship, intimacy, family, sense of connection

Safety needs
personal security, employment, resources, health, property

Physiological needs
air, water, food, shelter, sleep, clothing, reproduction

Maslow's hierarchy of needs

Plateresca/Shutterstock.com

Socio-Cultural Theories

Researchers have argued that many of the traditional motivational theories do not address cultural factors (Zusho & Clayton, 2011). Culture plays an important role in all aspects of your life including your motivations (King et al., 2017; Sivan, 1986). Socio-cultural theorists focus on the fact that humans are social beings and believe that relationships with others and the environments where interactions with others take place significantly impact our motivation for tasks. It is critical to view motivation within the context of culture and situation. The ecological, sociocultural, and personal investment theories are examples of motivational theories that have relevance across cultures.

DisobeyArt/Shutterstock.com

- **Bronfenbrenner's ecological theory.** This theory emphasizes the role that the environment plays in your motivation and development. According to this theory, you are most impacted by those with whom you interact with on a regular basis. This includes your family and friends and is referred to as your microsystem; however, you are also impacted by many other layers of the environment. This theory states that the interaction of your complex environments influences your motivations, actions, and learning (McInerney, 2011). See Figure 7.4.
- **Vygotsky's sociocultural theory.** This theory highlights the importance of social and cultural variables on learning. According to the sociocultural theory,

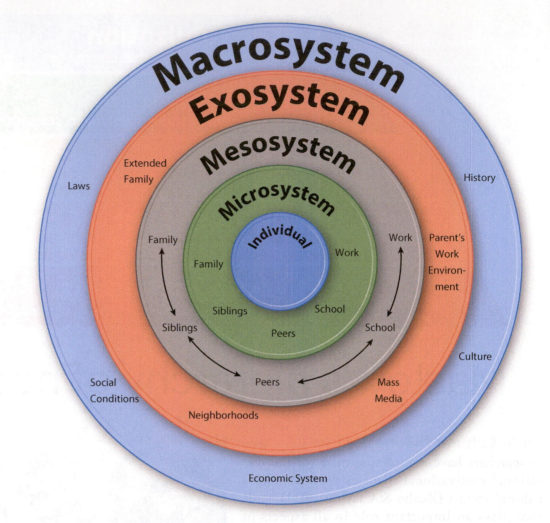

Figure 7.4   Bronfenbrenner's ecological theory.

Think Critically

1. What are some examples of how you can be influenced by various systems?

2. How might the impact of different systems vary across individuals and cultures?

motivation and learning are most likely when individuals are challenged to do tasks just beyond their reach while having support from others (McInerney, 2011). The area of challenge that is just outside one's current skill sets is called the zone of proximal development, and the support provided is called scaffolding. Social and cultural contexts play a particularly important role in scaffolding. The presence or absence of support and who is providing the support, for example, can make a big difference in terms of motivation, effort, and learning.

•   **Personal investment theory.** According to King and McInerney (2014), personal investment theory is a cross-culturally relevant motivational theory that "rests on the assumption that whether persons will invest themselves in particular activities or domains (e.g. academics, sports, work) depends on the interaction among three facets of meaning: sense of self (who am I?), perceived goals (what do I want to achieve?), and facilitating conditions (what is the environment like?)" (p. 177). According to this theory, students would be more likely to invest time and effort into tasks when the goal matters to them and the environment is inclusive and supportive.

Although your already established relationships with family, friends, and significant others play a huge role in your motivation, building new relationships with classmates, staff, and professors on campus can also be incredibly motivating. For example, when you see your roommate working in the library on a project, you may be more motivated to start working on an assignment. Enthusiasm and positive energy can be contagious. However, sometimes others can distract you from your goals. In a study conducted by Bahadir (2020), students reported their social circle was sometimes a contributor to their lack of success. Surrounding yourself with a social network that shares your commitment and passion for success can help you get and stay motivated.

iStockPhoto/Ridofranz

Celebrating Success

Celebrating your success is important. There are several benefits associated with celebrating success. Celebrating can increase motivation, positively impact your overall well-being, improve your self-efficacy, increase the likelihood of future success, and inspire others. Fogg (2020) emphasized how celebrating can help you develop and stick with new habits.

Celebrate with others. Tell others in your network about your accomplishments. Your support team will be proud and will want to help you celebrate your achievement. Consider sharing your accomplishments on professional social media sites such as LinkedIn, too. By posting your accomplishments such as earning Dean's list status, having your work published or highlighted, or receiving an award, others in your network will know about your successes and can join in on the celebration.

Celebrating on social media sites has many benefits. It helps you market yourself. It also helps you keep track of your accomplishments. When it is time to look for a job, you can easily remind yourself of your accomplishments by visiting your social media page. This can make writing cover letters and updating resumes a much easier task. When employers visit your social media pages, they will see a long history of your accomplishments. Another incredibly important benefit is that you can serve as a role model for others. Others, especially those who identify as the same gender or race can be inspired by your actions. By posting your accomplishments, you can motivate others to excel.

The bottom line is that celebrating is important. When you have worked hard to achieve a goal, take time to enjoy the rewarding feeling and share this experience with others, especially those who are important to you. Success takes effort and work; be proud of your accomplishments!

Being Resilient and Developing Grit Quick Quiz

1. What is resilience?

2. What is grit?

3. What are some basic, but effective stress management techniques?

4. Based on what you learned about mindset, what is the most important piece of advice you would give to a friend?

5. What role does support play in being resilient and gritty?

6. What is mindfulness?

7. What strategies can you use to combat racial battle fatigue?

8. According to behaviorists, what should you do to motivate yourself?

9. According to cognitive psychologists, what motivates us?

10. How does Maslow's hierarchy of needs relate to motivation?

11. From a socio-cultural perspective, what influences our motivation?

12. Why is it important to celebrate our accomplishments?

Chapter
7

Chapter Summary: Note-Taking Model

• Let us summarize what you have learned in this chapter. The matrix model is used for this chapter. Remember, it is not expected that your notes will look like this right after class or reading. It takes time to organize your notes and repackage them. It is time well spent, though, because you learn the content better as you organize it, and you will have a fabulous foundation from which to study for your exams! There are several ways to use this section:

• **Preview:** Read the model before reading the chapter to familiarize yourself with the content.

• **Compare:** Compare the notes you took on the chapter to the model provided.

• **Study:** The model along with your notes and other course materials are great resources for studying.

Matrix Notes Model

Creating Academic Plans and Monitoring Progress

Actions to Take	Terms to Know
Connect with an Advisor	Educational plan—map of what courses will be taken and when
Understand Curriculum	General education—core courses to build knowledge and essential skills for life and career Major courses—courses required in your academic major, builds career specific knowledge and skills Electives—can choose a variety of courses or select a minor or double major
Explore Experiential Learning Opportunities	Internships—gain valuable work experience Study abroad—earn credits by learning in another country Service learning—learn course content while providing a service to the community
Reflect on Progress	Self-regulation—set goals, assess progress, adjust as needed Cognitive feedback—feedback during the study process (ex. practice quiz performance) Outcome feedback—feedback after assignment is submitted Attributions—what you attribute successes and failures to

Being Resilient and Developing Grit

Term	Definition
Resilience	the ability to bounce back after stressful events
Grit	persevering and sticking with tasks that matter even when faced with setbacks

Stress Management Techniques

Stress Management Technique	Key Concepts
Sleep, Eating Healthily, and Exercising	Get a good quality sleep every night Choose healthy foods Exercise every day
Mindset	Fixed mindset—intelligence cannot be changed Growth mindset—intelligence is malleable Optimistic, hopeful attitude is best Challenge negative thoughts
Support System	Quality over quantity Expand to include others who understand current challenges Professional counselors are available
Relaxation and Mindfulness	Progressive muscle relaxation works Mindfulness—being in the moment
Combatting Microaggressions and Racial Battle Fatigue	Use a reflective, problem-solving approach Find a mentor and use current support system Engage in self-care and take breaks from stressors
Avoiding Unhealthy Behaviors	Avoid using substances to manage stress as this often results in other risky behaviors and can have long-term consequences

Staying Motivated

Theory	Description	Strategies
Behavioral	• Consequences motivate you • Motivation increases when you are rewarded	• Reward yourself after completing tasks • Enjoy the positive feeling you experience after accomplishing a task
Cognitive	• Thoughts and interpretations motivate you • Having higher self-efficacy (the belief in your ability to successfully achieve tasks) motivates you	• Challenge negative, unproductive thinking (look for data or evidence) • Keep the situation in perspective • Identify action steps to achieve your goal • Access help when needed to increase likelihood of success • Interpret mistakes productively
Humanistic	• Everyone will achieve their potential (self-actualization) if needs are met • Basic needs must be met first (physiological, safety, belonging, esteem, self-actualization)	• Eat nutritious meals and get enough sleep • Connect with others and become a part of the campus community • Express your ideas and thoughts to others • Accomplish tasks and learn new skills

Sociocultural	• Your interactions with others and the culture and environments in which you interact matter • Family and friends have the strongest influence on our motivation, but your motivation is impacted by many social and cultural factors	• Maintain relationships with friends and family • Build new relationships • Surround yourself with support

Celebrating Success

Benefits	Strategies
Improve well-being	Share with others
Increase self-efficacy	Post on social media
Improve success	
Inspire others	

Glossary

3R method is a reading strategy that involves reading, reciting, and reviewing.

abstract is another word for summary.

academic integrity refers to engaging in academically honest behaviors.

academic planning involves mapping out a plan for completing all the academic requirements needed for graduation.

active listening requires that you give your full attention to the person.

activism is a term that refers to acting on your values in ways that result in political or social change.

advisor refers to a support person on campus who can help you engage in academic and career planning.

aspirations are hopes or ambitions.

audience engagement refers to the involvement and attentiveness of your audience members.

chunking refers to organizing content into meaningful units.

civic engagement involves engaging in actions for the good of others and society.

concept mapping is a note-taking technique that visually organizes content.

congruence is the basic premise of the person-environment theory that if you can identify a work environment or career that matches well with your personality and interests, then you will be satisfied with your career choice.

corequisites are courses that you need to take at the same time, or before, as another desired course.

Cornell method is a note-taking method that involves writing key points on the left side of the page, notes on the right, and a summary at the bottom of the page.

correlation refers to the relationship between two variables.

credit score is a number that signifies whether you have engaged in good financial behaviors and will be likely to repay a loan.

critical thinking has been defined as the ability "to think in a sophisticated manner—to ask questions, define terms, examine evidence, analyze assumptions, avoid emotional reasoning, resist oversimplification, consider alternative interpretations, and tolerate uncertainty" (Wade, 2008, p. 11).

cultural competence is the ability to understand, communicate with, and effectively interact with people across cultures.

cultural humility is a process of being open, self-aware, egoless, and incorporating self-reflection when interacting with diverse individuals, groups, or communities.

direct costs are any costs associated with obtaining the degree.

discussion refers to the last section of a research article that describes key findings and their value.

diversity refers to the differences among and between individuals.

dual-encoding process involves using visual images and verbal language to remember.

dual-tasking means you are engaging in two actions at the same time.

elaboration is a memory strategy that involves determining examples and meaning of the content.

elevator speeches are brief explanations of one's career or goals.

emotional intelligence can be defined as perceiving, understanding, and managing your own emotions as well as the emotions of others.

encoding refers to how you get memories into your memory system.

ethics refers to whether choices are morally right or wrong.

ethnicity refers to a shared ancestry, history, and culture.

exam wrappers are reflective assignments that students complete after an exam.

gender is defined as "the attitudes, feelings, and behaviors that a given culture associates with a person's biological sex" (American Psychological Association, 2015, p. 20).

general education are core courses that all students must take regardless of major.

happenstance is a career theory that emphasizes the role of unplanned events.

hidden job opportunities refer to jobs that are never advertised but are instead filled through connections.

incidental information refers to information that we encounter when not actively looking for it.

information literacy is "the set of integrated abilities encompassing the reflective discovery of information, the understanding of how information is produced and valued, and the use of information in creating new knowledge and participating ethically in communities of learning" (Association of College and Research Libraries, 2016, p. 12).

informational interview is a brief meeting between a person who wants to investigate a career and a person working in that career.

intentional information seeking is when you take action to learn something new, such as when you search the Internet.

interests refer to activities that you enjoy doing; sports, gaming, reading, traveling, fitness, gardening, cooking, drawing, and music are some examples.

internships are opportunities for you to gain work experience in your field of study while also earning credit toward graduation.

intersectionality refers to how your various group memberships intersect and define your identity.

introduction is the first official section after the abstract in a peer-reviewed journal article.

leadership involves the ability to build and maintain relationships, cope with change, motivate and inspire others, and deploy resources.

linear note-taking method is an ineffective note-taking strategies that involves writing content in a notebook without much, if any, organization.

matrix method is a note-taking method in the form of a table.

mean is another word for average.

method is the section of a peer-reviewed article that focuses on how the study was conducted.

microaggressions are subtle, negative statements or behaviors about a person based on their membership in a group.

multiple intelligence refers to how individuals have varied abilities.

multitasking is attempting to complete more than one task at a time.

networking involves connecting with professionals in a field of interest.

opportunity costs refer to what is lost because of an action.

oppression refers to disadvantages associated with group membership.

outcome feedback is provided to students after they complete an assignment or other learning task.

peer-reviewed journal articles are theoretical or research-written work that has been deemed worthy of publication by experts in the field.

performance anxiety is anxiety related to giving a speech or engaging in another type of performance.

person-environment model is a career theory that focuses on the importance of a person's interests aligning with the job tasks and environment.

picture superiority effect refers to memory being stronger for pictures as compared to words.

prejudice refers to your negative feelings or attitudes about a group or members of a group.

prerequisite courses are courses that must be taken before you will be allowed to register for and take another course.

privilege refers to advantages that are automatically given to individuals who belong to a certain group.

professionalism refers to behaviors in the workplace.

race refers to a social construct where individuals with similar physical traits, language, and ancestry are grouped together.

race salience refers to how prominent or important race is to you.

results in a peer-reviewed journal articles focuses on the findings of the research study.

resume is a snapshot of your professional skills and accomplishments and is used by hiring managers to decide if you should be interviewed for an open position.

retrieval is the act of locating a previously stored memory.

return on investment refers to the financial benefits associated with investing your money in something such as education or the stock market.

reviewing involves looking over your notes, text, and other resources.

revising a paper involves adding, deleting, and modifying the information in your first draft for the purpose of improvement.

self-efficacy refers to your belief about whether you can successfully complete a task such as critical thinking.

self-regulation refers to monitoring learning progress.

service learning involves learning while supporting the community in some way.

sexual orientation refers to "a component of identity that includes a person's sexual and emotional attraction to another person and the behavior that may result from this attraction" (American Psychological Association, 2015, p. 22).

short-term goals are goals that you can complete within days, weeks, or months.

single-tasking requires you give your full attention and effort to one task at a time.

social capital refers to the collective value of all social networks and the trust, reciprocity, information, and cooperation generated by those social networks.

social cognitive theory of career focuses on how self-efficacy, goals, and expectations impact career decisions.

social construct means that it is not biologically determined but rather determined by humans in society.

spaced practice is defined as studying in small chunks over time.

SQ3R method is a reading technique that involves surveying, questioning, reading, reciting, and reviewing.

stereotype threat refers to when a member of a group performs lower because of their awareness of a stereotype.

stereotypes are judgments you make about a person based on beliefs you have about a group.

storage refers to how you hold onto and save your memories.

studying abroad involves going to another country to learn and continue your studies.

subsidized loans are loans that do not accrue interest for individuals still attending college.

task-switching refers to switching back and forth between two or more tasks.

technical skills are career-specific skills.

testing effect refers to the fact that testing improves memory.

time traps are activities that take up a lot of your time and are often unproductive in nature.

topic sentence is a sentence that captures the main idea of the paragraph.

traditional outline format involves organizing content using headings.

transformational leaders are change agents who motivate and inspire others.

unsubsidized loans begin to accrue interest immediately.

value-based theory for career choice and satisfaction emphasizes the powerful role that values play in career decisions.

values refer to what you believe is important.

vicarious learning experiences means that you can learn from watching others.

working memory is where memories are temporarily stored and if the individual engages with the content in a meaningful way, the content can shift to long-term memory.

Exploring the Research in Depth Appendix

Tovar-Murray, D., Jenifer, E. S., Andrusyk, J., D'Angelo, R., & King, T. (2012). Racism-related stress and ethnic identity as determinants of African American college students' career aspirations. *Career Development Quarterly, 60*(3), 254–262. https://doi.org/10.1002/j.2161-0045.2012.00021.x

Engage via Research Prediction

- Do you think racism-related stress and ethnic identity impact career aspirations?

Read for Key Points

- What question did the researcher seek to answer? (Introduction)
- Who participated in the study and what did the participants do? (Method)
- What was the answer to the research question? (Results)

Critically Think about the Research

- Why are these findings important?
- Why do you think ethnic identity acted as a buffer against racism-related stress?
- Based on these findings, what recommendations do you have for students of color?

Build Information Literacy Skills

- Are these findings consistent with other research investigating racism-related stress, ethnic identity, and career goals and aspirations?

Research Study

Tovar-Murray, D., Jenifer, E. S., Andrusyk, J., D'Angelo, R., & King, T. (2012). Racism-related stress and ethnic identity as determinants of African American college students' career aspirations. *Career Development Quarterly, 60*(3), 254–262.

Drawing primarily on the construct of psychological buffer, the purpose of this study was to explore the extent to which racism-related stress and ethnic identity are determinants of career aspirations. A total of 163 African American college students from a predominately White Midwestern university participated in the study. A moderation regression analysis was conducted. Results indicate that ethnic identity interacted with racism-related stress (p = .04) to predict career aspirations. In other words, as racism-related stress increases in the context of low identity de velopment, career aspirations decrease. Conversely, as perceived racism increases in the context of high identity development, career aspirations increase. Implications for professionals and future research in the field of career counseling are discussed.

Keywords: African American, career aspirations, ethnic identity, racism-related stress

Career counseling is defined as "the process of assisting individuals in the development of a life-career with focus on the definition of the worker role and how that role interacts with other life roles" (Fouad & Byars-Winston, 2005, p. 224). One goal of career counseling is to help students set goals toward their career aspirations. Career aspirations refer to students finding incentives to set objectives toward and be motivated to meet their occupational goals (Quaglia & Cobb, 1996). To better accomplish this mission, career counselors have begun to consider the sociocultural contexts (i.e., identity and racism) that influence students' career goal-setting processes (Fouad & Byars-Winston, 2005).

Recently, researchers have theorized that identity and racism may enhance or detract racial and ethnic minorities from specific occupational goals (e.g., Fouad & Byars-Winston, 2005). To further extend the career counseling literature, this study amalgamates career aspirations with two areas of research: racism and identity. Similar to other scholars (e.g., Helms & Piper, 1994), we postulated that racism would have a negative impact on African American college students' career goals. We also assumed that identity would moderate the relationship between racism and career aspirations. Although the extent to which identity buffers against the attacks of racism has received recent attention (Cross & Vandiver, 2001), we found no study that identified ethnic identity as a protective-reactive factor for career aspirations. Therefore, it was predicted that the more African American college students identified with their ethnic identity, the weaker the effect of racism-related stress would be on their career aspirations.

Racism: A Career Barrier on Career Aspirations

Recent developments in the career counseling literature have focused at tention on how *career barriers* influence African American college students' career development (Neblett, Shelton, & Sellers, 2004). Career barriers are defined as "events or conditions, either within the person or in his or her environment, that make career progress difficult" (Swanson & Woitke, 1997, p. 434). In their recent meta-analysis, Fouad and Byars-Winston (2005) examined racial and ethnic differences on career aspirations and barriers. The results of their study showed (a) no significant difference in career hopes among racial and ethnic groups and (b) that racial and ethnic minorities were more likely to be exposed to career barriers. In other words, career barriers such as racism or racial-related stress might preclude racial and ethnic minorities from meeting their occupational goals.

Darrick Tovar-Murray, Jara Andrusyk, Ryan D'Angelo, and Tia King, College of Education, DePaul University, Chicago; Ericka S. Jenifer, Mental Health Clinic, United States Air Force, Goodfellow Air Force Base, San Angelo, Texas. Correspondence concerning this article should be addressed to Darrick Tovar-Murray, College of Education, De Paul University, 2320 North Kenmore Avenue, Chicago, IL 60614–3250 (e-mail: dtovarmu@depaul.edu).

However, only recently have scholars considered racism-related stress as a potential career barrier (Neblett et al., 2004). *Racism-related stress* is defined as "the race-related transactions between individuals or groups and their environment that emerge from the dynamics of racism, and that are perceived to tax or exceed existing individual and collective resources or threaten well-being" (Harrell, 2000, p. 44). Racism-related stress merges Jones's (1997) tripartite model of racism (e.g., individual, institutional, and cultural) with Lazarus and Folkman's (1984) transactional model of stress and coping (Harrell, 2000). Drawing directly on these well-defined models, Harrell posited that individuals and environmental factors are constantly interacting with each other and that, when a race-related event threatens an individual's personal resources to cope, it is perceived as a psychological barrier.

Ethnic Identity and Career Aspirations

Ethnic identity is also reported to have an influence on the career development process. Phinney (1992) described ethnic identity as individuals sharing a common origin and participating in shared cultural activities. Within this context, ethnic identity is a social construct that is coupled with the identification of and the identification with meanings and expectations associated with belonging to a group (Phinney, 1996). This may include adopting the thinking, perceptions, feelings, and behaviors that are associated with group membership and the investment of time and energy with one's social group (Jaret & Reitzes, 2009). Ethnic identity also includes both a commitment to one's group and participation in social activities of one's group (Phinney & Ong, 2007).

Much of the research connecting identity to career development has explored the effect of racial and ethnic identity on vocational maturity and career goals. For instance, Jackson and Neville (1998) were the first researchers to empirically investigate how identity predicts African American college students' vocational identity and hope to achieve goals. The results of their study indicated that African American college students who conformed to White cultural standards and values reported lower levels of vocational identity. Conversely, African American college students who accepted healthy aspects of both the American society and their own racial identity reported higher levels of vocational identity and career hopes. More recently, Duffy and Klingaman (2009) conducted a cross-sectional study and examined the extent to which ethnic identity was a determinant of career development progress among 2,432 first-year college students. The results suggest that, when African Americans strongly identify with their ethnic identity, they tended to report higher levels of career decidedness.

Identity as a Psychological Buffer Against Racism Regarding Career Aspirations

A *psychological buffer* is defined as "any psychological act of protection, which Blacks employ when they encounter Whites who are explicitly acting in a racist and insulting manner" (Cross & Vandiver, 2001, p. 379). Consistent with the construct of a psychological buffer, this study postulated that ethnic identity would psychologically safeguard African American college students' career aspirations from racism. As previously noted, we found no empirical studies that examined these variables simultaneously. However, empirical evidence does suggest that identification with one's ethnic background serves as a buffer for other important psychological variables. For example, research conducted with African Americans suggested that racial and ethnic identity moderated the negative effects of perceived racism on indicators of psychological health, such as self-worth (Cross & Vandiver, 2001; Neblett et al., 2004; Sellers & Shelton, 2003). Evidence has demonstrated clearly the buffering effects of identity, and we postulated that the same would be true for career aspirations.

Purpose of This Study

Examining how racism-related stress and ethnic identity are determinants of African American college students' career aspirations is imperative for gaining a picture of barriers to their career possibilities. By focusing on these variables simultaneously, we may determine whether racism-related stress leads to a lack of career goal-setting or a perception of the opportunity structure in their career-related choices among this population. Given that ethnic identity is a construct that is related to important psychological domains, further investigation of its importance for African American college students' career progress is needed. Therefore, we predicted that ethnic identity would moderate the relationship between racism-related stress and career aspirations. In other words, as African American college students experienced increased racism, we expected that they would strongly identify with their ethnic identity as a means to psychologically protect their career aspirations.

Method
Participants

A total of 163 African American college students from an urban, predominately White midwestern university volunteered for this study. A convenience sampling procedure was used to recruit participants who self-identified as African American. Demographic information indicated that 83 (50.9%) were women and 80 (49.1%) were men.

The ages of the participants ranged from 18 to 26, with an average age of 23 years.

Procedure

Prior to data collection, the university's institutional review board (IRB) approved the research proposal and measures used for this study. After receiving approval, the research team contacted student organizations and student affairs offices on campus to coordinate the survey distribution. The survey instruments were counterbalanced to reduce the chance of order effect. Data also were collected at the university student center and online using Survey Monkey. All of the participants were informed that the research project involved an investigation of factors that influence a person's career aspirations. Before questionnaires were administered, participants read a consent form that stated that the study was voluntary, being conducted anonymously, and approved by the university's IRB.

Independent Variables

Index of Race-Related Stress-Brief Version (IRRS-B). The IRRS-B (Utsey, 1999) is a self-report scale rooted in the idea that racism (individual, institutional, and cultural) is a unique source of stress. The IRRS-B is composed of 22 items that are rated on a 5-point Likert-type scale, ranging from 0 (*this never happened to me*) to 4 (*this event happened and I was extremely upset*). Completing the IRRS-B required participants to rate race-related events in their daily lives. There are three subscales (Individual Racism, Institutional Racism, and Cultural Racism) and a Global Racism scale. Scoring the IRRS-B is performed by summing the total of the weighted subscale scores. Higher scores on the IRRS-B are indicative of experiences of greater levels of racism-related stress. Utsey (1999) reported the Cronbach's alpha as .78 for Cultural Racism, .69 for Institutional Racism, and .78 for Individual Racism. In this study, the alpha coefficient for the Global Racism scale was .88.

Multigroup Ethnic Identity Measure (MEIM). The MEIM (Phinney, 1992) consists of a total of 15 items with 12 questions measuring ethnic identity. For this study, the 12 items measuring ethnic identity were used. The items are measured on a 4-point Likert-type scale (4 = strongly agree, 3 = somewhat agree, 2 = somewhat disagree, 1 = strongly disagree). Scoring for the MEIM is derived by reversing the negatively worded items, summing across the 12 items, and dividing by the number of items to obtain a mean. Ponterotto, Gretchen, Utsey, Stracuzzi, and Saya (2003) found that the Cronbach's alphas for the MEIM tended to range from .81 to .92. For this study, the alpha coefficient for ethnic identity was .81.

Dependent Variable-Career Aspiration Scale (CAS)

The CAS (Quaglia & Cobb, 1996) comprises 10 items that measure goals that students set for their career choices. Scoring the CAS requires that four of the items be reverse scored and added together to determine a total. This total is then divided by the number of items, computing the mean. Higher scores on the CAS are indicative of a stronger career goal and achievement orientation, and lower scores indicate less motivation toward career goals and achievement. The Cronbach's alpha for the CAS on a sample of 329 students, of whom 30.7% were African Americans, was .92. Studies on the internal consistency of the CAS found it to be moderate to moderate high (.77 to .80). For this study, the alpha coefficient was .82.

Analysis

A moderation regression analysis was used to test whether ethnic identity moderated the relationship between racism-related stress and career aspirations (Cohen & Cohen, 1983). Following the recommendations of Frazier, Tix, and Barron (2004), the continuous predictor and moderator variables were centered and plotted. Values within 1 *SD* below the mean were considered low, and values 1 *SD* above the mean were considered high. For the analysis, the participant variables were entered as a block of variables in the first step. In the second step, racism-related stress and ethnic identity were added. In the third step, the interaction term of Ethnic Identity x Racism-Related Stress was entered. The F test for significance of change in R^2 with a *p* value of .05 and effect size of .06 or greater was used to determine a moderation effect of ethnic identity on racism-related stress and career aspirations.

Results

Preliminary Data Analysis and Pearson Correlations

As recommended by Field (2005), preliminary data analysis was conducted to determine if the assumptions of moderation analysis were met. To test for normality, the normal probability plot was used. The results showed no violations of normality. Multicollinearity was tested by looking at the variance inflation factor (VIF) scores and tolerance values. The VIF values were less than 10, and the tolerance values were greater than 2, suggesting that multicollinearity was not an issue. To check for homogeneity of the variance, we plotted the ZRESID against ZPRED. The results indicated this assumption was met. The Durbin-Watson statistic was used to test the assumption of independence of the errors; the results support the conclusion that the residuals were uncorrelated. Pearson's product correlations were conducted and revealed that career aspirations had a significant and positive relationship with ethnic identity ($r = .170$, $p = .034$) and age ($r = .173$, $p = .03$). The results also showed that racism-related stress was related to ethnic identity ($r = .087$, $p = .05$) and age ($r = .312$, $p = .05$).

Moderation Analysis With Career Aspirations as the Criterion Variable

To test whether ethnic identity moderated the relationship between racism related stress and career aspirations, a moderation regression analysis was conducted. The results for this analysis are presented in Table 1. The demographic variables of age, gender, and education were entered as a block of variables in the first step and did not account for any significant variance ($p = ns$) in career aspirations. In the second step, the model was improved when the racism-related stress ($p = .04$) and ethnic identity ($p = .03$) variables were entered. These variables accounted for 7.5% of additional variance in career aspirations. In the third step, the interaction term Racism-Related Stress x Ethnic Identity was entered. The results showed an interaction effect, $\Delta F(6, 156) = 4.09$, $p = .04$, indicating that the effect of racism-related stress on career aspirations is conditional upon levels of identity development. The additional interaction term explained 2.6% of the significant portion of the variance in career aspirations. Although the effect size (R^2 change $= .026$) for the interaction effect was small, the beta weight coefficient for the interaction term was positive and significant, suggesting that, as racism related-stress increases in the context of low identity development, career aspirations decrease. Conversely, as perceived racism increases in the context of high identity development, career aspirations increase. Figure 1 also provides further evidence of an interaction effect of ethnic identity.

Discussion

In this study, we hypothesized that as African American college students experienced increased racism, their ethnic identity would serve as a psychological armor to protect their career aspirations. The results support the psychological buffer construct and demonstrated that the effect of racism-related stress on African American college students' career aspirations is conditional upon their levels of identity development. In other words, as racism related-stress increases in the context of low identity development, career aspirations decrease. Conversely, as perceived racism increases in the context of high identity development, career aspirations increase. This is evident by ethnic identity interacting with racism-related stress to predict career aspirations in a positive direction. This could suggest that ethnic identity is a cultural adaptation

Table 1
Hierarchical Regression Analysis for Variables Predicting Career Aspirations: Ethnic Identity as a Moderator

Variable	Model 1			Model 2			Model 3		
	B	SEB	β	B	SEB	β	B	SEB	β
Demographic Variables									
Age	−.01	.00	−15	−.01	.01	−.09	−.01	.01	−.18
Gender	−.08	.06	−.11	−.07	.06	−.09	−.09	.03	−.09
Education	−.00	.03	−.01	−.01	.03	−.04	−.00	.02	−.04
Step 2 (Main Effect)									
Racism-Related Stress (RRS)				−.23	.08	−.21*	−.27	.08	−.20*
Ethnic Identity (EI)				.21	.09	.18*	.27	.09	.18*
Step 3 (Interaction Effect)									
RRS 3 EI							.68	.31	.17*
R2		.04			.08			.03	
F∆R²		.90			6.64*			4.09*	

Note. N = 163. Variables were centered at their means. Gender coded as a dichotomous variable: male = 1 and female = 2; Education coded as an ordinal variable: 1 = freshmen, 2 = sophomore, 3 = junior, and 4 = senior; Age was coded as a continuous variable. *$p < .05$.

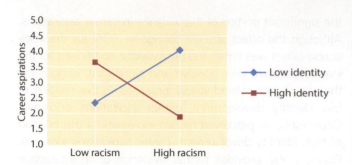

Figure 1 Plotted interaction between ethnic identity and racism-related stress for career aspirations.

that buffers against the threats of racism-related stress and results in African American college students finding incentives to achieve their occupational goals.

Our findings add to the body of literature on the moderation value of ethnic identity (i.e., Neblett et al., 2004; Sellers & Shelton, 2003), by supporting the assertion that identity is a psychological buffer against the attacks of racism on career aspirations. The results also could mean that African American college students who have high career aspirations may expect that, because of their increased aspirations, they will have more racism-related challenges to encounter along their career trajectories. Thus, they might look for support from where it will more likely come—the group with whom they identify. It also may be that African American college students who are more sensitized to racism are also more sensitized to their own racial and ethnic identity, particularly if their career aspirations are high. These notions are consistent with the identity development theory (Phinney, 1992, 1996; Sellers & Shelton, 2003).

Current findings indicate that racism-related stress plays an important role in African American college students' career goals. When racism-related stress was entered in the moderation equation, it was identified as a statistically significant predictor of career aspirations. The beta coefficient for racism related stress was negative, suggesting an inverse relationship. Our findings are consistent with past studies that suggest that African American college students suffer career deficits as a function of experiencing racism (Neblett et al., 2004). Additionally, age and identity had a positive relationship with racism-related stress, suggesting that older African American college students who embrace their ethnic identity reported experiencing more racial stressors.

As expected, the results of this study provide support for ethnic identity as a determinant of career aspirations. Compared to racism-related stress, ethnic identity displayed the strongest significant and positive correlation

with career aspirations. The beta coefficient for ethnic identity was also larger than the coefficient for racism-related stress, and it accounted for more of the significant proportion of the variance. Furthermore, the beta weight coefficient for ethnic identity was positive, suggesting that African American college students who strongly sought out their ethnic group were more likely to be motivated to set career goals. The results of this study are consistent with past studies that have demonstrated that African American college students who have a strong racial and ethnic identity reported higher levels of vocational identity, career hopes, and career decidedness (Duffy & Klingaman, 2009; Jackson & Neville, 1998). Additionally, career aspirations were positively correlated with age, suggesting that older African Americans were more likely to be motivated to achieve their career goals.

Implications for Practice

We believe that these findings make an important contribution to the career counseling literature and have implications for counseling African American college students. First, we expanded the concept of psychological buffer by applying it to career aspirations. Our findings support the notion of a psychological buffer of ethnic identity against racism-related stress regarding career aspirations. Second, because embracing one's identity buffered against the stressors of racism, this study invites career counselors to gain an understanding of the cultural factors related to African American college students' career aspirations. This means that career counselors might need to explicitly discuss the importance of identity in career progression with their African American clients. Next, this study points to the importance of career counselors using theoretical models that are situated in a culturally specific context. Readers are directed to the work of Fouad and Bingham (1995), who examined best practices for counseling ethnic and racial minorities. Finally, given that the relationship among age, identity, and career aspirations was positive, career counselors might consider connecting African American college students with older peers of the same ethnic background. By connecting them with older African Americans on campus, career counselors may afford younger African American students the opportunity to engage in a process whereby their career aspirations are valued and realized.

Limitations of the Current Study

Although we believe these findings add to the emergent literature on career aspirations, caution is warranted. First, the generalizability of this study is limited to the university setting in which the study took place. Further research could replicate this study at other universities. A second caveat to this study is the research design. The research analysis used for this study was moderated regression analysis; therefore, no direct causal relationship was established. Third, this study used self-report measures, which rely on participants' responses to questions. As with all self-report measures, consistency biases and social desirability might be evident. In other words, the participants might have skewed the results by portraying themselves in a more negative or positive direction. However, we believe this was not the case, considering that the scores on the measures were normally distributed. A final caution is the small effect size, suggesting that the moderating term played a small part in understanding career aspirations. To this end, we recommend that future studies include other measures of identity (i.e., Black Racial Identity Scale) and racism (i.e., Perceived Racism Scale) to better understand how sociocultural variables affect African Americans college students' career aspirations. ■

References

Cohen, J., & Cohen, P. (1983). *Applied multiple regression/correlation analysis for the behavioral sciences* (2nd ed.). Hillsdale, NJ: Erlbaum.

Cross, W. E., & Vandiver, B. J. (2001). Introducing the Cross Racial Identity Scale. In J. Ponterotto, M. Casas, L. Suzuki, & C. Alexander (Eds.), *Handbook of multicultural counseling* (2nd ed., pp. 371–393). Thousand Oaks, CA: Sage.

Duffy, R. D., & Klingaman, E. A. (2009). Ethnic identity and career development among first-year college students. *Journal of Career Assessment, 17*, 286–297.

Field, A. (2005). *Discovering statistics using SPSS for windows* (2nd ed.). Thousand Oaks, CA: Sage.

Fouad, N. A., & Bingham, R. (1995). Career counseling with racial/ethnic minorities. In W. B. Walsh & S. H. Osipow (Eds.), *Handbook of vocational psychology* (2nd ed., pp. 331–366). Hillsdale, NJ: Erlbaum.

Fouad, N. A., & Byars-Winston, A. M. (2005). Cultural context of career choice: Meta analysis of race/ethnicity differences. *The Career Development Quarterly, 53*, 223–233.

Frazier, P. A., Tix, A. P., & Barron, K. E. (2004). Testing moderator and mediator effects in counseling psychology. *Journal of Counseling Psychology, 51*, 115–134.

Harrell, S. P. (2000). A multidimensional conceptualization of racism-related stress: Implications for the well-being of people of color. *American Journal of Orthopsychiatry, 70*, 42–57.

Helms, J. E., & Piper, P. (1994). Implications of racial identity theory for vocational psychology. *Journal of Vocational Behavior, 44*, 124–138.

Jackson, C. C., & Neville, H. A. (1998). Influence of racial identity attitudes on African American college students' vocational identity and hope. *Journal of Vocational Behavior, 53*, 97–113.

Jaret, C., & Reitzes, D. (2009). Currents in a stream: College student identities and ethnic identities and their relationship with self-esteem, efficacy, and grade point average in an urban university. *Social Science Quarterly, 90*, 345–367.

Jones, J. M. (1997). *Prejudice and racism* (2nd ed.). New York, NY: McGraw-Hill.

Lazarus, R. S., & Folkman, S. (1984). *Stress, appraisal, and coping.* New York, NY: Springer.

Neblett, E. W., Shelton, J. N., & Sellers, R. M. (2004). The role of racial identity in man aging daily racial hassles. In G. Philogine (Ed.), *Racial identity in context: The legacy of Kenneth B. Clark* (pp. 77–90). Washington, DC: American Psychological Association.

Phinney, J. S. (1992). The multigroup ethnic identity measure: A new scale for use with adolescents and young adults from diverse groups. *Journal of Adolescent Research, 7*, 156–176.

Phinney, J. S. (1996). When we talk about American ethnic groups, what do we mean? *American Psychologist, 51*, 918–927.

Phinney, J. S., & Ong, A. D. (2007). Conceptualization and measurement of ethnic identity: Current status and future directions. *Journal of Counseling Psychology, 54*, 271–281.

Ponterotto, J. G., Gretchen, D., Utsey, S. O., Stracuzzi, T., & Saya, R. (2003). The multigroup ethnic identity measure (MEIM): Psychometric review and further validity testing. *Educational and Psychological Measurement, 63*, 502–515.

Quaglia, R. J., & Cobb, C. D. (1996). Toward a theory of student aspirations. *Journal of Research in Rural Education, 12*, 127–132.

Sellers, R. M., & Shelton, J. N. (2003). The role of racial identity in perceived discrimination. *Journal of Personality and Social Psychology, 84*, 1079–1092.

Swanson, J. L., & Woitke, M. B. (1997). Theory into practice in career assessment for women: Assessment and interventions regarding perceived barriers. *Journal of Career Assessment, 5*, 443–462.

Utsey, S. O. (1999). Development and validation of a short form of the Index of Race Related Stress (IRRS)-Brief Version. *Measurement & Evaluation in Counseling & Development, 32*, 149–167.

Travis, T. (2011). From the classroom to the boardroom: The impact of information literacy instruction on workplace research skills. *Education Libraries, 34*(2), 19–31.

Engage via Research Prediction

- What percentage of college graduates reported using information literacy or research skills in their current position on at least a monthly basis?

Read for Key Points

- What question did the researcher seek to answer? (Introduction)

- Who participated in the study and what did the participants do? (Method)

- What was the answer to the research question? (Results)

Critically Think about the Research

- Why are these findings important? How can you use this research to guide your actions as a college student?

- Why do you think the students who did not have a required information literacy requirement have higher confidence in their skills?

- Based on these findings, what recommendations would you make to your college president about information literacy skill development? Why?

- What future research in this area would you suggest?

Build Information Literacy Skills

- Are the beliefs of alumni consistent with the beliefs of employers?

- How do colleges and universities teach information literacy skills?

- How can information literacy skills be helpful to you in your personal life?

Research Study

Travis, T. (2011). From the classroom to the board-room: The impact of information literacy instruction on workplace research skills. *Education Libraries, 34(2), 19–31.*

"Many businesses are knowledge driven. Even entry level employees have to know how to identify information problems and go about solving them" ~ unidentified employer 2000.

Topsey Smalley, Workplace Quotes www.cabrillo.edu/~tsmalley/WorkplaceQuotes.html

Introduction

Since the wide-scale adoption of the ACRL *Information Literacy Standards* (2000), there have been numerous students who have graduated from universities that have formal library instruction programs. Currently there has been very little assessment of their post-graduate research skills or what role information literacy plays on workplace performance. The effect libraries have on graduates is not only of interest to librarians; the skills students gain in college have a significant impact on costs and productivity in the workplace. Within the last five years, the corporate world has acknowledged the importance of information literacy on workplace success. This has largely been linked to the growth of the knowledge management sector coinciding with the ability to access large amounts of unfiltered information on the internet.

The report, *Are they really ready to work?: Employers' perspectives on the basic knowledge and applied skills of new entrants to the 21st century U.S. workforce* (Casner-Lotto, 2006) delineated 21st century skills needed by baccalaureates. While information literacy was not specifically mentioned in the report, the areas of critical thinking/problem solving, information technology application, and lifelong learning certainly correspond to the ACRL standards. The following year, information literacy was listed as an Essential Learning Outcome by the *Association of American Colleges and Universities (2007). The AACU* (2007) states these outcomes, "reflect an important emerging consensus—among educators and employers—about the kinds of learning needed for a complex and volatile world" (p. 13). Since then, variations of 21st century skills have been increasingly adopted by universities to ensure their graduates possess the proficiencies needed to function in a knowledge-based society.

The purpose of this study is to examine various factors that may contribute to continued and sustained use of information literacy skills beyond the college experience, and specifically, what competencies students identify as essential for their work.

Literature Review
Information Literacy in the Workplace

The most significant research regarding information literacy in the workplace has been published by Christine Bruce (Bruce 1999; McMahon, C., & Bruce, C., 2002). Using her seminal seven faces framework, Bruce examined information seeking behaviors in the workplace. Seven faces of information literacy in the workplace were identified: using information technology for awareness and communication; finding information from appropriate sources; executing a process; controlling information; building a personal knowledge base in a new area of interest; working with knowledge and personal perspectives to gain novel insight; and using information wisely for the benefit of others (Bruce, 1999). What is underscored is the importance of lifelong learning and the position information literacy has in all work sectors, not solely knowledge management. In 2002, Carmel O'Sullivan surmised that the term information literacy is "at best sporadic outside the isolation of the library and teaching professions" (p. 7). O'Sullivan also found that the corporate literature that did exist regarding information-gathering in the workplace focused on computer literacy or was framed in the context of lifelong learning. Other research laid the groundwork linking information literacy and knowledge management (Hughes, Middleton, Edwards, Bruce Mcallister, 2005; Kirton and Barham 2005; O'Farril 2008; Ferguson, 2009). Lloyd examined information literacy through the lens of sociocultural practice, specifying the ranges of information modalities involved within the context of work (Lloyd, 2007). Lloyd conducted studies that examined the work of ambulance drivers and fire-fighters and questioned whether the information literacy skills in the traditional settings of education and in the library had the same characteristics as the workplace (Lloyd, 2008).

Studies that have quantified information literacy skills in the workplace focus mainly on current practices of employees and corporate needs (Smalley, 2000;

Cheuk, 2008). Using Bruces' seven faces framework (1999), Cheuk modeled an approach for information literacy training of employees at a large consulting firm (2008). For obvious reasons, professions that deal with the collection and creation of written product are more likely to be engaged in information gathering. However, as the importance of evidence-based practice has become a staple in medical fields and other on-the-job decision making, information literacy can conceivably be important in many other work environments.

As the body of information literacy research has expanded, several perspectives in the context of work have emerged (Halford, Lotherington, Obstefelder and Dyb, 2008; Hepworth and Smith, 2008; Somerville and Howard, 2008; Klusek and Bournstein, 2006). Again the focus has been on information-dependent professions. However, from the literature one key point emerges. Information seekers in the workplace require more advanced navigation and evaluation skills since often they do not have information experts to rely on nor do they always have access to vetted information sources like databases and knowledge management systems (Bruce, 1999; Lloyd, 2008; Ochs, 1991).

Assessing the Transferability of Information Literacy

Information literacy has been extensively evaluated in the K-16 settings. Standardized tests and various direct assessment tools have been developed to determine which skills students have mastered and attempt to measure the impact of information literacy skills or usage of library materials on academic success (Oakleaf and Owen, 2010; de Jager, 1997; Schulte, 2008; Shepherd, 2011; Walsh, 2011; Whitemire, 2002; Wong, 2011). What is lacking in the literature is a focus on what information competencies in the academic setting transfer to the workplace.

While previous research advocates collaboration between business managers and librarians to align information literacy with corporate needs, very few have tried to correlate the skills learned in college with actual use in the workplace. The most applicable methodology to use for such research is referred to as postcampus assessment (Rockman, 2002). This form of assessment measures the degree of skills students retain from their college research experience. Additionally, it helps identify which skills students and their employers' value. Ilene Rockman notes, "this post campus assessment technique can be used for gaining valuable feedback about the usefulness and applicability of course content, instructional strategies, and the campus learning environment" (p. 193). Three studies have employed this form of data collection to analyze the transferability of information seeking skills of alumni (Smalley, 2000;

Crawford and Irving, 2006; Wu, 2008). One of the earliest examples of this data collection technique was conducted by Ochs (1991). Ochs distributed surveys to both employers and alumni regarding use of information literacy and technology skills. Employers identified skill levels they expected of students while alumni rated their own skill set and where they felt they gained them. Of the most frequently identified sources of skill attainment, "Cornell classes" or "on the job" and "on my own" often rate higher than Mann library instruction program as students' sources of information management skills" (p. 17). Ochs surmised that it was probably due to lack of librarian contact time with students. Another "postcampus" survey by Crawford and Irving (2006) was conducted after the widespread use of the internet in libraries. Alumni from Glasgow Caledonian were asked to identify which skills and to what extent research skills gained as students applied to their current workplace activities. The findings indicated that students felt the research skills they used in the university made a significant impact on their job performance.

These results raise a core issue that libraries struggle to substantiate: what impact does information literacy really have on students, especially once they no longer have to conduct research for courses?

Models of Information Literacy Instruction

While most institutions strive for the perfect combination of tiered, embedded, curricular integration at the programmatic level, the reality is usually far removed. Stephanie Sterling Brasely examined models of information literacy in academic institutions and described the landscape as "collaborations that run along a continuum from the informal and episodic or scattershot to the formal, sequential, and programmatic." (Brasley, 2008, p. 77). Sue Curzon defined various models of information literacy integration including general education; credit courses; online tutorials; faculty-led; and the most common, on-demand instruction (Curzon, 2004). These models can be divided into two categories: direct and indirect information literacy instruction. Direct information literacy is curriculum-centric and either manifested as a requirement for graduation and integrated systematically at the university level. Indirect information literacy instruction is defined as library-centric and not fully diffused into the curriculum but rather intermittently throughout the university. Typically, the latter model may have an instruction plan adopted by the library; however, without curricular requirements, there is no full integration of information literacy outcomes at the university level. Very few institutions of higher education have the "perfect" model of information literacy nevertheless; several examples of direct and indirect information literacy programs exist. Perhaps one of the first examples of a systematic approach to building more direct information literacy instruction is found in the California State University system. The California State University (CSU) system has had an advantage in the area of information literacy in large part due to a centralized approach to integration. The report *Information Competence in the CSU* (1995) developed a blueprint for providing financial and institutional support at individual campuses for inclusion of information literacy into the curriculum. Rockman (2002) described a multi-campus approach that focused on providing grants, interdepartmental and cross-campus collaboration as well as faculty development opportunities. The approach was designed to take advantage of the trends in general education (GE) reform. The result was to enable many campuses in the system to create various configurations of information literacy instruction. Currently, half the libraries in the CSU System "have information literacy and competency learning outcomes as part of the institutional requirements for general education" (Travis, 2008, p. 18). The models that have been adopted at various CSU campuses can be categorized as both indirect and direct. Some examples of direct information literacy inclusion are CSU Northridge and CSU Los Angeles. Both have information literacy requirements for graduation which are fulfilled through GE courses. These are courses which are seamlessly embedded in course content, rather than a stand-alone tutorial, instruction session, or assignment. Other libraries in the system provide examples of indirect forms of information literacy integration. For example, Sonoma State has infused the first-year program with information literacy outcomes. CSU Long Beach has adopted information literacy outcomes for general education; however, there is currently no requirement in place for graduation. CSU Monterey Bay offers majors which have information literacy outcomes built into the overall departmental outcomes. Still other schools like San Diego State have established library instruction programs but no embedded information literacy curriculum. In many cases, a variety of information literacy integration can exist on the same campus. For example, CSU Long Beach has GE outcomes, some departmental outcomes, as well as faculty led information literacy instruction (Brasley, 2008). With such varying campuses and multi-pronged efforts, it is important to assess which models may have a greater or lesser impact on skills of alumni in the workplace.

Due to the variety of information literacy programs in existence, it is expected that student use of information literacy skills in the workplace will vary depending upon the method of information literacy integration. By comparing alumni from campuses with and without information literacy requirements, this study will explore the following research questions:

RQ1: Does an information literacy requirement at a campus effect research skills?

RQ2: Do alumni attribute their information literacy skills to the library or other aspects of their education?

RQ3: How much do information literacy skills learned in college impact their use in the workplace?

Background & Methodology

The model for this research study is based on the work of Crawford and Irving (2006). To modify the original survey for distribution in the United States, the language was changed from British to American English; questions were adjusted to current internet use trends; and a question about LEAP 21st century skills was added. These skills identified by Association of American Colleges and Universities have recently been adopted by the CSU system in the revision of the GE curriculum (CSU, 2008) and mirror similar GE curriculum revisions nationwide. Part of this study examined which of the 21st century skills participants identified as learning during college.

The instrument contained forty three questions divided into five sections (Figure 1):

The purpose of this study was to:

Alumni Profile: brief demographic survey regarding school, major, and current employment.

Information Literacy/Library Instruction: information regarding the mode and level of exposure to information literacy concepts as college students.

Information Sources You Used at Your Campus: questions about the types and names of specific resources alumni used as students.

Information Sources You Use in the Workplace: information sources and information needs questions.

Self-Assessment of Information Literacy/Research Skills: participants' overall judgment of their research skills before college, after college, and in the workplace.

Figure 1 Five sections of the instrument.

- Determine the extent to which graduates use information literacy/research skills in the workplace
- Explore any impact different models of information literacy curriculum integration has on these skills
- Compare differences between use of information sources for academic and workplace research
- Evaluate the distinction alumni make between research skills learned as college student with current research skills in the workplace

Results: Key Findings

Demographics

In order to examine any patterns that may exist, the data was analyzed by population. Due to the low response rate, the results can only be used as a starting point of the discussion of the impact information literacy has on performance in the workplace and cannot be used to generalize all alumni experiences. This convenience sample provides descriptive data that can give insight into how information literacy has impacted respondents after they become members of the workforce.

The survey was distributed twice. The first dissemination was to graduates of the CSU system and the second was open to anyone that attended a four-year institution in the United States. There were 62 surveys started by CSU respondents with 54 usable surveys. There were 71 surveys started by the non-CSU respondents with 44 usable surveys. Eleven different CSU campuses were represented while over 24 campuses overall made up the total. Fifty-one percent of total respondents obtained master's degrees with less than one percent getting a Ph.D. The disciplines for undergraduates were varied with most of the students majoring in social science programs, arts & humanities, followed by business, and the sciences. The core numbers of graduates responding to the survey were psychology and library science degree holders with social sciences, education, business administration, social work and nursing respondents as well.

The majority of the respondents were female (71%). 58% of the respondents could be described as Millennials (born between the years of 1980–2000) while next largest age group were between the ages of 31–40.

RQ1: Does an information literacy requirement at a campus make a difference in research skills?

The data was examined to determine if there were significant differences between the populations that fulfilled information literacy requirements with those that did not. From the data collected the results are mixed. Twenty-eight percent of respondents answered that they had an information literacy requirement. Forty-nine percent had no requirement while 23% couldn't remember if they had such a requirement. Of the 28% who had a requirement, a surprising 85% satisfied the requirement by completing a credit course. Six percent of those who indicated that they had information literacy (IL) requirements in college listed their most advanced degree as library science. Eleven percent of those who responded they had no information literacy requirement or didn't remember also identified their highest degree as library science.

When comparing specific questions related to research there were no major differences in their self-rating of information literacy skills (Figure 2 and Figure 3). The students who attended college without an IL requirement were more confident in their skills both before and after college. This furthers the implication that students feel research skills increase as a result of attending college.

Another area of the survey where there was an expected difference was in responses to the questions regarding evaluation and application of information (Figure 4).

Most respondents stated they used advanced searching features when using the internet but less in subscription databases. The criteria they list for finding websites offers insight into what criteria is used to select sites found on the internet (Figure 5).

Figure 2
Before starting my coursework at a 4-year College/University, my information literacy/research skills were:

Answer Options	IL Required Response Percent	IL Not Required Response Percent
Poor	19%	19%
Average	44%	41%
Good	33%	29%
Very good	3%	10%
		N=95

Figure 3
When I completed my coursework at a 4-Year college/University my information literacy/research skills were:

Answer Options	IL Required Response Percent	IL Not Required Response Percent
Poor	0%	0%
Average	15%	9%
Good	48%	39%
Very good	37%	52%
		N=94

Figure 4
Please mark all of the statements that best apply to you.

Answer Options	IL Required Response Percent	IL Not Required Response Percent
I use advanced search options when I search online resources.	84%	75%
I use advanced search options when I search subscription databases.	72%	69%
I use specific criteria for evaluating information I find using Internet information sources.	52%	75%
I use more than one source to verify the accuracy of information I find using Internet information sources.	76%	81%
I regularly manipulate or otherwise incorporate information I find using Internet information sources into presentations or reports for work.	40%	41%
		N=89

Figure 5
When searching for information, how do you select which sites to use? Please mark all that apply.

Answer Options	IL Required Response Percent	IL Not Required Response Percent
I am already familiar with the site.	81%	87%
URL listed for the site.	23%	30%
Information has been rated by other users.	15%	19%
Information is contrary to what I think.	4%	12%
See what sources the author used.	58%	67%
If the source is listed on the first page of search results.	27%	19%
Consult the credentials listed for the author(s).	50%	48%
Information confirms my assumptions.	4%	16%
Site is well designed and easy to use.	50%	60%
I was referred to the site by a colleague or friend.	69%	76%
		N=93

Being familiar with a site and a referral to a site were the highest-ranking responses. Other findings regarding information-seeking behavior and undergraduates mirrors these results (Head & Eisenberg, 2010). It is interesting to note that "information has been rated by other users" is significantly lower than other referral-type answers due to the prevalence of user-generated rankings on sites such as *Amazon, Yahoo Answers, and Yelp*. Site design, while often identified in the literature as the least reliable way to evaluate site content, is still ranked by 50% or more of respondents, equal to credentials of the author. Selecting a source because it's on the first page of results is also a significant finding and should be investigated further to determine which search engines are being used and if there is any user understanding of how page rankings are calculated.

Also notable is the low number of respondents who regularly manipulate or incorporate information as part of their job (Figure 4). It begs to question what they do with the information they find in the workplace, especially when reports and presentations were ranked highest in response to the question "for which work related projects did you perform research to complete."

RQ2: Do alumni attribute their information literacy skills to the library or other aspects of their education?

Information Literacy Exposure

The results for questions relating to information literacy exposure were very revealing. Sixty-eight percent of those who had no IL requirement recall attending a library-led research session. Sixty-three percent of those with no course-related interaction with librarians stated they consulted with librarians at some point in their career. Of those that had, 97% stated they got help at the reference desk with 29% using email and 5% using instant message.

In terms of conducting research while attending university, 67% answered they used the library website to access information "often" with 18% responding "seldom" or "never". Thirty-nine percent replied they used the print collection "often" with 32% responding "seldom" or "never". All respondents affirmed using research databases in college. Seventy-six percent of respondents agreed with the statement "research databases were very important for completing my academic research." Fifteen percent disagreed or strongly disagreed with this statement.

When asked what respondents felt contributed most to developing information literacy skills in college the results were interesting. "Writing research papers" and "figuring it out myself" were cited most often with "using the library resources" referenced by 55% of respondents (Figure 7). Librarians were ranked 8th below "professors" and "general education" as resources. "Library instruction," "credit courses by the library," and "online research tutorials" ranked lowest on the list. These findings from the study are reminiscent of Ochs' (1991) finding that "Cornell courses" and "on my own" ranked higher than library instruction.

21st Century and Information Literacy Skill Areas

When asked to select LEAP 21st century skills and specific information literacy concepts they felt they currently used in the workplace, the answers had interesting implications for integrating these skills into the curriculum (Figure 8).

Respondents felt that college helped them gain critical thinking skills and problem solving the most, with "oral communication" and "writing" identified by more than 50% of respondents. What they felt it helped the least was "global awareness," "creativity," and "self-awareness." This isn't surprising, as these concepts are not something people typically "learn" in a classroom or through a specific assignment or course.

Of the information literacy skills, "finding relevant information" and "evaluating information" were chosen most

Figure 6
Library's subscription research databases (e.g. Lexis Nexis, Academic Search Elite, JSTOR etc.) were very important for the completion of my academic research.

Answer Options	All Respondents
Strongly agree	53%
Agree	23%
Neutral	9.0%
Disagree	4%
Strongly disagree	11%
	N = 92

Figure 7
What do you feel contributed most to developing your information literacy/research skills in college?

Task	All Respondents
Writing research papers	84%
Figuring it out myself	70%
Using library resources	55%
General education	52%
Professors	49%
Research methods course	43%
Curriculum in my major	42%
Librarians	33%
Fellow students	29%
Library instruction session(s)	27%
Online research tutorial	12%
Credit course offered by the library	0%

N=92

Figure 8
As a result of attending a 4-year College/University, which skills do you think you gained from your college experience that you use most often in the workplace? (please mark all that apply)

Skill Area	All Respondents
Finding relevant information	78%
*Critical thinking	78%
Evaluating information	69%
*Problem solving	65%
*Oral communication	64%
*Writing	61%
Recognizing bias	56%
*Methods of inquiry	48%
*Quantitative reasoning	48%
*Teamwork	47%
*Intercultural competence	42%
Determining an information need	40%
*Social responsibility	40%
Using information ethically	39%
*Self-understanding	36%
*Creativity	33%
*Global awareness	28%
Information cycle	13%

N=89

*Denotes LEAP 21st century skill

often; the "information cycle" and "using information ethically" ranked lowest. "Determining an information need," which previous research identified as the most difficult information-seeking task, was marked by only 40% of respondents (Head, 2010).

RQ3: How much do information literacy skills learned in college impact use in the workplace?

Research in the Workplace

All Respondents

The transmission of information literacy skills to the workplace is also examined in this survey. One- third of all respondents use research skills to perform job daily; 30% weekly, and 19% monthly. 10% never use research skills in the workplace.

The job occupations listed by respondents who never used their research skills in the workplace included servers, sales, correctional officer, counselor, and registered nurses. Most of these respondents also indicated they spent most of their work day away from the computer. All of these respondents in this category indicated their research skills were unchanged before and after attending college.

Another indicator of the transferability of information literacy skills to the workplace setting are the responses indicating the evaluation and application of information into their work lives. Fifty-three percent believe their research skills played a role in getting hired for their current position, while 36% did not feel research skills played any role in their current employment. In the workplace, respondents were more likely to use free internet sources than subscription databases. Free sources most often cited in open-ended responses were Google, trade websites, education databases, PubMed, and blogs.

The most-cited types of information looked for at work were current news, empirical research, and statistics while office supplies and medical information ranked lowest. The most-often cited work-related projects were reports and presentations. Open-ended responses included computer fixes, lesson plans, design work, patient care, emergency preparedness, lab research, research help, engineering projects, patient diagnosis, images/graphics, and legal research (Figure 9).

In terms of rating their current research skills, 51% of respondents reported their skills had "gotten better" while 31% responded "unchanged." Very few reported their skills as becoming worse, which corresponds with the finding that the majority of respondents were not interested in receiving continuing education to increase their information-seeking skills. Those that stated they would

Figure 9
What types of information do you typically search for in the workplace? (please check all that apply)

Answer Options	Response Percent
Current news	57%
Empirical research	46%
Product information	36%
Statistics	36%
Other (please specify)	30%
Information for my supervisor	27%
Law	24%
Price comparison	23%
Medical	22%
Licensing information	17%
Software	17%
Travel	14%
Human resources	12%
Office supplies	11%
Employment ads	10%
	N=83

want more training identified "keeping up to date" as their justification.

Discussion

The results of this study offer insights for both librarians and the corporate world. When comparing results to Crawford and Irving, there are similarities. In the Crawford study, the majority of alumni also believed research skills improved as a result of attending a university and felt their research skills improved once they were employed. In related research of Millennials (individuals born between 1980–2000) at work, it was reported that 77% of respondents felt that "technology helps me improve my work." In the same study 76% felt technology made them more successful in their career (O'Dell, 2010). This study found 48% felt their information literacy skills were a factor for getting hired in their current position and 77% of respondents felt "finding information is an essential part of my work." This indicates the usefulness of information literacy skills in the workplace is acknowledged as much by graduates as it is by businesses.

Another study of information-seeking behavior of college students found most turned to friends (87%) for help while only 14% asked librarians for assistance (Head & Eisenberg, 2010). Likewise, the results of the present study indicate this pattern of help-seeking continues after graduation. Of note in this study was the large number of students who consulted librarians in person (97%) versus via email (27%). The increased access to instant messaging and services such as LibAnswers may impact help-seeking patterns and deserves further research due to the visibility of the products and growing usage of both library services.

The findings regarding evaluation of information can provide insight into areas that should be studied further. The number of students using "site design" to assign credibility to a website is troubling. Alison Head and Michael Eisenberg found similar results as 71% use interface design as part of their source selection (2010). There is also prevalence for alumni to use previous knowledge of a site as selection criteria. What should be examined is how individuals balance previous site content with new information needs. Research has found that students will select sites based on previous success regardless of if it appropriate for the topic. If this tendency continues after college, it may have implications, as librarians are not regularly employed in the workplace environment.

Another important aspect of the findings is the low ranking of librarians, online tutorials, and library instruction sessions as contributing to the growth of information literacy skills. What was identified most were tasks that required demonstrated use of information literacy concepts. "Writing research papers," "figuring it out myself," and "using library resources" are all active learning processes.

It appears significant that students rated doing research contributed more to gaining which skills rather than passive learning activities such as sitting through a presentation or using an online tutorial. This strengthens the argument that information literacy should be embedded in courses and assignments rather than as a stand-alone or one-shot model.

Any research conducted to see how individuals interact with information and employ information literacy skills can be used to strengthen our instructional programs. The results of this study cannot definitively determine if an information literacy requirement is the best method to approach this. However, the results indicate that students are employing research skills in the workplace; they value and use library resources; and most importantly, they value the skills they gain from engaging in the finding, evaluating and applying information. As Bruce (1999) eloquently states, librarians need to "find ways to help learners reflect on their use of information, so that they become aware of their experiences and transfer these ways of working to a wide range of situations" (p. 45). This concept of transferability not only applies to work but to contribute to a society of lifelong learners.

Limitations and Future Directions

This study had several limitations. Initially, this survey was designed to be distributed only to alumni of the California State University system. This would have allowed the research to focus on known models of information literacy, and also allow for a comparison between direct and indirect information literacy programs. The low response rate made this comparison impossible, therefore it was distributed via social media outlets (Twitter, Facebook, listservs, etc.) to a nationwide audience. The issues with distributing the survey via social media meant a disproportionate amount of respondents had library science degrees and a population that regularly uses the internet for socializing. Any future studies should be distributed to a broader, diverse population.

In addition, future research should focus on examining the different information literacy skills between students who have completed credit courses versus those who have had no formal library instruction. While it is impossible to control for other sources of information literacy skill building, longitudinal studies examining participants both in the university and workplace settings will provide greater insight. The results of this study suggest there are other sources outside of library instruction where students feel they gain research skills that should be examined further.

Additionally, comparing knowledge management professions with less information-intensive professions would further define the differences in use of information by the two groups. Using a combination of outcomes based measures and phenomenography, data can be compiled to provide a definitive assessment of the libraries role in preparing individuals for lifelong learning. ■

References

Association of American Colleges and Universities., & National Leadership Council (U.S.). (2007). *College learning for the new global century: A report from the National Leadership Council for Liberal Education & America's Promise*. Washington, D.C:

Association of American Colleges and Universities. Available: http://www.aacu.org/leap/documents/Global Century_final.pdf

Association of College and Research Libraries., & American Library Association. (2000). *Information literacy competency standards for higher education*. Chicago, IL: ACRL.

Brasley, S. (2008). Effective librarian and discipline faculty collaboration models for integrating information literacy into the fabric of an academic institution. *New Directions for Teaching and Learning, 114*, 71–88.

Bruce, C. S. (1999). Workplace experiences of information literacy. *International Journal of Information Management, 19*, 33–47.

California State University. California State University retools general education courses to focus on core values of liberal education (Press Release) Available at http://www.calstate.edu/pa/news/2008/leaps.html

California State University. (1995). *Information competence in the CSU: A report submitted to Commission on Learning Resources and Instructional Technology Work Group on Information Competence*. Sacramento, CA: California State University.

Casner-Lotto, J., Conference Board., Partnership for 21st Century Skills., Corporate Voices for Working Families., & Society for Human Resource Management (U.S.). (2006). *Are they really ready to work?: Employers' perspectives on the basic knowledge and applied skills of new entrants to the 21st century U.S. workforce*. United States: Conference Board.

Cheuk, B. (2008). Delivering business value through information literacy in the workplace. *Libri, 58*. 137–143.

Crawford, J. (2006). The use of electronic information services and information literacy: A Glasgow Caledonian University study. *Journal of Librarianship & Information Science, 38*(1), 33–44. doi:10.1177/0961000606060958

Curzon, S. C. (2004). Developing faculty-librarian partnerships in information literacy. In Rockman, I. F. (Eds.). Integrating information literacy into the higher education curriculum: Practical models for transformation. San Francisco: Jossey-Bass.

de Jager, K. (1997). Library use and academic achievement. *South African Journal of Library & Information Science, 65*, 26–30.

Ferguson, S. (2009). Information literacy and its relationship to knowledge management. *Journal of Information Literacy, 3*, 6–24.

Halford, S., Lotherington, A. T., Obstfelder, A., & Dyb, K. (2010). Getting the whole picture? *Information, Communication & Society, 13*, 442–465.

Head A., Eisenberg M. (2010) Truth be told: How college students evaluate and use information in the digital age. Project Information Literacy Progress Report. Available http://projectinfolit.org/pdfs/PIL_Fall2010_ Survey_FullReport1.pdf

Hepworth, M., & Smith, M. (2008). Workplace information literacy for administrative staff in higher education. *Australian Library Journal, 57*, 212–236.

Hughes, H. , Middleton, M. , Edwards, S. , Bruce, C. and McAllister, L. (2005). Information literacy research in Australia 2000— 2005, Bulletin des *Bibliothèques de France* 50, 1–23. Available http://eprints.qut.edu.au/archive/00002832/0 1/BdesB_submission.pdf

Kirton, J., & Barham, L. (2005). Information literacy in the workplace. *Australian Library Journal, 54*, 365–376.

Klusek, L., & Bornstein, J. (2006). Information literacy skills for business careers: Matching skills to the workplace. *Journal of Business & Finance Librarianship, 11*, 3–21.

Lloyd, A. (2007). Recasting information literacy as sociocultural practice: Implications for library and information science researchers. *Information Research, 12*, 1–13.

Lloyd, A. (2009). Informing practice: Information experiences of ambulance officers in training and on-road practice. *Journal of Documentation, 65*, 396–419.

McMahon, C., & Bruce, C. (2002). Information literacy needs of local staff in cross-cultural development projects. *Journal of International Development, 14*, 113–127.

Oakleaf, M., & Owen, P. L. (2010). Closing the 12 - 13 gap together: School and college librarians supporting 21st century learners. *Teacher Librarian, 37*(4), 52–58.

Ochs, M. (1991). Assessing the value of an information literacy program. Ithaca, NY: Cornell University. ERIC EDRS340385. Available http://www.eric.ed.gov/PDFS/ED340385.pdf

O'Dell, J. (February 9, 2010). How millenials use tech at work. *Read Write Web*. Available http://www.readwriteweb.com/archives/how_millenials_use_tech_at_work.php

O'Farril, R. T. (2008). Information literacy and knowledge management: Preparations for an arranged marriage. Libri: *International Journal of Libraries & Information Services, 58*, 155–171.

O'Sullivan, C. (2002). Is information literacy relevant in the real world?. *Reference Services Review, 30*, 7–14.

Rockman, I. F. (2002). Strengthening connections between information literacy, general education, and assessment efforts. *Library Trends, 51*, 185–98.

Schulte, S. J. (2008). High self-efficacy and high use of electronic information may predict improved academic performance. *Evidence Based Library & Information Practice, 3*, 35–37.

Shepherd, P. T. (2011). Journal usage factor - a promising new metric. *Serials, 24*, 64–68.

Somerville, M. M., & Howard, Z. (2008). Systems thinking: An approach for advancing workplace information literacy. *Australian Library Journal, 57*, 257–273.

Smalley, T. (2000). Investigating information age realities in the world of work. Available http://www.cabrillo.edu/~tsmalley/WorldOf Work.html

Travis, T. (2008). Librarians as agents of change: Working with curriculum committees using change agency theory. New Directions for *Teaching and Learning, 114*, 17–33.

Walsh, T. R. (2011). Evolution of an information competency requirement for undergraduates. *Journal of Web Librarianship, 5*, 3–23.

Whitmire, E. (2002). Academic library performance measures and undergraduates' library use and educational outcomes. *Library & Information Science Research, 24*, 107–128.

Wong, S. H. R., & Webb, T. D. (2011). Uncovering meaningful correlation between student academic performance and library material usage. *College & Research Libraries, 72*, 361–370.

Wu, D. (2008). Aligning information literacy with workplace expectations. 12th Biennial CARL Conference. Irvine, CA.

Tiffini A. Travis

Director of Information Literacy & Outreach

Services, University Library

California State University, Long Beach

Voice: 562- 985-7850

Fax: 562–985-1703

ttravis@csulb.edu

Woods, D. M. (2020). Using goal setting assignments to promote a growth mindset in IT students. *Information Systems Education Journal, 18*(4), 4–11.

Engage via Research Prediction

- Will a growth-minded goal setting activity in class help students develop a growth mindset and develop skills?

Read for Key Points

- What question did the researcher seek to answer? (Introduction)
- Who participated in the study and what did the participants do? (Method)
- What was the answer to the research question? (Results)

Critically Think about the Research

- Why do you think this growth-minded goal setting class activity led to positive outcomes?
- What are some other ways an instructor can foster growth mindset and goal setting skill development?

Build Information Literacy Skills

- Are these findings consistent with other research studies?
- How can college instructors teach growth mindset?

Research Study

Woods, D. M.* (2020). Using goal setting assignments to promote a growth mindset in IT students. *Information Systems Education Journal, 18*(4), 4–11.

This paper explores how goal-setting activities in a course were used to promote a growth mindset in students. Research shows many benefits for students with a growth mindset that emphasizes learning and addressing challenges by focusing on effort and process rather than judgments about success or ability. Activities designed to prompt students to improve general skills that would make them better students and prepare them to be life-long learners were introduced in two upper level IT courses. The activities were designed to promote a growth mindset by focusing on the efforts made and processes used rather than the outcomes. Assessment of the activities found that students demonstrated a growth mindset in their work, saw clear value in the activities, and made progress in improving specific skills.

Keywords: growth mindset, goal setting, life-long learning, IT education, pedagogy

Introduction

We teach, but our real goal is for students to learn and prepare for success in life. For instructors, there are many parts to this. We must learn about the latest technologies and update classes to add technologies that employers seek. We need to adjust content and delivery to address the move to hybrid and online courses. Ever present concerns about retention and completion statistics mean that we must ensure that students are actively engaged in our programs and institutions. In addition, all fields, but especially IS/IT must prepare students to be lifelong learners.

At the center of all of these efforts are our students, with the instructor in the classroom as the main person engaged in helping the student learn. The instructor can't do it all, so institutions provide a range of services to support students – learning assistance centers, tutoring, study skills courses, etc. Some students take advantage of these support services, and others may not need them, but there are students who need to improve their skills but fail to make use of these services.

This failure to develop needed skills is puzzling. Students are given clear feedback about skills they need to improve – writing, time management, etc. – along with information about where they could find assistance, but no improvement is seen. Discussions with students offered many explanations for not developing these skills that would help them in all of their courses. Two themes stood out. First were the students who knew that poor skills were limiting their ability to succeed, but did not feel that they could improve these skills, demonstrating the fixed mindset identified by Dweck (2016). Another theme was students who set goals for improvement but struggled to take action and make progress towards their goals.

This information prompted thought about expanding course activities and assignments to help students foster a growth mindset, set goals, and make progress towards achieving these goals. These efforts serve many purposes, but fundamentally, the goal is to help students improve their skills as students. Improved skills will help them learn more in a specific course, help them in later courses, and make them more confident in their ability to complete their degree program. After they graduate, employers will benefit from new employees who can take ownership of planning and executing the learning and improvement necessary to remain valuable employees.

* David M. Woods, Woodsdm2@miamioh.edu, Computer & Information Technology Department, Miami University Regionals, Hamilton, OH 45011

Motivation

Mindset

Work looking at individuals' attitudes has identified two mindsets that affect how people respond to the challenges they encounter in their life (Dweck, 2016). People with a fixed mindset believe that their "qualities are carved in stone" (Dweck, 2016, p. 6) and feel they have a fixed intelligence and personality. People with a growth mindset believe that these qualities can be developed through their efforts, strategies, and the help of others.

The two mindsets drive significant differences in an individual's behavior and how they react to challenges. People in the fixed mindset feel they are constantly being evaluated – are they smart or dumb, will they succeed or fail, will they win or lose? A challenge is seen as a test where they must succeed or fail. They focus on the judgment and may ignore feedback about how to improve their performance. If they do not succeed in their first effort, they may give up. With the growth mindset, people are not interested in proving themselves, but rather improving themselves. The person with the growth mindset feels smart when "learning something over time: confronting a challenge and making progress (Dweck, 2016, p. 24). The person with a growth mindset seeks to overcome a challenge by working harder, trying different strategies, and seeking help from others.

There are connections between mindset and the concept of grit, defined as "perseverance and passion for long-term goals" (Duckworth and Peterson, 2007, p. 1087)" which has been shown to predict success factors beyond those predicted by IQ. Duckworth (2013) identified the growth mindset as "the best idea I've heard about building grit in kids."

A growth mindset seems ideal for learning, and studies have explored the impact of mindset in education. A recent study by the Center for Community College Student Engagement explored many aspects of mindset. One finding was that "More students have fixed mindsets for math than for either English or overall intelligence" (CCCSE, 2019, p. 6). The growth mindset also correlates with higher GPAs in both math and English. These findings could affect student success and retention and have specific interest for IS/IT educators since math is seen as a closely related field. Another finding from the study is a relationship between maturity and mindset, with non-traditional age students showing more optimism when facing challenges.

Research on connections between mindset and poverty shows how a growth mindset helps poor students overcome some of the obstacles they face. Research on a national scale looked at the mindset of public school students in Chile (Claro, Paunesku, & Dweck, 2016). This work found that mindset and socioeconomic factors are both strong predictors of academic achievement. The study found that a growth mindset was more common with students from higher income families. The finding that "students in the lowest 10th percentile of family income who exhibited a growth mindset showed academic performance as high as that of fixed mindset students from the 80th income percentile" highlights the potential value of promoting the growth mindset (Claro, Paunesku, & Dweck, 2016, p. 8664).

The mindset of faculty can have a significant impact on students. Recent work that looked at a sample of 150 STEM instructors and 15,000 students found that students in courses taught by instructors with a fixed mindset earned lower grades (Canning, Muenks, Green, & Murphy, 2019). In addition, while students from underrepresented minorities had lower average grades than White or Asian peers, the study found that this racial achievement gap was twice as large in courses taught by instructors with a fixed mindset. This work also reviewed course evaluations and found that students were less motivated in courses taught by faculty with a fixed mindset, and were less likely to recommend a course taught by an instructor with a fixed mindset.

Dweck notes that "in truth we're all a mixture of the two" mindsets, and that various events or situations may trigger a specific mindset (2016, p. 211). Grant and Dweck (2003) performed five studies that looked at the impact of goals on mindset. Ability or performance goals predict fixed mindset results where student performance and engagement suffer in the face of a challenge. In contrast, goals focused on learning and gaining new knowledge predict growth mindset behavior - "active coping, sustained motivation, and higher achievement in the face of a challenge (Grant & Dweck, 2003, p. 541)." This finding shows the importance of focusing on learning goals rather than performance, providing feedback focused on effort, and offering processes to support students' efforts.

Several efforts have explored applying mindset thinking to technology courses (Murphy & Thomas, 2008; Cutts, Cutts, Draper, O'Donnell, & Saffrey, 2010; Lovell, 2014; Payne, Babb, & Abdullat 2018). An obvious starting point is an initial programming course, which can present students with many unexpected challenges along with the potential for technology-generated feedback, including syntax errors, compiler errors, and run-time errors, that are presented in a fixed mindset type success/failure format. One study found that teaching students about mindset and providing growth mindset motivated feedback to students during a six-week period had a positive impact on student's mindset and test scores (Cutts et al., 2010).

Goals Setting

With the value of processes like goals in supporting a growth mindset, it is interesting to look at research on goal setting. Research finds that goal setting in the workplace has a positive impact on employee engagement, workplace optimism, and individual performance – signs of a growth mindset (Medlin & Green, 2009).

Research on the use of goal setting in the classroom also shows benefits. When students in a management course used a goal setting worksheet to develop goals for a group project, instructors found that students actively used the goals to improve project quality and team performance (Lawlor & Hornyak, 2012).

Both of these studies found value in formal, structured goal setting processes. Lawlor & Hornyak specifically used the SMART goal approach. The first published discussion of SMART goals defined the acronym as Specific, Measurable, Assignable, Realistic, and Time-related (Doran, 1981). Since then, several useful variations have developed (SMART criteria, n.d.), including a format that uses Achievable in place of Assignable (SMART Goals, n.d.).

Goal Setting Activities

How can we promote a growth mindset in students and encourage them to develop skills that make them better students, and in the future, better employees? The growth mindset's focus on effort and process suggests exploring the use of goal setting as a specific process to support the growth mindset. Goal setting activities designed to promote a growth mindset and help students build general skills, rather than skills specific to one course, were developed. The goal setting activities were used in two different upper-level IT courses but were not tied to specific course projects. In addition to the goal of promoting a growth mindset, a second goal was to measure student perceptions of the goal setting activities to guide further use and development of the activities. Students in both courses are a mix of traditional age and older, non-traditional students, with many students working part-time or full-time while taking courses.

Personal Improvement Project

The Current Practices in Information Technology course is the first course in a three-semester self-directed capstone experience. For their capstone, students use technology to develop and implement a solution to a specific problem. During the first capstone course, students work individually to research potential capstone project ideas. In addition to learning about a problem, the research often involves exploring technologies and tools for potential solutions.

During the semester, students complete four three-week long research projects. Each project includes assignments for a project proposal, in-class project pitch, intermediate work product, final work product, reflection, and in-class project presentation. A challenge of this course is that students must take ownership of planning and managing their projects. Additionally, oral and written communication skills are important for the project pitch, in-class presentation, and final project report. A Personal Improvement Project activity was developed to provide a process to promote a growth mindset in the development of the soft skills used in this class.

The activity had three graded assignments during the course of the semester. In the second week of the semester, students submitted a proposal setting a goal to improve a specific non-technical skill along with a discussion of why they chose the specific skill. The proposal assignment prompted students to think about how they would measure and report on their progress in later assignments. The assignment also provided examples of soft skills and potentially useful on-campus and online resources.

In the middle of the semester, students completed a status check assignment. Using a growth mindset approach, the assignment prompted students to think about effort and process. Students submitted a reflection about what they had done, whether they wanted to make updates to their initial goal, whether they needed help to work towards their goal, and their plans for working on their goal during the rest of the semester.

The final assignment was an end of the semester wrap up. Again, students reflected on their work to achieve their goal and discussed whether they would continue working on the goal or add a new goal.

Student Performance Planning

Goal setting was also used in a course that covers IT strategy and management. This course covers a wide range of topics, but one specific learning outcome covers the management of IT staff. Material supporting this learning outcome includes hiring, promotion, and employee performance planning and evaluation. To help students understand employee performance planning and appraisal, student performance planning and evaluation activities were developed. These activities are spread throughout the semester and provide processes to promote a growth mindset.

The course text uses a novel like format to follow a business leader unexpectedly thrust into the role of Chief Information Officer (CIO) at a fictional company (Austin, Nolan, & O'Donnell, 2016). The book starts with this leader moving into his new role, similar to students starting a new class. In the first week of class, a discussion of goal setting and performance planning for the main character in the book is used to support a discussion of goal setting and performance planning for students. The discussion introduces the SMART goal concept, along with examples of writing SMART goals.

In the first performance planning assignment, students develop a student performance plan for their work in the course during the semester. Students are provided a performance planning template and develop goals organized into three groups, with examples provided for each group:

- General Student Activities – activities a student might do in any course they take.
- Achievement of Course Learning Outcomes – activities to help the student achieve this specific course's learning outcomes.
- Teamwork – goals to support team assignments in the course.

The class has several team assignments, and students work in the same teams for all assignments. While students are developing their teamwork goals, the teams are also working on a team organization and planning assignment and are encouraged to connect their personal teamwork goals with the plans developed by their team.

In the middle of the semester, students complete a two-part midterm performance assessment. First, students assess their progress for at least two goals in each of the three groups in the performance plan. Students are encouraged to submit data to support their self-assessment. For example, one student with a goal about the number and quality of classroom contribution submitted a spreadsheet documenting and assessing each of their classroom contributions. Secondly, students reflect on how creating and following a performance plan has helped their overall performance in the class, with specific discussion of:

- Their execution of activities to support their goals.
- Whether they wrote the right goals.
- How they might improve their goals or their work to achieve them.

The final assignment in the performance planning activities was an end of semester assessment of the performance plan. The assignment had two parts. The first was the same as the midterm assessment – an assessment of progress on the goals, ideally supported with data. The second part asked students to reflect on how the performance planning activities had helped their performance in the class. Students also discussed how they might use performance planning, including specific goals, in future courses or a work environment. All of the performance planning assignments contributed to the student's final course grade.

Assessment

Two methods were used to assess the two goal setting activities. The student submissions were reviewed to determine how students engaged in the activities and assess their mindset. An end-of-semester survey collected data about student views on the value of the activities and effort required.

Personal Improvement Project

Students in two successive semesters completed the personal improvement project. The course enrollment was thirty-one (31) in the first semester and eleven (11) in the second. In both semesters, student goals covered a range of topics. The most popular covered time management (procrastination, scheduling, and work/life balance), self-care (meditation, exercise, and stress management), and communication (writing and public speaking).

The end of semester wrap up assignment was reviewed to assess what mindset students exhibited in discussing their work on the personal improvement project. Of the thirty-three (33) students who consented to participate in the research, all but one completed this assignment.

The student submissions provided clear discussions of what the student learned and the impact of the projects. Students showed pride and even surprise in what they were able to accomplish. All of the student discussions addressed one or more concepts associated with the growth mindset. These included the effort they made, the processes they used, and the progress they made. Many also discussed plans to continue work on their goal.

Nine of the responses included judgments or similar content associated with a fixed mindset. Four of these were positive – noting the accomplishment of a goal or the success of the project. The other five submissions used terms reflecting disappointment, failure, or scoring their effort poorly. At the same time, all of these submissions also included discussion of the effort and progress that the student had made in working on their goal, and all of these students exhibited signs of a growth mindset by discussing how they would continue to work on their goal.

Students completed a short, anonymous survey on the last day of class. In the first semester, twenty-three (23) of the students completed the survey (74% response rate), and in the second semester, ten (10) students completed the survey (91% response rate).

The first four questions used a 5 point Likert scale, asking students to agree or disagree with the statements:

1. I felt that the personal improvement project helped me improve my skills as a student.
2. I felt that the mid-semester status check on the personal improvement project helped me assess how I was doing with my improvement project.
3. I saw the value of the personal improvement project for improving my work as a student.
4. The feedback provided by the instructor encouraged my efforts to work on this project.

For all four questions, the average response was at least 4.0, with at least 75% of students agreeing or strongly agreeing, indicating that students saw clear value in the activities and that instructor feedback promoted a growth mindset.

The remaining questions used a 7 point Likert scale for students to rate (not much to very much):

5. How effortful was it for you to work on your personal improvement project?
6. How much did the personal improvement project help your ability to complete the research projects in the course?
7. How much did you enjoy the personal improvement project?
8. How much would you like to do a similar personal improvement project in future courses?

For question 5, the average was 5.2, showing the project required some effort. The results from the remaining questions were all positive (4.8–4.9) showing that the work was beneficial and enjoyable. Question 8 had the widest distribution of answers, with ten (30%) very much wanting to do a similar project in a future course, but also with thirteen (39%) unsure.

Student Performance Planning

The student performance planning activities were used in a recent semester of the course with twenty-four (24) students. Goal setting and the assignment to write a student performance plan were introduced in the first week. The SMART goal concept was also introduced with in-class discussions and examples and supporting online material. Students identified good goals but struggled to document them as SMART goals. The main issues were goals that were not measurable or were not specific. To address these problems, specific feedback was provided. Students were encouraged to discuss their goals with the instructor and allowed to resubmit their student performance plan.

It was a pleasure to read the student reflections submitted with the final performance evaluation. The reflections showed that students had made clear progress in accomplishing their goals. The student reflections also showed that students had put significant effort into working on their goals. For many students, their discussion of how goal setting had helped them improve as students matched what was observed in their class participation and submitted assignments.

All of the student discussions addressed the effort and process concepts linked to the growth mindset. All of the students mentioned goal setting and performance planning as a valuable process. Many also mentioned how the performance plan motivated them to be accountable to make an effort to work on the goals. Two students did make clear judgments that they were not able to achieve their goals, but their discussions focused on lack of effort, a sign of a growth mindset, rather than lack of ability, a sign of a fixed mindset.

An anonymous end of semester survey was used to collect information about several class activities, including the student performance plan, and sixteen students completed the survey (67% response rate).

The first five questions on the survey used a 5 point Likert scale, asking students to agree or disagree with the statements:

1. I saw the value of the performance planning activities for learning how to write good performance goals for the course.
2. I saw the value of the performance planning activities for evaluating my own performance.
3. I saw the value of the performance planning activities for planning to improve my own performance.
4. I saw the value of the performance planning activities to prepare me for performance planning I might do in a professional workplace.
5. I felt that the performance planning activities engaged me in thinking about how to improve my performance as a student.

For questions 1 – 4, a clear majority (69 – 88%) of students agreed that they saw value in the different goals of the activities. For question 5, the majority (69%) also agreed that the activities prompted them to engage in the process of self-improvement.

The remaining questions about the performance planning activities used a 7 point Likert scale for the students to rate (not much to very much):

6. How effortful was it for you to write your initial performance plan?

7. How effortful was it for you to complete your mid-term performance evaluation?

8. How effortful was it for you to complete your final performance evaluation?

9. How much did you enjoy the performance planning activities?

10. How much did you learn about setting good goals?

11. How much did you learn about a planning process for improving your work in a class or similar long term activity?

12. How much would you like to do similar performance planning activities in future courses?

For questions 6 – 8 about the effort for the activities, averages were 4.1 – 4.5, with writing the initial performance plan requiring the most effort. The response for question 9 about the enjoyment was overall neutral – 4.1. For questions 10 and 11, the averages show students learned about both processes that could be used to support a growth mindset - goal setting (5.1) and performance planning (4.9). For the final question, 50% of the students wanted to do similar activities in future courses. Several students in the course were about to graduate, which may have affected the responses to this question.

Conclusions and Future Plans

Students in both classes demonstrated a growth mindset and saw value in the goal setting activities. The presence of a growth mindset is not clearly linked to the class activities, but both activities met the goals set when the activities were developed. The activities were beneficial to the majority of the students, did not require too much effort, and were well received by students. From the instructor's perspective, the time required to develop and grade the assignments was minimal, and the student submissions provided good insight into the effort and progress students were making. There was also clear evidence that students appreciated and acted on the feedback they received.

The results are encouraging, supporting further efforts to use goal setting in the future. The design of these activities to focus on general, non-technical skills should allow use in a wide range of courses.

Goal setting activities are being developed for two introductory courses. These will use a version of the personal improvement project with more frequent status updates. One of the introductory courses also includes first-year experience content that all new students at the university are required to take, which will provide an excellent opportunity to discuss the mindset and SMART goal concepts.

Goal setting is just one process that can support a growth mindset. Further work will review other aspects of the course environment to identify additional opportunities to encourage the growth mindset. ∎

References

Austin, R. D, Nolan, R. L., & O'Donnell, S. (2016). The Adventures of An IT Leader. Harvard Business Review Press, Boston.

Canning, E. A., Muenks, K., Green, D. J., & Murphy, M. C. (2019). STEM Faculty Who Believe Ability is Fixed Have Larger Racial Achievement Gaps and Inspire Less Student Motivation in Their Classes. Science Advances, 5(2), EAAU4734.

Center for Community College Student Engagement (CCCSE) (2019). A mind at work: Maximizing the relationship between mindset and student success. The University of Texas at Austin, College of Education, Department of Educational Leadership and Policy, Program in Higher Education Leadership, Austin, TX. Retrieved from http://www.ccsse.org/center/NR2019/Minds et.pdf

Claro, S., Paunesku, D., & Dweck, C. S. (2016). Growth Mindset Tempers the Effects of Poverty on Academic Achievement. Proceedings of the National Academy of Sciences, 113(31), 8664–8668.

Cutts, Q., Cutts, E. Draper, S., O'Donnell, P., & Saffrey, P. (2010). Manipulating Mindset to Positively Influence Introductory Programming Performance. In SIGCSE 10: Proceedings of the 41st ACM technical symposium on computer science education, Milwaukee (WI), USA, 10–13.03.2010. Association for Computing Machinery, New York.

Doran, G. T. (1981). There's A S.M.A.R.T. Way to Write Management's Goals and Objectives. Management Review, 70(11), 35.

Duckworth, A. & Peterson, C. (2007). Grit: Perseverance and Passion for Long-Term Goals. Journal of Personality and Social Psychology, 92(6), 1087–1101.

Duckworth, A. (2013). Grit: The Power of Passion and Perseverance. TED Talks Education, retrieved from https://www.ted.com/talks/angela _lee_duck worth_grit_the_power_of_passion_and_pers everance

Dweck, C. (2016). Mindset: The New Psychology of Success, Updated Edition. Ballantine Books, New York.

Grant, H. & Dweck, C. S. (2003). Clarifying Achievement Goals and Their Impact. Journal of Personality and Social Psychology, 85(3), 541–553.

Lawlor, K. B. & Hornyak, M. J. (2012). SMART Goals: How the Application of SMART Goals can Contribute to Achievement of Student Learning Outcomes. Developments in Business Simulation and Experiential Learning, 39, 259–267.

Lovell, E. (2014). Promoting Constructive Mindsets for Overcoming Failure in Computer Science Education. In ICER '14 Proceedings of the tenth annual conference on International computing education research. Association for Computing Machinery, New York.

Medlin, B. & Green Jr., K. W. (2009). Enhancing Performance through Goal Setting, Engagement, and Optimism. Industrial Management & Data Systems, 109(7), 943–956.

Murphy, L. & Thomas, L. (2008). Dangers of a Fixed Mindset: Implications of Self-theories for Computer Science Education. In ITiCSE 08: Proceedings of the 13th Annual Conference on Innovation and Technology in Computer Science Education: Madrid, Spain, June 30-July 2, 2008. Association for Computing Machinery, New York.

Payne, K. C., Babb, J., & Abdullat, A. (2018). Reflections on Applying the Growth Mindset Approach to Computer Programming Courses. In 2018 Proceedings of the EDSIG Conference Norfolk, VA USA, 4(4641).

SMART criteria (n.d.) In Wikipedia. Retrieved July 9, 2019, from https://en.wikipedia.org/wiki/SMARTcriteria

SMART Goals: How to Make Your Goals Achievable. (n.d.). Retrieved from https://www.mindtools.com/pages/article/s mart-goals.htm

Deepa, S., & Seth, M. (2013). Do soft skills matter? Implications for educators based on recruiters' perspective. *The IUP Journal of Soft Skills, 7*(1), 7–20.

Engage via Research Prediction

- What percentage of mid-level and top-level executives believe soft skills are essential to success?

Read for Key Points

- What question did the researcher seek to answer? (Introduction)
- Who participated in the study and what did the participants do? (Method)
- What was the answer to the research question? (Results)

Critically Think about the Research

- Why do most employers report graduates coming to the world of work without having developed essential soft skills?
- How can college students put this research into practice? How are soft skills developed?
- How might the value of soft skills vary based on culture or discipline?

Build Information Literacy Skills

- Are these findings consistent with research studies conducted in different countries, including the United States, and across different disciplines?
- How do colleges and universities teach soft skills?
- What strategies or approaches work best at helping students build and strengthen soft skills?

Research Study

Deepa, S.*, & Seth, M**. (2013). Do soft skills matter? Implications for educators based on recruiters' perspective. *The IUP Journal of Soft Skills, 7*(1), 7–20.

Soft skills are very critical in the workplace today. These skills mirror the ability to communicate and interact with others. They are unique because they emphasize on action. They have become indispensable for every person in the present context. This paper deals with the significance of soft skills for getting a job and for further promotions and progress in the workplace. People who are flexible and have the zeal to understand and learn new technologies are sought after by organizations as part of their growth process. The need to provide training in soft skills is seriously being considered today. This study is an attempt to find out the importance that middle to top level executives, who are involved in recruiting employees, attach to soft skills.

Introduction

Organizations today have transformed into places where people cannot function in seclusion. Teamwork or group work is the need of the day in most industries. There are many organizations that do not necessarily design jobs on the basis of a team. Nonetheless, they require a fair amount of interaction between people within and across functional realms to successfully carry out a piece of work. The opportune discoveries made through the Hawthorne studies are now accepted as basic and universal principles of life in any organization. In this setting, soft skills have become indispensable to function competently in any interpersonal relationship.

'Soft skills' is an umbrella term covering various survival skills such as communication and interpersonal skills, emotional intelligence, leadership qualities, team skills, negotiation skills, time and stress management, and business etiquettes. In recent years, the corporate world felt that soft skills are crucial at the workplace and its training must be a part of the curriculum during education. In career terms, soft skills soften the edges and provide a competitive advantage over others. However, those who ignore this critical aspect of personality learn its importance the hard way when their promotion is overlooked.

Soft skills are "attitudes and behaviors displayed in interactions among individuals that affect the outcomes of various interpersonal encounters" (Muir, 2004). These are skills that refer to the ability to communicate and interact with other employees in a positive manner.

Soft skills are necessary in the workplace for professional success. They are vital at every level of an organization if it is to function smoothly and productively. Hard skills are technical competencies and domain knowledge, while soft skills are a combination of people skills, interpersonal skills, communication skills and emotional intelligence. Companies search for a mélange of both soft and hard skills among their employees to deliver goods and services effectively to their clients. It is rightly said that people rise in organizations because of their hard skills and fall due to a shortage of soft skills.

Kelly Pierce points out in "eSight Trend Watch: Increased Value in Soft Skills," that "There is a growing recognition that interpersonal skills are not simply helpful in business today; they are essential in today's highly focused, downsized and streamlined organizations where people tend to work in a series of small, often temporary workgroups or teams organized to accomplish short-term objectives." He lists such qualities as "attitude, initiative, cooperation, teamwork, communication, perception" among the skills that are valued in the contemporary workplace.

Soft skills deal with these behavioral aspects relevant in personal and corporate life. Today, we find employers taking hard skills as a given or as the basic requirement and the soft skills 'including communicating, relationship building, work ethic and problem solving' (Johnson, 2006), as an important consideration in deciding upon the choice of a candidate for any job.

The purpose of this paper is to understand the prospective employers' perception about importance of soft skills while hiring MBAs and provide information that may be utilized by educators to enhance the soft skills of students entering the workforce.

* Assistant Professor, Managerial Communication, Indian Institute of Management, Kozhikode, Kerala, India; and is the corresponding author. E-mail: deepa@iimk.ac.in

** Assistant Professor, Human Resource Management, Jaipuria Institute of Management, Lucknow, Uttar Pradesh, India. E-mail: manisha.seth@jaipuria.ac.in

Literature Review

Rainsbury et al. (2002) categorized the competencies of superior managers identified by Spencer and Spencer (1993) as hard skills or soft skills. Only three of the 20 competencies were classified as hard skills, while the remaining 17 were organized as soft skills. The categories of soft skills, include achievement and action, impact and influence, managerial (team management and developing others), and personal effectiveness.

The last few years have witnessed a growing awareness and a need to identify the intangible factors which play a very important role in an individual's success at the workplace. Varied studies have been done in the past related to such areas. Many experts have in the past worked on and concluded that these extra skills which help to attain success at the workplace are certainly precious. Jacobs and Marshall discussed the importance of the definite class of skills that allow value additions to a person's worth. Though none of them uses the term, they actually deem it to be soft skill.

For decades, the center of management was on the so-called 'hard' skills, i.e., the emphasis centered on technical skills imperative to effectively perform within the organization. These skills tended to be more job-specific or more closely related to the actual task being performed.

Today, employers look for managers with the vital soft skills. These skills tend to be more generic in nature. In other words, these are skills strategic to effective performance across all job categories. And these soft skills have come to play an even more central role in management positions in today's setting. As the world has changed and the nature of work has changed, the skill set required for managers has also undergone a change.

Studies by Stanford Research Institute and the Carnegie Mellon Foundation among Fortune 500 CEOs found that 75% of long-term job success depended on people skills and only 25% on technical skills. In fact, this stands true at other levels as well. For effective performance in the workplace, companies need their employees to not only have domain knowledge, technical and analytical skills, but also skills to deal with the external world of clients, customers, vendors, the government and public, and to work in a collaborative manner with their colleagues.

The annual rankings of MBA colleges often place communication and interpersonal skills as the most decisive skills needed for success in the corporate world.

Distinguished academician Prof. Henry Mintzberg, while speaking on the importance of soft skills for MBAs, referred to the crucial 'soft skills'—leadership, teamwork, communication and the ability to think 'outside the box' of a discipline—that separate the rest in the management world.

In a poll on Melcrum's Black Belt Training website, the skill that was voted the most vital for internal communicators to master in order to carry out their roles with utmost efficacy was building effective relationships.

Other surveys and studies also show that employers are often more concerned about soft skills or attitudes rather than technical knowledge or competencies. Empirical studies of work find that employers and workers also feel generic skills, such as problem solving, communications and the ability to work in teams, are more significant for workplace success. Another study on developing soft skills in vocation high school graduates talks about the importance of developing soft skills in students for their betterment and future career growth.

A 2007 study of recruiters found that communication skills are the most desired characteristics needed in a candidate for an ideal job.

According to a survey by Harvard University, 80% achievements in career are determined by soft skills and only 20% by hard skills. In the book, *Lessons from the Top* by Neff and Citrin, the duo talk about 10 top success tips, out of which eight are concerned with soft skills and only two criteria talk about hard skills.

Similarly, a literature review undertaken by researchers to understand best practices revealed that soft skills are given much importance by the employers worldwide. Luthans et al. (1985 and 1998), on the basis of their study conducted on more than 450 managers, ascertained that the average managers spend most of their time in traditional management activities, whereas in the case of managers who were successful (defined in terms of speed of promotion within their organization), networking skills made the largest contribution to their success. In the case of effective managers (defined in terms of the quantity and quality of their performance and the satisfaction and commitment of their subordinates and coworkers), communication skills made the largest contribution.

A literature review undertaken by researchers to understand best practices made known that soft skills are given much importance by the employers universally. According to them, it was found that in IT companies, projects failed not due to the lack of technical skills but due to the lack of interpersonal and communication skills. Bill (2004) showed that communication skills, self-esteem, and work ethics are the main factors that determine one's achievement in his/her work. Several other works, especially on customer-focused services, have shown that customer-focused soft skills can make a big contribution to profitability even in industries regarded as highly technical.

To achieve success in today's job market, employees need a combination of occupation-specific hard skills and soft skills.

According to Duncan and Dunifon (1998), "soft skills are as good a predictor of labor market success as level of formal education." Similarly, commenting on the need for high school students to develop such skills, experts have agreed on several hard skills. And over and above that, the two most important soft skills are the ability to communicate effectively and the ability to work productively with people from different backgrounds. Thus, the review of literature shows that there is a need for other types of skills than the routine hard skills to succeed in the work place, but none has completely and satisfactorily understood the skill requirements; and there is limited research done to generate specific guidance that is useful to educators and students.

According to Harvey and Knight (1996), "employers are not looking for trainees but people equipped to learn and deal with change. Employers want graduates who are adaptable and flexible, who can communicate well and relate to a wide range of people, who are aware of, but not indoctrinated into, the world of work and the culture of organizations, and who, most importantly, have inquiring minds, are willing and quick to learn, are critical, can synthesize and are innovative."

Contrary to the popular belief, soft skills do make a difference in the business world (Workforce, 1999). Even though managers still need typical techniques taught in MBA programs, they need additional tools to be effective. Today's managers need a variety of soft skills in communication, negotiation, and team building to effectively manage technological change and corporate stress resulting from downsizing and rapid growth (Deverell, 1994). Another study conducted by Caudrin (1999) revealed that while hiring MBAs, corporations seek the three most desired capabilities—communication skills, interpersonal skills and initiative—all of which are elements of emotional intelligence.

For a long time, recruitment and selection processes concentrated on finding people with the right technical or domain expertise. The focus was on the so-called hard skills. So, the requirements normally spelt out the area and the technical expertise required for a job. The person-job fit was measured typically on the basis of these qualifications. Later, employers realized that while the core skills are present, successful interpersonal relationships played a major role in achieving results. The success of a department or an organization depended on domain knowledge and also as much, if not more, on the ability of a group of individuals to work in a team and optimize their individual resources.

The 21st century workforce has experienced tremendous changes due to advances in technology; consequently, the 'old way' of doing things may be effective but not efficient (Redmann & Kotrlik, 2004). The National Business Education Association (NBEA) stated that the shortage of skills confronting today's dynamic workforce goes beyond the academic and hands-on occupational skills. Therefore, the best way to prepare potential employees for tomorrow's workforce is to develop not only technical, but also human-relation abilities (Policies Commission for Business and Economic Education (PCBEE), 2000).

Defining 'soft skills', Perreault (2004) stated that these are personal qualities, attributes, or the level of commitment of a person that set him or her apart from other individuals who may have similar skills and experience. According to James and James (2004), 'soft skills' is a new way to describe a set of abilities or talents that an individual can bring to the workplace. Soft skills characterize certain career attributes that individuals may possess such as team skills, communication skills, leadership skills, customer service skills and problem solving skills. "Employers Value Communication and Interpersonal Abilities" (2004) suggests that one who communicates effectively, gets along with others, embraces teamwork, takes initiative, and has strong work ethics is considered to have an accomplished a set of soft skills. Sutton (2002) found that soft skills are so important that employers identify them as 'the number one differentiator' for job applicants in all types of industries (p. 40). According to Sutton, soft skills have become extremely important in all types of occupations. Glenn (2008) added that hiring individuals who possess soft skills is instrumental for high-performing organizations to retain a competitive edge. Wilhelm (2004) agreed and claimed that employers rate soft skills highest in importance for entry-level success in the workplace.

Literature supports the conclusion that proficiency in soft skills is extremely important from employers' perspective. However, many employees in business are reported to be lacking in soft skills. Also, literature revealed that research is needed in the area of soft skills so that enhanced instructional methodology may be developed and applied by business educators.

The paradigm shift in the 21st century workforce has forced employees to be well armed with soft skills (Ganzel, 2001). James and James (2004) confirmed that soft skills have become extremely crucial even in technical environments. This endorses the view of Evenson (1999) who believed that equipping students with soft skills could make the difference in obtaining and retaining the jobs for which they have been prepared.

The NBEA believes that skills emphasized in the 20th century must be refocused. To ensure success, students entering the 21st century workforce must possess non-technical soft skills along with technical competence (PCBEE, 2000). A complex labor market has been generated due to the multifaceted 21st century business world; therefore, organizations are seeking versatile individuals, who possess professional skills, even for entry-level jobs (Employers Value Communication and Interpersonal Abilities, 2004). According to Christopher (2006), employers want graduates with strong interpersonal abilities. Quite a lot of researchers (Sutton, 2002; Glenn, 2003; NBEA, 2004; and Wilhelm, 2004) substantiated that mastery of soft skills is instrumental to success for individuals entering the 21st century workforce.

With time, companies aren't just assessing their current staff and future recruits on their business skills. They are now evaluating them on a multitude of soft skills like how well they relate to and communicate with others. It is a bit shocking and somewhat disturbing when someone exhibits the old autocratic style of bullying management tactics.

Measuring these soft skills is not easy. But in the most progressive companies, managers are looking for people's ability to communicate clearly and openly, and to listen and respond empathetically. They also want them to have equally well-honed written skills so that their correspondence (including e-mails) does not undo all the good work their face-to-face communication creates.

A few companies are untouched by the ever-widening authority of other cultures and good soft skills ease better communication and people's ability to manage differences efficiently. Already everyone has some form of soft skills (probably a lot more than they realize). They just need to look at areas in their personal life where they get on with others, feel confident in the way they interact, can solve problems, are good at encouraging, and can network with the best of them. All these skills are soft skills and all of them are transferable to the workplace.

It is unfortunate that people lightly esteem the significance of soft skills. In fact, the concept of soft skills is a developing ambit that people must take seriously; people have to be educated about them. Whenever a new discipline surfaces, people resist and mostly do not respect it because there is no strong research to substantiate its relevance. However, over a period of time people start accepting and respecting the discipline. For example, there were many people who initially did not take management as a discipline seriously and expressed their reservations. Today, management as a discipline is a reality, having a sacred and respectable position like many other disciplines in the world. Similarly, soft skills will evolve as a discipline during the course of time when more research is done. It is often difficult to quantify soft skills (unlike hard skills), but soft skills are both intrapersonal and interpersonal competencies that determine a person's ability to gel well with others and excel in the corporate world (Rao, 2012).

Research Methodology

Data regarding the views of employers and managers involved in interviewing and recruiting people and their expectations from new recruits was collected with the help of a questionnaire (Appendix), comprising questions on how much importance is being given to soft skills while recruiting new persons or experienced persons. The respondents were asked to rate the seven broad categories of skills included in 'soft skills' and the typical soft skills they look for when recruiting. About 160 mid-level to top level executives from about 4–5 sectors located in Delhi, Noida, Nasik, Lucknow, Indore and Mumbai were sent questionnaires. 135 responses were received, out of which 100 were found complete in all respects. Finally, the data collected through the questionnaire was analyzed and the results were compared to the previously held beliefs and theories. Telephonic discussions with some recruiters also provided insights into their perception of soft skills.

Findings and Analysis

The findings were generally on expected lines, with 86% respondents agreeing that soft skills are indeed very important to succeed at the work place (Figure 1).

But when asked about the quality of new entrants entering the workforce today, 60% said that the new entrants do not possess the necessary soft skills to succeed at the workplace. And an overwhelming majority, that is 82% respondents, agreed that there were gaps between the industry requirements and the products churned out by the colleges and universities of today. On the question whether they thought that the new entrants can acquire soft skills on joining a good organization, 50% felt that they would. And 85% strongly felt that adding soft skills in college curricula will improve the quality of the workforce.

When asked what ratio they would offer to soft skills and work experience while recruiting, 68% of the respondents stated 60:40 if it is an entry level job, 50:50 if it is a mid level management position and 60:40 in case of a higher management position.

The respondents were also asked to divide a percentage score of 100 among the six must-have soft skills

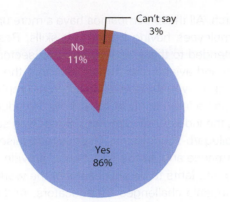

Figure 1   Are soft skills important at the workplace?

to succeed at the workplace. The results showed that communication skills received the maximum weightage of 22%, while interpersonal skills followed a close second with 20%, teamwork and leadership qualities received 16% and 15%, respectively, time management got 13%, while conflict management received 14% weightage (Figure 2).

While expressing his thoughts on how much importance is attached to soft skills while recruiting candidates for entry level jobs in Management, Himojyoti Sengupta, Human Resources – North, Reliance General Insurance Company Ltd., opines, "The said skill set is very much important for an entry level position but it is hard to find. The same gives an edge over other candidates." When asked whether the organization got the candidates with required soft skills, he stated that they needed to provide the necessary training.

In this regard, Khyati Seth, Assistant Manager – HR, Abhitech IT Solutions Private Limited states, "Soft skills are a very important aspect considered while selecting a candidate, especially for the freshers. As observed, the quality of the candidates is deteriorating day by

day, they lack basic skills like communication and social behavior." She further says, "We do not get candidates with the required set of soft skills. Also, the time and resources involved in the training of the candidates are very high."

Mohit Kumar, AVP – HR, Aditya Birla Group said, "We hire candidates from management institutes under Young Leaders' program. We have a competency framework in our organization. We believe that soft skills like communication, influencing, teamwork, getting things done, and developing self and others are very important for people to successfully perform and excel in the various roles in the organization. Proficiency levels for these competencies for various roles in job hierarchy are very much defined, including that for entry level roles. We look forward to people demonstrating these competencies appropriately while we make a hiring decision." He added, "We get the candidates with required soft skills. Training is a continuous process and it is equally important for people having these competencies to further hone their skills to the next level."

Tanmay Panda, Head HR, National Payment Corporation of India, said that soft skills are indeed very important while recruiting candidates for entry level jobs in management. He added that they are generally required to train the employees in the crucial soft skills.

Nidhi Bhatnagar, Human Resources, Fidelity Info Services, while expressing her views on the importance of soft skills in recruiting stated, "It is always important to be really good at soft skills. However, the weightage of this parameter actually depends on the role that one is appearing for. For instance if one has appeared for a HR job, soft skills will be given high weightage along with the other prerequisites, lack of soft skills might even result in elimination/rejection, since a HR professional needs to cater to the aspirations and emotions of human capital, it is important that one has excellent soft skills. On the other hand, if one applies for a sales job, soft skills need to be modified in a way where the person is able to crack a deal, the conviction required over there will be slightly different, the weightage of soft skills parameter might differ/might be less as well, however it will carry its due importance."

On probing whether they got candidates with the required soft skills or they needed to train them, Nidhi Bhatnagar said, "We cannot expect excellent soft skills in candidates applying for entry level jobs, as it will be quite unfair to them since they do not hold a practical exposure to the corporate world. We certainly believe in training the candidate in case we feel that he/she has all the prerequisites for the role and needs slight polishing on soft skills. We too would not want to lose such good

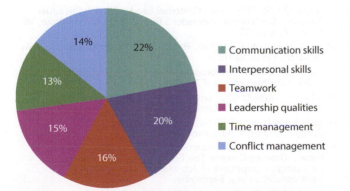

Figure 2   Must-Have Soft Skills to Succeed at the Workplace.

resources, yes; they need to have that aptitude and attitude to learn which paves way for us to make them shine as any other seasoned employees. Training them on soft skills is something which is always an option as that is a very softer aspect which can be evolved in a person to bring about that desired change in one's personality, both professionally and personally."

Conclusion

Recruitment managers respect and expect technical expertise. Results show that they do prefer people with experience, but at the same time, they also look for certain other qualities in them. However, technical or the so-called hard skills soon become outdated when there is no motivation to keep learning new ones. So, they also look for people who are flexible and have the passion to appreciate and learn new technologies as part of their growth process. And as Beck and Yaeger pointed out, "The ability to effectively communicate with the managers, superiors, bosses and coworkers plays a definite role in workplace success." Furthermore, "the interpersonal skills, alignment with the corporate culture, the ability to work as an effective and contributing team member and the political savvy to know how to get things done in the organization" also determine a person's long-term success in an organization. Therefore, our results have shown that in generic terms, hiring managers are not happy with the new workforce coming out of the colleges and they do think that they should be much better equipped with soft skills in addition to hard skills. On the basis of these results, we have made an attempt to provide to the educators a guideline to design the soft skills course curriculum in such a way so as to bridge the gap that exists between the existing one and the industry expectations. The results also pointed out that the basic skills should include good communication style along with the ability to work in teams and ability to get things done on time as well as manage conflicts tactfully.

This study may be quite useful to business educators because the findings reported help to recognize the most important workforce skills. In addition, this information may allow educators to more effectively include employability skills in their courses.

Scope for Further Research: This study was basically a preliminary (probing) research to tap into the minds of recruiters across Indian companies and find out the importance of soft skills in their scheme of things, particularly the recruitment process. Although an attempt was made to take samples from across India from the banking, insurance, automobile, real estate and retail sectors, there is a lot of scope for further research. All these companies have a more urgent need for employees having better soft skills. Research can be extended to these as well as other sectors like hospitality and aviation, to further look into the difference these skills would make to their career graph. Besides, it would be interesting to know how the educators feel about the industry requirement of teaching soft skills at the college/b-school level. The desire to raise academic performance and, at the same time, provide opportunities for students to be successful at the workplace creates sizeable challenges for educators. And expanding the curriculum to meet the new skill demands raises several questions such as: What should be the college and university curriculum that can inculcate problem solving, teamwork, interpersonal and communication skills in students? Further research in this area could provide exciting ideas to bridge the existing gap between education curricula and industry demands. ■

Bibliography

Buhler P M (2001), "The Growing Importance of Soft Skills in the Workplace", *Supervision*, Vol. 62, No. 6, p. 13, available at http://connection.ebscohost.com/c/ articles/4514272 /growing-importance-soft-skills-workplace

Caudrin S (1999), "The Hard Case for Soft Skills", *Workforce*, Vol. 78, No. 7, pp. 60–64.

Christopher D A (2006), "Building Better Communicators: Integrating Writing into Business Communications Courses", *Business Education Forum*, Vol. 61, No. 2, pp. 40–43.

Coplin B (2004), "For New Graduates, "Soft-Skills'' Are The Secret Weapon in Job Hunt", June 9, available at http://usatoday30. usatoday.com/news/opinion/editorials/ 2004-06-09-coplin_x.htm

Deverell J (1994), "The Most Valuable Quality in a Manager", *Fortune*, Vol. 136, No. 12, pp. 279–280.

Duncan G J and Dunifon R (1998), "Soft Skills and Long-Run Labor Market Success", *Research in Labor Economics*, Vol. 17, pp. 123–150, JAI Press, London.

"Employers Value Communication and Interpersonal Abilities" (2004), *Keying In*, Vol. 14, No. 3, pp.1–6.

Evenson R (1999), "Soft Skills, Hard Sell. Techniques: Making Education and Career Connections", Vol. 74, No. 3, pp. 29–31.

Ganzel R (2001), "Hard Training for Soft Skills", *Training*, Vol. 38, No. 6, pp. 56–60.

Glenn J L (2003), "Business Success Often Depends on Mastering the 'Sixth R' Relationship Literacy", *Business Education Forum*, Vol. 58, No. 1, pp. 9–13.

Glenn J L (2008), "The 'New' Customer Service Model: Customer Advocate, Company Ambassador", Business Education Forum, Vol. 62, No. 4, pp. 7–13.

Harvey L and Knight P T (1996), *Transforming Higher Education*, Open University Press, SRHE.

http://www.melcrum.com/products/training_courses/bbinternational /index. html?mxmroi=23962826/24254731/false

http://www.softskillsindia.com/why develop softskills /importanceofsoftskills.html

Huba M E and Freed J E (2000), *Learner Centered Assessment on College Campuses*, Allyn and Bacon, MA.

Information Technology Association of America (2004), "Adding Value… Growing Careers: The Employment Outlook in Today's Increasingly Competitive IT Job Market", Annual Workforce Development Survey, September.

Jacobs J (1969), *The Economy of Cities*, Vintage, New York.

James R F and James M L (2004), "Teaching Career and Technical Skills in a 'Mini' Business World", *Business Education Forum*, Vol. 59, No. 2, pp. 39–41.

Johnson J (2006), "More Employers are Focusing on Soft Skills When Seeking out New Employees", *Colorado Springs Business Journal (CO)*, September 29. Retrieved on November 25, 2008, from Regional Business News database.

Kane T E (2009), "Soft Skills are Hard and Critical to Career Success", available at http://www.chartresource.com/featurekane.htm.

Kennedy and Kathy (2005), "Integrating Technical Skills and Soft Skills to Ensure Student Success", *Best Practices*, Summer, pp. 1–3.

Luthans F (1988), "Successful vs Effective Real Managers", *The Academy of Management Executive*, Vol. 11, No. 2, pp. 127–132.

Luthans F, Rosenkrantz S A and Hennessey H W (1985), "What do Successful Managers Really Do? An Observation Study of Managerial Activities", *Journal of Applied Behavioral Science*, Vol. 21, No. 3, pp. 255–270.

Marshall A (1890), *Principles of Economics*, MacMillan, London.

Meenakshi S (2009), "How Important are Soft Skills from the Recruiter's Perspective", *The IUP Journal of Soft Skills*, Vol. III, No. 2.

Muir C (2004), "Learning Soft Skills at Work", *Business Communication Quarterly*, Vol. 67, No. 1, pp. 95–101.

Perreault H (2004), "Business Educators Can Take a Leadership Role in Character Education", *Business Education Forum*, Vol. 59, No. 1, pp. 23–24.

Polack-Wahl J A (2000), "It is Time to Stand up and Communicate", Proc. 30th ASEE/ IEEE Frontiers in Educ. Conf., pp. F1G-16-F1G-21, Kansas City, USA.

Policies Commission for Business and Economic Education (2000), "This we Believe About Teaching Soft Skills: Human Relations, Self-Management, and Workplace Enhancement", Statement No. 67.

Rainsbury E, Hodges D, Burchell N and Lay M (2002), "Ranking Workplace Competencies: Student and Graduate Perceptions", *Asia-Pacific Journal of Cooperative Education*, Vol. 3, No. 2, pp. 8–18.

Rao M S (2012), "Soft Versus Hard Skills", *T+D*; Vol. 66, No. 5, pp. 48–51.18 The IUP Journal of Soft Skills, Vol. VII, No. 1, 2013

Redmann D H and Kotrlik J W (2004), "Technology Integration into the Teaching-Learning Process by Business Education Teachers", *The Delta Pi Epsilon Journal*, Vol. 46, No. 2, pp. 76–91.

Sireesha M (2009), "Use of Portfolios in a Soft Skills Course", *The IUP Journal of Soft Skills*, Vol. III, No. 1, pp. 7–18.

Stasz C, Ramsey K, Eden R et al. (1996), *Workplace Skills in Practice: Case Studies of Technical Work* (MDS-773), National Center for Research in Vocational Education, University of California, Berkeley.

Sutton N (2002), "Why Can't We All Just Get Along?", *Computing Canada*, Vol. 28, No. 16, p. 20.

Thomas Neff J and Citrin James M (1999), *Lessons from the Top: The Search for America's Best Business Leaders*, p. 448, Doubleday, New York.

Timm J A (2005), "Preparing Students for the Next Employment Revolution", *Business Education Forum*, Vol. 60, No. 2, pp. 55–59.

Wilhelm W J (2004), "Determinants of Moral Reasoning: Academic Factors, Gender, Richness of Life Experiences and Religious Preferences", *The Delta Pi Epsilon Journal*, Vol. XLVI, No. 2, pp. 105–121.

Appendix

Questionnaire

Name (Optional): Mr./Ms.: _____

Designation: _____

Organization: _____

Location: _____

Gender: _____

Age Group (Years): 20–30 ☐   30–40 ☐   40–50 ☐   >50 ☐

Mark your perception on the following statements where 1 - Strongly Agree, 3 - Neutral and 5 - Strongly Disagree

S. No.	Statements	1	2	3	4	5
1.	Soft skills are crucial to achieve success at the workplace.					
2.	Soft skills are important criteria when interviewing job applicants.					
3.	Soft skills are more important than experience in similar position.					
4.	New entrants/joiners possess the required soft skills to be successful at the workplace.					
5.	There is a gap between the industry requirements and the products of the colleges today.					
6.	Recruiters are satisfied with the current workforce available for their industry/sector.					
7.	Soft skills can be acquired even after joining a good company or an organization.					
8.	Adding soft skills in the college curricula will provide better equipped personnel.					

Appendix (Cont.)

What ratio would you offer to soft skills and work experience?

S. No.	Statements	40:60	50:50	60:40
1.	For considering lower level management positions			
2.	For considering middle level management positions			
3.	For considering higher management positions			

Rate the following soft skills in order of their importance (1–6) with 1 being the topmost essential skill and 6 the least essential that a new job applicant/fresher must possess to join an organization:

S. No.	Soft Skill	Order					
		1	2	3	4	5	6
1.	Team Work						
2.	Conflict Management						
3.	Communication Skills						
4.	Time Management						
5.	Interpersonal Skills						
6.	Leadership Qualities						

Reference # 50J-2013-03-01-01

Orndorff, H. N., III. (2015). Collaborative note-taking: The impact of cloud computing on classroom performance. *International Journal of Teaching and Learning in Higher Education, 27*(3), 340–351.

Engage via Research Prediction

- Does engaging in collaborative note-taking improve academic performance?

Read for Key Points

- What question did the researcher seek to answer? (Introduction)
- Who participated in the study and what did the participants do? (Method)
- What was the answer to the research question? (Results)

Critically Think about the Research

- Why do you think the collaborative note-taking resulted in better performance?
- How can faculty use these findings to support student learning?
- Would the results be different for different disciplines?

Build Information Literacy Skills

- What additional evidence exists for collaborative note-taking?
- What technology tools would best support collaborative note-taking?

Research Study

Orndorff, H. N., III*. (2015). Collaborative note-taking: The impact of cloud computing on classroom performance. *International Journal of Teaching and Learning in Higher Education, 27(3), 340–351.*

This article presents the early findings of an experimental design to see if students perform better when taking collaborative notes in small groups as compared to students who use traditional notes. Students are increasingly bringing electronic devices into social science classrooms. Few instructors have attempted robustly and systematically to implement this technology to facilitate student learning. This study examines the efficacy of using technology to improve student note-taking. Cloud-based collaborative software makes it possible for the first time to break down the most basic walls that separate students during the process of taking and encoding notes. Collaborative note participants used Google Drive under direction of an instructor to assess performance differences. Strong evidence is found that such groups improve grades and related learning outcomes.

Content in most social science classrooms is still primarily delivered via lecture. That quintessential collegiate institution, the classroom, remains familiar in its static delivery of content. Students individually and in isolation take notes while a professor speaks. If students are encouraged to collaborate, that interaction is solely outside the confines of the class and typically not encouraged during the lecture. While there are often times of group discussion or interaction, these are not typically during the lecture, movie, or multimedia event. Current research demonstrates that interaction actually decreases the amount of note-taking during a class session (Boch & Piolat, 2005). From chalk to PowerPoint, technology has not disrupted the normal classroom environment.

Yet there are pedagogical reasons for wanting to overcome the isolation inherent in the contemporary classroom. Modern cognitive theory has uncovered that "learners must be actively engaged in learning" to achieve deep understanding (Barkley, Cross, & Major, 2005, p. 10). Pedagogical research has demonstrated that good undergraduate education includes meaningful and extensive contact between students as well as between students and faculty, both of which encourage active learning. As early as 1994 there was evidence that collaboration could advance problem solving and critical thinking skills (Alavi, 1994). Earlier still Johnson, Mesch, and Johnson (1988) found that cooperative learning arrangements increase measures of achievement, higher-level reasoning, frequency of new ideas, and situational transfer. In his seminal work on writing across the curriculum, critical thinking, and active learning, Bean (2011) emphatically emphasized the need for small group collaboration in the classroom. In short, there is an emerging consensus that our creativity and learning are enhanced by social interactions (Resta & Laferrière, 2007).

Nowhere has the isolating effects, so devastating for critical thinking, been so pronounced as during the act of note-taking. Note-taking, at its most basic, has been defined by educational psychology as the condensation of material while simultaneously interacting in other ways with a given material set (Piolat, Olive, & Kellogg, 2005). During a traditional lecture students have time limitations which requires unique summarization and leads to "much diversification in note-taking practices" (Piolat et al., 2005, p. 293). But how effective are these practices? What are students actually gaining from this skill set quantitatively?

Typically, students are involved in a form of "copy-regurgitate" strategies (Boch & Piolat, 2005, p. 102). Students copy lecture material down in order to later perform well on tests. These kinds of notes are about the passive production of information, and the notes are a process of enhancing internal storage (Kiewra, 1987). It is also a way to focus attention. Note-taking requires a listener to be more connected to a speaker or document (Piolat et al., 2005). The problem is that although students rely on this method, its efficacy has been demonstrated to be inadequate in the classroom setting (Ambruster, 2000; Kiewra, 1985; Makany, Kemp, & Dror, 2009). The problem found in the literature is that students are not efficient note takers, meaning they only successfully capture information about 20% of the time, and they are organizationally flawed and therefore miss how information should fit together. These shortcomings, efficiency and organization, are particularly acute in individuals taking notes on a computer alone (Mueller & Oppenheimer, 2014). Mueller and Oppenheimer (2014) specifically find that computers – when used in isolation – lead to lower levels of information retention, and they postulate this is due to students trying to be

*Harold N. Orndorff III, Daytona State College

stenographers with keyboards instead of actively engaging with the material.

Given the numerous problems of normal note-taking practices, much research has examined the effects of particular note-taking techniques in order to assess how it might be improved (Makany et al., 2009). Makany et al. (2009) are particularly interested in finding ways to help improve information retention. These include clustering, concept mapping, the Cornell system, idea mapping, instant replays, knowledge maps, learning maps, mind mapping, model maps, and others. There is a consensus emerging that the key to note-taking is the ability to select, encode, and organize information (Robinson, Katayama, DuBois, & DeVaney, 1998; Samarawickrema & O'Reilly, 2003) and that well-structured notes lead to better learning outcomes (Titsworth & Kiawra, 1998, 2004). Traditional lectures and notes have been demonstrated to lead to less information transfer, less structure, and less learning than was previously thought.

Within the context of these many options, much pedagogical research has focused on creating and proposing systems for improving note-taking. Among the suggestions is the use of collaborative notes (Kam et al., 2005; Kobayashi, 2006; Miyake & Masukawa, 2000; Wu, Chen, Chen, & Chiu, 2009). Collaborative notes are mechanisms by which students summarize lecture (or other material) jointly and simultaneously. Typically such collaboration occurs in small groups (three to four students) who work together to produce a single notes document.

Unfortunately, the techniques presented in the literature are often implemented by obscure, expensive, technical software or forms not immediately user friendly (Kittle & Hicks, 2009). Additionally, prior proposals have had pricing and familiarity issues. Expensive and unfamiliar software is simply not a realistic possibility for many universities and colleges. Despite many suggestions for changing how students take notes, none have displaced the normal model. The few suggestions that do exist are not readily available in most academic settings.

As a result of these shortcomings, those interested in writing pedagogy and collaboration have recently turned to Google Drive (Kittle & Hicks, 2009). Their reasoning is Google offers three primary services not available with other tools (like wikis or specialized software): (a) users can interact inside the program, (b) Google saves are made automatically and simultaneously, and (c) Google Drive informs users of changes by other writers. Writing pedagogy—highlighted by the now ubiquitous Writing Across the Curriculum (WAC) and Writing in the Disciplines (WID) programs—now makes a strong case for the use of digital collaboration, but that work has not yet extended its research to the broader classroom environment or the process of note-taking.

The goal of this work is twofold: to bring small groups into the classroom and improve student learning via collaborative notes using non-specialized software. Given that half of the variance of students' test scores are related to lecture notes (Titsworth & Kiewra, 1998), professors should be deeply interested in ways of improving the note-taking process. This project begins where the varying research threads have left off. How can we increase student collaboration while improving note-taking practices? Further, how is this accomplished without disadvantaging students and colleges who may not have access to expensive or specialized software? The current work attempts to bridge an unfortunate gap between the well-intentioned goal of collaboration and improved note-taking in earlier pedagogical work and the pragmatic reality that faculty face in the classroom.

Project Overview

One of the most important technological advances has been the advent of the *cloud*. Cloud computing has altered the way data is processed and stored. Instead of computers being isolated units, cloud computers run software and functions on remote servers that can be accessed by any local client. The unique possibility presented by such a paradigm shift is that multiple users can run the same program simultaneously and thereby interact with one another. For word processing, this means that multiple users could access, create, and edit the same document.

A variety of cloud software is available for word processing, but for the purposes of creating a collaborative space in which students can take notes together, Google Drive was chosen due to the literature on writing noted earlier (Kittle & Hicks, 2009). It must be noted that a variety of other software could also be used; the newest versions of iWork allow for collaborative real-time editing (including for tablets). Microsoft Office 360 is working on implementing real-time editing. Emergent tools such as QUIP are also becoming potential editing packages. For the purposes of this study the goal was something that was device agnostic: there are versions of Google Drive for iPhone, iPad, Android phones and tablets, and even for every variety of laptop including Linux. It was also desirable to use software that had been previously tested in earlier studies.

Google Drive is a hard drive in the cloud. It allows files to be stored remotely and accessed from any computer. In addition, Google Drive comes with a free tool, Google Documents. Documents allows for editing remotely in a word processor that is on any tablet or computer. Multiple users can edit the same document, chat, and work together in real time. Importantly for student buy-in, unlike other office suites (such as the dominant Microsoft Office), Google Drive is completely free. The no-cost entry means that any student, at any level of institution, can participate. Expensive software is possible at some universities, but for many teaching institutions such costs are prohibitive.

Unlike traditional, locally based word processors, Google Drive can be used by a nearly unlimited number of individuals at the same time. Central to the current context, users can actually edit a single document simultaneously. One of the key failings of traditional notes is trying to record information while simultaneously processing that same information. But what if more than one student were able to work together? Could this offload some of the mental shortcomings of traditional, individualized notes? This research tests the effects of collaborative note-taking on class performance both qualitatively and quantitatively across a spectrum of classes.

The experiment was relatively simple: allow students to use collaborative notes in small groups (three to four students) and compare experiences and performances between those who used collaborative notes and those who did not. Further, compare outcomes between classrooms that participated in the experiment and control classrooms. It was also possible to administer a pre-/post-test in order to evaluate if the notes themselves were a defining factor in learning outcomes. The classes in the experiment were introductory political science and psychology classes. All classes were from state colleges.

Students freely volunteered at the beginning of each semester to participate in the collaborative note-taking. Professors (or a teaching assistant) who participated would explain to their classes about Google Drive and the possibility of joining small groups to take notes simultaneously in class. This presentation was done during the first week of each semester. Students then opted into the study if they so chose and remained part of the process for the duration of the semester. From the larger body of participants, students then freely entered into smaller note-taking groups however they wished or were randomly assigned into smaller groups by the professor or teaching assistant.

Each professor (or teaching assistant) created a blank file in Google Drive for each small group in the class. As a result, classes had multiple small groups. One American government class in the fall of 2012, for example, had four small note-taking groups of three to four students. These collaborative note groups had their own independent Google Drive document. Therefore, each class had multiple collaborative small groups, and this was constant across all classes.

Letting the professor or teaching assistant author the file granted the instructor access and ownership of each group's notes in case of disputes or issues during the semester. It also allowed for the instructor to get real-time feedback on how well students understood any particular set of lectures. Professors were able to engage students in a new way by having the ability to tailor content and get a feeling for the performance of students by the notes they were taking—a feature not possible with traditional notes. For example, in the spring of 2013, I modified and altered lectures on a section on civil liberties due to the way students were taking notes (such changes were implemented the following semester).

Methodology and Results

In order to assess the effects of collaborative note-taking, the following two strategies were employed:

- A quantitative controlled study focused on a survey tool and student grade data to assess the actual impact of collaborative notes. Did students benefit from using collaborative notes? How did students' self-reports compare to received grades? To mitigate the issue of the self-selection bias there is also a comparison between participating classes and non-participating classes.
- Standardized open-ended interviews were administered to each student participant (Turner, 2010). These interviews involved asking students identical questions during the course of the semester while using collaborative notes. In this way it was possible to see how students themselves assessed collaborative note-taking, and what, if any, benefits or discouragements they encountered. Students were asked a serious of open ended-questions and were not restricted in how to respond.

Student Performance Findings

Phase one of the experiment looked for evidence that small groups taking notes collaboratively performed better than their peers. There were two primary measures: grades and independent learning outcome performance. Ten classes participated in the experiment that included a total of 247 students where 51 students were in an experimental group (small groups using collaborative notes) and 196 students were in the control group (students in the same class who took notes individually). The benefit of the first control group was that all participants received an identical stimulus. The problem is that, given the voluntary nature of student involvement, there is a potential for selection bias. To account for the issue of selection bias a second control group, a class of an additional 32 students, was used. The control class was taught identically to the experimental sections, but the offer to take notes collaboratively was never extended. By using two control groups it was possible to minimize selection bias.

A final experimental design looked to content knowledge measures outside grades. In one of the experimental classes the college performed a student learning outcomes pre-test and post-test. These tests are designed by a panel of instructors to assess the effectiveness of classes in achieving their learning outcomes. In conjunction with the experimental design, the pre-tests and post-tests helped to detect if either the experimental or control population started at different baseline knowledge levels and to compare – apart from grades – how the groups performed after the stimuli.

Table 1 shows the class breakdowns. Unsurprisingly, each section had slightly larger female populations. The largest population of students came from American government sections. All students were either freshmen or sophomores. Further demographic information was not collected due to privacy concerns.

Table 2 shows that the average grade across all classes and groups (experimental and control) was 72.02%. Students in the experimental group had an average grade of 79.66%, while the control group average was a 71.87% (a difference of 7.79%). Students who participated in collaborative notes performed nearly a single letter grade better than did their peers in the same classes. The ANOVA result found significance at the .01 level (F = 5.47, p < 0.01). Further, Bartlett's test for equal variance returned a non-significant value, indicating a reliable ANOVA model. It is possible to say there was a statistically significant difference between the control group and the experimental group.

Is this difference due to a selection bias? The control class (a population of 32 as noted earlier) was compared to the experimental group. The average grade for the control class was 70.3%, nearly identical to that of the average control group (71.87%), and there was no significant difference in ANOVA results. As a result, it is possible to say that the grade data is probably not skewed and that the improvement to grades was likely due to the influence of collaborative notes as a variable. See Table 3.

But did the notes result in additional learning? In one experimental class, as already described, a pre-test and post-test, independent of the instructor, was administered by the department. The college in question administers these tests to students during the first week of classes to assess their baseline knowledge of a particular subject. During the last week of the semester students are then given the same test again. The post-test is required to be worth a certain percentage of a student's grade. This allows the school to measure student-learning outcomes. These tests are applied to all instructors and are not created by any one instructor but a panel of faculty in the discipline. One of the experimental classes for collaborative notes was also selected by the department to be administered a pre-/post-test. It was possible to use this data to see how the experimental group compared to the control group on an independent, professor agnostic, metric. Results are shown on Table 4.

Students who were part of the experimental group (35.41%, N = 7) performed worse than their peers (38.54%, N = 43) on the pre-test. On the post-test students who participated in collaborative note-taking did significantly better (72.49%) than their peers (64.17%). Presumably this means that the students who participated in the study had lower levels of baseline knowledge at the outset, but they had a more robust level of knowledge by the end of the class and the experiment than did their peers who had taken notes individually. The difference of 8.28% is strikingly similar to the difference in grades. As the results indicate, these are difficult tests for students. The experimental group did not just perform almost a letter grade better in grades; they also performed almost a letter grade better on the pre/post tests.

In addition to grade and pre-/post-test data, additional questionnaires were distributed to students online at the end of each semester to see what students believed about their performance and technological skill. Students were asked about the propensity to use technology, to self-report on the usefulness of collaborative notes, to consider the likelihood of using collaborative notes in the future, and to identify the areas in which they self-reported improvements using collaborative notes compared to other methods. Unsurprisingly, students who participated were at least moderately interested in technology overall. Students who participated indicated they at least sometimes turned to technology to solve problems. See Figure 1.

In order to assess student outcomes, we asked a series of questions with Likert scale responses. It was important to assess students' perception of usefulness, likelihood of using again, likelihood of use in future classes, and areas of use. The first question asked students for their enjoyment. Did students like using collaborative notes? If students did not find the experience likable, the probability that they would employ them would be low—an important measure if a faculty member wants to implement a practical solution. On this measure students overwhelmingly said yes. Seventy students (71.43%) agreed, or strongly agreed, that they enjoyed collaborative notes. See Figure 2.

Table 1
Class Overviews

Class	Student Participants		Number of Sections	Male	Female
	Total	Test Group			
American Government	120	29	4	55	65
State and Local Politics	50	7	2	20	30
Comparative Politics	27	4	2	10	17
Introduction to Psychology	26	5	1	10	16
Research Methods (Psychology)	24	6	1	11	13
Total	247	51	10	106	141

Table 2
Class Grades

	Total Participants	Average Grade	Std. Dev.	Minimum Grade	Maximum Grade
All Students	247	72.02%	16.47	35.33%	99.97%
Test Group	51	79.66%	9.33	59.74%	91.57%

Table 3
Control Class

	Total Students	Average Grade	Std. Dev.	Minimum Grade	Maximum Grade
Control Class (American Government)	32	70.30%	15.32	44.46%	93.50%

Table 4
Pre-Post Test Results

State and Local Politics	Total Participants	Pre Test Avg. (Control Group)	Post Test Avg. (Control Group)
Control Group	43	38.54%	64.17%
Experimental Group	7	35.41%	72.49%

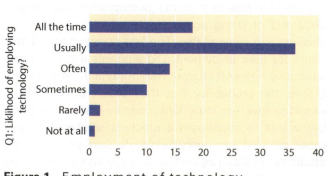

Figure 1   Employment of technology.

Another important question was whether students would want to use this method in another class. Even if under testing conditions students found the notes useful, would they continue to employ the tool without assistance or aid from the professor? Again overwhelmingly students answered yes. Sixty-seven students (81.71%) indicated they were planning on using collaborative notes again in a future class. See Figure 3.

Would students have used notes again in the current class? Almost universally participants said yes. This is interesting because it means that students increased

Third, students who take notes together can spend more cognitive energy on class material. This particular insight should help faculty who worry about the rows of computers they face in today's classroom and the potential shortcoming traditional, individualized, notes have in that environment. As Mueller and Oppenheimer (2014) have demonstrated, students who take notes individually on computers do worse at learning material than their longhand counterparts. The data here indicates that these effects might disappear if students take notes together in small groups. Given that the laptop is not likely to be toppled by the pen, it would be fruitful if future research compared student cognitive performance on laptops in small groups. The assumption in the Mueller and Oppenheimer study was that students would be taking notes in isolation. Under such conditions they apparently become stenographers and not deep thinkers. But as the qualitative research shows here, collaborative notes force students to do one job only and one job well during note-taking. In this environment, no one student is wasting cognitive energy writing everything down. Instead, they are simply playing their individual role, leaving the rest of their time to think more deeply on the material presented.

Software, Realism, and Education

Another insight is that software selection for higher education needs a healthy dose of realism. Most prior experiments concerning technology have used expensive and obscure software (Kittle & Hicks, 2009). Further studies are rarely conducted, and the average college cannot afford the potential solution even if more data could be collected. Any collegiate institution, in contrast, can implement free consumer-based software such as Google Drive (or QUIP or iWork). Far too much experimentation in previous research has focused on tools that the average classroom cannot access. Software needs to be targeted at widespread adoption if it is to be considered a realistic tool. Future research would do well to expand on the size of the experiment performed here. Such an experiment, by design, is easily performed at a wide range of schools given the low entry cost.

Classrooms of all types—from lecture based to flipped—assume that students are, and are capable of, taking effective notes. Yet very little time is spent pedagogically attempting to improve this aspect of student learning. The data here indicates that investing more time in note-taking strategies could continue to improve student success, which is an area of deep concern in higher education today and will likely remain so for the foreseeable future. Imagine the possibilities if student success could be shifted—even slightly—by a low cost intervention such as collaborative note-taking. Small groups and Google Drive can be implemented and tested anywhere.

Limitations

There are also several limitations of the current research. As is often the case with pedagogical studies, the total population of the study is relatively low. Further, despite the attempts to control for the issue of selection bias, the lower sample size increases the probability of extreme results. Future research, however, by starting from the basic model presented here, could expand the work to a larger population to see if the effects found continue to measure significantly. The findings are also limited in their scope: social science classes. While it is reasonable to assume the effects would manifest themselves across the curriculum, the limited nature of the study cannot demonstrate that possibility with certainty. But there are two big reasons to be optimistic in the face of these limitations. First, by having classes across a number of content areas it is possible to control for professorial variation. Many pedagogical studies are often limited to a single case study. Here, while the total population is limited, it does extend across a number of classes, fields, and professors. Second, the pre-and post-test data helps demonstrate that the sample population did not start off with higher baseline knowledge. To the contrary, the experimental population apparently had lower knowledge levels. Future research could expand on the pre- and post-test measures to see how deep or widespread this collaborative learning penetrates. Given this, the results of such a significant difference are encouraging for future research.

Conclusion

The early evidence indicates that collaborative student note-taking in small groups has improved student performance both as measured by grades and by external student learning outcomes. Collaborative note-taking appears to improve note-taking skills which are crucial in academia. The data suggests there is a potentially simple and pragmatic way for faculty to improve student learning and implement laptops and mobile devices in their classrooms. Small groups learning and taking notes together appear to be a potent academic tool.

Students will continue to use computers and mobile devices, and they will increasingly use these devices in class. The rise in use is inevitable as more digital natives, and post-digital natives, enter higher education. How will faculty manage this shift? One possibility, and the easiest, is to simply continue the classical formula: lecture and individualized notes. The data here suggestions that professors should not be passive agents as mobile technologies enter into the classroom. Instead, they should harness this new technology to improve student note-taking and in the process improve student success.

Students will be most successful if we recognize the importance of small groups. Students need a space to learn how to take notes. Small groups create a space where students can not only better learn the current content, but also improve on the skill of note-taking itself. Mobile technology is allowing students to interact in a way never before possible. Faculty will need to assist if we want these devices used in positive ways that will enhance and not detract from learning. In short, it might be worth considering using small groups for taking notes together online in your next class. ■

References

Alavi, M. (1994). Computer-mediated collaborative learning: An empirical evaluation. *MIS Quarterly, 18*(2), 59–174.

Armbruster, B. B. (2000). Taking notes from lectures. In R.A. Flip & D.C. Cavalry (Eds.), *Handbook of college reading and study strategy research* (175–199). Yahweh, NJ: Erlbaum.

Barkley, E. F., Cross, K. P., & Major, C. H. (2005). *Collaborative learning techniques: A handbook for college faculty.* San Francisco, CA: Jossey-Bass.

Bean, J. C. (2011). *Engaging ideas: The professor's guide to integrating writing, critical thinking, and active learning in the classroom* (2nd ed.). San Francisco, CA: Jossey-Bass.

Boch, F. & Piolat, A. (2005). Note-taking and learning : A summary of research. *The WAC Journal, 16*(September), 101–113.

Johnson, W., Mesch, D., & Johnson, R. (1988). Impact of positive interdependence and academic group contingencies on achievement. *The Journal of Social Psychology, 128*(3), 345–352.

Kam, M., Wang, J., Iles, A., Tse, E., Chiu, J., Glaser, D., ... Hall, S. (2005). *Livenotes: A system for cooperative and augmented note-taking in lectures.* Retrieved from http://www.cs. berkeley .edu/~jfc/papers/05/CHILivenotes/CHI200 5.pdf

Kiewra, K. A. (1987). Note-taking and review: The research and its implications. *Journal of Instructional Science, 16*(3), 233–249.

Kittle, P., & Hicks, T. (2009). Transforming the group paper with collaborative online writing. *Pedagogy: Critical Approaches to Teaching Literature, Language, Composition, and Culture, 9*(3), 525– 538. doi:10.1215/15314200-2009-012

Kobayashi, K. (2006). Combined effects of note-taking/reviewing on learning and the enhancement through interventions: A meta-analytic review. *Educational Psychology, 26*(3), 459–477. doi:10.1080/01443410500342070

Makany, T., Kemp, J., & Dror, I. E. (2009). Optimising the use of note-taking as an external cognitive aid for increasing learning. *British Journal of Educational Technology, 40*(4), 619–635.

Mueller, P. A., & Oppenheimer, D. M. (2014) The pen is mightier than the keyboard: Advantages of longhand over laptop note-taking. *Psychological Science, 25*(6), 1159–1168.

Miyake, N., & Masukawa, H. (2000). Relation-making to sense-making: Supporting college students' constructive understanding with an enriched collaborative note-sharing system. In B. Fishman & S. O'Connor-Divelbiss (Eds.). *Proceedings of the Fourth International Conference of the Learning Sciences* (pp. 41–47). Mahwah, NJ: Lawrence Erlbaum.

Piolat, A., Olive, T., & Kellogg, R. T. (2005). Cognitive effort during note-taking. *Applied Cognitive Psychology, 19*(3), 291–312. doi:10.1002/acp.1086

Resta, P., & Laferrière, T. (2007). Technology in support of collaborative learning. *Educational Psychology Review, 19*(1), 65–83. doi:10.1007/s10648-007-9042-7

Robinson, D. H., Katayama, A. D., DuBois, N.F. & DeVaney, T. (1998). Interacive effects of graphic organizers and delayed review in concept acquisition. *The Journal of Experimental Education, 67*, 17–31.

Samarawickrema, G., & O'Reilly, J. (2003). Using concept maps to improve the quality of learning law at a distance. In G. Davis & E. Stacey (Eds.), *Quality education @ a distance*, Vol. 259 (pp. 161–168). Boston, MA: Kluwer Academic Publishers.

Titsworth, B. S. & Kiewra, K. A. (1998, April). *By the numbers: The effect of organizational lecture cues on note-taking and achievement.* Paper presented at the meeting of the American Educational Research Association, San Diego, CA.

Titsworth, B. S. & Kiewra, K. A. (2004). Organizational lecture cues and student note-taking as facilitators of student learning. *Contemporary Educational Psychology, 29*(4), 447–461.

Turner, D. W. (2010). *Qualitative interview design: A practical guide for novice investigators, 15*(3), 754–760.

Wu, C., Chen, S., Chen, C., & Chiu, C. (2009). *The effect of integrating web 2.0 technology in collaborative note-taking on elementary students' science learning.* Paper presented at the World Conference on Educational Multimedia, Hpermedia, and Telecommunications, Honolulu, Hawaii.

HAROLD N. ORNDORFF III, PhD is an Assistant Professor of Political Science at Daytona State College in Daytona Beach, FL. where he also works inside the QUANTA honors program. His research areas include presidential politics, social media, and student learning.

Oliver, J., & Kowalczyk, C. (2013). Improving student group marketing presentations: A modified Pecha Kucha approach. *Marketing Education Review, 23*(1), 55–58.

Engage via Research Prediction

- Does the Pecha Kucha presentation approach work better than traditional PowerPoint presentations?

Read for Key Points

- What question did the researcher seek to answer? (Introduction)

- Who participated in the study and what did the participants do? (Method)

- What was the answer to the research question? (Results)

Critically Think about the Research

- Why do you think the Pecha Kucha approach resulted in better performance? What are the most important elements of the Pecha Kucha approach?

- Would the results be different for different disciplines or different purposes?

- How does this research finding connect to Mayer's (2009) multimedia principles?

Build Information Literacy Skills

- What additional evidence exists for Pecha Kucha? What does the research say about effective PowerPoint presentations?

- What type of presentation works best in the world of work?

Research Study

Oliver, J.*, & Kowalczyk, C.** (2013). Improving student group marketing presentations: A modified Pecha Kucha approach. *Marketing Education Review, 23*(1), 55–58.

Student presentations can often seem like a formality rather than a lesson in representing oneself or group in a professional manner. To improve the quality of group presentations, the authors modified the popular presentation style of Pecha Kucha (20 slides, 20 seconds per slide) for marketing courses to help students prepare and deliver professional business presentations. Data were collected and analyzed from marketing student presentations that used two different presentation styles: the proposed modified Pecha Kucha and traditional PowerPoint presentations. The authors' modified version of Pecha Kucha resulted in higher individual and group assessments along with other key findings relevant to marketing courses.

Students can often view project presentations as a formality, something that they just have to do as a requirement of a course. This can lead to behaviors such as reading from PowerPoint slides, including too much text on the slides, presenting for more than the allotted time or not enough time, and not knowing who should be presenting next. These are only a few of the challenging issues professors are confronted with when marketing students make group presentations.

As marketing graduates enter the business world, employers are seeking more than just marketing knowledge and skills, but also effective communication, presentation, and teamwork skills (Taylor, 2003; Young & Murphy, 2003). Team selling has become a popular approach, and the importance of effective public speaking, both individually and as a group, has never been more crucial. Marketing students may need to present or sell ideas to clients, customers, as well as internal and external stakeholders. However, many students are not natural presenters; for some, it is a skill that must be learned (Anderson & Anderson, 2010).

In order to better prepare marketing students for their careers, recommendations have been made to enhance the effectiveness of student oral presentations through a comprehensive and systematic approach (Bonnici & Luthar, 1996; Calcich & Weilbaker, 1992; Haley, 1993; Martin, 1990). These recommendations included discussions with the instructor, the number of presentations per semester, as well as dress rehearsals. In addition, research has suggested how student presentations should be evaluated by instructors and their peers (Carroll, 2006). To our knowledge, no marketing article addresses the modified Pecha Kucha presentation style in undergraduate marketing courses.

Pecha Kucha (which means "chitchat" in Japanese) was created in 2003 in Tokyo by Astrid Klein and Mark Dytham of Klein–Dytham Architecture, who hoped to attract people to their special events venue. The Pecha Kucha Night events allowed young designers an opportunity to show their work in a concise and fast-paced environment. Each presenter was only allowed 20 PowerPoint slides to be shown for 20 seconds each on a timer, limiting the presentation time to 6 minutes and 40 seconds. Ideas were explained visually with graphics and little text. Since 2003, Pecha Kucha Nights have become a worldwide phenomenon in more than 460 cities worldwide because of its fast-paced and powerful imagery, which often yields entertaining, energetic presentations (www.pechakucha.org). We wanted to bring that energy into the classroom and address the other presentation challenges. Therefore, we decided to adapt and utilize this unique presentation style in three different marketing courses.

***Jason Oliver** (Ph.D., University of Rhode Island), Assistant Professor, Department of Marketing and Supply Chain Management, College of Business, East Carolina University, Greenville, NC, oliverj@ecu.edu.

****Christine Kowalczyk** (Ph.D., University of Memphis), Assistant Professor, Department of Marketing and Supply Chain Management, College of Business, East Carolina University, Greenville, NC, kowalczykc@ecu.edu.

The Need To Innovate Student Presentations

In the business world, presentation skills are imperative. This innovation of using Pecha Kucha is one way to address the need to improve the quality of student marketing presentations. The Pecha Kucha format requires students to practice presenting so they can more effectively and efficiently address their projects' main points. In the past, we observed students frequently spending too much time talking about their background information and not enough time talking about critical facts, key takeaways, and their analyses.

Further, we noted that students were not as well prepared as they should be for professional presentations in class. Students frequently used PowerPoint slides as note cards, turning their backs to the audience as they read from the slides, or relied heavily on actual note cards. They also stumbled over transitions, often filling the awkward moment, where they were unsure who was supposed to go next, with laughter that changed the professional tone of the presentation. Therefore, Pecha Kucha was introduced as a group presentation style to strengthen presentation skills and encourage more extensive preparation.

As mentioned, the traditional Pecha Kucha presentation style utilizes 20 PowerPoint slides in 6 minutes and 40 seconds with each slide only being presented for 20 seconds. In addition, Pecha Kucha was intended for individual presentations. We hypothesized the Pecha Kucha approach would increase student preparation and

Table 1		
Original and Author-Modified Pecha Kucha		
	Original Pecha Kucha	**Modified Pecha Kucha**
Number of Presenters	1	3–5
Time per Slide	20 seconds	Variable
PowerPoint Setup	Timed slides	Use of remote to advance slides
Total Time	6 minutes, 40 seconds	6 minutes, 40 seconds

Marketing Education Review, vol. 23, no. 1 (spring 2013), pp. 55–58.
ISSN 1052-8008 (print) / ISSN 2153-9987 (online)
DOI: 10.2753/MER1052-8008230109

force them to focus more on the key arguments and the solutions instead of background information that was less critical to the presentation. We also hypothesized that students would spend more time preparing for the Pecha Kucha presentations since this format took them out of their comfort zone, where they used slides as note cards or used note cards as a crutch.

The Teaching Innovation: Modifying Pecha Kucha

The innovation is a modified version of the presentation style Pecha Kucha. The basic rules of Pecha Kucha are 20 slides to be presented in 6 minutes and 40 seconds, resulting in 20 seconds per slide. Traditionally, Pecha Kucha was completed as an individual presentation via timed PowerPoint slides that are automatically advanced.

We modified the traditional rules of Pecha Kucha to be used in group presentations. We wanted to make sure the presentations were engaging, concise, and visual. Twenty slides were still the requirement. However, based on previous research that suggested the time limitation was too restrictive and had a negative impact on communication effectiveness (e.g., Lehtonen, 2011), we modified the rules by allowing the time allotted per slide to vary as long as it did not affect the total presentation length of 6 minutes 40 seconds. In other words, the students could "borrow" time from one slide to focus more time on other important points. The students were also given the option to use a remote to advance the slides.

The students were encouraged to focus on the visual aspect of each slide, instead of text and bullet points, and to spend time on the main points rather than background information. For example, if a group project involved a new product or service, the slides would incorporate pictures that represented the new product or service. Sometimes the pictures were accompanied with a few bullet points to emphasize the most important parts of the project's presentation. Further, the students were encouraged to spend time together as a team to practice their Pecha Kucha presentations. Practicing their presentations built confidence and allowed the students to feel like experts on the marketing project. The specific adaptations to the original Pecha Kucha presentation style are summarized in Table 1.

The modification of the original Pecha Kucha format allowed for more flexibility in a classroom setting. It still kept the fast-paced presentation environment, but it did not force the students to structure the presentations at 20 seconds per slide. Although some students used the timing feature in PowerPoint, we observed that the more structured timing would often lead to students getting ahead or behind the slides, which distracted from the overall presentation, so using the remote was more effective than using the PowerPoint timing feature. The presentation remote allowed for more flexibility for possible interruptions, which may take place in the business environment. We also used the format for group presentations instead of individual presentations, which is where Pecha Kucha is more commonly used.

The course assignment required a paper along with a presentation. The paper provided an outlet for more in-depth background and analysis of the course-specific marketing project so the presentation could focus on key takeaways.

The students presented the big idea(s), which allowed for more time for elaboration during the question-and-answer session. This process mimics professional presentations where the presenter may want the energy level to be high while presenting the key ideas, but also allow ample time for more detail to address client/colleague inquiries.

Because the Pecha Kucha presentation format is unique and new to many students, it was important to provide students with additional training and support prior to the final presentations. Guidelines were provided to each team, including the specific number of slides (20) and the time range for presenting the topic. Moreover, sample presentations via YouTube examples allowed students to view Pecha Kucha. Also, students were referred to the Pecha Kucha Web site (www.pechakucha.org), which provides more examples on a variety of topics as well as a listing of local Pecha Kucha nights, enabling students see live examples of this presentation style. A review of this information was completed several times throughout the semester. References were made throughout the semester to the development of the Pecha Kucha group presentations, reminding the students to capture favorite images and outline the main points of the presentation.

Assessment: Modified Pecha Kucha Contributes to Student Presentation Success

The modified Pecha Kucha presentation style was utilized in three different marketing courses: customer relationship management, sustainability marketing, and cultural environments in international business. Feedback on the modified Pecha Kucha was compared to feedback on more traditional group presentations in three other marketing courses: advertising and promotion management, marketing strategy, and consumer behavior. All the courses had a required group project and presentation.

After the group presentations, the students were provided with a questionnaire to evaluate their marketing presentations, including questions about their presentation work as individuals and as a group as well as their anticipated grade and practice time. There were also questions designed to measure respondent anxiety and vanity (physical concern, achievement concern). Finally, there were basic demographics (age, gender, class standing), and a few open-ended questions were included in the survey.

A total of 132 students responded to the survey. There were some responses from students who were assigned to a group project but did not actually participate in the presentation their responses were not included in our analysis. In addition, incomplete surveys were removed, resulting in a total of 114 usable responses (68 Pecha Kucha presentations and 46 traditional presentation).

The results were analyzed using ANCOVA (analysis of covariance). The students were asked to rate their performance based on their group presentation style (Pecha Kucha versus traditional PowerPoint presentations) compared to other group presentations that semester. The students responded to a seven-point Likert scale ranging from "much weaker" to "much stronger." Those assigned to the modified Pecha Kucha presentation style rated their individual performance to be significantly stronger ($M = 4.96$, $N = 68$) as compared to the traditional presentation group ($M = 4.01$, $N = 46$; $F = 6.47$, $p < 0.01$). The same was found when students were asked to evaluate their group's performance. The Pecha Kucha groups had stronger ratings ($M = 5.10$, $N = 68$) of relative group performance than the traditional presentation style ($M = 4.26$, $N = 46$; $F = 4.76$, $p < 0.01$). None of the covariates (anxiety, vanity/physical concern, vanity/achievement concern) were found to be significant in either model.

We also evaluated student's confidence by comparing their anticipated grades across presentation styles. Presentation style was a significant predictor of anticipated grade ($F = 3.810$, $p < 0.05$). Those who presented with the Pecha Kucha style anticipated a higher grade than those in the traditional presentation groups. The covariate vanity/physical concern was a significant predictor in this model ($p < 0.01$), which seemed to make sense given that the dependent variable was the student's confidence in anticipated grade.

Lastly, we compared the amount of presentation practice across presentations styles. When considering the number of hours students practiced for their presentations, the Pecha Kucha presentation style was found to be significantly different from the traditional presentation style ($F = 3.69$, $p < 0.05$). Students who presented with the Pecha Kucha style, on average, practiced more than two hours, whereas the traditional presentation groups practiced, on average, an hour or less. None of the covariates (anxiety, vanity/ physical concern, vanity/achievement concern) were found to be significant in the model.

The survey also allowed students to provide written comments about their presentation experiences. The following are highlighted comments:

I like the presentation method because it really forces you to prepare for presentations. You really have to know what you are going to say without having to rely on the slides.

I thought it went very well because I felt that everyone in the group was prepared.

Loved this new way of doing a presentation. I felt very prepared.

I thought the presentation ran a lot smoother and asked for more preparation time due to the necessary preparedness of the presentation style.

Instructor Perspective: Challenges to Adopting Pecha Kucha

Implementing Pecha Kucha into marketing courses came with some challenges. Utilizing the traditional Pecha Kucha was too restrictive for students; however, we found that adapting the guidelines for the students based on the courses and project needs made for more successful and engaging presentations. Even so, getting students to properly apply the principles of Pecha Kucha was challenging. Many times students are not provided with guidelines for marketing project presentations, and they prefer the flexibility, perhaps they feel they can "wing it." The modified Pecha Kucha format forced students to collaborate with their teams and spend more time practicing as a group. Further, the student audiences were more engaged in the presentations, asking questions and providing insight to the project presentations.

Challenges were not limited to the students. As professors, we were challenged with properly communicating the Pecha Kucha style to the students. At the time, there was a lack of student examples of Pecha Kucha in a classroom setting. We recorded outstanding examples to show in future semesters on a voluntary basis. In addition, we dedicated time throughout the semester to reiterate the guidelines of the Pecha Kucha style and meet with teams to review and practice their presentations. It should be noted that the resulting improvement in student presentations indicates that adapting this presentation style and spending the time during class to go over the structure was worth the effort.

Conclusion: Future Adaptation of Pecha Kucha for Marketing Courses

Utilizing a modified Pecha Kucha presentation style increased students' evaluations of their marketing project presentations. Pecha Kucha challenges students to focus on developing visually entertaining presentations. It allows students to more critically think about the information they are presenting and focus on the main takeaways in the time frame they have to present. Any marketing course with business-related presentations could utilize this unique presentation format. It also develops a good work ethic for public speaking and presentations. The students who used our modified Pecha Kucha presentation style took time to prepare and work together. The students' hard work was evident in the quality level of their presentations as observed by their professors and in their own self-assessments.

This adaptation of the popular Pecha Kucha presentation style resolves concerns about Pecha Kucha restrictions hindering communication and should help bring marketing students' presentation skills to the next level. The students came across as experts who knew their subject matter inside and out, which was evident, even in 6 minutes and 40 seconds. ∎

References

Anderson, Randy J., and Lydia E. Anderson (2010). "Professorial Presentations: The Link Between the Lecture and Student Success in the Workplace," *Academy of Educational Leadership Journal*, 14(1), 55–62.

Bonnici, Joseph, and Harsh K. Luthar (1996). "Peer Evaluated Debates: Developing Oral Communication Skills Through Marketing Case Studies," *Marketing Education Review*, 6(2), 73–81.

Calcich, Stephen E., and Dan C. Weilbaker (1992). "Selecting the Optimum Number of In-Class Sales Presentations," *Marketing Education Review*, 2(1), 31–33.

Carroll, Conor (2006). "Enhancing Reflective Learning Through Role-Plays: The Use of an Effective Sales Presentation Evaluation Form in Student Role-Plays," *Marketing Education Review*, 16(1), 9–13.

Haley, Debra A. (1993). "Optimizing the Graduate Sales Management Seminar: Enhancing Presentation Skills and Expanding Knowledge," *Marketing Education Review*, 3(2), 40–43.

Lehtonen, Miikka (2011). "Communicating Competence Through Pechakucha Presentations," *Journal of Business Communication*, 48(4), 464–481.

Martin, Charles L. (1990). "Enhancing the Effectiveness of Student Oral Presentations," *Marketing Education Review*, 1 (November), 56–60.

Taylor, Kimberly A. (2003). "Marketing Yourself in the Competitive Job Market: An Innovative Course Preparing Undergraduates for Marketing Careers," *Journal of Marketing Education*, 25(2), 97–107.

Young, Mark R., and J. William Murphy (2003). "Integrating Communications Skill into the Marketing Curriculum: A Case Study," *Journal of Marketing Education*, 25(1), 57–70.

Saleh, D., Camart, N., Sbeira, F., & Romo, L. (2018). Can we learn to manage stress? A randomized controlled trial carried out on university students. *PLoS ONE, 13*(9), 1–20.

Engage via Research Prediction

- Can an internet-based stress management program help students manage stress more effectively?

Read for Key Points

- What question did the researcher seek to answer? (Introduction)
- Who participated in the study and what did the participants do? (Method)
- What was the answer to the research question? (Results)

Critically Think about the Research

- How can you put these research findings into action?
- Do you think the results would be the same if there were more male students? Why or why not?
- How can colleges and universities use this research to support the success of their students?

Build Information Literacy Skills

- What are some other ways to learn to manage stress?
- What stress management techniques work best?

Research Study

Saleh, D.[1,2¤a]*, Camart, N.[1¤b], Sbeira, F.[2¤a], & Romo, L[13¤b]. (2018). Can we learn to manage stress? A randomized controlled trial carried out on university students. *PLoS ONE, 13*(9), 1–20.

In our research, we examined the efficacy of an Internet-based stress management program. Our interest in evaluating this type of intervention is based on the increasing accessibility of the Internet today, the growth of Internet-based interventions for various psychopathological problems, and the observation that despite the prevalence of stress among university students, only a fraction of students ever seek professional help. Methodology: "I'm managing my stress" ("Je gère mon stresse"), an Internet-based self-help program composed of four sessions, was examined in this study. The aforementioned program is based on cognitive-behavioral therapy and was inspired by the "Funambule" program in Quebec. Four questionnaires (Perceived Stress Scale, Rosenberg Self-Esteem Scale, Scale of Satisfaction in Studies, and General Health Questionnaire) uploaded online were answered thrice: during "preintervention", "postintervention", and "follow-up" stages, the latter of which occurred three months after the intervention. The sample comprised 128 university students, with the majority being women (81.25%). The subjects were divided randomly into two groups (an experimental group and a control group that did not follow the program). Results: The self-esteem scores of the control group were significantly higher than those of the experimental group at the preintervention stage, but this difference disappeared at the postintervention and follow-up stages. There were also significantly lower scores on the General Health Questionnaire subfactors of somatic symptoms and anxiety/insomnia in the experimental group than in the control group during the postintervention stage, though no differences

1 EA4430 CLIPSYD, UFR SPSE, Paris Nanterre University, Nanterre, France, 2 Counseling Psychology, Tishreen University, Latakia, Syria, 3 CMME, Centre Hospitalier Sainte Anne, Unité Inserm U864, CPN, Paris, France

¤a Current address: Department of Counseling Psychology, Tishreen University, Latakia, Syria

¤b Current address: Department of Psychology, Paris Nanterre University, Nanterre, France * dalia_saleh84@yahoo.com

Open Access

Citation: Saleh D, Camart N, Sbeira F, Romo L (2018) Can we learn to manage stress? A randomized controlled trial carried out on university students. PLoS ONE 13(9): e0200997. https://doi.org/10.1371/journal.pone.0200997

Editor: Jacobus P. van Wouwe, TNO, NETHERLANDS, **Received:** March 9, 2017, **Accepted:** July 3, 2018, **Published:** September 5, 2018

Data Availability Statement: The data underlying this study can not be made publicly available as the data are protected by the National Commission on Informatics and Liberty (CNIL), the national data protection authority for France. CNIL is an independent French administrative regulatory body whose mission is to ensure that data privacy law is applied to the collection, storage, and use of personal data. As the database of this study was authorized by the CNIL, we cannot make available data without prior agreement of the CNIL. More information can be found here: https://www.cnil.fr/ en/home. In addition, the researchers of this paper can also be contacted for assistance requesting data (Dalia Saleh: dalia_saleh84@yahoo.com, Nathalie Camart: nathalie_camart@hotmail.com, Lucia Romo: romodesprez@gmail.com).

Funding: The incentives (in the form of gift vouchers to all participants who fully participated in the research) in this study were funded by The Scientific Interest Group « Jeu et société». The funders had no role in study design, data collection and analysis, decision to publish, or preparation of the manuscript.

Competing interests: The authors declare that the research was conducted in the absence of any commercial or financial relationships that could be construed as a potential conflict of interest.

Abbreviations: ESDE, Satisfaction in Studies; GHQ-28, General Health Questionnaire; PSS-10, Perceived Stress Scale; RSES, Rosenberg Self-Esteem Scale.

were observed before the intervention. These differences no longer remained after three months. ANOVA revealed significant effects of the intervention over time in the experimental group. Effects were observed at both the postintervention and follow-up stages for self-esteem, perceived stress, satisfaction in studies, and in the somatic symptoms, anxiety and insomnia and severe depression aspects of the General Health Questionnaire (Cohen's d = 0.38 to 4.58). In contrast, no effects were observed in the control group. Conclusion: This type of Internet-based program has the ability to reach a large number of students due to its rather short format and accessibility. It has already shown improvements in terms of the levels of perceived stress, psychological distress, and satisfaction with studies. The option of online interventions could appeal specifically to students who do not seek professional help. However, even though these results are promising at the postintervention stage, they are limited, as indicated by the lack of significant differences between the two groups after the initial three months of follow-up. We still, specifically, need to improve this intervention program and, generally, need more research to address the methodological problems raised by this type of intervention.

Trial registration: *ISRCTN registry, ISRCTN13709272*

Introduction

University students are a category of people who are particularly vulnerable to stress [1–3] and present, according to scientific literature, high levels of stress [4–9]. They are prone to stress-related issues such as anxiety, depression [10–12], eating disorders [13–15], consumption of psychoactive substances [16,17], and sleep disorders [12,18,19]. The rates of psychological morbidity among university students are higher than those seen in the general population [10,11,20–24].

According to the literature, 83% of university students feel tired [25], 60% have low self-esteem [26] and 15% harbor suicidal thoughts [27]. In fact, the prevalence of several mental health issues among university students is always high, regardless of the issue. For example, the mental health distress rate ranges from 21% to 82% [26,28–30], the depression rate between 13% and 53% [31–34], anxiety between 34% and 47% [34–36], and stress between 33% and 79% [8,23,37,38]. More than half of students suffer from at least one mental health problem according to a study undertaken by Zivin and his team. In their study, 50% of students who declared having mental health issues, such as depression, anxiety and suicidal thoughts, did not seek help [39].

The link between stress and psychological distress has been theoretically presented in Lazarus and Folkman's transactional model in 1984 [4]. Their work is often applied in stress-management programs [40].

Finding efficient strategies to reinforce the feeling of personal efficacy and the efficient management of difficulties in certain groups such as students are essential to help these groups adapt to challenges and maintain a good standard of living [41]. Different types of interventions have already proven their efficacy [42–44].

The Internet has become an essential tool in the field of "self-help" interventions in mental health. These interventions can be defined by the fact that they allow online access to a therapeutic-aimed program [45]. This type of intervention via the Internet has several goals, such as reducing the risks leading to targeted problems [45], such as the levels of stress, anxiety and depression [46]; raising the level of well-being [47]; enhancing adaptation strategies [48]; and even increasing weekly physical activity [49]. The advantages of these online trials are their accessibility, continuous availability, confidentiality, and discretion, especially for people who do not want to seek medical help in a health center, as well as the opportunity to extend the program to a large population in an economical way [45].

Online application studies in this field are being developed to treat several problems, such as panic disorder [50], depression [51–53], anxiety [54–56], insomnia [57], post-traumatic stress [58], alcohol abuse [59], binge drinking [60], social phobia [61,62], and behavioral problems [63]. Stress management is one of the applications that has been suggested for diverse population groups [64–67].

Online stress management interventions aim to manage stress as well as other psychopathological issues [45] such as anxiety [68,69], prevention of obesity [70] and psychological distress [71]. In our literature review, according to a meta-analysis conducted in 2016 [45], only six studies had stress management as their principal goal [46–49,72], and only three of these studies were carried out with university students [45,46,48,49].

Despite its clear efficacy and numerous advantages [46,48], this type of intervention for stress management has its limits [73] and a major methodological problem, that is, a high attrition rate [45].

The aim of the current research is to measure the efficacy of an online stress management program for university students based on several mental health variables: self-esteem, perceived stress and its two subfactors (perceived helplessness and perceived self-efficacy), psychological distress and its four subfactors (somatic symptoms, anxiety/insomnia, social dysfunction, severe depression) and satisfaction with studies.

Materials and Methods

Design of Study

This protocol used a randomized controlled trial to determine the efficacy of an online stress management intervention for university students (Fig 1). The inclusion criteria included the following: being a student at a French university, having mastered the French language, being aged between 18 and 30, and having an e-mail address and access to the Internet.

The subjects were randomly allocated into one of the two groups: an experimental group (those who followed the program) and a control group (those who did not follow the program). The subjects in the control group were informed that they had been randomly assigned to a waiting group, that they would not be following the program during the study, and that they could follow it afterwards if they so wished. The study followed the CONSORT 2010 Statement's advice about randomized controlled trials [74].

Participants

A total of 142 students voluntarily signed up for baseline assessments, and 16 participants were excluded (aged under 18 or over 30). The sample consisted of 128 university students (64 in the experimental group and 64 in the control group), with a female majority (81.25% in the whole sample, 82.81% in the experimental group and 79.69% in the control group). The mean age of the whole sample was 22.54 years (Standard Deviation or SD: 3), with no difference between the two groups in terms of age. The students were from all academic years, from the first year at university to PhD-level, and from different study programs: Philosophy, Languages, Literature, Economy, Management, Mathematics, Computing, Psychology, Law and Political Science, Medicine, etc. (Table 1).

Recruitment and Procedure

The research was presented as an assessment of a stress management intervention carried out with university students, whose participation was anonymous and voluntary. The recruitment occurred mostly on the

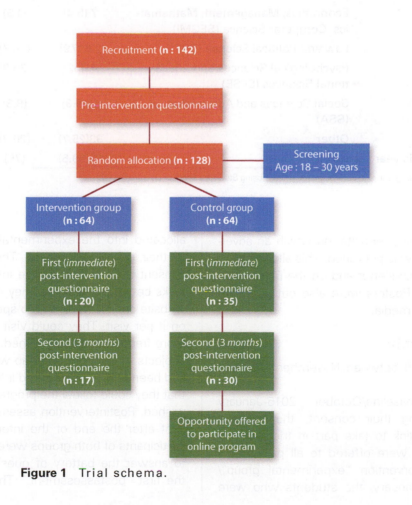

Figure 1 Trial schema.

Table 1
Participant Characteristics n (%)

Participants' characteristics		Total (n = 128)	Group 1 (n = 64)	Group 2 (n = 64)	p
Gender	Women	104 (81.2)	(82.8)	(79.6)	0.6
	Men	24 (18.7)	(17.1)	(20.3)	
Home university	Paris Nanterre La Defense	99(77.3)	(79.6)	(75)	0.5
Year of studies	L1: First academic year	17(13.2)	(15.6)	(10.9)	0.5
	L2: Second academic year	15 (11.7)	(14)	(9.3)	
	L3: Third academic year	33(25.7)	(21.8)	(29.6)	
	M1: First year of Master's degree	31(24.2)	(28.1)	(20.3)	
	M2: Second year of Master's degree	18 (14)	(12.5)	(15.6)	
	PhD	14(10.9)	(7.8)	(14)	
Academic sector according to UFR classification	Foreign cultures and languages (LCE)	2.3(2.3)	(3.1)	(1.5)	0.1
	Philosophy, Information-Communication, Language, Literature, Performing Arts (PHILLIA)	9 (7)	(10.9)	(3.1)	
	Economics, Management, Mathematics, Computer Science (SEGMI)	7 (5.4)	(1.5)	(9.3)	
	Law and Political Science (DSP)	23(17.9)	(18.7)	(17.1)	
	Psychological Sciences and Educational Sciences (SPSE)	41(32)	(35.9)	(28.1)	
	Social Sciences and Administration (SSA)	12(9.3)	(9.3)	(9.3)	
	Other	33(25.7)	(20.3)	(31.2)	
Repetition of academic year	No	89(69.5)	(75)	(64)	0.2

Group 1 = experimental group; group 2 = control group. P<0.05 using Student's t-test or chi-squared test.

Paris Nanterre University website, on which an advertisement for research was published. This allowed publicity in the student newsletter and on the university's social media outlets. Posters were also put up in the campus and on social media.

Stages of Research

The research occurred between November 2015 and June 2016.

Preintervention (baseline/October 2015-January 2016): After providing their consent, the subjects received an Internet link to take part in the research online. Gift vouchers were offered to all participants as an incentive. Intervention "experimental group"/ "control group": In January, the students who were allocated into the experimental group were informed of their group assignment. They then provided their consent to participate in the intervention and perform tasks between sessions. They were invited to visit the website once a week and to spend at least 20 minutes on it per visit. They could visit the page for longer or more frequently if they wished. At the same time, the subjects in the control group were informed that they had been randomly allocated into the control group and that they could follow the program afterwards if they so wished. Postintervention assessment (February 2016): Just after the end of the intervention in March, the participants of both groups were simultaneously invited to answer the battery of questionnaires by email for the first "postassessment." The "follow-up" (second postassessment) occurred three months later for both groups, in June. Reminder emails were sent in cases of no response.

Intervention (« *I'm managing my stress* ») (February 2016)

We created an online stress management pilot program entitled "I'm managing my stress". It was inspired by the "*Funambule*" program for teenagers developed by Dumont and his team [40] in Canada, in which cognitive-behavioral therapy techniques are used over 8 sessions.

The **"Funambule, for balanced stress management" program**, developed by Dumont and his team [40,75], is an intervention program designed to help young people aged 12 to 18 manage their stress better. It is undertaken in 8 weekly sessions of at least an hour and a half each. The content of the sessions is organized into 4 parts to target 4 goals: the perception of stress, the body, thoughts, and adaptation strategies [40,75]. The conception of the program was inspired by the transactional theory of stress developed by Lazarus and Folkmans in 1984, which aimed to strengthen protective resources [76]. Beneficial effects and a significant improvement of stress management in the experimental group were noted for participants using this program [75].

The "I'm managing my stress" program that we developed has the same objectives and aims, but as it is a pilot program inspired by "Funambule", we therefore reworked and adapted it to fit the Internet and our study population (adults, not children as in the original program). The program consists of four sessions, each 20 minutes long, including psycho-education, practical exercises and one to two weekly activities that the participant is asked to complete (prescription of tasks, as is customary in cognitive-behavioral techniques). The goal is for the students to learn easy techniques to help them handle stressful situations better.

The first session is "psycho-education", with information for the participants on how to identify and understand stress, measure stress levels, and determine stress sources. The second session aims to develop body relaxation using practical exercises adapted for the Internet, such as a contraction and relaxation method or diaphragmatic breathing. The third session is based on cognitive-behavioral techniques, such as Beck's three columns, the Meichenbaum method, and problem solving. The objective of this session is to develop positive thinking [40]. The fourth session focuses on adaptation strategies such as time management, exam preparation, and the use of DIY anti-stress cards [40,75]. The final session is used to collect the participants' opinions on the program in order to assess the program.

This program is interactive to the extent that the participants are invited to provide comments and opinions after each exercise and at the end of each session, at every stage of the program.

An email was sent to invite the participants at the start of each session to go online if they had not visited the website spontaneously; the first reminder was sent within three days after the start of the sessions. The students could contact us any time via a specific email address with any questions or complementary information on the program. Responses were sent within 48 hours.

Measures

We split the questionnaires used in our study into two sections. First, the students provided socio-demographic data concerning gender, age, place of residence, current year of study, study program and university of origin. The second part was a collection of questionnaires, including four uploaded ones during the preintervention, postintervention, and follow-up (3 months after the intervention) stages.

- Stress was assessed with the Perceived Stress Scale (PSS-10) using the 10-item version. This method was established by Cohen and his team [77] It was subsequently translated and validated in French by Bellinghausen and his team. Using a 5-point scale, from 1 (which means "never") to 5 ("very often"), each variable's frequency is rated. This scale includes two subfactors: perceived helplessness and perceived self-efficacy [78]. Two thresholds were decided upon: a score over 24 indicated anxiety, and a score over 26 indicated depression [79]. The Cronbach's alpha coefficient calculated for this assessment was (.84).

- To measure self-esteem, we decided to use a 10-item version of the Rosenberg Self-Esteem Scale (RSES), which was established by Morris Rosenberg [80] and then later translated and validated in French by Vallieres and his team. The participants were invited to use a 4-point Likert scale format, with their answers to the items ranging from "strongly agree" to "strongly disagree" [81]. Low self-esteem was indicated by a score under 30 [82] In this study, Cronbach's alpha coefficient was (.9).

- To evaluate the participants' satisfaction in their studies, we opted for the 5-item version of the ESDE, developed by Bissonnette and Vallerand, which was translated into French and validated by Vallerand and his team. In this assessment, five items are answered on a scale that ranges from 1 ("strongly disagree") to 7 ("strongly agree") [83]. The higher the score, the higher the participant's satisfaction in their studies [84]. In this study, Cronbach's alpha coefficient was (.79).

- We measured psychological distress using the 28-item General Health Questionnaire (GHQ-28), a questionnaire developed by Goldberg [85] and then translated and validated in French by Bolognini and his team [86]. It consists of 4 sub-scales that evaluate somatic symptoms, anxiety/insomnia, social dysfunction and severe depression [85]. In each of these sections, participants are invited to answer 7 items using a 4-point Likert scale [86]. Psychological distress is indicated by a score greater than or equal to 5 [87]. In this study, Cronbach's alpha coefficient was (.65).

Ethics

The ethics committee of the Psychological Science and Learning Science Department at the University of Paris Ouest Nanterre La Défense, UFR SPE (Department of Psychology and Education) in May 2015 and the CNIL (National Commission for Computing and Freedom) in November 2014 [n°: 1811031 v 0] gave their approval for our study protocol. We also obtained written consent from each student prior to their participation, as required by the Helsinki Declaration.

The research team obtained written permission from the creators of "Funambule", giving us the right to take inspiration from their program to create an intervention program adapted to the Internet. A report on the study was sent to the creators of "Funambule" after each stage.

The authors confirm that all ongoing and related trials for this intervention are registered.

Feasibility Study

The feasibility of the study was tested in a pilot study between January and March 2015, in which a first group of 18 students (mean age = 23.64, SD = 5.62) underwent an intervention.

During the feasibility study, we noted a high level of attrition, meaning a loss of participants over time. In response to this problem, we decided to offer an incentive in the form of gift vouchers to all participants who fully participated in the research [88].

This approach was based on the results of a study by Fridric and his team [89], who encountered this problem in similar experiments. The participants' comments also allowed us to improve our program's form.

Statistics

To allocate the participants into two groups (intervention/experimental and control), we used SPSS (IBM v. 23) random sampling software.

A standard descriptive analysis assessed sample characteristics (in general and by group), and Student's t-tests and chi-squared test were used to measure the homogeneity between the two groups. To compare the two groups (intervention and control) at each stage (T1 = preassessment, T2 = postassessment and T3 = follow-up), we used the Mann-Whitney U test because the variables: *self-esteem, life satisfaction in studies, perceived stress and its two sub factors (perceived helplessness and perceived self-efficacy), psychological distress and its 4 sub factors (somatic symptoms, anxiety/insomnia, social dysfunction, severe depression)*, did not follow a normal distribution.

To examine intra-group changes in the mental health variables' scores studied in our research, that is, self-esteem, life satisfaction in studies, perceived stress and its two subfactors (perceived helplessness and perceived self-efficacy), and psychological distress and its 4 subfactors (somatic symptoms, anxiety/insomnia, social dysfunction, severe depression), for each group over time (T1, T2 and T3), we used a repeated measures ANOVA for the variables that followed a normal distribution and the nonparametric equivalent, the Friedman test, for the variables that did not follow a normal distribution. Effect sizes and 95% confidence intervals (95% CI) were calculated using Cohen's d for the data from participants who completed the questionnaire at baseline and at follow-up. A value of 0.2 is generally interpreted as being suggestive of a small effect size, 0.5 of a medium effect size, and 0.8 of a large effect size [89].

A total of 63 students will be recruited for each group to detect 5% level of significance with 80% power in order to answer the research question (alpha: 0.05; Beta: 0.20 Power: 0.80; The variability (estimated) in (PSS /main variable): 2; Past experience (Feasibility Study), with similar experiments, with similar measurement method (PSS) and similar subjects, suggests that the data will be fairly distributed with an SD of 4; So, n = 2 × [(1.96 + 0.842)^2 × 4^2] / 2^2 = 62.809632).

The significance level was fixed at 0.05. All analyses were performed with SPSS (IBM v. 23) and Statistica (v. 12).

Results

Participants' Characteristics

The data in (Table 1) describe the study population, illustrating that the randomization protocol succeeded in balancing the intervention assignments and ensuring equal representation of important characteristics in the study's population. There were no significant statistical differences between the two groups.

Attrition

A total of 90 participants started the research study after being allocated into the two groups and sending an email confirming their participation after this stage, with 49 participants in the experimental group and 41 in the control group. A total of 55 students finished the study up to the first postassessment (of whom 20 were in the experimental group and 35 in the control group), and 47 students completed the second follow-up postassessment three months later (17 in the experimental group and 30 in the control group).

From the start of the intervention, in the experimental group (first session: 36 participants), there was a rate of general follow-up (for both groups) of 64.94% at the postassessment and 61.04% at the three-month follow-up (Table 2).

The attrition during the intervention went from 36 participants in the first session to 21 participants in the fourth session, with a follow-up rate of 58.33%.

Preliminary Analyses

Table 3 shows the means and SDs of the outcome variables at baseline and one-month and three-month follow-ups for the intervention and control groups.

Table 4 shows the comparisons between the two groups at each of the three stages. We noted only one significant difference at baseline between the two groups (U test: −2.49, p = 0.01): the self-esteem score (M = 28.12, SD = 5.9) was significantly higher in the control group than in the experimental group (M = 25.4, SD = 5.7).

At the postassessment stage, there were three significant differences between the two groups in global General Health (U test: −2.16, p = 0.03), with significantly lower scores in the experimental group (M = 10.45, SD = 3.7) than in the control group (M = 12.28, SD = 3.1). Regarding the two subfactors of the GHQ-28, the scores were significantly lower in the experimental group than in the control group for somatic symptoms (U test: -3.6 3, p = 0.001), with (M = 2.1, SD = 1.4) for the experimental group and (M = 3.82, SD = 1.3) for the control group, and for anxiety/insomnia (U test: −2.78, p = 0.04), with (M = 2.45, SD = 2.7) in the experimental group and (M = 3.48, SD = 2.07) in the control group.

The significant difference in self-esteem between the two groups at baseline disappeared at the postassessment and follow-up stages (Table 4).

Intervention Effects

Table 5 shows the means, standard deviations and effect sizes (Cohen's d) of the variables at baseline and at one-month (or immediate) and three-month follow-ups in both the intervention and control groups.

ANOVA (repeated-measures or Friedman) (Table 6) revealed significant effects of the intervention over time for self-esteem ($F_{2,32}$ = 7.23, p = 0.02); perceived stress ($F_{2,32}$ = 5.28, p = 0.006) and its two subfactors "perceived helplessness" ($F_{2,32}$ = 4.51, p = 0.1) and "perceived self-efficacy" ($F_{2,32}$ = 5.31, p = 0.01); satisfaction in studies ($F_{2,32}$ = 3.39, p = 0.02); and the global GHQ score (X^2 N = 17, dl = 2 = 15.11, p = 0.001) and three of its subfactors: somatic symptoms ($F_{2,32}$ = 3.87, p = 0.03), anxiety/insomnia ($F_{2,32}$ = 7.85, p = 0.001), and social dysfunction (X^2 N = 17, dl = 2 = 17.73, p = 0.001).

However, in the control group, we found significant changes over time regarding self-esteem ($F_{2,58}$ = 1.18,

Table 2					
Number of Participants in Each Trial					

Trial		Experimental group			Control group
Preinterventions/*Recruitment* November 2015 to January 2016		64			64
Start/January 2016		49			41
Intervention		Session			
January to February 2016	1st	2nd	3rd	4th	
	36	29	21	21	
		Participants			
Postintervention/March 2016		20			35
Follow-up/June 2016		17			30

Table 3
Statistics for All Outcome Measures at Baseline, Postintervention and Follow-Up

Variables	Preintervention								Post intervention								Follow-up M(SD)							
	G1/n = 64				G2/n = 64				G1/n = 20				G2/n = 35				G1/n = 17				G2/n = 30			
	M (SD)	Md	Q1	Q3	M (SD)	Md	Q1	Q3	Md	Q1	Q3	M (SD)	Md	Q1	Q3	M (SD)	M (SD)	Md	Q1	Q3	M (SD)	Md	Q1	Q3
Self esteem	25.4 (5.7)	24	22	30	28.12 (5.9)	29.5	24	33	28	24	32	27.7 (5.9)	29	26	33	28.57 (5.6)	29 (3.1)	28	27	31.5	29.56 (6.02)	31	27.75	34.25
Perceived stress																								
Global	33.75 (6.3)	34	30	38	32.27 (5.7)	32.5	29	36	31	25	36	30.2 (7.2)	32	26	37	31.74 (6.5)	29.52 (5.6)	31	24.5	33.5	30.63 (7.09)	29.5	25.75	34.25
Perceived helplessness	22.06 (4.3)	22	19	25	21.1 (4.06)	21	18.25	24	19	16	23	19.5 (4.5)	20	16	24	20.71 (4.4)	19.17 (4.3)	19	16	21.5	19.86 (4.5)	18	17	24
Perceived self-efficacy	11.68 (2.5)	12	11	13	11.62 (2.3)	11	10	12.75	11	7.75	13	10.7 (3.2)	11	9	13	11.02 (2.4)	10.35 (2.1)	11	9	12.5	10.76 (3.09)	10.5	8	12.25
Satisfaction in studies	20.56 (6.6)	21	16	25	21.06 (5.5)	21	18	25.75	26	16	30	23.9 (8.2)	24	16	27	21.88 (7.1)	24 (7.2)	27	20	29	22.43 (7.6)	24	17.75	30
General health																								
Global	12.95 (4.2)	14	9	16	11.87 (3.8)	12	9	15	9.5	7	13	10.45 (3.7)	13	10	14	12.28 (3.1)	5.82 (4.1)	5	3	7	8.06 (6.7)	6	4	8.5
Somatic symptoms	3.35 (1.4)	3.5	2	4	3.01 (1.6)	3	2	4	1.5	1	3	2.1 (1.4)	4	3	5	3.82 (1.3)	2.05 (1.5)	2	1	3	2.4 (2.1)	2	1	4
Anxiety and insomnia	3.93 (2.4)	5	2	6	3.93 (2.1)	4	2	6	1.5	0	5.5	2.45 (2.7)	3	2	5	3.48 (2.07)	1.82 (2.3)	1	0	3.5	2.9 (2.1)	3	1	4
Social dysfunction	4.07 (1.7)	4	3	5.7	3.87 (1.7)	4	2	5.75	5	4	6	4.85 (1.5)	4	2	6	3.91 (1.9)	1.47 (1.6)	1	0	2	1.63 (1.8)	1	0	2.25
Severe depression	1.57 (1.9)	1	0	2	1.04 (1.7)	0	0	2	0.5	0	1	1 (1.4)	0	0	1	1.05 (1.7)	0.47 (0.87)	0	0	1	1.13 (2.33)	0	0	0.5

G1 = experimental group. G2 = control group. Italics = subfactor. M: mean. Md: median. Q1: first quartile. Q3: third quartile.
* Although we performed non-parametric tests, we chose to present the means and standard deviations in the tables for clarity of results. However, we also added the median and first and third quartiles as Summary statistics in the article.

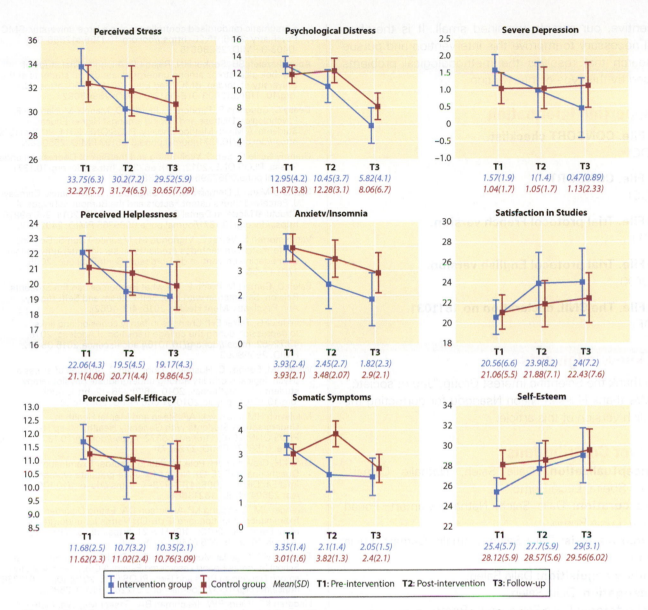

Figure 2 Mean scores over time based on the experimental condition for both groups and the studied mental health variables.

and anxiety/insomnia) and an interesting improvement in all the studied variables, such as stress, depression and satisfaction in studies, at a follow-up three months later in the experimental group but not in the control group.

This online program could therefore be offered to students showing problems with stress who have not yet sought professional help. However, even though these results are similar to those obtained in the original program that inspired us, there are time constraints, as indicated by the absence of significant differences between groups three months after the intervention. To better determine the effects of time, a follow-up assessment at six months should be considered. The fact that the

control group knows that they may benefit from the intervention should also be kept in mind.

Limitations

Our work has a certain number of limitations: the size of the sample, the measures given by questionnaire only, a follow-up of only 3 months later, and the attacks of November 13th, 2015 in Paris, which could have had a psychological impact on the studied sample.

Moreover, over time there was a loss of participants; we faced this problem during the feasibility study in 2015, which led us to use an incentive, as Fridric and his team recommended [90]. Nevertheless, despite this incentive, our sample remained small. It is therefore still necessary to improve this intervention and pursue research that resolves the methodological problems raised by this type of intervention.

Supporting Information

S1 File. CONSORT checklist.
(DOC)

S2 File. CONSORT.
(DOC)

S3 File. Trial protocol French version.
(PDF)

S4 File. Trial protocol English version.
(DOCX)

S5 File. The CNIL declaration no 1811031.
(PDF)

Acknowledgments

We thank the Scientific Interest Group "Jeu et société"

We thank Hassan Njifon Nsangou for correcting the English version of this article.

Author Contributions

Conceptualization: Dalia Saleh, Nathalie Camart, Fouad Sbeira, Lucia Romo.

Data curation: Dalia Saleh, Nathalie Camart, Fouad Sbeira, Lucia Romo.

Formal analysis: Dalia Saleh, Nathalie Camart, Lucia Romo.

Funding acquisition: Dalia Saleh.

Investigation: Dalia Saleh.

Methodology: Dalia Saleh, Lucia Romo.

Project administration: Dalia Saleh, Lucia Romo.

Resources: Dalia Saleh.

Software: Dalia Saleh.

Supervision: Dalia Saleh, Nathalie Camart, Fouad Sbeira, Lucia Romo.

Validation: Dalia Saleh.

Visualization: Dalia Saleh.

Writing – original draft: Dalia Saleh.

Writing – review & editing: Nathalie Camart, Fouad Sbeira, Lucia Romo. ■

References

Robotham D, Julian C. Stress and the higher education student: a critical review of the literature. J Furth High Educ. 2006; 30(2):107–17.

Lovell GP, Nash K, Sharman R, Lane BR. Across-sectional investigation of depressive, anxiety, and stress symptoms and health-behavior participation in Australian university students. Nurs Health Sci. 2015; 17(1):134–42. https://doi.org/10.1111/nhs.12147 PMID: 24799077

Crawford G, Burns SK, Chih HJ, Hunt K, Tilley PM, Hallett J, et al. Mental health first aid training for nursing students: a protocol for a pragmatic randomised controlled trial in a large university. BMC Psychiatry. 2015; 15:26. https://doi.org/10.1186/s12888-015-0403-3 PMID: 25886615

Abu-Ghazaleh SB, Sonbol HN, Rajab LD. A longitudinal study of psychological stress among undergraduate dental students at the University of Jordan. BMC Med Educ. 2016; 16:90. https://doi.org/10.1186/s12909-016-0612-6 PMID: 26968682

Deasy C, Coughlan B, Pironom J, Jourdan D, Mannix-McNamara P. Psychological Distress and Coping amongst Higher Education Students: A Mixed Method Enquiry. PLOS ONE. 2014; 9(12):e115193. https://doi.org/10.1371/journal.pone.0115193 PMID: 25506825

Grant F, Guille C, Sen S. Well-Being and the Risk of Depression under Stress. PLOS ONE. 2013; 8(7): e67395. https://doi.org/10.1371/journal.pone.0067395 PMID: 23840872

Montero-Marín J, Demarzo MMP, Stapinski L, Gili M, García-Campayo J. Perceived Stress Latent Factors and the Burnout Subtypes: A Structural Model in Dental Students. PLOS ONE. 2014; 9(6):e99765. https://doi.org/10.1371/journal.pone.0099765 PMID: 24927260

Vandentorren S, Verret C, Vignonde M, Maurice-Tison S. Besoins d'information en santédes étudiants au service inter-universitaire de médecine préventive de Bordeaux. SantéPublique. 2005; 17(1):47–56.

Saleh D, Camart N, Romo L. On what Resources can the Students Rely on: Satisfaction with Life, Self-Esteem and SelfEfficacy. Ann Psychiatry Ment Health. 2016; 4(2: 1062).

Moreira JFG, Telzer EH. Changes in family cohesion and links to depression during the college transition. J Adolesc. 2015; 43:72–82. https://doi.org/10.1016/j.adolescence.2015.05.012 PMID: 26058003

Walsh JM, Feeney C, Hussey J, Donnellan C. Sources of stress and psychological morbidity among undergraduate physiotherapy students. Physiotherapy. 2010; 96(3):206–12. https://doi.org/10.1016/j.physio.2010.01.005 PMID: 20674652

Milojevich HM, Lukowski AF. Sleep and Mental Health in Undergraduate Students with Generally Healthy Sleep Habits. PLOS ONE. 2016; 11(6):e0156372. https://doi.org/10.1371/journal.pone.0156372 PMID: 27280714

Luce KH, Crowther JH, Pole M. Eating Disorder Examination Questionnaire (EDE-Q): Norms for undergraduate women. Int J Eat Disord. 2008; 41(3):273–6. https://doi.org/10.1002/eat.20504 PMID: 18213686

Lavender JM, De Young KP, Anderson DA. Eating Disorder Examination Questionnaire (EDE-Q): Norms for undergraduate men. Eat Behav. 2010; 11(2):119–21. https://doi.org/10.1016/j.eatbeh.2009.09.005 PMID: 20188296

Torstveit MK, Aagedal-Mortensen K, Stea TH. More than Half of High School Students Report Disordered Eating: A Cross Sectional Study among Norwegian Boys and Girls. PLOS ONE. 2015; 10(3): e0122681. https://doi.org/10.1371/journal.pone.0122681 PMID: 25825877

Lindgren KP, Wiers RW, Teachman BA, Gasser ML, Westgate EC, Cousijn J, et al. Attempted Training of Alcohol Approach and Drinking Identity Associations in US Undergraduate Drinkers: Null Results from Two Studies. PLOS ONE. 2015; 10(8):e0134642. https://doi.org/10.1371/journal.pone.0134642 PMID: 26241316

Rogowska AM. Problematic use of psychoactive substances in undergraduates: a comparison of four patterns of substance use. J Subst Use. 2016; 21(3):304–8.

Choueiry N, Salamoun T, Jabbour H, Osta NE, Hajj A, Khabbaz LR. Insomnia and Relationship with Anxiety in University Students: A Cross-Sectional Designed Study. PLOS ONE. 2016; 11(2):e0149643. https://doi.org/10.1371/journal.pone.0149643 PMID: 26900686

Pilcher JJ, Ginter DR, Sadowsky B. Sleep quality versus sleep quantity: Relationships between sleep and measures of health, well-being and sleepiness in college students. J Psychosom Res. 1997; 42(6):583–96. PMID: 9226606

Adlaf EM, Gliksman L, Demers A, Newton-Taylor B. The Prevalence of Elevated Psychological Distress Among Canadian Undergraduates: Findings from the 1998 Canadian Campus Survey. J Am Coll Health. 2001; 50(2):67–72. https://doi.org/10.1080/07448480109596009 PMID: 11590985

Baykan Z, Naçar M, Cetinkaya F. Depression, anxiety, and stress among last-year students at Erciyes University Medical School. Acad Psychiatry J Am Assoc Dir Psychiatr Resid Train Assoc Acad Psychiatry. 2012; 36(1):64–5.

Bewick B, Koutsopoulou G, Miles J, Slaa E, Barkham M. Changes in undergraduate students' psychological well-being as they progress through university. Stud High Educ. 2010; 35(6):633–45.

O'Brien L, Mathieson K, Leafman J, Rice-Spearman L. Level of stress and common coping strategies among physician assistant students. J Physician Assist Educ Off J Physician Assist Educ Assoc. 2012; 23(4):25–9.

Stallman HM. Psychological distress in university students: A comparison with general population data. Aust Psychol. 2010; 45(4):249–57.

Maniecka-Bryła I, Bryła M, Weinkauf A, Dierks M-L. The international comparative study of the health status of medical university students in Lodz and Hanover. Przegl Lek. 2005; 62(3):63–8.

Strenna L, Chahraoui K, Vinay A. Santépsychique chez les étudiants de première année d'école supérieure de commerce: liens avec le stress de l'orientation professionnelle, l'estime de soi et le coping. Orientat Sc Prof. 2009;(38/2):183–204.

Lafay N, Manzanera C, Papet N, Marcelli D, Senon J. Les états dépressifs de la post-adolescence. Résultats d'une enquête menée chez 1521 étudiants de l'universitéde Poitiers. Ann Med Psychol (Paris). 2003; 161(2):147–51.

Humphris G, Blinkhorn A, Freeman R, Gorter R, Hoad-Reddick G, Murtomaa H, et al. Psychological stress in undergraduate dental students: baseline results from seven European dental schools. Eur J Dent Educ. 2002; 6(1):22–9. PMID: 11872070

Nerdrum P, Rustøen T, Rønnestad MH. Student Psychological Distress: A psychometric study of 1750 Norwegian 1st-year undergraduate students. Scand J Educ Res. 2006; 50(1):95–109.

Dyrbye LN, Harper W, Durning SJ, Moutier C, Thomas MR, Massie FS Jr, et al. Patterns of distress in US medical students. Med Teach. 2011; 33(10):834–9. https://doi.org/10.3109/0142159X.2010 .531158 PMID: 21942482

Boujut E, Koleck M, Bruchon-Schweitzer M, Bourgeois ML. Mental health among students: A study among a cohort of freshmen. Ann Méd-Psychol. 2009; 167(9):662–8.

Furr SR, Westefeld JS, McConnell GN, Jenkins JM. Suicide and depression among college students: A decade later. Prof Psychol Res Pract. 2001; 32(1):97.

Dahlin M, Joneborg N, Runeson B. Stress and depression among medical students: across-sectional study. Med Educ. 2005; 39(6):594–604. https://doi.org/10.1111/j.1365-2929.2005.02176.x PMID: 15910436

Wong JGWS, Cheung EPT, Chan KKC, Ma KKM, Tang SW. Web-based survey of depression, anxiety and stress in first-year tertiary education students in Hong Kong. Aust N Z J Psychiatry. 2006; 40 (9):777–82. https://doi.org/10.1080/j.1440-1614.2006.01883.x PMID: 16911753

Bayram N, Bilgel N. The prevalence and socio-demographic correlations of depression, anxiety and stress among a group of university students. Soc Psychiatry Psychiatr Epidemiol. 2008; 43(8):667–72. https://doi.org/10.1007/s00131-008-0345-x PMID: 18398558

Shamsuddin K, Fadzil F, Ismail WSW, Shah SA, Omar K, Muhammad NA, et al. Correlates of depression, anxiety and stress among Malaysian university students. Asian J Psychiatry. 2013; 6(4):318–23.

Bughi SA, Sumcad J, Bughi S. Effect of brief behavioral intervention program in managing stress in medical students from two southern California universities. Med Educ Online. 2006; 11:1–8.

Koochaki GM, Charkazi A, Hasanzadeh A, Saedani M, Qorbani M, Marjani A. Prevalence of stress among Iranian medical students: a questionnaire survey. East Mediterr Health J. 2011; 17(7):593–8. PMID: 21972483

Zivin K, Eisenberg D, Gollust SE, Golberstein E. Persistence of mental health problems and needs in a college student population. J Affect Disord. 2009; 117(3):180–5. https://doi.org/10.1016/j.jad.2009.01 .001 PMID: 19178949

Dumont M. Funambule Pour une gestion équilibrée du stress [Internet]. Québec: Septembre éditeur; 2012. http://www .septembre.com/livres/funambule-1259.html

Leppin AL, Bora PR, Tilburt JC, Gionfriddo MR, Zeballos-Palacios C, Dulohery MM, et al. The Efficacy of Resiliency Training Programs: A Systematic Review and Meta-Analysis of Randomized Trials. PLOS ONE. 2014; 9(10):e111420. https://doi.org/10.1371/journal .pone.0111420 PMID: 25347713

de Brouwer SJM, Kraaimaat FW, Sweep FCGJ, Donders RT, Eijsbouts A, van Koulil S, et al. Psychophysiological Responses to Stress after Stress Management Training in Patients with Rheumatoid Arthritis. PLOS ONE. 2011; 6(12):e27432. https://doi.org/10.1371/journal .pone.0027432 PMID: 22162990

Lai ESY, Kwok C-L, Wong PWC, Fu K-W, Law Y-W, Yip PSF. The Effectiveness and Sustainability of a Universal School-Based Programme for Preventing Depression in Chinese Adolescents: A Follow-Up Study Using Quasi-Experimental Design. PLOS ONE. 2016; 11(2):e0149854. https://doi.org/10.1371/ journal .pone.0149854 PMID: 26921275

Lay B, Drack T, Bleiker M, Lengler S, Blank C, Rössler W. Preventing Compulsory Admission to Psychiatric Inpatient Care: Perceived Coercion, Empowerment, and Self-Reported Mental Health Functioning after 12 Months of Preventive Monitoring. Front Psychiatry [Internet]. 2015 [cited 2016 Aug 26]; 6(161). Available from: http://www.ncbi.nlm.nih.gov/pmc/articles/PMC4650287/

Saleh D, Camart N, Romo L. Intervention de gestion du stress par Internet chez les étudiants: revue de la littérature. Ann Méd-Psychol Rev Psychiatr. 2016; 5.

Zetterqvist K, Maanmies J, Ström L, Andersson G. Randomized controlled trial of Internet-based stress management. Cogn Behav Ther. 2003; 32(3):151–60. https://doi.org/10.1080/16506070302316 PMID: 16291546

Vliet HV, Andrews G. Internet-based course for the management of stress forjunior high schools. Australas Psychiatry. 2009; 43(4):305–9.

George DR, Dellasega C, Whitehead MM, Bordon A. Facebook-based stress management resources for first-year medical students: A multi-method evaluation. Comput Hum Behav. 2013; 29(3):559–62.

Chiauzzi E, Brevard J, Thurn C, Decembrele S, Lord S. MyStudentBody–Stress: An online stress management intervention for college students. J Health Commun. 2008; 13(6):555–72. https://doi.org/10. 1080/10810730802281668 PMID: 18726812

Gajecki M, Berman AH, Sinadinovic K, Andersson C, Ljótsson B, Hedman E, etal. Effects of Baseline Problematic Alcohol and Drug Use on Internet-Based Cognitive Behavioral Therapy Outcomes for Depression, Panic Disorder and Social Anxiety Disorder. PLOS ONE. 2014; 9(8):e104615. https://doi. org/10.1371/journal .pone.0104615 PMID: 25122509

Broman-Fulks J. Internet-Based Interventionsfor Traumatic Stress-Related Mental Health Problems: A Review and Suggestion for Future Research. 2009;

Ebert DD, Zarski A-C, Christensen H, Stikkelbroek Y, Cuijpers P, Berking M, et al. Internet and Computer-Based Cognitive Behavioral Therapy for Anxiety and Depression in Youth: A Meta-Analysis of Randomized Controlled Outcome Trials. PLOS ONE. 2015; 10(3):e0119895. https://doi.org/10.1371/ journal.pone.0119895 PMID: 25786025

Imamura K, Kawakami N, Furukawa TA, Matsuyama Y, Shimazu A, Umanodan R, et al. Effects of an Internet-Based Cognitive Behavioral Therapy (iCBT) Program in Manga Format on Improving Subthreshold Depressive Symptoms among Healthy Workers: A Randomized Controlled Trial. PLOS ONE. 2014; 9(5):e97167. https://doi.org/10.1371/journal.pone.0097167 PMID: 24844530

Hedman E, Andersson G, Lindefors N, Gustavsson P, Lekander M, Rück C, etal. Personality Change following Internet-Based Cognitive Behavior Therapy for Severe Health Anxiety. PLOS ONE. 2014; 9 (12):e113871. https://doi.org/10.1371/journal.pone.0113871 PMID: 25437150

Hoek W, Schuurmans J, Koot HM, Cuijpers P. Effects of Internet-Based Guided Self-Help Problem-Solving Therapy for Adolescents with Depression and Anxiety: A Randomized Controlled Trial. PLOS ONE. 2012; 7(8):e43485. https://doi .org/10.1371/journal.pone.0043485 PMID: 22952691

Morgan AJ, Rapee RM, Bayer JK. Prevention and early intervention of anxiety problems in young children: A pilot evaluation of Cool Little Kids Online. Internet Interv. 2016; 4:105–12.

Ye Y, Zhang Y, Chen J, Liu J, Li X, Liu Y, et al. Internet-Based Cognitive Behavioral Therapy for Insomnia (ICBT-i) Improves Comorbid Anxiety and Depression—A Meta-Analysis of Randomized Controlled Trials. PLOS ONE. 2015; 10(11):e0142258. https://doi .org/10.1371/journal.pone.0142258 PMID: 26581107

Amstadter AB, Broman-Fulks J, Zinzow H, Ruggiero KJ, Cercone J. Internet-based interventions for traumatic stress-related mental health problems: a review and suggestion for future research. Clin Psychol Rev. 2009; 29(5):410–420. https://doi.org/10.1016/j .cpr.2009.04.001 PMID: 19403215

Sundström C, Gajecki M, Johansson M, Blankers M, Sinadinovic K, Stenlund-Gens E, et al. Guided and Unguided Internet-Based Treatment for Problematic Alcohol Use–A Randomized Controlled Pilot Trial. PLOS ONE. 2016; 11(7):e0157817. https://doi .org/10.1371/journal.pone.0157817 PMID: 27383389

Moore MJ, Soderquist J, Werch C. Feasibility and Efficacy of a Binge Drinking Prevention Intervention for College Students Delivered via the Internet Versus Postal Mail. J Am Coll Health. 2005; 54(1): 38–44. https://doi.org/10.3200/JACH.54.1.38ØPMID: 16050327

Alaoui SE, Ljótsson B, Hedman E, Kaldo V, Andersson E, Rück C, et al. Predictors of Symptomatic Change and Adherence in Internet-Based Cognitive Behaviour Therapy for Social Anxiety Disorder in Routine Psychiatric Care. PLOS ONE. 2015; 10(4):e0124258. https://doi.org/10.1371/journal.pone. 0124258 PMID: 25893687

Carlbring P, Furmark T, SteczkóJ, Ekselius L, Andersson G. An open study of Internet-based bibliotherapy with minimal therapist contact via email for social phobia. Clin Psychol. 2006; 10(1):30–8.

Hughes JA, Phillips G, Reed P. Brief Exposure to a Self-Paced Computer-Based Reading Programme and How It Impacts Reading Ability and Behaviour Problems. PLOS ONE. 2013; 8(11):e77867. https:// doi.org/10.1371/journal.pone.0077867 PMID: 24223125

Billings DW, Cook RF, Hendrickson A, Dove DC. A web-based approach to managing stress and mood disorders in the workforce. J Occup Environ Med. 2008; 50(8):960–8. PMID: 18695455

Servant D. Les programmes de gestion du stress au travail sont-ils efficaces? Lett Psychiatre. 2011; 7 (1):25–8.

Jung Y-H, Ha TM, Oh CY, Lee US, Jang JH, Kim J, et al. The Effects of an Online Mind-Body Training Program on Stress, Coping Strategies, Emotional Intelligence, Resilience and Psychological State. PLOS ONE. 2016; 11(8):e0159841. https://doi.org/10.1371 /journal.pone.0159841 PMID: 27479499

Hoch DB, Watson AJ, Linton DA, Bello HE, Senelly M, Milik MT, et al. The Feasibility and Impact of Delivering a Mind-Body Intervention in a Virtual World. PLOS ONE. 2012; 7(3):e33843. https://doi.org /10.1371/journal.pone.0033843 PMID: 22470483

Currie SL, McGrath PJ, Day V. Development and usability of an online CBT program for symptoms of moderate depression, anxiety, and stress in post-secondary students. Comput Hum Behav. 2010; 26 (6):1419–26.

Day V, McGrath PJ. Internet-based guided self-help for university students with anxiety, depression and stress: A randomized controlled clinical trial. Behav Res Ther. 2013; 51(7):344–351. https:// doi.org/ 10.1016/j.brat.2013.03.003 PMID: 23639300

LaChausse RG. My Student Body: Effects of an Internet-Based Prevention Program to Decrease Obe-sity Among College Students. J Am Coll Health. 2012; 60(4):324–30. https://doi .org/10.1080/ 07448481.2011.623333 PMID: 22559092

Arpin-Cribbie C, Irvine J, Ritvo P. Web-based cognitive-behavioral therapy for perfectionism: A randomized controlled trial. Psychother Res. 2012; 22(2):194–207. https://doi.org/10.1080/10503307.2011. 637242 PMID: 22122217

Fridrici M, Lohaus A. Stress-prevention in secondary schools: online-versus face-to-face-training. Health Educ. 2009; 109(4):299–313.

Baumeister H, Reichler L, Munzinger M, Lin J. The impact of guidance on Internet-based mental health interventions—A systematic review. Internet Interv. 2014; 1(4):205–15.

Schulz KF, Altman DG, Moher D. CONSORT 2010 Statement: updated guidelines for reporting parallel group randomised trials. BMJ. 2010; 340:c332. https://doi.org/10.1136/bmj.c332 PMID: 20332509

Dumont M, Leclerc D, MasséL, McKinnon S. Étude de validation du programme Funambule: pour une gestion équilibrée du stress des adolescents. Éducation Francoph. 2015; 43(2):154.

Lazarus RS, Folkman S. Coping and adaptation. Handb Behav Med. 1984;282–325.

Cohen S, Kamarck T, Mermelstein R. A global measure of perceived stress. J Health Soc Behav. 1983; 24(4):385–96. PMID: 6668417

Bellinghausen L, Collange J., Botella M., Emery J-L, Albert É. Factorial validation of the French scale for perceived stress in the workplace. SantéPublique. 2009; 21(4):365–73. PMID: 20101815

Collange J, Bellinghausen L, ChappéJ, Saunder L, Albert E. Stress perçu: à partir de quel seuil devient-il un facteur de risque pour les troubles anxiodépressifs? Arch Mal Prof Environ. 2013; 74(1):7–15.

Rosenberg M. Society and the adolescent self-image. [Internet]. Princeton University Press. 1965. 326 p. https://www.vitalsource .com/en-uk/products/society-and-the-adolescent-self-image -morris-rosenberg-v9781400876136

Vallieres EF, Vallerand RJ. Traduction et validation canadienne-française de l'échelle de l'estime de soi de Rosenberg. Int J Psychol. 1990; 25(2):305–16.

Chabrol H, Carlin E, Michaud C, Rey A, Cassan D, Juillot M, et al. Étude de l'échelle d'estime de soi de Rosenberg dans un échantillon de lycéens. Neuropsychiatr Enfance Adolesc. 2004; 52(8):533–6.

Blais MR, Vallerand RJ, Pelletier LG, Brière NM. L'échelle de satisfaction de vie: Validation canadienne-française du "Satisfaction with Life Scale". Can J Behav Sci Can Sci Comport. 1989; 21(2):210– 23.

Vallerand RJ, Bissonnette R. Construction et validation de l'Échelle de Satisfaction dans les Études (ESDE). [Construction and validation of the Scale of Satisfaction in Studies]. Can J Behav Sci Can Sci Comport. 1990; 22(3):295–306.

Goldberg DP, Hillier V. A scaled version of the General Health Questionnaire. Psychol Med. 1979; 9 (01):139–45.

Bolognini M, Bettschart W, Zehnder-Gubler M, Rossier L. The validity of the French version of the GHQ-28 and PSYDIS in a community sample of 20 year olds in Switzerland. Eur Arch Psychiatry Neurol Sci. 1989; 238(3):161–8. PMID: 2721534

Guelfi J-D. L'évaluation clinique standardisée en psychiatrie. Lavaur, France: Éd. médicales Pierre Fabre; 1993. 411 p.

Saleh D, Camart N, Sbeira F, Romo L. Internet-Based Stress Management Intervention: Feasibility Study. EC Psychol PSYCHIATRYShort. 2017 Jun; 4(1):27–33.

Cohen J. A power primer. Psychol Bull. 1992; 112(1):155–9. PMID: 19565683

Fridrici M, Lohaus A, Glass C. Effects of incentives in web-based prevention for adolescents: Results of an exploratory field study. Psychol Health. 2009; 24(6):663–75. https://doi.org/10.1080 /08870440802521102 PMID: 20205019

Answer Key Appendix

Introduction: Getting Started

Value of College Education Quick Quiz

1. As a college graduate, you are more likely to engage in healthy behaviors such as exercising and less likely to engage in unhealthy behaviors such as smoking. College graduates are more likely to be healthy, both physically and mentally. It is also more likely that you will have access to healthcare and benefits such as vacation time. College graduates, on average, earn more than those without a college degree. A person with a bachelor's degree, as compared to a person with a high school diploma, earns approximately $23,000 more per year.

2. There are many societal benefits associated with you getting a college education. For example, you are more likely to be engaged in the community and vote. You are also more likely to engage in productive parenting behaviors that can positively impact society. In addition, you will likely be earning a higher salary so can contribute more taxes that can be used to benefit your community.

Financing Your Education, Return on Investment, and Financial Actions Quick Quiz

1. You can pay for college with various types of financial aid or with personal funds. There are important differences in the various types of aid. Need-based aid is based on financial situation. You typically do not need to repay most need-based aid, with loans being the primary exception. Merit-based aid is given to high-achieving students, often in the form of a scholarship. You will often need to meet certain academic requirements to continue receiving the merit aid.

2. Return on investment refers to whether there is a financial benefit associated with an investment. For example, if you put your money in the stock market, how much do you expect to gain? If you invest in your education, is this a wise financial choice? Education has one of the highest returns at approximately 14%–15%.

3. To help you stay within your budget, investigate whether you have the best deals on current expenses such as on your cell phone. It is also a good idea to determine where you can reduce expenses such as not paying a gym membership and instead using the fitness center on campus.

4. To establish good credit, only charge up to 25% of the maximum allowed, and pay your bill on time.

Chapter 1

Intersectionality Quick Quiz

1. Your identity is based on many factors including your group memberships, your group roles, and personal characteristics and interests.

2. Intersectionality is a term that can help you see your many different identities and how these diverse aspects of your identity connect.

Values, Activism, and Aspirations Quick Quiz

1. Being an activist means you take actions such as participating in a protest or voicing concerns in another way to encourage change related to an issue of importance to you.

2. Our aspirations are influenced by those in our social networks and others visible to us via the media.

Chapter 2

Information Literacy Quick Quiz

1. In order to make good decisions, you will need to be able to sort through the endless amount of information that is available. Information literacy is a skill desired by employers because many positions will require you to find, evaluate, and use information.

2. Intentional information is when you actively look for information. Incidental information is information you encounter when you are not looking for it.

3. You can follow professionals and organizations on social media to learn about current issues in the field.

4. A peer-reviewed research article is an article published in a professional journal that has been reviewed and approved by experts in the field of study for that topic.

5. To determine if a source is credible, you will need to determine if the author was qualified, the reason or purpose of the information, how related and useful the information is to the task at hand, whether the information is consistent with other sources, and whether the information is current.

Critical Thinking Quick Quiz

1. Critical thinking involves taking in and evaluating information, viewing the information from multiple perspectives, and drawing conclusions.

2. The six levels from lowest to highest are remembering, understanding, applying, analyzing, evaluating, and creating.

3. The three foundational conditions are having a strong knowledge base, high self-efficacy, and desire and drive.

4. The two learning conditions are challenging tasks and opportunities and learning strategies and support.

Chapter 3

Setting Goals Quick Quiz

1. Examples of short-term goals include earning an A on an assignment or test, exercising 30 minutes every day for a week, and writing an outline for a paper or project. Examples of long-term goals include earning an A in a course, graduating in four years, and saving at least $20,000 for a down payment on a house.

2. Action-based goals have target actions associated with them. Target actions are steps that the individual can take to reach the goal.

3. The ABCS of effective goal setting refers to aiming high, believing in yourself, caring and committing to your goals, and specifying and self-reflecting.

4. "Do your best" goals do not work. Because these goals are not specific enough, they result in less effort being put forth, which in turn leads to lower achievement levels.

Career Exploration and Decision-Making Quick Quiz

1. According to the social cognitive theory, the people we care about play an important role in our decisions. Others can encourage and motivate us to pursue a particular career path.

2. According to values-based theory, your cultural and work values influence your decisions.

3. According to the happenstance theory, planned and unplanned events play an important role in how you make career decisions. By taking action steps, you never know what doors may open.

4. Holland's person-environment fit theory focuses on how individuals who choose careers that match their interests and personality will be more satisfied.

5. Career specialists will help you explore your options and make a decision that matches your interests and values. Students who work with a career counselor are less likely to change majors, which can save them time and money.

6. The Big Five personality factors are openness, conscientiousness, extraversion, agreeableness, and neuroticism. Finding a career that matches your personality style will lead to higher levels of career satisfaction.

7. The informational interview is when you interview a person who works in a career that you are interested in learning more about. The purpose of the interview is to learn about the career from that person's perspective. This information can help you learn about careers and will ultimately help you make an informed career decision.

Chapter 4

Networking Quick Quiz

1. Networking is establishing and nurturing relationships that are beneficial to both parties.

2. Joining clubs or organizations is a great way to expand your network. You can also attend professional workshops or conferences.

3. To maintain and strengthen your relationships within your network, take time to stay in touch. A brief call or e-mail to inquire about how someone in your network is doing or to share exciting news can keep relationships strong.

4. Employers often view social media sites before making hiring decisions. Employees can also be fired for using social media in a way that is not consistent with company policies.

5. Review current social media posts and delete posts that may be viewed negatively by employers. Create a LinkedIn account, sharing positive work, volunteer, or other professional activities.

6. An elevator speech is a very brief overview of your goals and skills. Make it brief enough to share on a quick elevator ride. To develop an elevator speech, identify just one or two key goals and skills. Keep it simple and stay focused on what is most important. Package the information in a creative way that is meaningful to the audience.

Essential Skills Quick Quiz

1. Some of the most valued essential skills include professionalism, communication, interpersonal skills, planning, and problem-solving skills.

2. Professionals complete tasks on time and produce high-level products. In other words, others can count on those with high levels of professionalism to do what it takes to successfully complete a project or assignment. Professionals are also respectful and honest.

3. Creating a to-do list with priority items at the top of the list is a very helpful time management strategy. Another strategy is scheduling tasks. Finally, focusing on only one task at a time is best.

4. Multitasking does not work. In fact, it often results in both tasks taking longer and can also increase your stress.

5. To develop cultural competence, you can become more aware of own beliefs and attitudes and learn about different cultures and populations. You can also develop your overall interpersonal skills.

6. Cultural humility means that you are open and self-aware and that you regularly reflect on how you interact with those who are different from you.

7. Emotional intelligence is the ability to manage one's own emotions and the emotions of others.

8. The 5R approach to group work includes establishing rapport, determining rules, identifying roles, getting ready to work, and remembering to evaluate.

9. Transformational leaders are charismatic, inspire and motivate others, promote intellectual stimulation, and are respectful of others.

Chapter 5

Note-Taking and Reading Skills Quick Quiz

1. The matrix has been found to be the most effective note-taking model.

2. According to research conducted by Recht and Leslie (1988), prior knowledge is more important than reading skills when it comes to reading comprehension. If you know a lot about the subject, it will be easier for you to understand what you read.

3. During the second R, you should close your book and recall what you just read. Writing down this summary works best.

4. Highlight only important points during the third R.

Memory and Study Strategies Quick Quiz

1. According to research conducted by Miller, you can only hold onto approximately seven pieces of information at a time.

2. Researchers have found that testing is a powerful memory tool. You learn the most when you test yourself and try to recall information.

3. You are more likely to remember pictures versus words. When you look at images related to the content, you learn the material better.

4. Research shows that studying in a group leads to higher achievement.

5. Be sure to select members for the study group who share your goals and passion for learning. Develop rules and consider assigning roles to different members.

Chapter 6

Academic Integrity Quick Quiz

1. Academic integrity refers to engaging in honest actions. It means that you have done your own work independently and have given credit to those who shaped or guided your work.

2. Academic integrity benefits everyone. Community partners are more likely to provide internships and other experiential learning experiences to students at colleges and universities with good reputations. You will also learn more when you engage in honest actions. Your character matters much more than your grade.

3. You always need to cite the source. The only two situations where a source is not needed is when an idea is entirely your own or the information is general knowledge.

4. Paraphrasing involves summarizing someone else's work into your own words. It requires more than changing a few words and should relate to the big ideas presented, not sentences.

Assignments and Tests Quick Quiz

1. When you begin the revision process, start with the big picture. In other words, focus on purpose, audience, and the overall organization.

2. The best way to combat performance anxiety is to practice. The more you know your material and feel prepared, the more confidence and less anxiety you will have.

3. You can begin with a hook such as an interesting story or statistic. During the presentation, you can take very brief active learning breaks using techniques such as polling or asking audience members to briefly discuss what they learned with a partner.

4. According to Mayer's (2009) research, use images, put only essential information on the slide, draw attention to what is most important, use conversational language, and allow audience members the opportunity to read slides if there is a need for a lot of words.

5. High-performing students anticipate the answer, read all answer choices, skip difficult questions, eliminate wrong choices, write on their exams, and change their answer if they have a good reason for doing so.

6. The three steps involved with writing a good essay response are planning, writing, and proofreading.

7. Take-home and online exams can be more challenging and time-consuming. While you may be less anxious, it is still important to prepare well. There may be no time limit, which means you may have to devote more time to this type of assessment.

Chapter 7

Creating Academic Plans and Monitoring Progress Quick Quiz

1. Students who meet with their advisors are more likely to be successful.

2. Most bachelor's degrees consist of general education courses, courses required for your selected major and elective credits, which can be used for a double major or minor.

3. Structured learning experiences such as internships or co-ops will give you valuable work experience that employers desire and will also give you the opportunity to learn skills and network.

4. Academic self-regulation involves goal setting, identifying learning strategies, and then monitoring progress and making changes as needed.

5. Attribution theory refers to how you interpret your successes and mistakes.

6. The most productive way to interpret a mistake is to attribute it to something that is internal and changeable, such as effort.

Being Resilient and Developing Grit Quick Quiz

1. Resilience is the ability to bounce back and be successful after facing a traumatic or very challenging situation.

2. Grit refers to your passion and commitment to a goal and your willingness to do whatever it takes to accomplish the goal.

3. Getting a good night's sleep, eating healthy, exercising, and talking to others are all very effective stress management techniques.

4. It is very important to have a positive mindset and to focus on what is within your control such as how much effort you put into a task.

5. Support is a key factor in being resilient and gritty. Those with a high level of support are more likely to be resilient and achieve goals.

6. Mindfulness is being aware of what is happening in the moment, noticing your breathing and other reactions to the environment.

7. A reflective, problem-solving coping style works best to combat racial battle fatigue. It is also helpful to talk with others about experiences and to problem-solve, and to take needed breaks.

8. Behaviorists suggest giving yourself a reward when you successfully accomplish a task or reach a goal.

9. Cognitive psychologists believe our thoughts play a powerful role in motivation. How you interpret experiences will have a positive or negative impact on motivation.

10. According to Maslow, everyone strives for self-actualization, being the best one can be. You can achieve this when your basic needs are met. The basic needs that need to be met, in hierarchical order from most basic, are physiological needs such as hunger, safety, love and belonging, esteem, and self-actualization.

11. According to sociocultural theorists, your motivation is impacted by social and cultural factors. Although you are most influenced by family and friends, many social factors can impact your motivation. This can include the absence or presence of support from others and the nature of the environment.

12. Celebrating increases your motivation and self-efficacy, both of which play an important role in future experiences.

References Index

Page numbers provided in purple refer to where the referenced material appears within the text.

AACC, Association of Community Colleges (2014). 2014 Fact Sheet. www.aacc.nche.edu. 13

Abel, J. R., & Deitz, R. (2014). Do the benefits of college still outweigh the costs? *Current Issues in Economics & Finance, 20*(3), 1–12. 6, 12

Abu, S. H. M., Aroury, A. M. A., Alsharari, A. F., Al, G. S. H., & Esaileh, A. A. (2020). Relationship between sleep quality, using social media platforms, and academic performance among university students. *Perspectives in Psychiatric Care, 56*(2), 415–423. doi:10.1111/ppc.12450 195

Alaoui SE, Ljótsson B, Hedman E, Kaldo V, Andersson E, Rück C, et al. Predictors of Symptomatic Change and Adherence in Internet-Based Cognitive Behaviour Therapy for Social Anxiety Disorder in Routine Psychiatric Care. PLOS ONE. 2015; 10(4):e0124258. https://doi.org/10.1371/journal.pone. 0124258 PMID: 25893687 266

Abu-Ghazaleh SB, Sonbol HN, Rajab LD. A longitudinal study of psychological stress among undergraduate dental students at the University of Jordan. BMC Med Educ. 2016; 16:90. https://doi.org/10. 1186/s12909-016-0612-6 PMID: 26968682 266

Adlaf EM, Gliksman L, Demers A, Newton-Taylor B. The Prevalence of Elevated Psychological Distress Among Canadian Undergraduates: Findings from the 1998 Canadian Campus Survey. J Am Coll Health. 2001; 50(2):67–72. https://doi.org/10.1080/07448480109596009 PMID: 11590985 266

Alavi, M. (1994). Computer-mediated collaborative learning: An empirical evaluation. *MIS Quarterly, 18*(2), 59–174. 248

Albion, M. J., & Fogarty, G. J. (2002). Factors influencing career decision making in adolescents and adults. *Journal of Career Assessment, 10*(1), 91–126. 81

Albitz, R. S. (2007). The what and who of information literacy and critical thinking in higher education. *Portal: Libraries and the Academy, 7*(1), 97–109. 159

Algharaibeh, S. A. S. (2020). Should I ask for help? The role of motivation and help-seeking in students' academic achievement: A path analysis model. *Cypriot Journal of Educational Sciences, 15*(5), 1128–1145. 201, 204

Alpizar, D., Adesope, O. O., & Wong, R. M. (2020). A meta-analysis of signaling principle in multimedia learning environments. *Educational Technology Research & Development, 68*(5), 2095–2119. doi:10.1007/s11423-020-09748-7 170

Alvarado, A. R., & Olson, A. B. (2020). Examining the relationship between college advising and student outputs: A content analysis of the NACADA journal. *NACADA Journal, 40*(2), 49–62. doi:10.12930/NACADA-19-33 182

American Association of Community Colleges. (2021). AACC 2021 Fast facts. https://www.aacc.nche.edu/research-trends/fast-facts/ 13

American Psychological Association. (2015). *Key terms and concepts in understanding gender diversity and sexual orientation among students.* https://www.apa.org/pi/lgbt/programs/safe-supportive/lgbt/key-terms.pdf 22

American Psychological Association. (2019, October 8). *Manage stress: Strengthen your support network.* https://www.apa.org/topics/stress/manage-social-support 21, 22, 198

American Psychological Association. (2008). Summary report of journal operations, 2007. *American Psychologist, 63*(5), 490–491. doi:10.1037/0003-066X.63.5.490 49

Amstadter AB, Broman-Fulks J, Zinzow H, Ruggiero KJ, Cercone J. Internet-based interventions for traumatic stress-related mental health problems: a review and suggestion for future research. Clin Psychol Rev. 2009; 29(5):410–420. https://doi.org/10.1016/j.cpr.2009.04.001 PMID: 19403215 266

Anderson, L., & Krathwohl, D. A. (2001). *Taxonomy for learning, teaching and assessing: A revision of Bloom's taxonomy of educational objectives.* Longman. 58, 60

Anderson, Randy J., and Lydia E. Anderson (2010). "Professorial Presentations: The Link Between the Lecture and Student Success in the Workplace," *Academy of Educational Leadership Journal, 14*(1), 55–62. 263

Anic, V., & Wallmeier, M. (2020). Perceived attractiveness of structured financial products: The role of presentation format and reference instruments. *Journal of Behavioral Finance, 21*(1), 78–102. doi:10.1080/15427560.2019.1629441 168

Appelbaum, S. H., Marchionni, A., & Fernandez, A. (2008). The multi-tasking paradox: Perceptions, problems and strategies. *Management Decision, 46*(9), 1313–1325. doi:10.1108/00251740810911966 115, 116

Archer, W., & Davison, J. (2008). Graduate employability: What do employers think and want? *The Council for Industry and Higher Education,* 1–20., 109

Armstrong, J. L. (2004). Seven keys for small groups success. *Adult Learning, 15*(1–2), 34–35. 123

Arnold, K. A. (2017). Transformational Leadership and Employee Psychological Well-Being: A Review and Directions for Future Research. *Journal of Occupational Health Psychology.* Advance online publication. http://dx.doi.org/10.1037/ocp0000062 125

Arpin-Cribbie C, Irvine J, Ritvo P. Web-based cognitive-behavioral therapy for perfectionism: A randomized controlled trial. Psychother Res. 2012; 22(2):194–207. https://doi.org/10.1080/10503307.2011.637242 PMID: 22122217 266

Artis, A. B. (2008). Improving marketing students' reading comprehension with the SQ3R method. *Journal of Marketing Education, 30*(2), 130–137. 140

Artuso, C., & Palladino, P. (2019) Long-term memory effects on working memory updating development. *PLOS One, 14*(5), 1–16. https://doi.org/10.1371/journal.pone.0217697 143

Ashford, K. (2014, August 29). 5 steps to calculating your college R.O.I. Forbes. Retrieved from: http://www.forbes.com/sites/learnvest/2014/08/29/5-steps-to-calculating-your-college-r-o-i/#72fa55b144c9 9, 12

Association of American Colleges and Universities., & National Leadership Council (U.S.) (2007). *College learning for the new global century: A report from the National Leadership Council for Liberal Education & America's Promise. Washington*, D.C. 221

Association of American Colleges and Universities. Available: http://www.aacu.org/leap/documents/Global Century _final.pdf 223

Atkinson, R. C., & Shiffrin, R. M. (1968). Human memory: A proposed system and its control processes. In K. W. Spence, & J. T. Spence, The Psychology of Learning and Motivation (Vol. 2, pp. 89–195). Academic Press. 141

Austin, R. D, Nolan, R. L., & O'Donnell, S. (2016). The Adventures of An IT Leader. Harvard Business Review Press, Boston. 235

Aydin, G. (2017). Personal factors predicting college student success. *Eurasian Journal of Educational Research, 69*, 93–112. 194

Ayeni, T. (2018, February 26). Exploring the relationship between experience, expectation, and academic performance. NACADA Academic Advising Today. https://nacada.ksu.edu/Resources /Academic-Advising-Today/View-Articles/Exploring-the -Relationship-between-Experience-Expectation-and-Academic -Performance.aspx 23–24, 98, 99, 117, 125, 185, 187, 203

Azmuddin, R. A., Nor, N. F. M., & Hamat, A. (2020). Facilitating online reading comprehension in enhanced learning environment using digital annotation tools. *IAFOR Journal of Education, 8*(2), 9–27. doi:10.22492/ije.8.2.01 139

Bahadir, F. (2020). University students' perceptions of the reasons for success and failure: A qualitative study. *Journal of Educational Issues, 6*(2), 214–231. 207

Baker, M. J. (2019). Pain or gain? How business communication students perceive the outlining process. *Business and Professional Communication Quarterly, 82*(3), 273–296. 162

Balsamo, M., Lauriola, M., & Saggino, A. (2013). Work values and college major choice. *Learning and Individual Differences, 24*, 110–116. 83

Bandura, A., & Walters, R. H. (1963). *Social learning and personality development*. Holt, Rinehart & Winston. 61, 73

Barnett, K. (2012). Student interns' socially constructed work realities: Narrowing the work expectation-reality gap. *Business Communication Quarterly, 75*(3), 271–290. 186

Barrington, L., Wright, M., Casner-Lotto, J. (2006). Are they really ready to work? Employers' perspectives on the basic knowledge and applied skills of new entrants to the 21st century U.S. workforce. *The Conference Board.* 109

Barkley, E. F., Cross, K. P., & Major, C. H. (2005). *Collaborative learning techniques: A handbook for college faculty*. San Francisco, CA: Jossey-Bass. 248

Bartsch, L. M., & Oberauer, K. (2021). The effects of elaboration on working memory and long-term memory across age. *Journal of Memory and Language, 118*, 1–16. https://doi.org/10.1016 /j.jml.2020.104215 145

Baum, S., Ma, J., & Payea, K. (2010). Education pays 2010: The benefits of higher education for individuals and society. *College Board Advocacy and Policy.* Retrieved from https://research.collegeboard.org/media /pdf/education-pays-2010-full-report.pdf 22 5

Baumeister H, Reichler L, Munzinger M, Lin J. The impact of guidance on Internet-based mental health interventions—A systematic review. Internet Interv. 2014; 1(4):205–15. 266

Bayram N, Bilgel N. The prevalence and socio-demographic correlations of depression, anxiety and stress among a group of university students. Soc Psychiatry Psychiatr Epidemiol. 2008; 43(8):667–72. https://doi.org /10.1007/s00127-008-0345-x PMID: 18398558 266

Baykan Z, Naçar M, Cetinkaya F. Depression, anxiety, and stressamong last-year students at Erciyes University Medical School. Acad Psychiatry J Am Assoc Dir Psychiatr Resid Train Assoc Acad Psychiatry. 2012; 36(1):64–5. 266

Bean, J. C. (2011). *Engaging ideas: The professor's guide to integrating writing, critical thinking, and active learning in the classroom* (2nd ed.). San Francisco, CA: Jossey-Bass. 248

Bell, A., Bhatt, R., Rubin, D. L., & Shiflet, C. (2021). Effects of education abroad on indices of student success among racial–ethnic minority college students. *Journal of Diversity in Higher Education.* Advance online publication. doi:10.1037/dhe0000327 188

Belter, R. W., & du Pre, A. (2009). A strategy to reduce plagiarism in an undergraduate course. *Teaching of Psychology, 36*, 257–261. doi:10.1080/00986280903173165 156

Bellinghausen L, Collange J., Botella M., Emery J-L, Albert É. Factorial validation of the French scale for perceived stress in the workplace. SantéPublique. 2009; 21(4):365–73. PMID: 20101815 269

Bercher, D. A. (2012). Self-monitoring tools and student academic success: When perception matches reality. *Journal of College Science Teaching, 41*(5), 26–32. 190

Bewick B, Koutsopoulou G, Miles J, Slaa E, Barkham M. Changes in undergraduate students' psychological well-being as they progress through university. Stud High Educ. 2010; 35(6):633–45. 266

Bidwell, A. (2014). Average student loan debt approaches $30,0000. US News. Retrieved from: https://www.usnews.com/news/articles /2014/11/13/average-student-loan-debt-hits-30-000 9

Billings DW, Cook RF, Hendrickson A, Dove DC. A web-based approach to managing stress and mood disorders in the workforce. J Occup Environ Med. 2008; 50(8):960–8. PMID: 18695455 266

Blair, B. F., & Millea, M. (2004). Student Academic Performance and Compensation: The Impact of Cooperative Education. *College Student Journal, 38*(4), 643–743. 186

Blais MR, Vallerand RJ, Pelletier LG, Brière NM. L'échelle de satisfaction de vie: Validation canadienne-française du "Satisfaction with Life Scale". Can J Behav Sci Can Sci Comport. 1989; 21(2):210– 23. 270

Blake, B. S., Bayne, M. L., Crosby, F. J., & Muller, C. B. (2011). Matching by race and gender in mentoring relationships: Keeping our eyes on the prize. *Journal of Social Issues, 67*(3), 622–643. doi:10.1111/j.1540-4560.2011.01717.x 102

Bledsoe, S., Baskin, J. J., & Berry, F. (2018). Fear not! How students cope with the fears and anxieties of college life. *College Teaching, 66*(3), 158–165. 198

Blikstad-Balas, M. (2016). "You get what you need": A study of students' attitudes towards using Wikipedia when doing school assignments. *Scandinavian Journal of Educational Research, 60*(6), 594–608. doi:10.1080/00313831.2015.106 6428 139

Blommaert, L., Meuleman, R., Leenheer, S., & Butkēviča, A. (2020). The gender gap in job authority: Do social network resources matter? *Acta Sociologica, 63*(4), 381–399. doi:10.1177 /0001699319847504 99

Bughi SA, Sumcad J, Bughi S. Effect of brief behavioral intervention program in managing stress in medical students from two southern California universities. Med Educ Online. 2006; 11:1–8. 266

Boch, F. & Piolat, A. (2005). Note-taking and learning : A summary of research. *The WAC Journal, 16*(September), 101–113. 248

Bodenlos, J. S., Noonan, M., & Wells, S. Y. (2013). Mindfulness and alcohol problems in college students: The mediating effects of stress. *Journal of American College Health, 61*(6), 371–378. doi:10.10 80/07448481.2013.805714 199

Bohnert, D., & Ross, W. H. (2010). The influence of social networking web sites on the evaluation of job candidates. *Cyberpsychology, Behavior, and Social Networking, 13*(3), 341–347. doi:10.1089/cyber.2009.0193 104

Bolognini M, Bettschart W, Zehnder-Gubler M, Rossier L. The validity of the French version of the GHQ-28 and PSYDIS in a community sample of 20 year olds in Switzerland. Eur Arch Psychiatry Neurol Sci. 1989; 238(3):161–8. PMID: 2721534 270

Bonanno, G. A., Galea, S., Bucciarelli, A., & Vlahov, D. (2007). What predicts psychological resilience after disaster? The role of demographics, resources, and life stress. *Journal of Consulting and Clinical Psychology*, 75(5), 671–682. doi:10.1037/0022-006X.75.5.671 198

Boujut E, Koleck M, Bruchon-Schweitzer M, Bourgeois ML. Mental health among students: A study among a cohort of freshmen. Ann Méd-Psychol. 2009; 167(9):662–8. 266

Bonnici, Joseph, and Harsh K. Luthar (1996). "Peer Evaluated Debates: Developing Oral Communication Skills Through Marketing Case Studies," *Marketing Education Review*, 6(2), 73–81. 260

Bowles, B., Gintis, H., & Osborne, M. (2001). The determinants of earnings: A behavioral approach. *Journal of Economic Literature*, 39, 1137–1176. 109

Bowman, L. L., Levine, L. E., Waite, B. M., & Gendron, M. (2010). Can students really multitask? An experimental study of instant messaging while reading. *Computers & Education*, 54(4), 927–931. doi:10.1016/j.compedu.2009.09.024 115, 116

Bowman, N. A., Jang, N., Kivlighan, D. M., Schneider, N., & Ye, X. (2020). The impact of a goal-setting intervention for engineering students on academic probation. *Research in Higher Education*, 61(1), 142–166. doi:10.1007/ s11162-019-09555-x 69

Brasley, S. (2008). Effective librarian and discipline faculty collaboration models for integrating information literacy into the fabric of an academic institution. *New Directions for Teaching and Learning*, 114, 71–88. 223

Breivik, P. (2005). 21st century learning and information literacy. *Change*, 37(2), 20–27. 159

Broda, M., Yun, J., Schneider, B., Yeager, D. S., Walton, G. M., & Diemer, M. (2018). Reducing inequality in academic success for incoming college students: A randomized trial of growth mindset and belonging interventions. *Journal of Research on Educational Effectiveness*, 11(3), 317–338. doi:10. 1080/19345747.2018.1429037 197

Broman-Fulks J. Internet-Based Interventionsfor Traumatic Stress -Related Mental Health Problems: A Review and Suggestion for Future Research. 2009 266

Brown, D. (2002). The role of work and cultural values in occupational choice, satisfaction, and success: A theoretical statement. *Journal of Counseling & Development*, 80(1), 48-56. doi:10.1002/j.1556-6678.2002.tb00165.x 79

Brown, J., & Vanable, P. (2007). Alcohol use, partner type, and risky sexual behavior among college students: Findings from an event-level study. *Addictive Behaviors*, 32(12), 2940–2952. doi:10.1016/j.addbeh.2007. 06.011 201

Brown, M. (2011). Effects of graphic organizers on student achievement in the writing process. *Online Submission*. 162

Brown-Kramer, C. R. (2021). Improving students' study habits and course performance with a "learning how to learn" assignment. *Teaching of Psychology*, 48(1), 48–54. doi:10.1177/0098628320959926 144

Bruce, C. S. (1999). Workplace experiences of information literacy. *International Journal of Information Management*, 19, 33–47. 45

Brusso, R. C., Orvis, K. A., Bauer, K. N., & Tekleab, A. G. (2012). Interaction among self-efficacy, goal orientation, and unrealistic goal-setting on videogame-based training performance. *Military Psychology (Taylor & Francis Ltd)*, 24(1), 1–18. doi:10.1080/089956 05.2012.639669 72

Bureau of Labor Statistics. (2019). Number of jobs, labor market experience, and earnings growth: Results from a national longitudinal survey. https://www.bls.gov/news.release/pdf/nlsoy .pdf 75

Burton, V. T., & Chadwick, S. A. (2000). Investigating the practices of student researchers: Patterns of use and criteria for use of internet and library sources. *Computers and Composition*, 17(3), 309–328. doi:10.1016/S8755-4615(00)00037-2 49

Byars-Winston, A., & Rogers, J. G. (2019). Testing intersectionality of race/ethnicity x gender in a social—cognitive career theory model with science identity. *Journal of Counseling Psychology*, 66(1), 30–44. doi:10.1037/cou0000309 36

Calcich, Stephen E., and Dan C. Weilbaker (1992). "Selecting the Optimum Number of In-Class Sales Presentations," *Marketing Education Review*, 2(1), 31–33. 260

Caligiuri, P., & Tarique, I. (2012). Dynamic cross-cultural competencies and global leadership effectiveness. *Journal of World Business*, 47(4), 612–622. doi:10.1016/j.jwb.2012.01.014 118

California State University. California State University retools general education courses to focus on core values of liberal education(Press Release) Available at http://www.calstate.edu/pa /news/2008/leaps.html 223

California State University. (1995). *Information competence in the CSU: A report submitted to Commission on Learning Resources and Instructional Technology Work Group on Information Competence*. Sacramento, CA: California State University. 223

Callanan, G., & Benzing, C. (2004). Assessing the role of internships in the career-oriented employment of graduating college students. *Education and Training*, 46(2), 82–89. doi:10.1108.00400910410525261 186

Canning, E. A., Muenks, K., Green, D. J., & Murphy, M. C. (2019). STEM Faculty Who Believe Ability is Fixed Have Larger Racial Achievement Gaps and Inspire Less Student Motivation in Their Classes. Science Advances, 5(2), EAAU4734. 233

Carlston, D. L. (2011). Benefits of student-generated note packets: A preliminary investigation of SQ3R implementation. *Teaching of Psychology*, 38(3), 142–146. 140

Carlbring P, Furmark T, Steczkó J, Ekselius L, Andersson G. An open study of Internet-based bibliotherapy with minimal therapist contact via email for social phobia. Clin Psychol. 2006; 10(1):30–8. 266

Carroll, Conor (2006). "Enhancing Reflective Learning Through Role-Plays: The Use of an Effective Sales Presentation Evaluation Form in Student Role-Plays," *Marketing Education Review*, 16(1), 9–13. 260

Carnevale, A. P., Chea, B., & van der Werf, M. (2020). A first try at ROI: Ranking 4,500 Colleges. Georgetown University Center on Education and the Workforce. https:// cew.georgetown.edu /cew-reports/collegeroi/ 12

Casad, B. J., & Bryant, W. J. (2016). Addressing stereotype threat is critical to diversity and inclusion in organizational psychology. *Frontiers in Psychology*, 7(8), 1–18. 172

Caudrin, S. (1999). "The hard case for soft skills", *Workforce*, 78(7), pp. 60–64. 241

Casner-Lotto, J., Conference Board., Partnership for 21st Century Skills., Corporate Voices for Working Families., & Society for Human Resource Management (U.S.). (2006). *Are they really ready to work?: Employers' perspectives on the basic knowledge and applied skills of new entrants to the 21st century U.S. workforce*. United States: Conference Board. 221

Caudrin, S. (1999). "The hard case for soft skills", Workforce, 78(7), pp. 60–64. 241

Cavanaugh, T., Lamkin, M. L., & Hu, H. (2012). Using a generalized checklist to improve student assignment submission times in an online course. *Journal of Asynchronous Learning Networks*, 16(4), 39–44. 114

Chabrol H, Carlin E, Michaud C, Rey A, Cassan D, Juillot M, et al. Étude de l'échelle d'estime de soi de Rosenberg dans un échantillon de lycéens. Neuropsychiatr Enfance Adolesc. 2004; 52(8):533–6. 269

Center for Community College Student Engagement (CCCSE) (2019). A mind at work: Maximizing the relationship between mindset and student success. The University of Texas at Austin, College of Education, Department of Educational Leadership and Policy, Program in Higher Education Leadership, Austin, TX. Retrieved from http://www.ccsse.org/center/NR2019/Minds et.pdf 233

Cheng and Cheou Pi-Yueh, C., & Wen-Bin, C. (2010). Achievement, attributions, self-efficacy, and goal setting by accounting undergraduates. *Psychological Reports*, 106(1), 54–64. doi:10.2466/PR0.106.1.54-64 73

Chiauzzi E, Brevard J, Thurn C, Decembrele S, Lord S. MyStudentBody–Stress: An online stress management intervention for college students. J Health Commun. 2008; 13(6):555–72. https://doi.org/10. 1080 /10810730802281668 PMID: 18726812 266

Cheuk, B. (2008). Delivering business value through information literacy in the workplace. *Libri*, 58. 137–143. 222

Chinyamurindi, W. T., Hlatywayo, C. K., Mhlanga, T. S., Marange, C. S., & Chikungwa-Everson, T. (2021). Career decision-making amongst high school learners: A descriptive- exploratory study from South Africa. *Cypriot Journal of Educational Sciences*, 16(1), 129–147. 76, 78

Chiou, C. C. (2008). The effect of concept mapping on students' learning achievements and interests. *Innovations in Education and Teaching International*, 45(4), 375–387. 137

Cholewa, B., & Ramaswami, S. (2015). The effects of counseling on the retention and academic performance of underprepared freshmen. *Journal of College Student Retention: Research, Theory and Practice*, 17(2), 204–225. doi:10.1177/1521025115578233 198

Choueiry N, Salamoun T, Jabbour H, Osta NE, Hajj A, Khabbaz LR. Insomnia and Relationship with Anxiety in University Students: A Cross-Sectional Designed Study. PLOS ONE. 2016; 11(2):e0149643. https://doi.org/10.1371/journal.pone.0149643 PMID: 26900686 266

Christian, T. Y., & Sprinkle, J. E. (2013). College student perceptions and ideals of advising: An exploratory analysis. *College Student Journal*, 47(2), 271–291. 182

Christopher, D. A. (2006). "Building better communicators: integrating writing into business communications courses", *Business Education Forum*, 61(2), pp. 40–43. 242

Chu, S. K. W., Hu, X., & Ng, J. (2020). Exploring secondary school students' self-perception and actual understanding of plagiarism. *Journal of Librarianship & Information Science*, 52(3), 806–817. doi:10.1177/0961000619872527 155

Clark, G., Marsden, R., Whyatt, J. D., Thompson, L., & Walker, M. (2015). 'It's everything else you do…': Alumni views on extracurricular activities and employability. *Active Learning in Higher Education*, 16(2), 133–147. doi:10.1177/1469787415574050 96, 109

Clark, K. R., & Buckley, M. B. (2017). Using a synthesis matrix to plan a literature review. *Radiologic Technology*, 88(3), 354–357. 161

Claro, S., Paunesku, D., & Dweck, C. S. (2016). Growth Mindset Tempers the Effects of Poverty on Academic Achievement. *Proceedings of the National Academy of Sciences*, 113(31), 8664–8668. 233

Clayson, D. E. (2013). Initial impressions and the student evaluation of teaching. *Journal of Education for Business*, 88(1), 26–35. 100

Coffelt, T. A., & Smith, F. L. M. (2020). Exemplary and unacceptable workplace communication skills. *Business and Professional Communication Quarterly*, 83(4), 365–384. 119

Cohen, M. T. (2012). The importance of self-regulation for college student learning. *College Student Journal*, 46(4), 892–902. 189, 190

Cohen S, Kamarck T, Mermelstein R. A global measure of perceived stress. J Health Soc Behav. 1983; 24(4):385–96. PMID: 6668417 269 Cohen J. A power primer. Psychol Bull. 1992; 112(1):155–9. PMID: 19565683 270

Cohen, J., & Cohen, P. (1983). *Applied multiple regression/correlation analysis for the behavioral sciences* (2nd ed.). Hillsdale, NJ: Erlbaum. 216

Cole, M. S., Rubin, R. S., Field, H. S., & Giles, W. F. (2007). Recruiters' perceptions and use of applicant resume information: Screening the recent graduate. *Applied Psychology: An International Review*, 56(2), 319–343. 108

Cole, Z. J., & Butler, D. L. (2020). Disentangling the effects of study time and study strategy on undergraduate test performance. *Psi Chi Journal of Psychological Research*, 25(2), 110–120. doi:10.24839/2325 -7342.jn25.2.110 144, 145

Collange J, Bellinghausen L, ChappéJ, Saunder L, Albert E. Stress perçu: à partir de quel seuil devient-il un facteur de risque pour les troubles anxiodépressifs? Arch Mal Prof Environ. 2013; 74(1):7–15. 269

Conkel-Ziebell, J. L., Gushue, G. V., & Turner, S. L. (2019). Anticipation of racism and sexism: Factors related to setting career goals for urban youth of color. *Journal of Counseling Psychology*, 66(5), 588–599. doi:10.1037/cou0000357 73

Cottringer, W. (2015). Setting the standards. *Supervision*, 76(7), 25–26. 110

Cranney, J., Morris, S., Spehar, B., & Scoufis, M. (2008). Helping first year students think like psychologists: Supporting information literacy and teamwork skill development. *Psychology Learning & Teaching*, 7(1), 28–36. doi:10.2304/plat.2008.7.1.28 122

Crawford, J. (2006). The use of electronic information services and information literacy: A Glasgow Caledonian University study. *Journal of Librarianship & Information Science*, 38(1), 33–44. doi:10.1177/0961000606060958 228

Crawford G, Burns SK, Chih HJ, Hunt K, Tilley PM, Hallett J, et al. Mental health first aid training for nursing students: a protocol for a pragmatic randomised controlled trial in a large university. BMC Psychiatry. 2015; 15:26. https://doi.org/10.1186/s12888-015-0403 -3 PMID: 25886615 266

Crosby, O. (2010). Informational interviewing: Get the inside scoop on careers. *Occupational Outlook Quarterly*, 54(2), 22–29. 90

Cross, W. E., & Vandiver, B. J. (2001). Introducing the Cross Racial Identity Scale. In J. Ponterotto, M. Casas, L. Suzuki, & C. Alexander (Eds.), *Handbook of multicultural counseling* (2nd ed., pp. 371–393). Thousand Oaks, CA: Sage. 214

Culham, R. (2018). *Teach writing well: How to assess writing, invigorate instruction, and rethink revision.* Stenhouse Publishers. 163

Currie SL, McGrath PJ, Day V. Development and usability of an online CBT program for symptoms of moderate depression, anxiety, and stress in post-secondary students. Comput Hum Behav. 2010; 26 (6):1419–26. 266

Cutts, Q., Cutts, E. Draper, S., O'Donnell, P., & Saffrey, P. (2010). Manipulating Mindset to Positively Influence Introductory Programming Performance. In *SIGCSE 10: Proceedings of the 41st ACM technical symposium on computer science education, Milwaukee (WI), USA, 10–13.03.2010.* Association for Computing Machinery, New York. 234

Curzon, S. C. (2004). Developing faculty-librarian partnerships in information literacy. In Rockman, I. F. (Eds.). Integrating information literacy into the higher education curriculum: Practical models for transformation. San Francisco: Jossey-Bass. 222

Dahlin M, Joneborg N, Runeson B. Stress and depression among medical students: across-sectional study. Med Educ. 2005;39(6): 594–604. https://doi.org/10.1111/j.1365-2929.2005.02176.xPMID: 15910436 266

Dansereau, D., Carmichael, L. E., & Hotson, B. (2020). Building first-year science writing skills with an embedded writing instruction program. *Journal of College Science Teaching*, *49*(3), 66–75. doi:10.2505/4/jcst20_049_03_66 165

Day V, McGrath PJ. Internet-based guided self-help for university students with anxiety, depression and stress: A randomized controlled clinical trial. Behav Res Ther. 2013; 51(7):344–351. https://doi.org/10.1016/j.brat.2013.03.003 PMID: 23639300 266

Day, T., & Tosey, P. (2011). Beyond SMART? A new framework for goal setting. *Curriculum Journal*, *22*(4), 515–534. 71

Deasy C, Coughlan B, Pironom J, Jourdan D, Mannix-McNamara P. Psychological Distress and Coping amongst Higher Education Students: A Mixed Method Enquiry. PLOS ONE. 2014; 9(12):e115193. https://doi.org/10.1371/journal.pone.0115193 PMID: 25506825 266

de Jager, K. (1997). Library use and academic achievement. *South African Journal of Library & Information Science*, *65*, 26–30. 222

de Janasz, S. C., & Forret, M. L. (2008). Learning the art of networking: A critical skill for enhancing social capital and career success. *Journal of Management Education*, *32*(5), 629–650. doi:10.1177/1052562907307637 71, 98, 106

De Vet, E., Nelissen, R. A., Zeelenberg, M., & De Ridder, D. D. (2013). Ain't no mountain high enough? Setting high weight loss goals predict effort and short-term weight loss. *Journal of Health Psychology*, *18*(5), 638–647. doi:10.1177/1359105312454038 71

deCarvalho, M., & Junior, R. (2015). Impact of risk management on project performance: the importance of soft skills. *International Journal of Production Research*, *53*(2), 321–340. doi:10.1080/00207543.2014.919423 109

Deem, J., Beyer, S., Dana, H., Chicone, R., Ringler, I., Ferebee, S., & Strouble, D. (2020). Increasing student success with team projects in the virtual classroom. *Online Journal of Distance Learning Administration*, *23*(3), 1–5. 122, 123

Deepa, S., & Seth, M. (2013). Do soft skills matter? Implications for educators based on recruiters' perspective. *The IUP Journal of Soft Skills*, *7*(1), 7–20. 109

de Brouwer SJM, Kraaimaat FW, Sweep FCGJ, Donders RT, Eijsbouts A, van Koulil S, et al. Psychophysiological Responses to Stress after Stress Management Training in Patients with Rheumatoid Arthritis. PLOS ONE. 2011; 6(12):e27432. https://doi.org/10.1371/journal.pone.0027432 PMID: 22162990 266

DeLaune, L. D., Rakow, J. S., & Rakow, K. C. (2010). Teaching financial literacy in a co-curricular service-learning model. *Journal of Accounting Education*, *28*(2), 103–113. doi:10.1016/ j.jaccedu.2011.03.002 188

Demirbilek, M., & Talan, T. (2018). The effect of social media multitasking on classroom performance. *Active Learning in Higher Education*, *19*(2), 117–129. doi:10.1177/1469787417721382 116

Demirdag, S. (2021). Communication skills and time management as the predictors of student motivation. *International Journal of Psychology and Educational Studies*, *8*(1), 38–50. 111

Dennick, R. (2012). Twelve tips for incorporating educational theory into teaching practices. *Medical Teacher*, *34*(8), 618–624. doi:10.3109/0142159X.2012.668244 57

deSmet, M. J. R., Broekcamp, H., Brand-Gruwel, S., & Kirschner. P. A. (2011). Effects of electronic outlining on students' argumentative writing performance. *Journal of Computer Assisted Learning*, *27*(6), 557–574. 162

DeVos, A., DeClippeleer, I., & Dewilde, T. (2009). Proactive career behaviours and career success during the early career. *Journal of Occupational and Organizational Psychology*, *82*, 761–777. 98

Deverell, J. (1994). "The most valuable quality in a manager", *Fortune*, 136(12), pp. 279–280. 241

Di Milia, L. (2007). Benefiting from multiple-choice exams: The positive impact of answer switching. *Educational Psychology*, *27*(5), 607–615. doi:10.1080/01443410701309142 173

Dickinson, D. J., & O'Connell, D. Q. (1990). Effect of quality and quantity of study on student grades. *Journal of Educational Research*, *83*(4), 227–231. 139, 145

Dobewell, H., & Rudnev, M. (2014). Common and unique features of Schwart'z and Inglehart's value theories at the country and individual levels. *Cross-cultural Research*, *48*(1), 45–77. doi:10.1177/1069397113493584 32–33

Doran, G. T. (1981). There's A S.M.A.R.T. Way to Write Management's Goals and Objectives. *Management Review*, 70(11), 35. 234

Doyle, A. (2016). Top 10 communication skills for workplace success. *The Balance*. https://www.thebalance.com/communication-skills-list-2063779 120 118

Duckworth, A. & Peterson, C. (2007). Grit: Perseverance and Passion for Long-Term Goals. *Journal of Personality and Social Psychology*, *92*(6), 1087–1101. 233

Duckworth, A. (2013). Grit: The Power of Passion and Perseverance. TED *Talks Education*, retrieved from https://www.ted.com/talks/angela_lee_duck worth_grit_the_power_of_passion_and_perseverance 233

Duckworth, A. (2016). *Grit: The power of passion and perseverance*. Scribner. 74, 198

Duncan, G. J., and Dunifon, R. (1998). "Soft skills and long-run labor market success", *Research in Labor Economics*, 17, pp. 123–150, JAI Press, London. 241

Duckworth, A. L., Peterson, C., Matthews, M. D., & Kelly, D. R. (2007). Grit: Perseverance and passion for long-term goals. *Journal of Personality and Social Psychology*, *92*(6), 1087–1101. 194

Dumont M, Leclerc D, MasséL, McKinnon S. Étude de validation du programme Funambule: pour une gestion équilibrée du stress des adolescents. Éducation Francoph. 2015; 43(2):154. 269

Dumont M. Funambule Pour une gestion équilibrée du stress [Internet]. Québec: Septembre éditeur; 2012. http://www.septembre.com/livres/funambule-1259.html

Duffy, R. D., & Klingaman, E. A. (2009). Ethnic identity and career development among first-year college students. *Journal of Career Assessment*, *17*, 286–297. 215

Dundes, L., & Marx, J. (2006). Balancing work and academics in college: Why do students working 10–19 hours per week excel? *Journal of College Student Retention: Research, Theory, and Practice*, *8*(1), 107–120. doi:10.2190/7UCU-8F9M-94QG-5WWQ 113

Dunlosky, J., Rawson, K. A., Marsh, E. J., Nathan, M. J., & Willingham, D. T. (2013). Improving students' learning with effective learning techniques: Promising directions from cognitive and educational psychology. *Psychological Science in the Public Interest (Sage Publications Inc.)*, *14*(1), 4–58. doi:10.1177/1529100612453266 141, 147–148

Dunn, D. Halonen, J. S., & Smith, R. A. (Eds.) (2008), *Teaching Critical Thinking in Psychology: A Handbook of Best Practices*, 11–22. Wiley-Blackwell. 57

Dweck, C. (2016). *Mindset: The New Psychology of Success, Updated Edition*. Ballantine Books, New York. 233

Dweck, C., Walton, G., & Cohen, G. (2014). *Academic Tenacity: Mindsets and Skills that Promote Long-Term Learning*. Bill & Melinda Gates Foundation. 197

Dyrbye LN, Harper W, Durning SJ, Moutier C, Thomas MR, Massie FS Jr, et al. Patterns of distress in US medical students. Med Teach. 2011; 33(10):834–9. https://doi.org/10.3109/0142159X.2010 .531158 PMID: 21942482 266

Earnest, D. R., Rosenbusch, K., Wallace-Williams, D., & Keim, A. C. (2016). Study abroad in psychology: Increasing cultural competencies through experiential learning. *Teaching of Psychology*, 43(1), 75–79. doi:10.1177/0098628315620889 188

Ebert DD, Zarski A-C, Christensen H, Stikkelbroek Y, Cuijpers P, Berking M, et al. Internet and Computer-Based Cognitive Behavioral Therapy for Anxiety and Depression in Youth: A Meta-Analysis of Randomized Controlled Outcome Trials. PLOS ONE. 2015; 10(3):e0119895. https://doi.org/10.1371/ journal. pone.0119895 PMID: 25786025 266

Edlund, J. E. (2020). Exam wrappers in psychology. *Teaching of Psychology*, 47(2), 156–161. 176, 191

Edmondson, M. (2016). Major in happiness: Debunking the college major myth. *NACE Journal*. 1–8. 81–82

Edmunds, S., & Brown, G. (2010). Effective small group learning: AMEE Guide No. 48. *Medical Teacher*, 32(9), 715–726. doi:10.310 9/0142159X.2010.505454 123

Einstein, G. O., Mullet, H. G., & Harrison, T. L. (2012). The testing effect: Illustrating a fundamental concept and changing study strategies. *Teaching of Psychology*, 38(3), 142–146. doi:10.1177/0098628312450432 145

El-Ghoroury, N. H., Galper, D. I., Sawaqdeh, A., & Bufka, L. F. (2012). Stress, coping, and barriers to wellness among psychology graduate students. *Training and Education in Professional Psychology*, 6(2), 122–134. doi:10.1037/a0028768 113

"Employers value communication and interpersonal abilities" (2004), *Keying In*, 14(3), pp.1–6. 242

End, C. M., Worthman, S., Mathews, M. B., & Wetterau, K. (2010). Costly cell phones: The impact of cell phone rings on academic performance. *Teaching of Psychology*, 37(1), 55–57. doi:10.1080/00986280903425912 111

Ericsson, K. A., Prietula, M. J., & Cokely, E. T. (2007). The making of an expert. *Harvard Business Review*, 85(7–8), 114. 102

Escorcia, D., Passerault, J.-M., Ros, C., & Pylouster, J. (2017). Profiling writers: Analysis of writing dynamics among college students. *Metacognition and Learning*, 12(2), 233–273. 161, 162, 164

Evenson, R. (1999). "Soft skills, hard sell. Techniques: making education and career connections", 74(3), pp. 29–31. 241

Eyal, N., & Sjostrand, M. (2020). On knowingly setting unrealistic goals in public health. *American Journal of Public Health*, 110(4), 480–484. doi:10.2105/AJPH.2019.305428 71, 72

Fedesco, H. N., Cavin, D., & Henares, R. (2020). Field-based learning in higher education: Exploring the benefits and possibilities. *Journal of the Scholarship of Teaching and Learning*, 20(1), 65–84. 185

Feldman, D. B., & Dreher, D. E. (2011). Can hope be changed in 90 minutes? Testing the efficacy of a single- session goal-pursuit intervention for college students. *Journal of Happiness Studies*, 13, 745–759. doi:0.1007/ s10902-011-9292-4 196

Ferguson, S. (2009). Information literacy and its relationship to knowledge management. *Journal of Information Literacy*, 3, 6–24. 221

Fernandes, M. A., Wammes, J. D., & Meade, M. E. (2018). The surprisingly powerful influence of drawing on memory. *Current Directions in Psychological Science*, 27(5), 302–308. doi:10.1177/0963721418755385 148

FICO. (2011). *Understanding your FICO score*. http://www.myfico.com /Downloads/Files/myFICO_UYFS_Booklet.pdf 15, 16

Furr SR, Westefeld JS, McConnell GN, Jenkins JM. Suicide and depression among college students: A decade later. Prof Psychol Res Pract. 2001; 32(1):97.266

Field, A. (2005). *Discovering statistics using SPSS for windows* (2nd ed.). Thousand Oaks, CA: Sage. 216

Fogg, B. J. (2020, January 6). How you can use the power of celebration to make new habits stick. *Ideas.TED.com* https://ideas.ted.com /how-you-can-use-the-power-of-celebration-to-make-new-habits -stick/ 207

Foos, P. W., & Goolkasian, P. (2008). Presentation format effects in a levels-of-processing task. *Experimental Psychology*, 55(4), 215–227. doi:10.1027/1618-3169.55.4.215 148

Forgeard, M. C., & Seligman, M. P. (2012). Seeing the glass half full: A review of the causes and consequences of optimism. *Pratiques Psychologiques*, 18(2), 107–120. doi:10.1016/j.prps.2012.02.002 196

Foronda, C., Porter, A., & Phitwong, A. (2021). Psychometric testing of an instrument to measure cultural humility. *Journal of Transcultural Nursing*, 32(4), 399–404. doi:10.1177/1043659620950420 118

Fouad, N. A., & Byars-Winston, A. M. (2005). Cultural context of career choice: Meta analysis of race/ethnicity differences. *The Career Development Quarterly*, 53, 223–233. 214

Fouad, N. A., & Bingham, R. (1995). Career counseling with racial/ ethnic minorities. In W. B. Walsh & S. H. Osipow (Eds.), Handbook of vocational psychology (2nd ed., pp. 331–366). Hillsdale, NJ: Erlbaum. 218

Fox, A. B., Rosen, J., & Crawford, M. (2009). Distractions, distractions: Does instant messaging affect college students' performance on a concurrent reading comprehension task? *Cyberpsychology and Behavior*, 12(1), 51–53. doi:10.1089/cpb.2008.0107 116

Franklin, J. D., Smith, W. A., & Hung, M. (2014). Racial battle fatigue for Latina/o Students: A quantitative perspective. *Journal of Hispanic Higher Education*, 13(4), 303–322. doi:10.1177/1538192714540530 200

Frazier, P. A., Tix, A. P., & Barron, K. E. (2004). Testing moderator and mediator effects in counseling psychology. *Journal of Counseling Psychology*, 51, 115–134. 216

Fridrici M, Lohaus A. Stress-prevention in secondary schools: online-versus face-to-face-training. Health Educ. 2009; 109(4):299–313. 266

Fridrici M, Lohaus A, Glass C. Effects of incentives in web -based prevention for adolescents: Results of an exploratory field study. Psychol Health. 2009; 24(6):663–75. https://doi. org/10.1080/08870440802521102 PMID: 20205019 277

Gajecki M, Berman AH, Sinadinovic K, Andersson C, Ljótsson B, Hedman E, etal. Effects of Baseline Problematic Alcohol and Drug Use on Internet-Based Cognitive Behavioral Therapy Outcomes for Depression, Panic Disorder and Social Anxiety Disorder. PLOS ONE. 2014; 9(8):e104615. https://doi. org/10.1371/journal. pone.0104615 PMID: 25122509 266

Galbraith, D., & Mondal, S. (2020). The potential power of internships and the impact on career preparation. *Research in Higher Education Journal*, 38, 1–9. 185–186

Galbraith, J., & Winterbottom, M. (2011). Peer-tutoring: What's in it for the tutor? *Educational Studies*, 37(3), 321–332. 148

Gardner, H. (1983). *Frames of mind: The theory of multiple intelligences*. Basic Books. 85

Gardner, M. P. (1985). Mood states and consumer behavior: A critical review. *Journal of Consumer Research*, 12(3), 281–300. doi:10.1086/208516 14

Garrison, D. R., Anderson, T., & Archer, W. (2000). Critical inquiry in a text-based environment: Computer conferencing in higher education. *The Internet and Higher Education*, 2(2-3), 87–105. 149

Garvey, J. C., Ballysingh, T. A., Dow, L. B., Howard, B. L., Ingram, A. N., & Carlson, M. (2020). Where I sleep: The relationship with residential environments and first-generation belongingness. *College Student Affairs Journal*, 38(1), 16–33. 25

Gati, I. (1986). Making career decisions- a sequential elimination approach. *Journal of Counseling Psychology*, 33(4), 408–417. 88

Gati, I., Krausz, M., & Osipow, S. H. (1996). A taxonomy of difficulties in career decision making. *Journal of Counseling Psychology*, 43(4), 510–526. 82

Gati, I., Tikotzki, Y. (1989). Strategies for collection and processing of occupational information in making career decisions. *Journal of Counseling Psychology*, 3(3), 430–439. 88

Ganzel, R. (2001). "Hard training for soft skills", *Training*, 38(6), pp. 56–60. 241

Gault, J., Leach, E., & Duey, M. (2010). Effects of business internships on job marketability: The employers' perspective. *Education and Training*, 52 (1), 76–88. doi:10.1.108/00400911011017690 186

George DR, Dellasega C, Whitehead MM, Bordon A. Facebook-based stress management resources for first-year medical students: Amulti-method evaluation. Comput Hum Behav. 2013; 29(3): 559–62. 266

George, D., Dixon, S., Stansal, E., Gelb, S. L., & Pheri, T. (2008). Time diary and questionnaire assessment of factors associated with academic and personal success among university undergraduates. *Journal of American College Health*, 56(6), 706–715. 112

Gier, V., Kreiner, D. S., & Natz-Gonzalez, A. (2009). Harmful effects of preexisting inappropriate highlighting on reading comprehension and metacognitive accuracy. *Journal of General Psychology*, 136(3), 287–300. doi:10.3200/ GENP.136.3.287-302 141

Glenn, J. L. (2003). "Business success often depends on mastering the 'sixth R' relationship literacy", *Business Education Forum*, 58(1), pp. 9–13. 242

Glenn, J. L. (2008). "The 'New' customer service model: customer advocate, company ambassador", Business Education Forum, 62(4), pp. 7–13. 241

Goesling, B. (2007). The rising significance of education for health? *Social Forces*, 85(4), 1621–1644. 5

Goldberg DP, Hillier V. A scaled version of the General Health Questionnaire. Psychol Med. 1979; 9 (01):139–45. 270

Goldman, D., Ayalon, O., Baum, D., & Haham, S. (2015). Major matters: Relationship between academic major and university students' environmental literacy and citizenship as reflected in their voting decisions and environmental activism. *International Journal of Environmental and Science Education*, 10(5), 671–693. 34

Goodman, D. J. (2010). Helping students explore their privileged identities. *Diversity and Democracy*, 13(2). https://www.aacu.org /publications-research/periodicals/ helping-students-explore-their-privileged-identities 21

Goodman, D. J. (2015). Oppression and privilege: Two sides of the same coin. *Journal of Intercultural Communication*, 18, 1–14. 26

Goodman, S., Keresztesi, M., Mamdani, F., Mokgatle, D., Musariri, M., Pires, J., & Schlechter, A. (2011). An investigation of the relationship between students' motivation and academic performance as mediated by effort. *South African Journal of Psychology*, 41(3), 373–385, 93. 74, 201

Goswami, U. (2008). Principles of learning, implications for teaching: A cognitive neuroscience perspective. *Journal of Philosophy of Education*, 42(3–4), 381–399. 60, 62, 145, 148

Goyer, J. P., Walton, G. M., & Yeager, D. S. (2021). The role of psychological factors and institutional channels in predicting the attainment of postsecondary goals. *Developmental Psychology*, 57(1), 73–86. doi:10.1037/dev0001142 194

Grant, H., & Dweck, C. (2003). Clarifying achievement goals and their impact. *Journal of Personality & Social Psychology*, 85(3), 541–553. doi:10.13514.85.3.541 192

Grant F, Guille C, Sen S. Well-Being and the Risk of Depression under Stress. PLOS ONE. 2013; 8(7): e67395. https://doi.org/10.1371 /journal.pone.0067395 PMID: 23840872 266

Greenbank, P. (2011). Improving the process of career decision making: An action research approach. *Education & Training*, 53(4), 252–266. 76, 82

Gregor, M., O'Brien, K. M., & Sauber, E. (2019). Understanding career aspirations among young men. *Journal of Career Assessment*, 27(2), 262–272. doi:10.1177/1069072717748957 38

Greguletz, E., Diehl, M.-R., & Kreutzer, K. (2019). Why women build less effective networks than men: The role of structural exclusion and personal hesitation. *Human Relations*, 72(7), 1234–1261. doi:10.1177/0018726718804303 100

Guelfi J-D. L'évaluation clinique standardisée en psychiatrie. Lavaur, France: Éd. médicales Pierre Fabre; 1993. 411 p. 270

Guerrero-Dib, J. G., Portales, L., & Heredia-Escorza, Y. (2020). Impact of academic integrity on workplace ethical behaviour. *International Journal for Educational Integrity*, 16(1), 1–18. doi:10.1007/s40979-020-0051-3 155

Gurung, R. A. R. (2005). How do students really study (and does it matter?). *Teaching of Psychology*, 32(4), 239–241. 144

Gurung, R. A. R., Mai, T., Nelson, M., & Pruitt, S. (2020). Predicting learning: Comparing study techniques, perseverance, and metacognitive Skill. *Teaching of Psychology*, 1-7. doi:10.1177/0098628320972332 148

Hadis, B. F. (2005). Why are they better students when they come back? Determinants of academic focusing gains in the study abroad experience. *Frontiers: The Interdisciplinary Journal of Study Abroad*, 11, 57–70. 188

Haley, Debra A. (1993). "Optimizing the Graduate Sales Management Seminar: Enhancing Presentation Skills and Expanding Knowledge," *Marketing Education Review*, 3(2), 40–43. 260

Halford, S., Lotherington, A. T., Obstfelder, A., & Dyb, K. (2010). Getting the whole picture? *Information, Communication & Society*, 13, 442–465. 222

Hall, N., Hladkyj, S., Perry, R., & Ruthig, J. (2004). The role of attributional retraining and elaborative learning in college students' academic development. *Journal of Social Psychology*, 144(6), 591–612. 145

Hansen, C. J., Stevens, L. C., & Coast, J. R. (2001). Exercise duration and mood state: How much is enough to feel better? *Health Psychology*, 20, 267–275. doi:10.1037/0278-6133.20.4.267 196

Hansen, R. S. (2006). Benefits and problems with student teams: Suggestions for improving team projects. *Journal of Education for Business*, 82(1), 11–19. 122, 123

Harkin, B., Webb, T. L., Chang, B. P. I., Prestwich, A., Conner, M., Kellar, I., Benn, Y., & Sheeran, P. (2016). Does monitoring goal progress promote goal attainment? A meta-analysis of the experimental evidence. *Psychological Bulletin*, 142(2), 198–229. doi:10.1037/bul0000025 189

Hartle, R., Baviskar, S., & Smith, R. (2012). A field guide to constructivism in the college science classroom: Four essential criteria and a guide to their usage. *Bioscene: Journal of College Biology Teaching*, 38(2), 31–35. 57

Hartshorne, J. K., & Makovski, T. (2019). The effect of working memory maintenance on long-term memory. *Memory and Cognition, 47*, 749–763. doi:10.3758/s13421-019-00908-6 143

Hartwell, C. J., & Campion, M. A. (2020). Getting social in selection: How social networking website content is perceived and used in hiring. *International Journal of Selection & Assessment, 28*(1), 1–16. doi:10.1111/ijsa.12273 104, 105

Harrell, S. P. (2000). A multidimensional conceptualization of racism-related stress: Implications for the well-being of people of color. *American Journal of Orthopsychiatry, 70*, 42–57. 2015 215

Harvey, L., and Knight, P. T. (1996). *Transforming Higher Education*, Open University Press, SRHE. 241

Hayati, A., & Shariatifar, S. (2009). Mapping strategies. *Journal of College Reading and Learning, 39*(2), 53–67. 141

Hayes-Bohanan, P., & Spievak, E. (2008). You can lead students to sources, but can you make them think? *College and Undergraduate Libraries, 15*(1–2), 173–210. doi:10.1080/10691310802177200 49

Head, A., & Eisenberg, M. (2010). Truth be told: How college students evaluate and use information in the digital age. Project Information Literacy Progress Report. Available http://projectinfolit.org/pdfs /PIL_Fall2010_ Survey_FullReport1.pdf

Head, A., & Eisenberg, M. (2010). Truth be told: How college students evaluate and use information in the digital age. Project Information Literacy Progress Report. Available http://projectinfolit.org/pdfs /PIL_Fall2010_ Survey_FullReport1.pdf

Head, A. J., & Eisenberg, M. B. (2009). What today's college students say about conducting research in the digital age. *Project Information Literacy Report*. Retrieved from http://libaq1.pbworks.com/f/PIL _ProgressReport_2_2009.pdf 159

Head, A. J., Wihbey, J., Metaxas, P. T., MacMillan, M., & Cohen, D. (2018, October 16). How students engage with news: Five takeaways for educators, journalists, and librarians. *The News Study Report*. https://projectinfolit.org/pubs/news-study/pil_news-study _2018-10-16.pdf 46, 47, 55

Hedman E, Andersson G, Lindefors N, Gustavsson P, Lekander M, Rück C, etal. Personality Change following Internet-Based Cognitive Behavior Therapy for Severe Health Anxiety. PLOS ONE. 2014; 9 (12):e113871. https://doi.org/10.1371/journal. pone.0113871 PMID: 25437150 266

Hefner, J., & Eisenberg, D. (2009). Social support and mental health among college students. *American Journal of Orthopsychiatry, 79*(4), 491–499. doi:10.1037/a0016918 198

Heikkila, A., & Lonka, K. (2006). Studying in higher education: Students' approaches to learning, self-regulation, and cognitive strategies. *Studies in Higher Education, 31*(1), 99–117. doi:10.1080/03075070500392433 70

Helms, J. E., & Piper, P. (1994). Implications of racial identity theory for vocational psychology. *Journal of Vocational Behavior, 44*, 124–138. 214

Henderson, F., Nunez-Rodriguez, N., & Casari, W. (2011). Enhancing research skills and information literacy in community college science students. *The American Biology Teacher, 73*(5), 270-275. 49

Hendry, G. D., Hyde, S. J., & Davy, P. (2005). Independent student study groups. *Medical Education, 39*(7), 672–679. doi:10.1111/ j.1365-2929.2005.02199.x 149

Henry, J., Martinko, M., & Pierce, M. (1993). Attributional style as a predictor of success in a first computer course. *Computers in Human Behavior, 9*(4), 341–352. doi:10.1016/0747-5632 (93)90027-P 196

Hernandez, P. R., Estrada, M., Woodcock, A., & Schultz, P. W. (2017). Protege perceptions of high mentorship quality depend on shared values more than on demographic match. *Journal of Experimental Education, 85*(3), 450–468. doi:10.10 80/00220973.2016.1246405 102

Hernandez, R. J., & Villodas, M. T. (2020). Overcoming racial battle fatigue: The associations between racial microaggressions, coping, and mental health among Chicana/o and Latina/o college students. *Cultural Diversity and Ethnic Minority Psychology, 26*(3), 399–411. doi:10.1037/cdp0000306 194, 200

Hepworth, M., & Smith, M. (2008). Workplace information literacy for administrative staff in higher education. *Australian Library Journal, 57*, 212–236. 222

Hidi, S. (2016). Revisiting the role of rewards in motivation and learning: Implications of neuroscientific research. *Educational Psychology Review, 28*(1), 61–93. 202

Hill, P. L., Jackson, J. J., Roberts, B. W., Lapsley, D. K., & Brandenberger, J. W. (2011). Change you can believe in: Changes in goal setting during emerging and young adulthood predict later adult well-being. *Social Psychological and Personality Science, 2*(2), 123–131. doi:10.1177/1948550610384510 69

Hoch DB, Watson AJ, Linton DA, Bello HE, Senelly M, Milik MT, et al. The Feasibility and Impact of Delivering a Mind-Body Intervention in a Virtual World. PLOS ONE. 2012; 7(3):e33843. https://doi.org/10.1371/journal.pone.0033843 PMID: 22470483 266

Hodges, L. C., Beall, L. C., Anderson, E. C., Carpenter, T. S., Cui, L., Feeser, E., Gierasch, T., Nanes, K. M., Perks, H. M., & Wagner, C. (2020). Effect of exam wrappers on student achievement in multiple, large STEM courses. *Journal of College Science Teaching, 50*(1), 69–79. 175, 191

Hoek W, Schuurmans J, Koot HM, Cuijpers P. Effects of Internet-Based Guided Self-Help Problem-Solving Therapy for Adolescents with Depression and Anxiety: A Randomized Controlled Trial. PLOS ONE. 2012; 7(8):e43485. https://doi 266

Holder, A. M. B., Jackson, M. A., & Ponterotto, J. G. (2015). Racial microaggression experiences and coping strategies of Black women in corporate leadership. *Qualitative Psychology, 2*(2), 164–180. http://dx.doi.org/10.1037/qup0000024 200

Holland, J. L. (1997). *Making vocational choices: Theory of vocational personalities and work environments*. Odessa, FL: Psychological Assessment Resources. 80, 81, 86, 87

Holmes, J. M., Bowman, N. A., Murphy, M. C., & Carter, E. (2019). Envisioning college success: The role of student identity centrality. *Social Psychology of Education: An International Journal, 22*(5), 1015–1034. 27, 28

Hopkins, M. M., & Yonker, R. D. (2015). Managing conflict with emotional intelligence: Abilities that make a difference. *Journal of Management Development, 34*(2), 226–244. doi:10.1108/JMD-04-2013-0051 121

Hopkins, R., Lyle, K., Hieb, J., & Ralston, P. (2016). Spaced retrieval practice increases college students' short- and long-term retention of mathematics knowledge. *Educational Psychology Review, 28*(4), 853–873. doi:10.1007/ s10648-015-9349-8 148

Hora, M. T., Benbow, R. J., & Smolarek, B. B. (2018). Re-thinking soft skills and student employability: A new paradigm for undergraduate education. *Change: The Magazine of Higher Learning, 50*(6), 30–37. 109, 119

Howard, R. M., Serviss, T., & Rodrigue, T. K. (2010). Writing from sources, writing from sentences. *Writing and Pedagogy, 2*(2), 177–192. doi:10.1558/wap.v2i2.177 158

Hughes JA, Phillips G, Reed P. Brief Exposure to a Self-Paced Computer-Based Reading Programme and How It Impacts Reading Ability and Behaviour Problems. PLOS ONE. 2013; 8(11):e77867. https:// doi.org/10.1371/journal.pone.0077867 PMID: 24223125 266

Hughes, H. , Middleton, M. , Edwards, S. , Bruce, C. and McAllister, L. (2005). Information literacy research in Australia 2000— 2005, Bulletin des Bibliothèques de France 50, 1–23. Available http://eprints.qut.edu.au/archive/00002832/0 1/BdesB_submission.pdf 221

Hughes, C., Toohey, S., & Velan, G. (2008). eMed Teamwork: A self-moderating system to gather peer feedback for developing and assessing teamwork skills. *Medical Teacher*, 30(1), 5–9. doi:10.1080/01421590701758632 125

Humphris G, Blinkhorn A, Freeman R, Gorter R, Hoad-Reddick G, Murtomaa H, et al. Psychological stress in undergraduate dental 266

Imamura K, Kawakami N, Furukawa TA, Matsuyama Y, Shimazu A, Umanodan R, et al. Effects of an Internet-Based Cognitive Behavioral Therapy (iCBT) Program in Manga Format on Improving Subthreshold Depressive Symptoms among Healthy Workers: A Randomized Controlled Trial. PLOS ONE. 2014; 9(5):e97167. https://doi.org/10.1371/journal.pone.0097167 PMID: 24844530 266

Iglesias, S. L., Azzara, S., Squillace, M., Jeifetz, M., Lores Arnais, M. R., Desimone, M. F., & Diaz, L. E. (2005). A study on the effectiveness of a stress management programme for college students. *Pharmacy Education*, 5(1), 27–31. doi:10.1080/15602210400028614 180, 194

Ingalls, V. (2018). Incentivizing with bonus in a college statistics course. *REDIMAT - Journal of Research in Mathematics Education*, 7(1), 93–103. 202

Irvine, J. (2018). A framework for comparing theories related to motivation in education. *Research in Higher Education Journal*, 35, 1–30. 202

Ishitani, T. T., & Association for Institutional, R. (2009). The effects of academic programs and institutional characteristics on post-graduate social benefit behavior. *Association for Institutional Research*. 5

Issa, N., Schuller, M., Santacaterina, S., Shapiro, M., Wang, E., Mayer, R., & DaRosa, D. (2011). Applying multimedia design principles enhances learning in medical education. *Medical Education*, 45(8), 818–826. doi:10.1111/j.1365-2923.2011.03988.x 161

Jackson, C. C., & Neville, H. A. (1998). Influence of racial identity attitudes on African American college students' vocational identity and hope. *Journal of Vocational Behavior*, 53, 97–113. 215

Jacques, A. (2017). You're hired: 8 secrets to help you in the job application process. *Public Relations Tactics*, 24(5), 21. 107

Jagger, L., Neukrug, E., & McAuliffe, G. (1992). Congruence between personality traits and chosen occupation as a predictor of job satisfaction for people with disabilities. *Rehabilitation Counseling Bulletin*, 36(1), 53–60. 81

Jaret, C., & Reitzes, D. (2009). Currents in a stream: College student identities and ethnic identities and their relationship with selfesteem, efficacy, and grade point average in an urban university. *Social Science Quarterly*, 90, 345–367. 215

Jason, Z. (2018). Student activism 2.0: A look back at the history of student activism and whether today's protesters are making a difference. *Harvard Ed. Magazine*. https://www.gse.harvard.edu/news/ed/18/08/student-activism-20 34, 35

James, R. F., and James, M. L. (2004). "Teaching career and technical skills in a 'Mini' business world", *Business Education Forum*, 59(2), pp. 39–41. 241

Jobvite. (2014), Available at: https://www.jobvite.com/wp-content/uploads/2014/10/Jobvite_SocialRecruiting_Survey2014.pdf 104

Johns, M., Schmader, T., & Martens, A. (2005). Knowing is half the battle: Teaching stereotype threat as a means of improving women's math performance. *Psychological Science*, 16(3), 175–179. doi:10.1111/j.0956-7976.2005.00799.x 104, 171

Johnson, J. (2006). "More employers are focusing on soft skills when seeking out new employees", *Colorado Springs Business Journal (CO)*, September 29. Retrieved on November 25, 2008, from Regional Business News database. 239

Johnson, W., Mesch, D., & Johnson, R. (1988). Impact of positive interdependence and academic group contingencies on achievement. *The Journal of Social Psychology*, 128(3), 345–352. 248

Johnson, E. C., Robbins, B. A., & Loui, M. C. (2015). What do students experience as peer leaders of learning teams? *Advances in Engineering Education*, 4(4), 1–22. 148

Johnson, M., & Ashton, B. (2015). Money matters on campus: Driving student success through financial literacy. *University Business*, 18(2), 22–23. 8

Jones, J. M. (1997). *Prejudice and racism* (2nd ed.). New York, NY: McGraw-Hill. 215

Jones, P. R. (2011). Reducing the impact of stereotype threat on women's math performance: Are two strategies better than one? *Electronic Journal of Research in Educational Psychology*, 9(2), 587–616. 171

Judge, T. A., Hurst, C., & Simon, L. S. (2009). Does it pay to be smart, attractive, or confident (or all three)? Relationships among general mental ability, physical attractiveness, core self-evaluations, and income. *Journal of Applied Psychology*, 94(3), 742–755. doi:10.1037/a0015497 84

Julian, T. A. and Kominski, R. A. (2011). Education and synthetic work–life earnings estimates. *American Community Survey Reports*, ACS-14. U.S. Census Bureau, Washington, DC. 24 12

Jung Y-H, Ha TM, Oh CY, Lee US, Jang JH, Kim J, et al. The Effects of an Online Mind-Body Training Program on Stress, Coping Strategies, Emotional Intelligence, Resilience and Psychological State. PLOS ONE. 2016; 11(8):e0159841. https://doi.org/10.1371/journal.pone.0159841 PMID: 27479499 266

Kahle, L. R. (1988). Using the List of Values (LOV) to understand consumers. *Journal of Services Marketing*, 2(4), 49–56. 33

Kam, M., Wang, J., Iles, A., Tse, E., Chiu, J., Glaser, D., ... Hall, S. (2005). *Livenotes: A system for cooperative and augmented note-taking in lectures.* Retrieved from http://www.cs. berkeley .edu/~jfc/papers/05/CHILivenotes/CHI200 5.pdf 249

Kamimura, T. (2019). Producing summaries of a narrative story under different conditions. *Journal of Pan-Pacific Association of Applied Linguistics*, 23(1), 85–102. 158

Kantamneni, N., McCain, M. R. C., Shada, N., Hellwege, M. A., & Tate, J. (2018). Contextual factors in the career development of prospective first-generation college students: An application of social cognitive career theory. *Journal of Career Assessment*, 26(1), 183–196. doi:10.1177/1069072716680048 26

Karkouti, I. M. (2014). Examining psychosocial identity development theories: A guideline for professional practice. *Education*, 135(2), 257–263. 29

Karpicke, J. D. (2016, June). A powerful way to improve learning and memory: Practicing retrieval enhances long-term, meaningful learning. *Psychological Science Agenda*. https://www.apa.org/science/about/psa/2016/06/learning-memory 144

Karpicke, J. D., & Blunt, J. R. (2011). Retrieval practice produces more learning than elaborative studying with concept maps. *Science*, 331, 772–772. doi:0.1126/science.1199327 144

Karpicke, J. D., & Roediger, H. L. (2006). Repeated retrieval during learning is the key to long-term retention. *Journal of Memory and Language*, 57, 151–162. 144, 145, 171

Kennedy, R., & Kennedy, D. (2004). Using the Myers-Briggs Type Indicator¨ in career counseling. *Journal of Employment Counseling, 41*(1), 38–44. 87

Ketonen, E. E., Haarala-Muhonen, A., Hirsto, L., Hanninen, J. J., Wahala, K., & Lonka, K. (2016). Am I in the right place? Academic engagement and study success during the first years at university. *Learning and Individual Differences, 51*, 141–148. 190

Kiewra, K. A. (1987). Note-taking and review: The research and its implications. *Journal of Instructional Science*, 16(3), 233–249. 248

Kiewra, K., DuBois, N., Christian, D., & McShane, A. (1988). Providing study notes: Comparison of three types of notes for review. *Journal of Educational Psychology, 80*(4), 595–597. doi:10.1037/0022-0663.80.4.595 136, 137

Kim, C., Tamborini, C. R., & Sakamoto, A. (2015). Field of study in college and lifetime earnings in the United States. *Sociology of Education, 88*(4), 320–339. doi:10.1177/0038040715602213 6

Kim, K., Sin, S J., & Lee, E. Y. (2014). Undergraduates' use of social media as information sources. *College & Research Libraries, 75*(4), 442–457. doi:10.5860/crl.75.4.442 47, 55

King, R. B., & McInerney, D. M. (2014). Culture's consequences on student motivation: Capturing cross-cultural universality and variability through personal investment theory. *Educational Psychologist, 49*(3), 175–198. doi: 10.1080/00461520.2014.926813 206

King, R., McInerney, D., & Nasser, R. (2017). Different goals for different folks: a cross-cultural study of achievement goals across nine cultures. *Social Psychology of Education, 20*(3), 619–642. doi:10.1007/s11218-017-9381-2 205, 206

Kirton, J., & Barham, L. (2005). Information literacy in the workplace. *Australian Library Journal, 54*, 365–376. 221

Kitsantas, A., Winsler, A., & Huie, F. (2008). Self-regulation and ability predictors of academic success during college: A predictive validity study. *Journal of Advanced Academics, 20*(1), 42–68. 70

Kittle, P., & Hicks, T. (2009). Transforming the group paper with collaborative online writing. *Pedagogy: Critical Approaches to Teaching Literature, Language, Composition, and Culture, 9*(3), 525– 538. doi:10.1215/15314200-2009-012 257

Klein, H. J., Lount, R. B., Jr., Park, H. M., & Linford, B. J. (2020). When goals are known: The effects of audience relative status on goal commitment and performance. *Journal of Applied Psychology, 105*(4), 372–389. doi:10.1037/apl0000441 74

Klonek, F. E., Kanse, L., Wee, S., Runneboom, C., & Parker, S. K. (2021). Did the COVID-19 lock-down make ss better at working in virtual teams? *Small Group Research, 1*, 1–22. doi:10.1177/10464964211008991 123

Klusek, L., & Bornstein, J. (2006). Information literacy skills for business careers: Matching skills to the workplace. *Journal of Business & Finance Librarianship, 11*, 3–21. 222

Knight, L. J., & McKelvie, S. J. (1986). Effects of attendance, note-taking, and review on memory for a lecture: Encoding vs. external storage functions of notes. *Canadian Journal of Behavioral Science, 18*(1), p. 52–61. 134

Kobayashi, K. (2006). Combined effects of note-taking/reviewing on learning and the enhancement through interventions: A meta-analytic review. *Educational Psychology, 26*(3), 459–477. doi:10.1080/01443410500342070 249

Kofoed, M. S., & McGovney, E. (2019). The effect of same-gender or same-race role models on occupation choice: Evidence from randomly assigned mentors at west point. *Journal of Human Resources, 54*(2), 430–467. doi:10.3368/jhr.54.2.0416.7838r1 78, 102

Kohnen, A. M., & Saul, E. W. (2018). Information literacy in the Internet age: Making space for students' intentional and incidental knowledge. *Journal of Adolescent & Adult Literacy, 61*(6), 671–679. doi:10.1002/jaal.734 46

Komarraju, M., & Nadler, D. (2013). Self-efficacy and academic achievement: Why do implicit beliefs, goals, and effort regulation matter? *Learning and Individual Differences, 2567–2572*. 73

Kornell, N., & Bjork, R. A. (2008). Optimising self-regulated study: The benefits—and costs—of dropping flashcards. *Memory, 16*(2), 125–136. doi:10.1080/09658210701763899 146–147

Koochaki GM, Charkazi A, Hasanzadeh A, Saedani M, Qorbani M, Marjani A. Prevalence of stress among Iranian medical students: a questionnaire survey. East Mediterr Health J. 2011; 17(7):593–8. PMID: 21972483 266

Kot, F. C. (2014). The impact of centralized advising on first-year academic performance and second-year enrollment behavior. *Research in Higher Education, 55*(6), 527–563. doi:10.1007/s11162-013-9325-4 182

Krings, F., Gioaba, I., Kaufmann, M., Sczesny, S., & Zebrowitz, L. (2021). Older and younger job seekers' impression management on LinkedIn: Similar strategies, different outcomes. *Journal of Personnel Psychology, 20*(2), 61–74. doi:10.1027/1866-5888/a000269 105, 107

Kristjansson, A., Sigfusdottir, I., & Allegrante, J. (2010). Health behavior and academic achievement among adolescents: The relative contribution of dietary habits, physical activity, body mass index, and self-esteem. *Health Education & Behavior, 37*(1), 51–64. doi:10.1177/1090198107313481 195, 196

Krumboltz, J. D. (2009). The happenstance learning theory. *Journal of Career Assessment, 17*(2), 135–154. 80, 81

Krumboltz, J., & Levin, A. (2004). *Luck is no accident: Making the most of happenstance in your life and career*. Impact. 80

Krumrei-Mancuso, E. J., Newton, F. B., Kim, E., & Wilcox, D. (2013). Psychosocial factors predicting first-year college student success. *Journal of College Student Development, 54*(3), 247–266. 114

Kulm, T. L., & Cramer, S. (2006). The relationship of student employment to student role, family relationships, social interactions and persistence. *College Student Journal, 40*(4), 927–938. 113

LaChausse RG. My Student Body: Effects of an Internet-Based Prevention Program to Decrease Obe-sity Among College Students. J Am Coll Health. 2012; 60(4):324–30. https://doi .org/10.1080 /07448481.2011.623333 PMID: 22559092 266

Lafay N, Manzanera C, Papet N, Marcelli D, Senon J. Les états dépressifs de la post-adolescence. Résultats d'une enquête menée chez 1521 étudiants de l'universitéde Poitiers. Ann Med Psychol (Paris). 2003; 161(2):147–51. 266

Lai ESY, Kwok C-L, Wong PWC, Fu K-W, Law Y-W, Yip PSF. The Effectiveness and Sustainability of a Universal School-Based Programme for Preventing Depression in Chinese Adolescents: A Follow-Up Study Using Quasi-Experimental Design. PLOS ONE. 2016; 11(2):e0149854. https://doi.org/10.1371/ journal .pone.0149854 PMID: 26921275 266

Lammers, W. J., Onwuegbuzie, A., & Slate, J. R. (2001). Academic success as a function of the gender, class, age, study habits, and employment of college students. *Research in the Schools, 8*(2), 71–81. 113

Larkin, J. E., LaPort, K. A., & Pines, H. A. (2007). Job choice and career relevance for today's college students. *Journal of Employment Counseling, 44*, 86–94. 113

Latham, G. P., & Locke, E. A. (2006). Enhancing the benefits and overcoming the pitfalls of goal setting. *Organizational Dynamics, 35*(4), 332–340. 74

Lazarus RS, Folkman S. Coping and adaptation. Handb Behav Med. 1984;282–325. 269

Lay B, Drack T, Bleiker M, Lengler S, Blank C, Rössler W. Preventing Compulsory Admission to Psychiatric Inpatient Care: Perceived Coercion, Empowerment, and Self-Reported Mental Health Functioning after 12 Months of Preventive Monitoring. Front Psychiatry [Internet]. 2015 [cited 2016 Aug 26]; 6(161). Available from: http://www.ncbi.nlm.nih.gov/pmc/articles/PMC4650287/ 266

Lavender JM, De Young KP, Anderson DA. Eating Disorder Examination Questionnaire (EDE-Q): Norms for undergraduate men. Eat Behav. 2010; 11(2):119–21. https://doi.org/10.1016/j.eatbeh.2009.09.005 PMID: 20188296 266

Lawlor, K. B. & Hornyak, M. J. (2012). *SMART Goals: How the Application of SMART Goals can Contribute to Achievement of Student Learning Outcomes. Developments in Business Simulation and Experiential Learning, 39,* 259–267. 234

Lazarus, R. S., & Folkman, S. (1984). *Stress, appraisal, and coping.* New York, NY: Springer. 215

Lee, B., Padilla, J., & McHale, S. (2016). Transmission of work ethic in African-American families and its links with adolescent adjustment. *Journal of Youth & Adolescence, 45*(11), 2278–2291. doi:10.1007/s10964-015-0391-0 32

Lee, E., & Kim, Y. (2019). Effect of university students' sedentary behavior on stress, anxiety, and depression. *Perspectives in Psychiatric Care, 55*(2), 164–169. doi:10.1111/ppc.12296 196

Lehtonen, Miikka (2011). "Communicating Competence Through Pechakucha Presentations," *Journal of Business Communication, 48*(4), 464–481. 261

Lent, R. W., Brown, S. D., & Hackett, G. (1994). Toward a unifying social cognitive theory of career and academic interest, choice, and performance. *Journal of Vocational Behavior, 45,* 79–122. 77, 78

Leppin AL, Bora PR, Tilburt JC, Gionfriddo MR, Zeballos-Palacios C, Dulohery MM, et al. The Efficacy of Resiliency Training Programs: A Systematic Review and Meta-Analysis of Randomized Trials. PLOS ONE. 2014; 9(10):e111420. https://doi.org/10.1371/journal.pone.0111420 PMID: 25347713 266

Levin, M. (2016, May 12). The most important rule of networking no one talks about. Inc. http://www.inc.com/marissa-levin/the-most-important-rule-of-networking-no-one-talks-about.html 100

Limniou, M. (2021). The effect of digital device usage on student academic performance: A case study. *Education Sciences, 11,* 1–15. 116

Linde, J. A., Jeffery, R. W., Finch, E. A., Ng, D. M., & Rothman, A. J. (2004). Are unrealistic weight loss goals associated with outcomes for overweight women? *Obesity Research, 12*(2), 569–576. doi:10.1038/oby.2004.65 71, 72

Lindgren KP, Wiers RW, Teachman BA, Gasser ML, Westgate EC, Cousijn J, et al. Attempted Training of Alcohol Approach and Drinking Identity Associations in US Undergraduate Drinkers: Null Results from Two Studies. PLOS ONE. 2015; 10(8):e0134642. https://doi.org/10.1371/journal.pone.0134642 PMID: 26241316 266

Linderholm, T. (2002). Predictive inference generation as a function of working memory capacity and causal text constraints. *Discourse Process, 34*(3), 259–280. 139

Liu, F. (2020, January 26). How information-seeking behavior has changed in 22 Years. *Nielson Norman Group.* https://www.nngroup.com/articles/information-seeking-behavior-changes/ 46, 47

Lloyd, A. (2007). Recasting information literacy as sociocultural practice: Implications for library and information science researchers. *Information Research, 12,* 1–13. 221

Lloyd, A. (2009). Informing practice: Information experiences of ambulance officers in training and on-road practice. *Journal of Documentation, 65,* 396–419. 221

Locke, E. A., & Latham, G. P. (2002). Building a practically useful theory of goal setting and task motivation: A 35-year odyssey. *American Psychologist, 57*(9), 705–717. doi:10.1037/0003066X.57.9.705 69, 71, 72, 74

Loes, C., Pascarella, E., & Umbach, P. (2012). Effects of diversity experiences on critical thinking skills: Who benefits? *Journal of Higher Education, 83*(1), 1–25. 62

Logan, G. D. (2021). Serial order in perception, memory, and action. *Psychological Review, 128*(1), 1–44. doi:10.1037/rev0000253 167

Lopes, P. N. (2016). Emotional intelligence in organizations: Bridging research and practice. *Emotion Review, 8*(4), 316-321. doi:10.1177/1754073916650496 121

LoSchiavo, F., & Shatz, M. (2002). Students' reasons for writing on multiple-choice examinations. *Teaching of Psychology, 29*(2), 138–140. 172

Luce KH, Crowther JH, Pole M. Eating Disorder Examination Questionnaire (EDE-Q): Norms for undergraduate women. Int J Eat Disord. 2008; 41(3):273–6. https://doi.org/10.1002/eat.20504 PMID: 18213686 266

Lovell, E. (2014). *Promoting Constructive Mindsets for Overcoming Failure in Computer Science Education.* In *ICER '14 Proceedings of the tenth annual conference on International computing education research.* Association for Computing Machinery, New York. 233

Lovell GP, Nash K, Sharman R, Lane BR. Across-sectional investigation of depressive, anxiety, and stress symptoms and health-behavior participation in Australian university students. Nurs Health Sci. 2015; 17(1):134–42. https://doi.org/10.1111/nhs.12147 PMID: 266 24799077

Lucero, J. E., Gallego, S., Hedgepeth, C., & Sanders, D. (2021). Structure and characteristics for successful outcomes: A review of community college internships programs. *Community College Journal of Research and Practice, 45*(2), 103–116, doi:10.1080/10668 926.2019.1647901 186

Luthans, F. (1988). "Successful vs effective real managers", *The Academy of Management Executive,* 11(2), pp. 127–132. 240

Luthans, F., Rosenkrantz, S. A., and Hennessey. H. W. (1985). "What do successful managers really do? An Observation Study of Managerial Activities", *Journal of Applied Behavioral Science,* 21(3), pp. 255–270. 240

Luo, L., Kiewra, K. A., Flanigan, A. E., & Peteranetz, M. S. (2018). Laptop versus longhand note taking: effects on lecture notes and achievement. *Instructional Science, 46*(6), 947–971. doi:10.1007/s11251-018-9458-0 134, 135

Lynch, D. J. (2006). Motivational strategies, learning strategies, and resource management as predictors of course grades. *College Student Journal, 40*(2), 423–428. 203

Ma, J., Pender, M., & Welch, M. (2019). Education pays: The benefits of education for the individual and society. College Board. https://research.collegeboard.org/media/pdf/education-pays-2019-full-report.pdf 5, 6, 7, 13

MacDonald, T., MacDonald, G., Zanna, M., & Fong, G. (2000). Alcohol, sexual arousal, and intentions to use condoms in young men: Applying alcohol myopia theory to risky sexual behavior. *Health Psychology, 19*(3), 290–298. doi:10.1037/0278-6133.19.3.290 201

Majali, S. A. (2020). Positive anxiety and its role in motivation and achievements among university students. *International Journal of Instruction, 13*(4), 975–986. doi:10.29333/iji.2020.13459a 166

Makany, T., Kemp, J., & Dror, I. E. (2009). Optimising the use of note-taking as an external cognitive aid for increasing learning. *British Journal of Educational Technology, 40*(4), 619–635. 249

Malik, A., Heyman-Schrum, C. & Johri, A. (2019). Use of Twitter across educational settings: A review of the literature. *International Journal of Educational Technology in Higher Education, 16* (36), 1–22. https://doi.org/10.1186/s41239-019-0166-x 48

Maniecka-Bryła I, Bryła M, Weinkauf A, Dierks M-L. The international comparative study of the health status of medical university students in Lodz and Hanover. Przegl Lek. 2005; 62(3):63–8. 266

Marco-Gardoqui, M., Eizaguirre, A., & Garcia-Feijoo, M. (2020). The impact of service-learning methodology on business schools' students worldwide: A systematic literature review. *PLOS One,* 15(12), 1–21. doi:10.1371/journal. pone.0244389 188

Marsay, G. (2020). A hope-based future orientation intervention to arrest adversity. *South African Journal of Education, 40*(1), 1–11. 196

Martin, Charles L. (1990). "Enhancing the Effectiveness of Student Oral Presentations," *Marketing Education Review,* 1 (November), 56–60. 261

Maslow, A. H. (1987). *Motivation and personality.* Harper & Row. 204

May, K. E., & Elder, A. D. (2018). Efficient, helpful, or distracting? A literature review of media multitasking in relation to academic performance. *International Journal of Educational Technology in Higher Education, 15*(1), 1–17. doi:10.1186/s41239-018-0096-z 115

Mayer, R. E. (2009). *Multimedia learning* (2nd ed.). Cambridge University Press. 148, 155, 168, 169

McArther, J. (2011). Reconsidering the social and economic purposes of higher education. *Higher Education Research & Development, 30*(6), 737–749. doi:10.1080/07294360.2010.539596. 4

McBride, D. M., & Dosher, B. (2002). A comparison of conscious and automatic memory processes for picture and word stimuli: A process dissociation analysis. *Consciousness and Cognition: An International Journal, 11*(3), 423–460. doi:10.1016/S1053-8100(02)00007-7 148

McCabe, D. L., Butterfield, K. D., & Trevino, L. K. (2012). *Cheating in college: Why students do it and what educators can do about it.* The John Hopkins University Press. 156

McCabe, J. A., & Lummis, S. N. (2018). Why and how do undergraduates study in groups? *Scholarship of Teaching and Learning in Psychology, 4*(1), 27–42. doi:0.1037/stl0000099 149

McCallum, S., & O'Connell, D. (2009). Social capital and leadership development." *Leadership & Organization Development Journal, 30*(2), 152–166. doi:10.1108/01437730910935756. 125

McCarty, J. A., & Shrum, L. J. (2000). The measurement of personal values in survey research: A test of alternative rating procedures. *Public Opinion Quarterly, 64*(3), 271–298. doi:10.1086/317989 33

McClain, L. (1983). Behavior during examinations: A comparison of 'A', 'C', and 'F' students. *Teaching of Psychology, 10*(2), 69. 172

McCorkle, D. E., Alexander, J. F., Reardon, J., & Kling, N. D. (2003). Developing self-marketing skills: Are marketing students prepared for the job search? *Journal of Marketing Education, 25*(3), 196–207. 101

McCorkle, D., & Alexander, J. F. (2019). Using a digital personal learning network assignment to teach social curation and lifelong learning in marketing. *Journal of Advertising Education, 23*(2), 108–120. 48

McCrae, R. R., & Costa, P. T., Jr. (1990). *Personality in adulthood.* Guildford. 86

McDaniel, M., Howard, D., & Einstein, G. (2009). The read-recite -review study strategy: Effective and portable. *Psychological Science, 20*(4), 516–522. doi:10.1111/j.1467-9280.2009.02325.x 139

McGuire, G. M. (2000). Gender, race, ethnicity, and networks: The factors affecting the status of employees' network members. *Work and Occupations, 27*(4), 501–524. 99, 100

McInerney, D. M. (2011). *Sociocultural theories of learning and motivation: Looking back, looking forward.* Information Age Publishing. 205–206

McMahon, C., & Bruce, C. (2002). Information literacy needs of local staff in cross-cultural development projects. *Journal of International Development, 14,* 113–127. 221

Medlin, B. & Green Jr., K. W. (2009). *Enhancing Performance through Goal Setting, Engagement, and Optimism. Industrial Management & Data Systems,* 109(7), 943–956. 234

Melton, J., Miller, R., Jensen, B. R., & Shah, V. (2018). Decisions, decisions: Cybervetting through the eyes of students. *Journal of Education for Business, 93*(5), 252–259. 105

Menzel, K., & Carrell, L. (1994). The relationship between preparation and performance in public speaking. *Communication Education, 43*(1), 17–26. doi:10.1080/03634529409378958 166

Meriam Library at California State University (2010). *Evaluating information: Applying the CRAAP test.* Retrieved from http://www.csuchico.edu/lins/handouts/eval_websites.pdf 55

Milojevich HM, Lukowski AF. Sleep and Mental Health in Undergraduate Students with Generally Healthy Sleep Habits. PLOS ONE. 2016; 11(6):e0156372. https://doi.org/10.1371/journal.pone.0156372 PMID: 27280714 266

Miller, A., Shoptaugh, C., & Wooldridge, J. (2011). Reasons not to cheat, academic-integrity responsibility, and frequency of cheating. *Journal of Experimental Education, 79*(2), 169–184. doi:10.1080/00220970903567830 156

Miller, G. A. (1956). The magical number seven, plus or minus two: Some limits on our capacity for processing information. *Psychological Review, 63,* 81–97. 143

Millis, B. J. (2002). Enhancing learning—and more!—through cooperative learning. *IDEA Paper #38.* Retrieved from https://ideacontent.blob.core.windows.net/content/sites/2/2020/01/IDEA_Paper_38.pdf 149

Mingo, M. A., Chang, H.-H., & Williams, R. L. (2018). Undergraduate students' preferences for constructed versus multiple-choice assessment of learning. *Innovative Higher Education, 43*(2), 143–152. doi:10.1007/s10755-017-9414-y 173

Miyake, N., & Masukawa, H. (2000). Relation-making to sense-making: Supporting college students' constructive understanding with an enriched collaborative note-sharing system. In B. Fishman & S. O'Connor-Divelbiss (Eds.). *Proceedings of the Fourth International Conference of the Learning Sciences* (pp. 41–47). Mahwah, NJ: Lawrence Erlbaum. 249

Moeller, A. J., Theiler, J. M., & Wu, C. (2012). Goal setting and student achievement: A longitudinal Study. *Modern Language Journal, 96*(2), 153–169. 69

Moen, K. C. (2021). The impact of multi-media presentation format: Student perceptions and learning outcomes. *Scholarship of Teaching and Learning in Psychology.* Advance online publication. http://dx.doi.org/10.1037/stl0000265 168

Moore MJ, Soderquist J, Werch C. Feasibility and Efficacy of a Binge Drinking Prevention Intervention for College Students Delivered via the Internet Versus Postal Mail. J Am Coll Health. 2005; 54(1): 38–44. https://doi.org/10.3200/JACH.54.1.38ØPMID: 16050327 266

Montero-Marín J, Demarzo MMP, Stapinski L, Gili M, García-Campayo J. Perceived Stress Latent Factors and the Burnout Subtypes: A Structural Model in Dental Students. PLOS ONE. 2014; 9(6):e99765. https://doi.org/10.1371/journal.pone.0099765 PMID: 24927260 266

Moreira JFG, Telzer EH. Changes in family cohesion and links to depression during the college transition. J Adolesc. 2015; 43:72–82. https://doi.org/10.1016/j.adolescence.2015.05.012 PMID: 26058003 266

Morehead, K., Dunlosky, J., Rawson, K. A., Blasiman, R., & Hollis, R. B. (2019). Note-taking habits of 21st Century college students: Implications for student learning, memory, and achievement. *Memory, 27*(6), 807–819. doi:10.1080/096 58211.2019.1569694 134

Morgan AJ, Rapee RM, Bayer JK. Prevention and early intervention of anxiety problems in young children: A pilot evaluation of Cool Little Kids Online. Internet Interv. 2016; 4:105–12. 266

Morisano, D., Hirsh, J. B., Peterson, J. B., Pihl, R. O., & Shore, B. M. (2010). Setting, elaborating, and reflecting on personal goals improves academic performance. *Journal of Applied Psychology, 95*(2), 255–264. doi:10.1037/a0018478 68, 69

Mostert, L. A., & Townsend, R. (2018). Embedding the teaching of academic writing into anthropology lectures. *Innovations in Education & Teaching International, 55*(1), 82–90. doi:10.1080/1470 3297.2016.1231619 161

Mou-Danha, S., Yakubova, M., & Vosen Callens, M. (2019). Answering the "Who Am I" question: Raising students' sense of self-competence with the 30-second elevator pitch. *Communication Teacher, 33*(4), 271–275. 106

Murphy, L. & Thomas, L. (2008). Dangers of a Fixed Mindset: Implications of Self-theories for Computer Science Education. In *ITiCSE 08: Proceedings of the 13th Annual Conference on Innovation and Technology in Computer Science Education: Madrid, Spain, June 30-July 2, 2008.* Association for Computing Machinery, New York. 233

Muir, C (2004). "Learning soft skills at work", B*usiness Communication Quarterly, 67*(1), pp. 95–101. 239

Mueller, P. A., & Oppenheimer, D. M. (2014) The pen is mightier than the keyboard: Advantages of longhand over laptop note-taking. *Psychological Science, 25*(6), 1159–1168. 248

Murre, J. M. J., & Dros, J. (2015) Replication and analysis of Ebbinghaus' forgetting curve. *PLOS One, 10*(7), 1–28. doi:10.1371/journal.pone.0120644 133

Myers, D. G. (2014). *Exploring psychology* (8th ed.). Worth. 142

Nardi, A., & Ranieri, M. (2019). Comparing paper-based and electronic multiple-choice examinations with personal devices: Impact on students' performance, self-efficacy and satisfaction. *British Journal of Educational Technology, 50*(3), 1495–1506. doi:10.1111/bjet.12644 175

National Institute on Alcohol Abuse and Alcoholism. (2021). *College drinking.* https://www.niaaa.nih.gov/publications/brochures-and-fact-sheets/college-drinking 201

Nauta, M. M. (2010). The development, evolution, and status of Holland's theory of vocational personalities: Reflections and future directions for counseling psychology. *Journal of Counseling Psychology, 57*(1), 11–22. doi:10.1037/a0018213 81

Neblett, E. W., Shelton, J. N., & Sellers, R. M. (2004). The role of racial identity in man aging daily racial hassles. In G. Philogine (Ed.), *Racial identity in context: The legacy of Kenneth B. Clark* (pp. 77–90). Washington, DC: American Psychological Association. 214

Neff, T. Thomas, and Citrin James, M. (1999). *Lessons from the Top: The Search for America's Best Business Leaders,* p. 448, Doubleday, New York. 240

Nelson, D. W., and Knight, A. E. (2010). The power of positive recollections: Reducing test anxiety and enhancing college student

efficacy and performance. *Journal of Applied Social Psychology, 40*(3), 732–745. doi:10.1111/j.1559-1816.2010.00595.x 171

Nerdrum P, Rustøen T, Rønnestad MH. Student Psychological Distress: A psychometric study of 1750 Norwegian 1st-year undergraduate students. Scand J Educ Res. 2006; 50(1): 95–109. 266

New, J. (2016, December 13). Looking for career help. Inside Higher Ed. Retrieved from: https://www.insidehighered.com/news/2016/12/13/only-17-percent-recent-graduates-say-career-centers-are-veryhelpful?utm_source=Inside+Higher+Ed&utm_campaign= b9ab9667e8-DNU20161213&utm_medium=email&utm_term=0_1fcbc04421-b9ab9667e8-199685953&goal=0_1fcbc04421-b9ab9667e8-199685953&mc_cid=b9ab9667e8&mc_eid=1bd4cf0705 101

Nonis, S. A., & Hudson, G. I. (2006). Academic performance of college students: Influence of time spent studying and working. *Journal of Education for Business, 81*(3), 151–159. 113

Nonis, S. A., Philhours, M. J., & Hudson, G. I. (2006). Where does the time go? A diary approach to business and marketing students' time use. *Journal of Marketing Education, 28*(2), 121–134. 112

O'Brien L, Mathieson K, Leafman J, Rice-Spearman L. Level of stress and common coping strategies among physician assistant students. J Physician Assist Educ Off J Physician Assist Educ Assoc. 2012; 23(4):25–9. 266

Oakleaf, M., & Owen, P. L. (2010). Closing the 12 - 13 gap together: School and college librarians supporting 21st century learners. *Teacher Librarian, 37*(4), 52–58. 222

Ochs, M. (1991). Assessing the value of an information literacy program. Ithaca, NY: Cornell University. ERIC EDRS340385. Available http://www.eric.ed.gov/PDFS/ED340385.pdf 226

O'Dell, J. (February 9, 2010). How millenials use tech at work. *Read Write Web.* Available http://www.readwriteweb.com/archives/how_millenials_use_tech_at_work.php 228

O'Farril, R. T. (2008). Information literacy and knowledge management: Preparations for an arranged marriage. Libri: *International Journal of Libraries & Information Services,* 58, 155–171. 221

O'Sullivan, C. (2002). Is information literacy relevant in the real world?. Reference Services Review, 30, 7–14. 221

O'Sullivan Sachar, C. (2020). Revising with metacognition to promote writing achievement: A case study. *Journal of the Scholarship of Teaching and Learning, 20*(3), 49–63. 164

Olafsdottir, G., Cloke, P., Schulz, A., van Dyck, Z., Eysteinsson, T., Thorleifsdottir, B., & Vogele, C. (2020). Health benefits of walking in nature: A randomized controlled study under conditions of real-life stress. *Environment & Behavior, 52*(3), 248–274. doi:10.1177/0013916518800798 196

Oley, N. (1992). Extra credit and peer tutoring: Impact on the quality of writing in Introductory Psychology in an open admissions college. *Teaching of Psychology, 19*(2), 78. 165

Orzech, K., Salafsky, D., & Hamilton, L. A. (2011). The state of sleep among college students at a large public university. *Journal of American College Health, 59*(7), 612–619. doi:10.10 80/07448481.2010.520051 195

Oswalt, S., Cameron, K., & Koob, J. (2005). Sexual regret in college students. *Archives of Sexual Behavior, 34*(6), 663–669. doi:10.1007/s10508-005-7920-y 201

Oviedo, V., Tornquist, M., Cameron, T., & Chiappe, D. (2015). Effects of media multi-tasking with Facebook on the enjoyment and encoding of TV episodes. *Computers in Human Behavior, 51*(Pt. A), 407–417. doi:10.1016/j.chb.2015.05.022 116

Oymak, C. (2018). High school students' views on who influences their thinking about education and careers. Stats in Brief. *National Center for Education Statistics.* 76

Ozer, M., & Perc, M. (2021). Impact of social networks on the labor market inequalities and school-to-work transitions. *Journal of Higher Education, 11*(1), 38–50. doi:10.2399/yod.21.868353 98, 99

Parsons, F. (1909). *Choosing a vocation.* Houghton Mifflin. 76

Pashler, H., McDaniel, M., Rohrer, D., & Bjork, R. (2008). Learning styles: Concepts and evidence. *Psychological Science in the Public Interest, 9*(3), 105–119. doi:10.111 1/j.1539.6053.2009.01038 76, 148

Pauk, W., & Ross, J. Q. O. (2008). *How to study in college* (9th ed.). Houghton Mifflin. 136

Payne, K. C., Babb, J., & Abdullat, A. (2018). Reflections on Applying the Growth Mindset Approach to Computer Programming Courses. In *2018 Proceedings of the EDSIG Conference Norfolk, VA USA, 4*(4641). 233

Peltzer, K., & Pengpid, S. (2016). Sleep duration and health correlates among university students in 26 countries. *Psychology, Health & Medicine, 21*(2), 208–220. doi:10.1080/135485 06.2014.998687 195

Perlman, B., McCann, L. I., & Prust, A. (2007). Students' grades and ratings of perceived effectiveness of behaviors influencing academic performance. *Teaching of Psychology, 34*(4), 236–240. doi:10.1080/00986280701700284 69

Perlman, M. (2018, October 23). The origin of the term intersectionality. *Columbia Journalism Review.* https://www.cjr. org/language_corner /intersectionality.php 21

Perreault, H. (2004). "Business educators can take a leadership role in character education", *Business Education Forum, 59*(1), pp. 23–24. 241

Perry, R. P., Stupnisky, R. H., Hall, N. C., Chipperfield, J. G., & Weiner, B. (2010). Bad starts and better finishes: Attributional retraining and initial performance in competitive achievement settings. *Journal of Social and Clinical Psychology, 29*(6), 668–700. 192

Perry, W. G. (1970). *Forms of intellectual and ethical development in the college years.* Holt, Rinehart and Winston. 57, 58

Petrone, P. (2018, February 14). Why you should have a personal elevator pitch (and how to structure one). *LinkedIn Learning Blog.* https://www.linkedin.com/business/learning/blog/productivity -tips/why-you-should-have-a-personal-elevator-pitch-and-how -to-do-it 106

Phinney, J. S. (1992). The multigroup ethnic identity measure: A new scale for use with adolescents and young adults from diverse groups. *Journal of Adolescent Research, 7,* 156–176. 215

Phinney, J. S. (1996). When we talk about American ethnic groups, what do we mean? *American Psychologist, 51,* 918–927. 215

Phinney, J. S., & Ong, A. D. (2007). Conceptualization and measurement of ethnic identity: Current status and future directions. *Journal of Counseling Psychology, 54,* 271–281. 215

Pierceall, E. A., & Keim, M. C. (2007). Stress and coping strategies among community college students. *Community College Journal of Research and Practice, 31*(9), 703–712. doi:10.1080/10668920 600866579 194

Pilcher JJ, Ginter DR, Sadowsky B. Sleep quality versus sleep quantity: Relationships between sleep and measures of health, well-being and sleepiness in college students. J Psychosom Res. 1997; 42 (6): 583–96. PMID: 9226606 266

Piolat, A., Olive, T., & Kellogg, R. T. (2005). Cognitive effort during note-taking. *Applied Cognitive Psychology, 19*(3), 291–312. doi:10.1002/acp.1086 249

Pluess, M., Conrad, A., & Wilhelm, F. (2009). Muscle tension in generalized anxiety disorder: A critical review of the literature. *Journal of Anxiety Disorders, 23*(1), 1–11. doi:10.1016 / j.janxdis. 2008.03.016 199

Policies Commission for Business and Economic Education (2000). "This we believe about teaching soft skills: human relations, self-management, and workplace enhancement", Statement No. 67. 241

Ponterotto, J. G., Gretchen, D., Utsey, S. O., Stracuzzi, T., & Saya, R. (2003). The multigroup ethnic identity measure (MEIM): Psychometric review and further validity testing. *Educational and Psychological Measurement, 63,* 502–515. 216

Poppick, S. (2015). Here's what the average grad makes out of college. Retrieved from: https://money.com/collection-post/heres-what-the -average-grad-makes-right-out-of-college/ 10

Prater, C. (2010). *A Guide to the Credit Card Act of 2009.* Retrieved from http://www.creditcards.com/credit-card -news/credit-card-law -interactive-1282.php 16

Prince, M. (2004). Does active learning work? A review of the research. *Journal of Engineering Education, 93*(3), 223–231. 149

Quaglia, R. J., & Cobb, C. D. (1996). Toward a theory of student aspirations. *Journal of Research in Rural Education, 12,* 127–132. 214

Quaye, S. J., Karikari, S. N., Allen, C. R., Okello, W. K., & Carter, K. D. (2019). Strategies for practicing self-care from racial battle fatigue. *Journal Committed to Social Change on Race and Ethnicity, 5*(2), 94–131. 200

Quimby, J. L., & DeSantis, A. M. (2006). The influence of role models on women's career choices. *Career Development Quarterly, 54*(4), 297–306. doi:10.1002/j.2161-0045.2006. tb00195.x 36, 78

Raffety, B., Smith, R., & Ptacek, J. (1997). Facilitating and debilitating trait anxiety, situational anxiety, and coping with an anticipated stressor: A process analysis. *Journal of Personality and Social Psychology, 72*(4), 892–906. doi:10.1037/0022-3514.72.4.892 166, 194

Raimes, A., & Jerskey, M. (2011). *Keys for writers* (6th ed.). Wadsworth. 50

Rainsbury, E, Hodges D, Burchell N and Lay M (2002). "Ranking workplace competencies: student and graduate perceptions", *Asia-Pacific Journal of Cooperative Education, 3*(2), pp. 8–18. 240

Ramler, T. R., Tennison, L. R., Lynch, J., & Murphy, P. (2016). Mindfulness and the college transition: The efficacy of an adapted mindfulness-based stress reduction intervention in fostering adjustment among first-year students. *Mindfulness, 7*(1), 179–188. doi:10.1007/s12671-015-0398-3 194, 199

Rampton, J. (2019, April 18). 9 ways to organize and manage your calendar properly. *LinkedIn.* https://www.linkedin.com/pulse /9-ways-organize-manage-your-calendar-properly-john-rampton/ 115

Rao, M. S. (2012). "Soft versus hard skills", *T+D; 66*(5), pp. 48–51.18 The IUP Journal of Soft Skills, VII(1), 2013 242

Rath, S. (2008). Converting distress into stress. *Social Science International, 24*(1), 98–103. 194

Rawes, E. (2014). 5 common unprofessional workplace behaviors. USA Today. Retrieved from: http://www.usatoday.com/story/money /business/2014/08/02/unprofessional-workplace-behaviors/ 13420381/ 111

Rawson, K. A., Dunlosky, J., & Thiede, K. W. (2000). The rereading effect: Absolute monitoring accuracy improves across reading trials. *Memory & Cognition, 28,* 1004–1010. 138, 139

Reardon, R. C., Peace, C. S., & Burbrink, I. E. (2021). College career courses and instructional research from 1976 through 2019. *Scholarship of Teaching and Learning in Psychology*. Advance Online Publication. doi:10.1037/stl0000254 76

Recht, D. R., & Leslie, L. (1988). Effect of prior knowledge on good and poor readers' memory of text. *Journal of Educational Psychology*, *80*, 16–20. doi:10.1037/00220663.80.1.16 138

Redmann, D. H., and Kotrlik, J. W. (2004). "Technology integration into the teaching-learning process by business education teachers", *The Delta Pi Epsilon Journal*, *46*(2), pp. 76–91. 241

Resta, P., & Laferrière, T. (2007). Technology in support of collaborative learning. *Educational Psychology Review*, *19*(1), 65–83. doi:10.1007/s10648-007-9042-7 248

Reynolds, J. R., & Baird, C. L. (2010). Is there a downside to shooting for the stars? Unrealized educational expectations and symptoms of depression. *American Sociological Review*, *75*(1), 151–172. 72, 73

Ritter, B. A., Small, E. E., Mortimer, J. W., & Doll, J. L. (2018). Designing management curriculum for workplace readiness: Developing students' soft skills. *Journal of Management Education*, *42*(1), 80–103. 109

Rix, J., Dewhurst, P., Cooke, C., & Newell, D. (2021). Nonacademic qualities as predictors of performance in an undergraduate healthcare program. *Journal of Chiropractic Education*, *35*(1), 106–115. doi:10.7899/JCE-19-3 194, 202

Robotham D, Julian C. Stress and the higher education student: a critical review of the literature. J Furth High Educ. 2006; 30(2):107–17. 266

Robb, C. A., Moody, B., & Abdel-Ghany, M. (2012). College student persistence to degree: The burden of debt. *Journal of College Student Retention: Research, Theory & Practice*, *13*(4), 431–456. 8

Roberts, R. E., Phinney, J. S., Masse, L. C., Chen, Y. R., Roberts, C. R., & Romero, A. (1999). The structure of ethnic identity of young adolescents from diverse ethnocultural groups. *The Journal of Early Adolescence*, *19*(3), 301–322. doi:10.1177/02724316990019003001 25

Robinson, D. H., Katayama, A. D., DuBois, N.F. & DeVaney, T. (1998). Interacive effects of graphic organizers and delayed review in concept acquisition. T*he Journal of Experimental Education*, *67*, 17–31. 249

Robles, M. M. (2012). Executive perceptions of the top 10 soft skills needed in today's workplace. *Business Communication Quarterly*, *75*(4), 453–465. 85, 109, 159

Rockman, I. F. (2002). Strengthening connections between information literacy, general education, and assessment efforts. *Library Trends*, *51*, 185–98. 222

Rode, J. C., Arthaud-Day, M. L., Mooney, C. H., Near, J. P., & Baldwin, T. T. (2008). Ability and personality predictors of salary, perceived job success, and perceived career success in the initial career stage. *International Journal of Selection & Assessment*, *16*(3), 292–299. doi:10.1111/j.1468-2389.2008.00435.x 86

Rodriguez, F., Kataoka, S., Janet Rivas, M., Kadandale, P., Nili, A., & Warschauer, M. (2021). Do spacing and self-testing predict learning outcomes? *Active Learning in Higher Education*, *22*(1), 77–91. 145

Rogowska AM. Problematic use of psychoactive substances in undergraduates: a comparison of four patterns of substance use. J Subst Use. 2016; 21(3):304–8. 266

Rohrer, D., & Pashler, H. (2012). Learning styles: Where's the evidence? *Medical Education*, *46*(7), 634–635. doi:10.1111/j.1365-2923.2012.04273.x 148

Roney, C. R., & O'Connor, M. C. (2008). The interplay between achievement goals and specific target goals in determining performance. *Journal of Research in Personality*, *42*(2), 482–489. doi:10.1016/j.jrp.2007.07.001 74

Roohr, K., Olivera-Aguilar, M., Ling, G., & Rikoon, S. (2019). A multi-level modeling approach to investigating students' critical thinking at higher education institutions. *Assessment & Evaluation in Higher Education*, *44*(6), 946–960. 57

Rosen, P. A., Solomon, S. J., McLarty, B. D., Esken, C. A., & Taylor, E. C. (2018). The use of Twitter profiles to assess personality and hireability. *Journal of Managerial Issues*, *30*(2), 256–272. 91, 104

Rosenberg M. Society and the adolescent self-image. [Internet]. Princeton University Press. 1965. 326 p. https://www.vitalsourcc.com/en-uk/products/society-and-the-adolescent-self-image-morris-rosenberg-v9781400876136 269

Rowland, A. L. (2008). The health challenges of urban Latino college students as revealed through student journaling. *Journal of Hispanic Higher Education*, *7*(2), 131–143. doi:10.1177/1538192707313937 195

Roy, S., & Saha, B. (2019). Goal setting as a motivator for student performance: Evidence from lab experiments. *Journal of Higher Education Theory & Practice*, *19*(3), 153–165. doi:10.33423/jhetp.v19i3.2123 70

Roychowdhury, H. S., Gerrits, R., Hull, K., Stowe, S., & Jensen, M. (2020). Benefits and challenges of assigned out-of-class group work in the community college setting. *HAPS Educator*, *24*(3), 23–33. 149

Russo, K. (2015). Hard skills vs. soft skills: What they mean to your job search and the weight they carry with HR. Huffington Post. Retrieved from: https://www.huffpost.com/entry/hard-skills-vs-soft-skill_b_8341566.html 109

Salame, I. I., & Thompson, A. (2020). Students' views on strategic note-taking and its impact on performance, achievement, and learning. *International Journal of Instruction*, *13*(2), 1–16. 133, 135

Salary.com. (2021). *Teacher elementary school, New York City and San Antonio*. Retrieved from http://swz.salary.com/SalaryWizard/Teacher-Elementary-School-Salary-Details-San-Antonio-TX.aspx 89

Saleh D, Camart N, Romo L. Intervention de gestion du stress par Internet chez les étudiants: revue de la littérature. Ann MédPsychol Rev Psychiatr. 2016; 5. 266

Saleh D, Camart N, Sbeira F, Romo L. Internet-Based Stress Management Intervention: Feasibility Study. EC Psychol PSYCHIATRYShort. 2017 Jun; 4(1):27–33. 270

Salisbury, F., & Karasmans, S. (2011). Are they ready? Exploring student information literacy skills in the transition from secondary to tertiary education. *Australian Academic and Research Libraries*, *42*(1), 43–58. 46, 49

Samarawickrema, G., & O'Reilly, J. (2003). Using concept maps to improve the quality of learning law at a distance. In G. Davis & E. Stacey (Eds.), *Quality education @ a distance*, Vol. 259 (pp. 161–168). Boston, MA: Kluwer Academic Publishers. 249

Sampson, J. P., Osborn, D. S., Kettunen, J., Hou, P., Miller, A. K., & Makela, J. P. (2018). The validity of social media– based career information. *Career Development Quarterly*, *66*(2), 121–134. doi:10.1002/cdq.12127 92

Samson, S. (2010). Information literacy learning outcomes and student success. *The Journal of Academic Librarianship*, *36*(3), 202-210. 45, 49

Sana, F., Weston, T., & Cepeda, N. J. (2013). Laptop multitasking hinders classroom learning for both users and nearby peers. *Computers and Education*, *62*, 24–31. 116

Sanchez Abril, P., Levin, A., & Del Riego, A. (2012). Blurred boundaries: Social media privacy and the twenty-first -century employee. *American Business Law Journal*, *49*(1), 63–124. doi:10.1111/j.1744-1714.2011.01127.x 104, 106

Sanders, M. L. (2012). *Becoming a learner: Realizing the opportunity of education.* Institute for Communication and Leadership. 5, 156

Sandoval-Lucero, E., Maes, J. B., & Klingsmith, L. (2014). African American and Latina(o) community college students' social capital and student success. *College Student Journal, 48*(3), 522–533. 100

Sarfo, F., & Elen, J. (2011). Investigating the impact of positive resource interdependence and individual accountability on students' academic performance in cooperative learning. *Electronic Journal of Research in Educational Psychology, 9*(1), 73–94. 124, 149

Sargent, L. D., & Domberger, S. R. (2007). Exploring the development of a protean career orientation: Values and image violations. *Career Development International, 12*(6), 545–564. doi:10.1108/13620430710822010 83

Schulte, S. J. (2008). High self-efficacy and high use of electronic information may predict improved academic performance. *Evidence Based Library & Information Practice, 3,* 35–37. 222

Schloemer, P., & Brenan, K. (2006). From students to learners: Developing self-regulated learning. *Journal of Education for Business, 82*(2), 81–87. 75, 189

Schreiber, L. M., & Valle, B. (2013). Social constructivist teaching strategies in the small group classroom. *Small Group Research, 44*(4), 395–411. doi:10.1177/1046496413488422. 118

Schultchen, D., Reichenberger, J., Mittl, T., Weh, T. R. M., Smyth, J. M., Blechert, J., & Pollatos, O. (2019). Bidirectional relationship of stress and affect with physical activity and healthy eating. *British Journal of Health Psychology, 24*(2), 315–333. doi:10.1111/bjhp.12355 196

Schulz KF, Altman DG, Moher D. CONSORT 2010 Statement: updated guidelines for reporting parallel group randomised trials. BMJ. 2010; 340:c332. https://doi.org/10.1136/bmj.c332 PMID: 20332509 267

Schunk, D. H. (1990). Goal setting and self-efficacy during self-regulated learning. *Educational Psychologist, 25*(1), 71–86. 70

Schutte, N. S., & Loi, N. M. (2014). Connections between emotional intelligence and workplace flourishing. Personality and Individual Differences, 66134–66139. doi:10.1016/j.paid.2014.03.031 121

Schuur, J., van Weerdenburg, M., Hoogeveen, L., & Kroesbergen, E. H. (2021). Social-emotional characteristics and adjustment of accelerated university students: A systematic review. *Gifted Child Quarterly, 65*(1), 29–51. 194

Schwartz, B. L., Son, L. K., Kornell, N., & Finn, B. (2011). Four principles of memory improvement: A guide to improving learning efficiency. *The International Journal of Creativity and Problem Solving, 21*(1), 7–15. 124, 150

Schwartz, S. H. (2012). An overview of the Schwartz theory of basic values. *Online Readings in Psychology and Culture, 2*(1), 1–20. https://scholarworks.gvsu.edu/cgi/viewcontent.cgi?article=1116 &context=orpc 32, 33

Schwartz, S. J., Zamboanga, B. L., Weisskirch, R. S., & Wang, S. C. (2010). The relationships of personal and cultural identity to adaptive and maladaptive psychosocial functioning in emerging adults. *The Journal of Social Psychology, 150*(1), 1–31. doi:10.1080/00224540903366784 21

Seifert, L. S. (1997). Activating representations in permanent memory: Different benefits for pictures and words. *Journal of Experimental Psychology: Learning, Memory, and Cognition, 23*(5), 1106–1121. doi:10.1037/0278-7393.23.5.1106 148

Seifert, T., Goodman, K., Lindsay, N., Jorgensen, J., Wolniak, G., Pascarella, E., & Blaich, C. (2008). The effects of liberal arts experiences on liberal arts outcomes. *Research in Higher Education, 49*(2), 107–125. doi:10.1007/s11162-007-9070-7 183

Seijts, G. H., & Latham, G. P. (2011). The effect of commitment to a learning goal, self-efficacy, and the interaction between learning goal difficulty and commitment on performance in a business simulation. *Human Performance, 24*(3), 189–204. doi:10.1080/08959285.2011.5 80807 74

Seirup, H., & Rose, S. (2011). Exploring the effects of hope on GPA and retention among college undergraduate students on academic probation. *Education Research International.* 1–7. doi:10.1155/2011/381429 196

Sellnow, D. D. (2005). *Confident public speaking* (2nd ed.). Wadsworth. 166

Sellers, R. M., & Shelton, J. N. (2003). The role of racial identity in perceived discrimination. *Journal of Personality and Social Psychology, 84,* 1079–1092. 215

Seo, E., & Patall, E. A. (2020). Feeling proud today may lead people to coast tomorrow: Daily intraindividual associations between emotion and effort in academic goal striving. *Emotion.* 1–6. doi:10.1037/emo0000752.supp 70

Seo, E., Patall, E. A., Henderson, M. D., & Steingut, R. R. (2018). The effects of goal origin and implementation intentions on goal commitment, effort, and performance. *Journal of Experimental Education, 86*(3), 386–401. doi:10.1080/002 20973.2016.1277334 70, 74

Servant D. Les programmes de gestion du stress au travail sont-ils efficaces? Lett Psychiatre. 2011; 7 (1):25–8. 266

Shamsuddin K, Fadzil F, Ismail WSW, Shah SA, Omar K, Muhammad NA, et al. Correlates of depression, anxiety and stress among Malaysian university students. Asian J Psychiatry. 2013; 6(4):318–23. 266

Shatz, M., & Best, J. (1987). Students' reasons for changing answers on objective tests. *Teaching of Psychology, 14*(4), 241. 173

Shell, M. D., Shears, D., & Millard, Z. (2020). Who am I? Identity development during the first year of college. *Psi Chi Journal of Psychological Research, 25*(2), 192–202. doi:10.24839/2325-7342.jn25.2.192 20

Shellenbarger, T. (2009). Time and project management tips for educators. *The Journal of Continuing Education in Nursing, 40*(7), 292–293. doi:10.3928/00220124-20090623-08 113, 114, 115

Shen, Z. (2015). Cultural competence models and cultural competence assessment instruments in nursing: A literature review. *Journal of Transcultural Nursing, 26*(3), 308-321. doi:10.1177/1043659614524790 117

Shepherd, P. T. (2011). Journal usage factor - a promising new metric. *Serials, 24,* 64–68.

Shimazoe, J., & Aldrich, H. (2010). Group work can be gratifying: Understanding and overcoming resistance to cooperative learning. *College Teaching, 58*(2), 52–57. doi:10.1080/87567550903418594 149

Sironi, M. (2012). Education and mental health in Europe: School attainment as a means to fight depression. *International Journal of Mental Health, 41*(3), 79–105. 5

Sivan, E. (1986). Motivation in social constructivist theory. *Educational Psychologist, 21,* 209–233. doi:10.1207/ s15326985ep2103_4 205

Smalley, T. (2000). Investigating information age realities in the world of work. Available http://www.cabrillo.edu/~tsmalley/WorldOfWork.html 222

Smart, J. C., Feldman, K. A., & Ethington, C. A., (2006). Holland's theory and patterns of college student success. *National Postsecondary Education Cooperative.* 1–44. 80–81

SMART criteria (n.d.) In Wikipedia. Retrieved July 9, 2019, from https://en.wikipedia.org/wiki/SMARTcriteria 235

SMART Goals: How to Make Your Goals Achievable. (n.d.). Retrieved from https://www.mindtools.com/pages/article/smart-goals.htm 235

Smith-Peavler, E., Gardner, G. E., & Otter, R. (2019). PowerPoint use in the undergraduate biology classroom: Perceptions and impacts on student learning. *Journal of College Science Teaching, 48*(3), 74–83. 168

Smith-Proulx, L. (2018). How the Linkedin profile should (and should not) align with the resume. *Career Planning & Adult Development Journal, 32*(2), 120–125. 107

So, J. Y., & Chan, A. S. (2009). Validity of highlighting on text comprehension. *AIP Conference Proceedings, 1177*(1), 217–224. doi:10.1063/1.3256250 140

Somerville, M. M., & Howard, Z. (2008). Systems thinking: An approach for advancing workplace information literacy. *Australian Library Journal, 57*, 257–273. 222

Son, L. K., & Metcalfe, J. (2000). Metacognitive and control strategies in study-time allocation. *Journal of Experimental Psychology: Learning, Memory, and Cognition, 26*(1), 204–221. doi:10.1037/0278-7393.26.1.204 115

Soria, K. M., & Stebleton, M. (2013). Major decisions: Motivations for selecting a major, satisfaction, and belonging. *NACADA Journal, 33*(2), 29–43. doi:10.12930/NACADA-13-018 28

Sparkman, L. A., Maulding, W. S., & Roberts, J. G. (2012). Non-cognitive predictors of student success in college. *College Student Journal, 46*(3), 642–652. 121

Spieker, C. J., & Hinsz, V. B. (2004). Repeated success and failure influences on self-efficacy and personal goals. *Social Behavior & Personality: An International Journal, 32*(2), 191–197. 73

Srivastava, T. K., Waghmare, L. S., Mishra, V. P., Rawekar, A. T., Quazi, N., & Jagzape, A. T. (2015). Peer teaching to foster learning in physiology. *Journal of Clinical and Diagnostic Research, 9*(8), 1–6. doi:10.7860/JCDR/2015/15018.6323 148

Stallman, H. M., Ohan, J. L., & Chiera, B. (2019). Reducing distress in university students: A randomised control trial of two online interventions. *Australian Psychologist, 54*(2), 125–131. doi:10.1111/ap.12375 194

Steele, C. M. (2011). *Whistling Vivaldi: How stereotypes affect us and what we can do.* W.W. Norton and Company. 171

Sterling, E., Bravo, A., Porzecanski, A. L., Burks, R. L., Linder, J., Langen, T., Fernandez, D., Ruby, D., & Bynum, N. (2016). Think before (and after) you speak: Practice and self-reflection bolster oral communication skills. *Journal of College Science Teaching, 45*(6), 87–99. doi:10.2505/4/jcst16_045_06_87 170

Stewart, J. (2006). Transformational leadership: An evolving concept examined through the works of Burns, Bass, Avolio, and Leithwood. *Canadian Journal of Educational Administration and Policy, 54*, 1–29. 125

Stewart, M. (2019, November 15). Connecting without social capital: How underserved students network despite barriers. *Insight into Diversity.* https://www.insightintodiversity.com/connecting-without-social-capital-how-underserved-students-network-despite-barriers/ 99

Stinebrickner, R., & Stinebrickner, T. R. (2004). Time-use and college outcomes. *Journal of Econometrics, 121*(1/2), 243–269. doi:10.1016/j.jeconom.2003.10.013 113

Stirratt, M. J., Meyer, I. H., Ouellette, S. C., & Gara, M. A. (2008). Measuring identity multiplicity and intersectionality: Hierarchical classes analysis (HICLAS) of sexual, racial, and gender identities. *Self and Identity, 7*(1), 89–111. doi:10.1080/15298860701252203 21, 22

Stallman HM. Psychological distress in university students: A comparison with general population data. Aust Psychol. 2010; 45(4):249–57 266

Stone, M. J., & Petrick, J. F. (2013). The educational benefits of travel experiences: A literature review. *Journal of Travel Research, 52*(6), 731–744. 185

Stowell, J., & Bennett, D. (2010). Effects of online testing on student exam performance and test anxiety. *Journal of Educational Computing Research, 42*(2), 161–171. doi:10.2190/EC.42.2.b 174–175

Strack, J., & Esteves, F. (2015). Exams? Why worry? Interpreting anxiety as facilitative and stress appraisals. *Anxiety, Stress & Coping, 28*(2), 205–214. doi:10.1080/10615806.2014.93 1942 194

Strang, K. (2011). How can discussion forum questions be effective in online MBA courses? *Campus-Wide Information Systems, 28*(2), 80–92. 61, 124

Strasser-Burke, N., & Symonds, J. (2020). Who do you want to be like? Factors influencing early adolescents' selection of accessible and inaccessible role models. *Journal of Early Adolescence, 40*(7), 914–935. doi:10.1177/0272431619880619 77

Strayhorn, T. L. (2019). *College students' sense of belonging: A key to educational success for all students. 2nd edition.* Taylor and Francis. 28

Strenna L, Chahraoui K, Vinay A. Santépsychique chez les étudiants de première année d'école supérieure de commerce: liens avec le stress de l'orientation professionnelle, l'estime de soi et le coping. Orientat Sc Prof. 2009;(38/2):183–204. 266

Stupnisky, R., Renaud, R., Perry, R., Ruthig, J., Haynes, T., & Clifton, R. (2007). Comparing self-esteem and perceived control as predictors of first-year college students' academic achievement. *Social Psychology of Education, 10*(3), 303–330. doi:10.1007/s11218-007-9020-4 203

Su, N., Buchin, Z. L., & Mulligan, N. W. (2021). Levels of retrieval and the testing effect. *Journal of Experimental Psychology: Learning, Memory, and Cognition, 47*(4), 652–670. doi:10.1037/xlm0000962 144

Sukkon, B. Z. (2016, June 20). Higher education's public purpose. Association of American Colleges & Universities. Retrieved from: https://www.aacu.org/leap/liberal-education-nation-blog/higher-educations-public-purpose 4

Sutton, N (2002). "Why can't we all just get along?", *Computing Canada, 28*(16), p. 20. 242

Sulastri, A., Handoko, M., & Janssens, J. M. A. M. (2015). Grade point average and biographical data in personal resumes: Predictors of finding employment. *International Journal of Adolescence and Youth, 20*(3), 306–316. doi:10.1080/02673843.2014.996236 100, 101

Sundström C, Gajecki M, Johansson M, Blankers M, Sinadinovic K, Stenlund-Gens E, et al. Guided and Unguided Internet-Based Treatment for Problematic Alcohol Use–A Randomized Controlled Pilot Trial. PLOS ONE. 2016; 11(7):e0157817. https://doi.org/10.1371/journal.pone.0157817 PMID: 27383389 266

Sundheim, K. (2011, July 27). Networking: It's not about who you know, it's about who knows you. Business Finder. Retrieved from: https://www.businessinsider.com/networking-its-not-about-who-you-know-its-about-who-knows-you-2011-5 100

Swanson, J. L., & Woitke, M. B. (1997). Theory into practice in career assessment for women: Assessment and interventions regarding perceived barriers. *Journal of Career Assessment, 5*, 443–462. 214

Tailab, M. M. K., & Marsh, N. Y. (2020). Use of self-assessment of video recording to raise students' awareness of development of their oral presentation skills. *Higher Education Studies, 10*(1), 16–28. 166

Tang, Y., Holzel, B. K., & Posner, M. I. (2015). The neuroscience of mindfulness meditation. *Nature Reviews Neuroscience, 16*(4), 213–225. doi:10.1038/nrn3916 199

Taylor, Kimberly A. (2003). "Marketing Yourself in the Competitive Job Market: An Innovative Course Preparing Undergraduates for Marketing Careers," *Journal of Marketing Education, 25*(2), 97–107. 260

Timberlake, S. (2005). Social capital and gender in the workplace. *The Journal of Management Development, 24*(1), 34–44. 99

Titsworth, B. S. & Kiewra, K. A. (1998, April). *By the numbers: The effect of organizational lecture cues on note-taking and achievement.* Paper presented at the meeting of the American Educational Research Association, San Diego, CA. 2249

Tope-Banjoko, T., Davis, V., Morrison, K., Fife, J., Hill, O., & Talley, C. (2020). Academic resilience in college students: Relationship between coping and GPA. *Anatolian Journal of Education, 5*(2), 109–120. 199

Torstveit MK, Aagedal-Mortensen K, Stea TH. More than Half of High School Students Report Disordered Eating: A Cross Sectional Study among Norwegian Boys and Girls. PLOS ONE. 2015; 10(3): e0122681. https://doi.org/10.1371/journal.pone.0122681 PMID: 25825877 266

Trail-Ross, M. (2012). Linking classroom learning to the community through service learning. *Journal of Community Health Nursing, 29*(1), 53–60. doi:10.1080/07370016.2012.645746 188

Travis, J., Kaszycki, A., Geden, M., & Bunde, J. (2020). Some stress is good stress: The challenge-hindrance framework, academic self-efficacy, and academic outcomes. *Journal of Educational Psychology, 112*(8), 1632–1643. 71, 72, 73, 194

Travis, T. (2008). Librarians as agents of change: Working with curriculum committees using change agency theory. New Directions for *Teaching and Learning, 114*, 17–33. 223

Travis, T., (2011). From the classroom to the boardroom: The impact of information literacy instruction on workplace research skills. *Education Libraries, 34*(2), 19–31. 45, 48

Triandis, H. C., & Gelfand, M. J. (2012). A theory of individualism and collectivism. In P. A. M. Van Lange, A. W. Kruglanski, & E. T. Higgins (Eds.), *Handbook of Theories of Social Psychology* (p. 498–520). Sage Publications Ltd. https://doi.org/10.4135/9781446249222.n51 32

Trockel, M., Barnes, M., & Egget, D. (2000). Health-related variables and academic performance among first-year college students: Implications for sleep and other behaviors. *Journal of American College Health, 49*(3), 125. 195

Tsang, A. (2020). Enhancing learners' awareness of oral presentation (delivery) skills in the context of self-regulated learning. *Active Learning in Higher Education, 21*(1), 39–50. 167

Turaga, R. (2020). Managing microaggressions at work. *IUP Journal of Soft Skills, 14*(3), 42–51. 117

Turner, D. W. (2010). *Qualitative interview design: A practical guide for novice investigators, 15*(3), 754–760. 250

Turner, E., & Rainie, L. (2020, March 5). Most Americans rely on their own research to make big decisions, and that often means online searches. Pew Research Center. https://www.pewresearch.org/fact-tank/2020/03/05/most-americans-rely-on-their-own-research-to-make-big-decisions-and-that-often-means-online-searches/ 45, 46

Turner, J. E., & Husman, J. (2008). Emotional and cognitive self-regulation following academic shame. *Journal of Advanced Academics, 20*(1), 138–173. 74

Ungar, M. (2013). Resilience, trauma, context, and culture. *Trauma, Violence, & Abuse, 14*(3), 255–266. 198

Utsey, S. O. (1999). Development and validation of a short form of the Index of Race Related Stress (IRRS)-Brief Version. *Measurement & Evaluation in Counseling & Development, 32*, 149–167. 216

Utz, S. (2016). Is LinkedIn making you more successful? The informational benefits derived from public social media. *New Media & Society, 18*(11), 2685–2702. 91

Valentine, B. (2001). The legitimate effort in research papers: Student commitment versus faculty expectations. *The Journal of Academic Librarianship, 27*(2), 107–115. doi:10.1016/S0099-1333(00)00182-8 48

Vandentorren S, Verret C, Vignonde M, Maurice-Tison S. Besoins d'information en santédes étudiants au service inter-universitaire de médecine préventive de Bordeaux. SantéPublique. 2005; 17(1): 47–56. 266

Vallieres EF, Vallerand RJ. Traduction et validation canadienne-française de l'échelle de l'estime de soi de Rosenberg. Int J Psychol. 1990; 25(2):305–16. 270

Vallieres EF, Vallerand RJ. Traduction et validation canadienne-française de l'échelle de l'estime de soi de Rosenberg. Int J Psychol. 1990; 25(2):305–16. 269

Van Hoye, G., van Hooft, E. A. J., & Lievens, F. (2009). Networking as a job search behavior: A social network perspective. *Journal of Occupational and Organizational Psychology, 82*, 661–682. doi:10.1348/096317908X360675 98

Velez, G. S., & Giner, G. R. (2015). Effects of business internships on students, employers, and higher education institutions: A systematic review. *Journal of Employment Counseling, 52*, 121–130. 186

Vertsberger, D., & Gati, I. (2015). The effectiveness of sources of support in career decision-making: A two-year follow up. *Journal of Vocational Behavior, 89*, 151–161. doi:10.1016/j.jvb.2015.06.004 82–83

Villar, E., Juan, J., Corominas, E., & Capell, D. (2000). What kind of networking strategy advice should career counsellors offer university graduates searching for a job? *British Journal of Guidance and Counselling, 28*(3), 389–409. 98, 99

Villiness, Z. (2020, November 1). What are the different types of memory? *Medical News Today.* https://www.medicalnewstoday.com/articles/types-of-memory#working-memory 142

Vliet HV, Andrews G. Internet-based course for the management of stress for junior high schools. Australas Psychiatry. 2009 266

Wade, C. (2008). Critical thinking: Needed now more than ever. In D. Dunn, J. S. Halonen, & R. A. Smith (Eds.), *Teaching critical thinking in psychology: A handbook of best practices*, 11–22. Wiley-Blackwell. 57

Walker, C. O., Greene, B. A., & Mansell, R. A. (2006). Identification with academics, intrinsic/extrinsic motivation, and self-efficacy as predictors of cognitive engagement. *Learning and Individual Differences, 16*(1), 1–12. doi:10.1016/ j.lindif.2005.06.004 201

Walker, I., & Crogan, M. (1998). Academic performance, prejudice, and the Jigsaw classroom: New pieces to the puzzle. *Journal of Community & Applied Social Psychology, 8*(6), 381–393. doi:10.1002/(SICI)1099- 1298(199811/12)8:6<381::AID-CASP457>3.0.CO;2-6 118

Walsh, T. R. (2011). Evolution of an information competency requirement for undergraduates. *Journal of Web Librarianship, 5*, 3–23. 222

Wallace, D. L., Hayes, J. R., Center for the Study of Writing, B. A., & Center for the Study of Writing, P. A. (1990). Redefining revision for freshmen. *Occasional paper no. 21.* 164

Walsh JM, Feeney C, Hussey J, Donnellan C. Sources of stress and psychological morbidity among undergraduate physiotherapy students. Physiotherapy. 2010; 96(3):206–12. https://doi.org /10.1016/j. physio.2010.01.005 PMID: 26620674652

Walters, G. D., & Kremser J. (2016) Differences in career aspirations, influences, and motives as a function of class standing: An empirical evaluation of undergraduate criminal justice majors. *Journal of Criminal Justice Education*, 27(3), 312–323, doi:10.1080/10511253. 2015.1125516 36

Warmuth, K. A. (2021). Pecha Kucha as an alternative to traditional student presentations. *Currents in Teaching & Learning, 12(2)*, 44–51. 170

Warr, P., & Pearce, A. (2004). Preferences for careers and organisational cultures as a function of logically related personality traits. *Applied Psychology: An International Review*, 53(3), 423–435. doi:10.1111/ j.1464-0597.2004.00178.x 86

Waseem, J., & Asim, M. (2020). Regression model on selfesteem, self-efficacy, locus of control as predictors of academic performance of students in higher education. *Journal of Education and Educational Development*, 7(2), 387–406. 203

Wayment, H., Bauer, J., & Sylaska, K. (2015). The Quiet Ego Scale: Measuring the Compassionate Self-Identity. *Journal of Happiness Studies*, 16(4), 999–1033. doi:10.1007/ s10902-014-9546-z 31

Weible, R. (2009). Are universities reaping the available benefits internship programs offer? *Journal of Education for Business*, 85(2), 59–63. 186

Werner, E. E. (1989). High-risk children in young adulthood: A longitudinal study from birth to 32 years. *American Journal of Ortho-psychiatry*, 59(1), 72–81. doi:10.1111/j.1939-0025.1989.tb01636.x 198

West, E. J. (2004). Perry's legacy: Models of epistemological development. *Journal of Adult Development*, 11(2), 61–70. doi:10.1023/B:JADE.0000024540.12150.69 58

West, N. M. (2019). By us, for us: The impact of a professional counterspace on African American women in student affairs. *Journal of Negro Education*, 88(2), 159–180. 100, 102

Wilcox, P., Winn, S., & Fyvie-Gauld, M. (2005). "It was nothing to do with the university, it was just the people": The role of social support in the first-year experience of higher education. *Studies in Higher Education*, 30(6), 707–722. doi:10.1080/03075070500340036 198

Wild, L., Canale, A. M., & Herdklotz, C. (2017). The power of many: Mentoring networks for growth and development. *College & University*, 92(2), 37–41. 102

Wilhelm, W. J. (2004). "Determinants of moral reasoning: academic factors, gender, richness of life experiences and religious preferences", *The Delta Pi Epsilon Journal*, XLVI(2), pp. 105–121. 241

Williams, C. L., Hirschi, Q., Sublett, K. V., Hulleman, C. S., & Wilson, T. D. (2020). A brief social belonging intervention improves academic outcomes for minoritized high school students. *Motivation Science*, 6(4), 423–437. doi:10.1037 /mot0000175.supp 27–28, 203

Williamson, G. L. (2008). A text readability continuum for postsecondary readiness. *Journal of Advanced Academics*, 19(4), 602–632. 138

Willingham, D. T. (2009). *Why don't students like school? A cognitive scientist answers questions about how the mind works and what it means for the classroom.* Jossey-Bass. 141-142, 148

Willingham, D. T. (2020). Ask the cognitive scientist: How can educators teach critical thinking? *American Educator*, 44(3), 41–45. 55, 57, 58, 60

Winston, C. N. (2016). An existential-humanistic-positive theory of human motivation. *The Humanistic Psychologist*, 44(2), 142–163. https://doi.org/10.1037/hum0000028 204

Wise, A., Saghafian, M., & Padmanabhan, P. (2012). Towards more precise design guidance: Specifying and testing the functions of assigned student roles in online discussions. *Educational Technology Research & Development*, 60(1), 55–82. doi:10.1007/s11423-011 -9212-7 124

Wu, C., Chen, S., Chen, C., & Chiu, C. (2009). *The effect of integrating web 2.0 technology in collaborative note-taking on elementary students' science learning.* Paper presented at the World Conference on Educational Multimedia, Hpermedia, and Telecommunications, Honolulu, Hawaii. 249

Wolfe, C. T., & Spencer, S. J. (1996). Stereotypes and prejudice: Their overt and subtle influence in the classroom. *American Behavioral Scientist*, 40(2), 176–185. doi:10.1177/00027642 96040002008 117, 118

Wolff, H., & Moser, K. (2009). Effects of networking on career success: A longitudinal study. *Journal of Applied Psychology*, 94(1), 196–206. 98

Wong, S. H. R., & Webb, T. D. (2011). Uncovering meaningful correlation between student academic performance and library material usage. *College & Research Libraries*, 72, 361–370. 222

Wong, S. S. H., & Lim, S. W. H. (2021). Take notes, not photos: Mind-wandering mediates the impact of note-taking strategies on video-recorded lecture learning performance. *Journal of Experimental Psychology*. Advance online publication. http://dx.doi.org/10.1037/xap0000375 134

Wong JGWS, Cheung EPT, Chan KKC, Ma KKM, Tang SW. Web-based survey of depression, anxiety and stress in first-year tertiary education students in Hong Kong. Aust N Z J Psychiatry. 2006; 40 (9):777–82. https://doi.org/10.1080/j.1440-1614.2006.01883.x PMID: 16911753 266

Wood, L., Harris, F. (2020, May 5). How to respond to racial microaggressions when they occur. *Diverse Issues in Higher Education*. https://diverseeducation.com/article/176397/ 117

Workman, J. L. (2015). Parental influence on exploratory students' college choice, major, and career decision making. *College Student Journal*, 49(1), 23–30. 76

Worrell, F. C., Mendoza-Denton, R., Vandiver, B. J., Phagen, P. E., & Cross, W. E. (2020). Incorporating a race salience subscale into the cross racial identity scale (CRIS). *Journal of Black Psychology*, 46(8), 638–658. doi:10.1177/0095798420967598 26

Wu, D. (2008). Aligning information literacy with workplace expectations. 12th Biennial CARL Conference. Irvine, CA. 222

Yakovlev, P., & Leguizamon, S. (2012). Ignorance is not bliss: On the role of education in subjective well-being. *Journal of Socio-Economics*, 41(6), 806–815. doi:10.1016/j. socec.2012.08.009 5

Yamashita, T., Bardo, A. R., Liu, D., & Cummins, P. A. (2020). Literacy, Numeracy, and Health Information Seeking Among Middle-Aged and Older Adults in the United States. *Journal of Aging & Health*, 32(1/2), 33–41. doi:10.1177/0898264318800918 45

Yavorsky, J. E., Keister, L. A., Qian, Y., & Nau, M. (2019). Women in the one percent: Gender dynamics in top income positions. *American Sociological Review*, 84(1), 54–81. doi:10.1177/0003122418820702 37

Young, Mark R., and J. William Murphy (2003). "Integrating Communications Skill into the Marketing Curriculum: A Case Study," *Journal of Marketing Education*, 25(1), 57–70. 260

Ye Y, Zhang Y, Chen J, Liu J, Li X, Liu Y, et al. Internet-Based Cognitive Behavioral Therapy for Insomnia (ICBT-i) Improves ComorbidAnxiety and Depression—A Meta-Analysis of RandomizedControlled Trials. PLOS ONE. 2015; 10(11):e0142258. https://doi.org/10.1371/journal.pone. 0142258 PMID: 26581107 266

Zhang, W., Chen, Q., McCubbin, H., McCubbin, L., & Foley, S. (2011). Predictors of mental and physical health: Individual and neighborhood levels of education, social well-being, and ethnicity. *Health & Place*, 17(1), 238– 247. doi:10.1016/j.healthplace.2010.10. 0085884.2008 .00370. 23 5

Zivin K, Eisenberg D, Gollust SE, Golberstein E. Persistence of mental health problems and needs in a college student population.

J Affect Disord. 2009; 117(3):180–5. https://doi.org/10.1016/j. jad.2009.01. 001 PMID: 19178949 266

Zimmerman, B. J. (2002). Becoming a self-regulated learner: An overview. *Theory into Practice*, 41(2), 64–72. Retrieved from ERIC database. Free Press. 71, 73, 75

Zetterqvist K, Maanmies J, Ström L, Andersson G. Randomized controlled trial of Internet-based stress management. Cogn Behav Ther. 2003; 32(3):151–60. https://doi.org/10.1080/16506070302316 PMID: 16291546 266

Zusho, A., & Clayton, K. (2011). Culturalizing achievement goal theory and research. *Educational Psychologist*, 46(4), 239–260. doi:10.1080/00461520.2011.614526 205

Subject Index